LINCOLN'S
BOYS

LINCOLN'S BOYS

JOHN HAY, JOHN NICOLAY,
AND THE WAR FOR
LINCOLN'S IMAGE

JOSHUA ZEITZ

VIKING

VIKING

Published by the Penguin Group
Penguin Group (USA) LLC
375 Hudson Street
New York, New York 10014

USA | Canada | UK | Ireland | Australia | New Zealand | India | South Africa | China
penguin.com
A Penguin Random House Company

First published by Viking Penguin, a member of Penguin Group (USA) LLC, 2014

A portion of Chapter 15 appeared in different form as "Rebel Redemption Redux" in *Dissent,*
Winter 2000.

PHOTOGRAPH CREDITS: Insert pages 1, 2 (top and bottom), 6: Library of Congress; 3 (top and bottom),
4 (top and bottom), 5 (top and bottom): From the Lincoln Financial Foundation Collection,
courtesy of the Indiana State Museum and Allen County Public Library; 7: Minnesota Historical
Society; 8 (top and bottom): John Hay Library, Brown University

LIBRARY OF CONGRESS CATALOGING-IN-PUBLICATION DATA
Zeitz, Joshua.
Lincoln's boys : John Hay, John Nicolay, and the war for Lincoln's image / Joshua Zeitz.
pages cm.
Includes bibliographical references and index.
ISBN 978-0-670-02566-4
1. Lincoln, Abraham, 1809–1865—Friends and associates. 2. Hay, John, 1838–1905. 3. Nicolay,
John G. (John George), 1832–1901. 4. Private secretaries—United States—Biography.
5. Presidents—United States—Staff—Biography. 6. Lincoln, Abraham, 1809–1865—Influence.
7. Presidents—United States—Biography. I. Title.
E457.2.Z45 2013
973.7092'2—dc23 2013017052

Printed in the United States of America
1 3 5 7 9 10 8 6 4 2

For Angela, Lily, and Naomi

Contents

PART IV

PART V

LINCOLN'S BOYS

Prologue

June 13, 1905

Less than three weeks before his death, John Milton Hay awoke in his cabin room on the RMS *Baltic* as the great ocean liner, still the jewel of the White Star Line, steamed a course from Liverpool to New York. He reached for his diary and composed one of its final entries.

It was June 1905. Electric lights and streetcars lined hundreds of American towns. Phonographs and telephones were quickly becoming common fixtures in middle-class living rooms, and for a nickel city folk could gaze into large wood and steel boxes and marvel at moving picture images of prizefighters, ballplayers, and ballerinas. John D. Rockefeller and Andrew Carnegie represented the extremes of American wealth and power. It had already been two years since the Wright brothers conducted the first manned test flight of an airplane. In Germany, the theoretical physicist Albert Einstein had recently published a paper on the "photoelectric effect" and was fast at work developing his theory of relativity. In Vienna, Sigmund Freud published his pathbreaking volume *Three Essays on the Theory of Sexuality*.

In his youth, John Hay could scarcely have imagined this world. A child of the western prairie, he was raised in the age of iron and grew to manhood in the age of steel. A noted poet and historian, former newspaper editor and railroad executive, Hay had served as U.S.

ambassador to Britain and, since 1898, secretary of state—first under President William McKinley and then, after 1901, under President Theodore Roosevelt. He was one of the most powerful men in the world. But his bright spirit was fast burning out a frail body. In his final weeks, his mind wandered back to the simpler world of his youth.

"I dreamed last night that I was in Washington," Hay confided to his diary, "and that I went to the White House to report to the President, who turned out to be Mr. Lincoln. He was very kind and considerate, and sympathetic about my illness. He gave me two unimportant letters to answer. I was pleased that this slight order was within my power to obey. I was not in the least surprised at Lincoln's presence in the White House. But the whole impression of the dream was one of overpowering melancholy."

This is the story of John Hay and John Nicolay, prairie boys who met in 1851 and forged a close friendship that endured over a half century. Fortune placed them in the right place (Springfield, Illinois) at the right time (1860) and offered them a front-row seat to one of the most tumultuous political and military upheavals in American history, then or since.

As Abraham Lincoln's private secretaries, they became, both literally and figuratively, closer to the president than anyone outside his immediate family. Still young men in their twenties, they lived and worked on the second floor of the White House, performing the roles and functions of a modern-day chief of staff, press secretary, political director, and presidential body man. Above all, they guarded the "last door which opens into the awful presence" of the commander in chief, in the words of Noah Brooks, a journalist and one of many Washington insiders who coveted their jobs, resented their influence, and thought them a little too big for their britches ("a fault for which it seems to me either Nature or our tailors are to blame," Hay once quipped). "These . . . Secretaries are young men," Brooks grumbled, "and the least said of them the better, perhaps."

In demeanor and temperament, they could not have been more different. Short-tempered and dyspeptic, Nicolay cut a brooding figure to those seeking the president's time or favor. William Stoddard, an

assistant secretary under their supervision, later remarked that Nicolay was "decidedly German in his manner of telling men what he thought of them . . . People who do not like him—because they cannot use him, perhaps—say he is sour and crusty, and it is a grand good thing, then, that he is."

Hay cultivated a softer image. He was, in the words of his contemporaries, a "comely young man with peach-blossom face," "very witty—boyish in his manner, yet deep enough—bubbling over with some brilliant speech." An instant fixture in Washington social circles, fast friend of Robert Todd Lincoln's, and favorite among Republican congressmen who haunted the White House halls, he projected a youthful dash that balanced out Nicolay's more grim bearing.

Hay and Nicolay were party to the president's greatest official acts and most private moments. They were in the room when he signed the Emancipation Proclamation, and they were by his side at Gettysburg, when he first spoke to the nation of a "new birth of freedom." When he could not sleep, which, as the war progressed, was often, Lincoln walked down the corridor to their private quarters and passed the time reciting Shakespeare or mulling over the day's political and military developments. When his son Willie passed away in 1862, the first person to whom Lincoln turned was John Nicolay. When the president drew his last breath in April 1865, John Hay was by his bedside.

For the rest of their lives, even as they built their own families and careers, Hay and Nicolay inspired a certain measure of wonder and awe. The greater Lincoln grew in death, the greater they grew for having known him so well, and so intimately, in life. Everyone wanted to know them, if only to ask what it had been like—what *he* had been like. It was a tough question to answer. Abraham Lincoln worked hard at being inscrutable. "The tones, the gestures, the kindling eye, and the mirth-provoking look defy the reporter's skill," wrote Brooks. William Herndon, Lincoln's law partner, could fairly claim to have known him as well as any man during the Springfield days. But to Herndon, the future president was the most "shut-mouthed man who ever lived." He "always told only enough of his plans and purpose to induce the belief that he had communicated all," observed another friend, "yet he

reserved enough to have communicated nothing." Even Lincoln acknowledged as much. "I am rather inclined to silence," he admitted, "and whether that be wise or not, it is at least more unusual now-a-days to find a man who can hold his tongue than to find one who cannot."

If anyone knew the inner mind of the president, it was the two secretaries. Witty and prolific letter writers, observant and incisive diarists, Hay and Nicolay left a remarkable record of Lincoln's evolution as chief executive. By their later account, they "came from Illinois to Washington with him, and remained at his side and in his service—separately or together—until the day of his death. We were the daily and nightly witnesses of the incidents, the anxieties, the fears, and the hopes which pervaded the Executive Mansion and the National Capital during the war." Better than anyone else, they knew where the president was, what he was doing, and what he was thinking at almost every turn. It is little wonder that historians of the era consult Hay's and Nicolay's writings freely and frequently. But their life's work after the Civil War is a largely forgotten story.

"The boys," as the president affectionately called them, became Lincoln's official biographers. Enjoying exclusive access to his papers, which the Lincoln family closed to the public until 1947, they undertook a twenty-five-year mission to create a definitive and enduring historical image of their slain leader. It became the great undertaking of their lives. The culmination of these efforts—their exhaustive, ten-volume biography, which was widely serialized between 1886 and 1890—constituted one of the most successful exercises in historical revisionism in American history. Writing against the rising currents of Southern apologia and a popular vogue for reunion and reconciliation, Hay and Nicolay pioneered the "Northern" interpretation of the Civil War—an interpretation whose influence waxed and waned but that created a standard against which every other historian and polemicist had to stake out his or her position.

Hay and Nicolay helped invent the Lincoln we know today:

the Great Emancipator
the sage father figure

the military genius
the greatest American orator
the brilliant political tactician
the master of a fractious cabinet who forged a "team of
 rivals" out of erstwhile challengers for the throne
the Lincoln Memorial Lincoln

That Abraham Lincoln was all of these things, in some measure, there can be no doubt. But it is easy to forget how widely underrated Lincoln the president and Lincoln the man were on the eve of his death and how successful Hay and Nicolay were in elevating his place in the nation's collective historical memory. While Lincoln prided himself on his deep connection to "the people"—that nebulous body politic in whose collective wisdom he developed an almost mystic faith—he never succeeded in translating his immense popularity with the Northern public into similar regard among the nation's political and intellectual elites. The profound emotional bond that he shared with Union soldiers and their families, and his stunning electoral success in two successive presidential elections, never fully inspired an equivalent level of esteem by the influential men who governed the country and guarded its official history. To many of these men, he remained in death what he was in life: the rail-splitter and country lawyer—good, decent, and ill-fitted to the immense responsibilities that befell him in time of war.

Leading into the 1864 election cycle, many prominent members of Lincoln's own party agreed with the Iowa senator James Grimes that the administration "has been a disgrace from the very beginning to every one who had any thing to do with bringing it into power." Charles Sumner, the radical antislavery leader, fumed that the nation needed "a president with brains; one who can make a plan and carry it out." From across the political spectrum, influential writers and politicians blamed Lincoln for four years of military stalemate and setbacks and for a series of political blunders that cost his party dearly in the 1862 midterm elections. John Andrew, the governor of Massachusetts, spoke for many Republicans when he explained his support

of Lincoln's reelection. The president, he said, was "essentially lacking in the quality of leadership," but now that he had been renominated, "correction is impossible . . . Massachusetts will vote for the Union Cause at all events and will support Mr. Lincoln so long as he remains the candidate."

Years later, Hay remarked that had Lincoln "died in the days of doubt and gloom which preceded his reelection," rather than in the final weeks of the war, as the Union moved to secure its great victory, he would almost certainly have been remembered differently, despite his great acts and deeds.

But that is not how it happened. Assassinated on Good Friday, Lincoln became a Christ figure to many Americans who sought to make sense of the carnival of death and destruction that had touched virtually every community over the preceding four years. But apotheosis was not Hay's or Nicolay's objective. They sought to canonize their boss as a great leader among men, not a saint or a martyr. They remembered him as an innate leader of men, with a powerful grasp of political and military strategy. He was steadfast where other men wavered; he saw the long game, where others staggered from crisis to crisis; he alone enjoyed the trust of the Northern people. Americans today understand Abraham Lincoln much as Nicolay and Hay hoped that they would. Theirs was a deliberate project of historical creation. They were "Lincoln men," Hay asserted, and they meant to tell their story so that the rest of the world would know the man as they had.

It was not an easy task to complete. Hay and Nicolay had to slug it out with lesser figures who entertained their own ideas about Lincoln's place in history. They were especially troubled by the historical amnesia that was quickly taking hold over the reunited states. In popular literature and journalism, the war was being recast as a brothers' squabble over abstract political principles like federalism and states' rights, rather than as a moral struggle between slavery and freedom. Magazines and newspapers commonly took to celebrating the military valor of both Confederate and Union soldiers, as though bravery, rather than morality, were the chief quality to be commemorated.

They also reimagined Lincoln as a conciliatory figure who was above politics and sectionalism, conveniently forgetting the social revolution unleashed by emancipation and ignoring his admonition—just weeks before his death—that "if God wills that [the war] continue until all the wealth piled by the bondsman's two hundred and fifty years of unrequited toil shall be sunk, and until every drop of blood drawn with the lash shall be paid by another drawn with the sword, as was said three thousand years ago, so still it must be said 'the judgments of the Lord are true and righteous altogether.'"

Nicolay and Hay viewed this revisionist tendency with alarm. While their editor and publisher hoped that the Nicolay-Hay volumes would "help unite the North and South as never before, around the story and experiences of the great President," the authors pointedly rejected the vogue for sectional reconciliation and emphasized the salient moral and political issues that divided the two sections before, and in many respects after, the war. The war had been caused by "an uprising of the national conscience against a secular wrong" that could never be blotted out by the romance of reunion. Though the influence of their interpretation of events would wax and wane over time, it established the terms of a historiographical debate that persists to this day. As the only authorized biographers of Abraham Lincoln, they played a central role in determining how future generations would understand and imagine the sixteenth president and the events over which he presided.

More than just a story of history and memory, this book also addresses the ideological journey traveled by many men who came of age during the Civil War. Jolted to consciousness by the national debate over slavery, they were America's first "hope and change" generation. They forged new and expansive ideas about national citizenship on the fields of Shiloh and Gettysburg and in the halls of Congress. Yet in the decades that followed the war, many young men who began public life as antislavery crusaders seemed to be evolving into relatively conservative adults.

In some respects, there was great consistency in this evolution. The

Republican Party, an organization that would remain central to the political identities of men like Hay and Nicolay, was founded on the laissez-faire proposition that free labor is always superior to slave labor. Regardless of color, people should be afforded the right to rise or fall on their talents and industry. Most Republicans continued to embrace this free-market understanding of the world, but by the 1870s that vision had grown estranged from its radical antislavery roots and become a natural point of opposition to labor unions and advocates of urban and working-class Americans. During the war, Republicans had forged a strong alliance with capital and industry to subdue the South. After the war, they saw no reason to divorce the party from its interests. Many men like Hay and Nicolay, who cut their teeth on antislavery politics, were comfortable with the inequalities that modern capitalism wrought. In their youth, they were reformers; as they grew old, they became conservatives. It was not their thinking that changed as much as the context.

A brief note about what this book is not—namely, a comprehensive biography of John Hay or John Nicolay, let alone Abraham Lincoln. Much has been written about Hay's literary career, his friendship with Henry Adams, and his service as secretary of state under McKinley and Roosevelt. In many ways, he was one of the most extraordinary men of his generation. He was seemingly everywhere at every turn. I touch on these topics insofar as they help to inform a discussion of his ideological progression and his enduring allegiance to a martyred president, but this is not a work of diplomatic or literary history. Little has been written about Nicolay's postwar career, as so much of it was devoted to preserving the memory of Lincoln. These pages fill in some of the gaps in his story.

Nicolay and Hay believed that writing good history required telling a good story. Ours begins some fifty years before John Hay's final passage across the sea, in Providence, Rhode Island, where a young poet has just completed a long journey from his boyhood home in Illinois.

PART I

Exile in the West

eptember 30, 1855. "As I am now all completely settled and arranged for the term," John Hay reported breathlessly to his family, "I proceed to give you notice of this important fact and to let you know that I still am an inhabitant of the earth."

For some, the journey is more important than the destination. Not for Hay. Just shy of his seventeenth birthday, the midwestern native had never spent any meaningful stretch of time in a city larger than Springfield, Illinois—then a town of roughly nine thousand people, where it was not altogether uncommon for hogs, chickens, and other farm animals to slog through streets perpetually caked in mud alongside the human beings who made their homes and earned their livelihoods in the capital's modest wood-frame houses and three-story brick office buildings. Providence, Rhode Island, where he would spend the next three years earning his bachelor's degree, was an intellectual mecca. With a heritage stretching back to the early colonial era and a population five times that of Springfield, it was home to Brown University, one of the premier colleges in the land. It was an eastern city, with eastern ideas and eastern sensibilities—a fitting place for a poet. And John Hay wanted quite badly to be a poet.

"I had a whirling, hustling time on the way here," the young man reported home, "but at last arrived without any accident on Tuesday evening, safe and sound in everything, except my eyes, mouth and ears were full of cinders and dust." At Brown, Hay lived on the second

floor of University Hall, an early Federal-style redbrick building
perched on a hill overlooking the city. The rent was $50 per year. He
found his room, with a window facing the grass-covered quadrangle,
"comfortable and conveniently furnished . . . My chum is a young man
from the State of New York, steady, studious, and good scholar, so I
stand a chance of doing a good deal of hard study this winter. It is not
here as in Springfield. Here I am acquainted with no one in the city
and have no inducements to leave the college, while in Springfield my
circle of acquaintance was far from limited, and entirely too agreeable
for my own good."

Sending his love to "Grandpa, aunts, uncles, cousins, and cats and
all inquiring friends," Hay bade his family to "write soon—soon—do
you hear? SOON" and began making his way in the wider world.

John Hay was born in Salem, Indiana, in 1838, in a one-story, four-
room brick house, the son of Charles Hay, a medical doctor, and his
wife, Helen Leonard. A close family of six children (one of whom,
Edward, died at age eight), the Hays were comfortable but far from
wealthy. When John was three years old, the family relocated to War-
saw, Illinois, a small town tucked along the banks of the Mississippi
River, near the westernmost part of the state. "The days of my boy-
hood were passed on the banks of the Mississippi, and the great river
was the scene of my early dreams," he later said. "The boys of my day
led an amphibian life in and near its waters in the summertime, and in
the winter its dazzling ice bridge, of incomparable beauty and purity, was
our favorite playground . . . We built forts and called them the Alamo;
we sang rude songs of the cane-brake and cornfield; and the happiest
days of the year to us who dwelt on the northern bluff of the river were
those that brought us, in the loud puffing and whistling steamers of
olden time, to the mecca of our rural fancies, the bright and busy me-
tropolis of St. Louis."

It was clear from the start that John was an unusually bright boy,
though given to daydreaming and flights of fancy. His sister remem-
bered that he developed the "habit of stringing words together into
rhymes," and his younger brother, Charles, recalled that when John

"was a small boy, a German of education called on my father to ask assistance in forming a class for the study of German[;] John listened with a great deal of interest and whispered to my father, 'I would like very much to study German.'" Always proud of his children and encouraging of their ambitions, Dr. Hay agreed. Though a mere child among a class of men, John surprised everyone by demonstrating an aptitude for the language.

In 1849, Hay's parents packed him off to Pittsfield, the seat of nearby Pike County. As Warsaw had no schools worth attending, his uncle Milton Hay had suggested that John live with him and attend a local academy managed by John D. Thomson, an Irishman who had graduated from Dublin University and somehow made his way as far as the Illinois prairie. There, Hay formed a fast friendship with John George Nicolay, a Bavarian immigrant six years his senior. No record exists of their earliest times together, but their association would soon evolve into the most important and enduring relationship in both men's lives.

After completing his course at Thomson's academy, Hay moved to Springfield in 1852, where he lived with his paternal grandfather and enrolled at Illinois State University, a new institution that, despite its name, was little more than a preparatory school meant to feed bright young men to more prominent colleges. Few traces survive of his time there, though by 1854 Hay had clearly discovered his métier. Writing to his sister, he offered that poetry was "one of the noblest faculties of our nature, and should be cultivated to its fullest extent. The true poet *will* cultivate this gift. One who is so highly gifted, can no more keep silent, and withhold from pouring out a flood of song, than can the songsters of the grove, refrain from warbling their notes of praise, or the rivulet refuse to flow."

Hay's course of study at Illinois State involved a healthy dose of Latin, Greek, algebra, and rhetoric, but his heart was never in it more than when he read "Milton, Byron, Moore & Burns . . . These I almost worship," or "the odes of Horace, which are beautiful." He professed to work every night except for Fridays and Sundays (on Friday evenings, he participated in salons, "for the purpose of debating, reading original essays, and criticizing"). But he would just as soon enjoy the

"exquisite happiness [of] contemplating the grandeur of the hoary mountain, the calm solicitude of the forest, the roar of the boundless ocean, the headlong career of the torrent, and the merry laugh of the dancing rill." This was John Hay at age fifteen.

Aside from his lofty aspirations to poetic glory, it was also clear that Hay shared with many teenagers then and since a burning desire to see more of the world. "In my opinion," he told his sister, "all the sentimental talk we hear from the poet and the novelist, about the simplicity & quiet ease of village life, is all humbug. The city is the only place to gain a knowledge of the world." By 1855, Springfield was no longer big enough to satisfy his ambitions. With backing from his uncle Milton, who agreed to pay the bill, John set off for Brown University, where he took his place as a sophomore.

One of his friends from around this time remembered Hay as a "red-cheeked, black-eyed, sunshiny boy, chock-full of fun and devilment that hurt nobody." Except for the description of his eyes (which were hazel), the sketch lined up well against the recollections of other contemporaries. Clark Carr, a friend from Brown, described Hay as "bright, rosy-faced, boyish-looking" and reflected that he had never before met "a young man or boy who charmed me as he did when he looked at me with his mischievous hazel eyes from under a wealth of dark brown hair. He was, for those days, elegantly dressed—better than any of us; so neatly, indeed, that he would . . . have been set down as a 'dude' at first sight." With his boyish features and small frame, Hay looked younger than his seventeen years, and it took some time before he cultivated enough savvy to replace his "western" garb with clothes more befitting the style preferred by the eastern college crowd. But it did not take him long to become tremendously popular, as would be the case almost everywhere he went in life. His classmate William Leete Stone credited him with "a singularly modest and retiring disposition," but "so winning a manner that no one could be in his presence, even for a few moments, without falling under the spell which his conversation and companionship invariably cast upon all who came within his influence."

Like most American colleges in the antebellum era, Brown University was a small institution, numbering only 225 students and nine faculty members. The curriculum favored Latin, Greek, and mathematics, and the pedagogy was heavy on recitation and repetition. "In those days, all text was memorized," explained one of Hay's classmates, "and it was the general opinion that Hay put his book under his pillow and had the contents thereof absorbed and digested by morning, for he was never seen 'digging,' or doing any other act or thing that could be construed as hard study. His quick perception, ready grasp of an idea and wonderfully retentive memory, made a mere pastime of study." Hay's senior-year roommate remembered that "often, after returning from a party late at night, when it was 'odds with morning which was which,' I . . . found him sitting up writing out a Latin or a French exercise for some classmate whose intellectual furnishment was not of the highest order." It was also during these years that Hay became a voracious consumer of books and ideas. College library records indicate that he was a faithful reader of British literary periodicals and that he devoured the works of Spenser, Beaumont, Fletcher, Percy, Wordsworth, and Goethe.

Hay's native intelligence was rivaled only by his outsized personality and charm. Years later, classmates still recalled with a smile the night that he delivered an impromptu toast at the freshman class dinner. "We don't want anything dry!" someone taunted from the rafters. "Hay that is green is never dry," he quickly retorted. Long remembered, too, was "the night that Johnny Hay took hasheesh." Inspired by Fitz Hugh Ludlow's book *The Hasheesh Eater* (1857), in which the author chronicled his frequent use of cannabis, Hay joined the legions of undergraduates before and since who experimented with artificial stimulants. Matters got sufficiently out of hand to warrant a visit by one of Brown's younger (and apparently more liberal) faculty members.

Hay's roommate remembered a young man with "boundless" enthusiasm and a "love for and appreciation of the beautiful in nature and in art . . . If he was smitten by the charms of a pretty girl he raved and walked the room, pouring out his sentiment in a flood of furious eloquence. He would apostrophize a beautiful sunset till the last glow

had expired. I remember being called out of bed by him one night to witness a beautiful display of Northern Lights. The display was gorgeous, but the night was cold, and after stating my view of the situation, I retired to my room leaving him with chattering teeth and eloquent language addressing Aurora B."

Northern lights were a rarity in Providence. Pretty girls were not. Hay was often smitten with them, and they were equally smitten with him. Anna Ridgely, who knew him a few years later in Springfield, remembered that John had "small, well-shaped hands which he had a habit of locking together interlacing the fingers, and carrying at arm's length, which the girls thought particularly fetching." Other times, "he wore a long, loose overcoat, flying open, his hands thrust into the pockets, which was also thought very graceful and attractive as he swung himself along the street, for he had a rocking walk in those days."

During his first year at Brown, Hay caught the eye of James Angell, then a young professor of modern languages. In and out of class, mentor and protégé worked through the canon of French and German classics, and by his senior year Hay had become a regular visitor at Angell's house. There, he met the professor's younger sister Hannah, who lived with her parents in nearby Scituate but frequently visited her brother in Providence. The attraction was instantaneous and mutual. Over fifty years later, Hannah could still vividly describe Hay's eyes, "which you could look into for a mile, and they looked through and through yours."

Hay's preferred method of flirtation involved excessive doses of purple prose and romantic verse. "I have no news to write you," he confessed in a typical letter, "and it would be utterly ridiculous to think of writing anything original on a day when the birds are too lazy to do more than to sleepily twitter in the shade, when the sky is like brass & the air sleeps in a sultry hush, & even the thunder lying in wait in the north utters ever & anon a drowsy growl and dies lazily in the hot silence. My only object is to get a letter from you." He visited Hannah on more than one occasion in Scituate, where her family's house looked out on a winding road shaded by tall maples and elms. As they

walked together by the Ponaganset River, he took a penknife from his pocket and carved the letters *HAY* (an amalgam of his surname and Hannah's initials) on the rail of a small footbridge. "I need not tell you how happy a day was yesterday," he wrote after one of their afternoon excursions. "As we rode home in silence the vanished hours passed before me in joyous review, lacking indeed, the warm and vivid beauty of the day but with a tender halo gathered of the starlight."

Hay's letters to Hannah frequently included lines of original verse. In them, he expressed a dread of his graduation and return to Illinois and got good mileage off a repertoire of self-effacing references to his western "barbarism." After three successful years in Providence, he still felt like a fish out of water. He knew the full extent of his talents. He was functionally fluent in German, Latin, Greek, and French, and he had mastered course work in chemistry, mathematics, physics, political economy, philosophy, rhetoric, modern history, and declamation—all by the age of nineteen. But he was still deeply self-conscious of his provincial roots. In later years, as Lincoln's secretary and as a journalist and poet of national renown, he was known for the clever simplicity of his prose and his free use of regional vernacular. That was an older, more confident man. At Brown, Hay was still imitating the romantic poets, writing long, flowery love letters, and apologizing just a little too frequently for his prairie origins. A typical effort began:

> In heathen wilds I soon shall pine
> Doomed to an exile worse than thine.
> When Mississippi madly roars
> In fury o'er his golden bars,
> And on the sleeping prairies pours
> The light of western stars;
> Day never gilded with his smile
> A land so fair, a race so vile.
> As diet horseshoe nails they use,
> And aqua fortis drink with glee;
> In milder moments they infuse

Corn whiskey in their tea.
On Sundays sally forth with dogs
To taunt their children in the bogs . . .
. . . The "Western District" may not boast
Men of a form and soul like those
(As soon on its clam haunted coast
You'll find the prairie rose.)
There country life & Yankee rum
Have wrought a milder heathendom.

Hannah surely knew that John was spending a great deal of his spare time in the company of several poets and prose writers who lived near College Hill. Chief among his new friends were Nora Perry, a young woman just seven years his senior who later served a long tenure as Boston correspondent for the *Chicago Tribune,* and Sarah Helen Whitman, an older writer who, ten years earlier, had been Edgar Allan Poe's romantic muse. With the encouragement of his literary mentors, Hay secured the honor of composing and delivering the class poem at the conclusion of his senior year. Writing to Hannah of his progress, he reported to be "in a remarkably good humor at present. I have freed myself from that fearful incubus which has been inflicting for the last month such acute Iambic torture."

The result won wide praise from Brown's faculty and student body. With his gaze fixed on a literary life, Hay extolled the virtues of the path that he wanted more badly than even before to pursue:

Oft let the poet leave his toil and care
To greet the spirits of the sky and air;
Let him go forth to learn of love and truth,
From Nature smiling in eternal youth;
To ponder long on infinite wealth and power,
Squandered to deck with gold one wayside flower;
And share the peaceful majesty that fills
The emerald circuit of the sunny hills.
Earth grows not old, nor niggard of her joys

But spells as genial on our souls employs
As when Greek sunsets poured their purple dyes
In wasteful splendor on blind Homer's eyes.

It was never likely that Hay's family could afford to indulge his pursuit of a writer's life, and he knew it. Still basking in the triumph of his poetic glory, John sent a good-bye letter to Hannah Angell. "When I look around me & see my trunk packed & observe the general look of confusion that a room has when everything is over, I begin to realize that I have completed my self-immolation," he confided to Hannah. "Today I am surprised, tomorrow I will be stunned, the next day I will see some friends whose faces will galvanize me into a mockery of life, in a week I will be at home sharing in the pathetic joy of kindred, & in a month I will be busy." With all the histrionics that a nineteen-year-old college graduate could muster, John hoped that he might "find rest and peace in the tumult of the West, & feel an inner calm . . . Whether I am 'snuffed' out young or die old & sordid, I shall remember that I lived one year in Providence [and] wrote a poem (you never saw it)." In closing, Hay reminded his college sweetheart that there would soon be "a young man in Warsaw, Illinois, that is going to the P.O. three times a day & looking like a pious Moslem, to the East."

August found Hay in a melancholy and melodramatic mood. Back home with his parents, he whiled away the last days of summer writing dreamy letters to his friends in Providence and longing for "the 'goodbye lands'" that he had left all of two weeks earlier. He told Nora Perry that he had cast off the world and was content to "go to my room to convene with shadows." He wrote love poems and sent them to Hannah Angell. He struck up a correspondence with William O'Connor, a Philadelphia poet of middling reputation. Counting himself as one of the "faithless nomads of the prairies," he predicted that all of his "ties and associations formed in the East" would soon be "dissolved by the air of Illinois." Four months later, he professed still to "turn my eyes Eastward, like an Islamite, when I feel prayerful," and told Nora that if she "loved Providence as I do, you would congratulate yourself hourly on your lot." The West, he complained, was

"a dreary waste of heartless materialism . . . [I]n time, I shall change.
I shall turn from 'the rose and the rainbow' to corner lots and tax-titles,
and a few years will find my eye not rolling in a fine frenzy, but steadily
fixed on the pole-star of humanity, $!" In an especially self-pitying dis-
patch to Whitman, he cast himself as "an exile in the West." It was
time, Hay decided—about two months into his postcollegiate career—
to "give up my dreams" and "turn my attention to those practical stud-
ies which are to minister to material wants in the West." In short, he
was miserable.

None of this was lost on Charles Hay, who indulged John's indefi-
nite summer vacation for several weeks but soon grew concerned by
his son's aimless drift. Charles admitted to his brother, Milton, that he
was "somewhat undecided as to what course" John should take. The
family discussed the idea of his entering the teaching profession, but
both Mrs. Hay and Augustus, the eldest of the Hay children, were op-
posed to the idea, as "it would neither suit his self-esteem nor his pe-
cuniary wants." Augustus wanted John to return to Brown, earn a
graduate degree, and write for "Eastern periodicals until a time and
opening offered for taking a high position *somewhere.*" But the family
could ill afford to subsidize another eastern adventure, and Charles
was not about to ask Milton (who had paid John's undergraduate ex-
penses) to foot the bill for another year. Some of John's friends urged
"him to turn his attention immediately to the law, while others, espe-
cially some valued ones at the East, advise him to turn his attention at
once and wholly to literature." Dr. Hay was not opposed to his son's
pursuit of a literary life, but he wanted him "to have some profession
upon which he can fall back, or rather rise upon, while he is rising,
higher. He is restless and wishes to know his destiny, although he ex-
pects me to decide for him entirely."

Charles and his brother agreed on a course of action that was de-
signed to please everyone. Guided by Milton, John would begin inde-
pendent legal studies, in preparation for a clerkship in his uncle's office.
At the same time, he would pursue whatever literary and scholarly
opportunities came his way. It was a good enough plan, but for one
problem: John had no interest in the profession.

"I am not making the most rapid progress in the law," he admitted to Milton in January 1859. "I have, as you advised, read all of Hume consecutively, and, to speak with moderation, remember *some* of it. I would then immediately have made an attack upon Blackstone, had I not been prevented for a while by the distemper that has troubled me more or less all season." What John had done, in lieu of working through Blackstone's *Commentaries,* was spend several weeks researching and writing a lecture on the history of the Jesuit order, for presentation to the local Warsaw "Literary Institute." In the wake of his lecture, close friends suggested in jest that he make a career of the pulpit. "I would not do for a Methodist preacher," he told Milton, "for I am a poor horseman. I would not suit the Baptists, for I dislike water. I would fail as an Episcopalian, for I am no ladies' man." Instead, he was politely resigned to furthering his legal studies. "They would spoil a first-class preacher to make a third-class lawyer of me," he quipped.

By spring, the family had decided that it was time for John to clerk for his uncle Milton, who had moved his law office to nearby Springfield. "I am hardly in a situation to begin anything," Hay complained to Hannah Angell. "I alternate between weeks of sickness and months of my normal condition of chronic worthlessness. How it will end does not seem difficult to say. The only question is one of time. In the meanwhile I will read the Law. John Doe & Richard Roe shall displace the airy forms that have guided my dreams."

Milton Hay's law office was on the second floor of a three-story brick building, directly in the center of town, on the western side of the city's State Capitol Square. In a nearby suite were the offices of Abraham Lincoln and William Herndon. (As a young man, Milton had clerked under Lincoln.) A former one-term congressman and twice-failed candidate for the U.S. Senate, Lincoln was a known personality in Springfield, but only a small group of loyalists thought he might be presidential timber. None of the chatter registered strongly with John. Even a year later, amid the tension and fever pitch of the 1860 presidential campaign, as Lincoln's political handlers were openly plotting a bold strategy to secure the nomination for their candidate, he wrote to Hannah that his "insanity has not yet changed its form from rhyme

to politics. Young men generally glide very naturally in their invocations from the muses to the masses and remove the shrine of their worship from Castalia to Congress. But I am as yet innocent of politics." Hay thought well enough of Lincoln but generally liked to "occupy myself very pleasantly in thoroughly hating both sides, and abusing the peculiar tenets of the company I happen to be in, and when the company is divided, in saying with Mercutio, 'A plague on both your houses.' This position of dignified neutrality I expect to hold for a very long time unless Lincoln is nominated at Chicago."

Though in the ensuing months he continued to write a flurry of self-pitying letters to his eastern correspondents, for the most part Hay buckled down and settled into his studies. In due course, Springfield offered charms of its own, and he developed a circle of friends and intimates. But he continued to view himself as a transient and an observer. "I am very easily contented, in whatever sphere I may be placed," he assured his uncle Milton before taking up his clerkship, "and can always wait for the tide of circumstances without any inconvenience."

Sometime during his first days in Springfield, with nothing better to do, John Hay took a walk over to the capitol building to visit his old friend John Nicolay. It was in this way that the tide of circumstances intervened.

The Homes of Free White People

While John Hay was hatching plans to achieve literary glory and escape indefinite exile in the "barbarous" West, the country in which he lived was consumed by an increasingly bitter debate over slavery. A contemporary observer noted that when one entered the home of even the most ordinary farmer, "the grand theme is politics; and you will be surprised by the sense and readiness with which he speaks on the most intricate national questions." Not so John Hay. Most striking about his papers in this period is the near-total absence of current affairs. Living in a decade of profound turmoil, he had little to say. In a letter to his uncle Milton, dated early 1856, John noted in passing that he had attended a Republican Party rally. But on the great topics of the day—the Fugitive Slave Act, the extension of slavery into the western territories, the rise of a new antislavery political movement—he was almost completely silent.

Over the preceding quarter century—from the late 1820s through the 1840s—American politics had been dominated by two political parties, Whigs and Democrats, who disagreed on a host of issues concerning political economy. Debates over the national banking system, tariffs, internal improvements, soft (that is, paper) versus hard (that is, metal) money, and workingmen's rights largely defined the antebellum political discussion, and for the most part both parties enjoyed strong bisectional support. By the late 1840s, the political system had come under severe strain, in part because many of the defining

questions of the era found resolution. Andrew Jackson had killed the Second Bank of the United States, thus sucking the air out of a highly charged debate over the institution's value and constitutionality. Broad consensus emerged that the states, not the national government, were chiefly responsible for financing infrastructure projects. The California gold rush flooded the country with additional "specie," temporarily alleviating the demand for paper currency and ending the debate over the propriety of printing it. The parties continued to debate tariff levels, but even that subject no longer inspired the passion that it had when Andrew Jackson occupied the White House. Increasingly, Whigs and Democrats strained to identify meaningful policy disagreements. All that it would take to loosen the voters' allegiances to the existing two parties was a new, salient issue. And that issue was ultimately slavery.

On the evening of Saturday, August 8, 1846, as Congress neared adjournment, David Wilmot, a Democratic congressman from northwestern Pennsylvania, approached the well of the House chamber and submitted an amendment to a routine military appropriations bill. It was an unusually hot and sticky night—even for Washington, D.C.—and most of Wilmot's colleagues were eager to flee the swamplike conditions of the capital city for cooler parts. At the time, the United States was engaged in a war with Mexico that it would ultimately win and that would bring the country into possession of lands that later formed all or part of modern-day California, Nevada, Utah, New Mexico, Arizona, Colorado, Texas, Oklahoma, Kansas, and Wyoming. The introduction of these vast new territories raised a question that Americans had not had to address for almost thirty years: Should Congress permit the institution of slavery to expand beyond its current borders? The Wilmot Proviso, as it came to be known, opened a Pandora's box by barring the institution in all newly acquired Mexican land. The amendment passed the House on a purely sectional vote, but Southern strength in the Senate prevented it from becoming law. Astute observers understood the significance of the event. Whigs and Democrats had failed to contain a burgeoning sectional conflict over the spread of slavery. "As if by magic," noted a reporter for the *Boston Whig*, "it

brought to a head the great question that is about to divide the American people." Even President James Polk, the chief architect of the Mexican War, privately feared that "the slavery question is assuming a fearful . . . aspect" and might "ultimately threaten the Union itself."

Since Congress enacted the Missouri Compromise in 1820, Americans had accepted as established fact that the 36°30′ parallel demarcated the line between the free and the slave states. Below the line, slavery was permitted; above it, it was banned. But the Missouri Compromise applied strictly to those territories that the United States had procured from France in the Louisiana Purchase. It had no bearing on the new lands that the United States acquired during the Mexican War. Because most of the Mexican cession fell beneath the Missouri Compromise line, many Southerners naturally felt that it ought to be open to slavery. Most Northerners disagreed. Foreseeing an inevitable conflict, Ralph Waldo Emerson warned at the outset of the war that "the United States will conquer Mexico, but it will be as the man swallows arsenic, which brings him down in turn. Mexico will poison us." Events later proved Emerson right.

As it had so many times in the past, Congress managed to delay the sectional clash by hammering out a series of accommodations. Originally conceived by Henry Clay and shepherded through the Senate by Stephen A. Douglas, a rising Democratic star from Illinois, the Compromise of 1850 split the baby in two. California entered the Union as a free state, but the citizens of other former Mexican territories were left to make their own determinations about slavery. Congress abolished the slave trade, but not slavery, in Washington, D.C., and created a more stringent fugitive slave law. Inasmuch as the compromise created a pathway to organize the former Mexican territories and temporarily settled the slavery question, it was a success. But storm clouds lurked on the horizon. Douglas was unable to secure passage of the compromise in "omnibus" form and had to break it into its component pieces to move it through the Senate. Majorities in each section opposed those provisions that were likely to offend their constituencies, raising quiet concern that the package was no compromise at all but rather a series of short-term expediencies meant to avoid civil war.

Despite its framers' hopes that the Compromise of 1850 would stanch sectional animosities, at least one of its components backfired. The new Fugitive Slave Act inspired widespread disgust throughout the North. The law stripped accused runaways of their right to trial by jury and allowed individual cases to be bumped up from state courts to special federal courts. As an extra incentive to federal commissioners adjudicating such cases, it provided a $10 fee when a defendant was remanded to slavery but only $5 for a finding rendered against the slave owner. Most obnoxious to many Northerners, the law stipulated harsh fines and prison sentences for any citizen who refused to cooperate with or aid federal authorities in the capture of accused fugitives.

Though resistance to the Fugitive Slave Act was not widespread, several high-profile cases caused a political firestorm. In Boston, an angry mob assailed two Georgians who came north to retrieve Ellen and William Craft, a black couple who had escaped from slavery two years earlier. The Crafts were celebrated runaways; nobody claimed that theirs was a case of mistaken identity. Citizens of Boston nevertheless held the slave catchers at bay while Theodore Parker and friends spirited them to Canada. A similar scene occurred months later, when slave catchers from Virginia came to retrieve Shadrach Minkins, a runaway from Norfolk. As the fugitive awaited his hearing before a federal magistrate, "we heard a shout from across the courthouse," recalled Richard H. Dana Jr., whose office window overlooked the melee, "continued into a yell of triumph, and in an instant after down the steps came two negroes bearing the prisoner between them with his clothes half torn off, and so stupefied by his sudden rescue and the violence of the dragging off that he sat almost dumb, and I thought had fainted . . . It was all done in an instant, too quick to be believed."

When federal marshals in Boston arrested Anthony Burns in 1854, a vigilance committee gathered at Faneuil Hall and declared that "resistance to tyrants is obedience to God." Heavily armed with axes and pistols, they marched to the courthouse, where, in the ensuing battle, a federal officer was killed. In response, President Franklin Pierce, a Northern Democrat, mobilized the U.S. Army and Navy to transport Burns back to Virginia, at a cost of $100,000 (roughly equivalent to

$4 million in 2012). As soldiers escorted the fugitive down the streets of Boston, church bells tolled in somber protest, and homeowners and shopkeepers turned their American flags upside down in a show of defiance. "I saw . . . the lawyers' offices hung in black," wrote a bystander. "I saw the cavalry, artillery, marines, and police, a thousand strong, escorting with shotted guns one trembling colored man to the vessel which was to carry him to slavery. I heard the curses, both loud and deep, poured over these soldiers; I saw the red flush in their cheeks as the crowd yelled at them, 'Kidnappers! Kidnappers!'" Even conservative "Cotton" Whigs—New Englanders with strong political and business ties to the plantation South—found the whole affair "odious and hateful." George Hillard, a prominent attorney, witnessed Burns's arrest firsthand. "When it was all over," he told a friend, "and I was left alone in my office, I put my face in my hands and wept. I could do nothing less." His townsman Amos Lawrence, a fellow Cotton Whig, spoke for many people when he wrote, "We went to bed one night old fashioned, conservative, Compromise Union Whigs & waked up stark mad Abolitionists."

Northern opposition to slavery sprang from diverse sources. On one end of the spectrum, abolitionists like Theodore Parker, William Lloyd Garrison, and Wendell Phillips believed that African Americans were human beings, entitled to the same rights and liberties as white men and women. Closely allied with these reformers were radical antislavery politicians like Thaddeus Stevens of Pennsylvania, Joshua Giddings and Salmon P. Chase of Ohio, and Charles Sumner of Massachusetts, whose moral opposition to slavery stemmed from a commitment to racial equality. In this position, they were well ahead of their time.

Somewhere on the other side of the spectrum, many conservative Whigs and Democrats harbored intensely negrophobic sentiments but opposed slavery because they believed that the institution placed white yeomen farmers at a disadvantage. If Southerners could import slave labor into the territories, free white homesteaders could never compete on a level playing field. Typical of this perspective was David Wilmot, who denied any "squeamish . . . sensitiveness" or "morbid

sympathy for the slave." Rather, he complained that "the negro race already occupy enough of this fair continent . . . I would preserve for free white labor a fair country . . . where the sons of toil, of my own race and own color, can live without the disgrace which association with negro slavery brings upon free labor."

The ideological lines were not always crystal clear. Abraham Lincoln, who built a career out of locating the political center, argued strongly for the slave's fundamental humanity, insisting that "no man is good enough to govern another man, *without the other's consent.*" Nevertheless, he agreed that Manifest Destiny was a white man's game. "The whole nation is interested that the best use shall be made of these territories," he wrote. "We want them for the homes of free white people. This they cannot be, to any considerable extent, if slavery shall be planted within them."

Most antislavery Northerners maintained that slavery was a local, rather than national, institution. By the tenets of natural law, all human beings were born free. States could enact "positive" laws establishing slavery, they conceded, but the institution enjoyed no force outside of its local boundaries. William Henry Seward, who served New York State as governor and in the U.S. Senate, gave voice to this idea when he denied that the "Constitution recognizes property in slaves." The original, unamended document made no direct reference to slaves or slavery. Instead, it referenced persons held in bondage and even counted them for purposes of assessing taxes and apportioning congressional seats—a clear sign (Seward claimed) that the founders recognized bondsmen as human beings rather than chattel. When Northerners flouted the Fugitive Slave Act, or when they fought to prevent the extension of slavery into federal lands, they did so in the firm belief that slaves ceased to be slaves the minute they crossed into free territory. The peculiar institution had no standing where it was not otherwise established by local law.

Aside from this emerging consensus that slaves were human beings, and not property, the common denominator of antislavery sentiment was opposition to the political and economic evils that the institution imposed on society. Perceiving deep social divisions between

the North, with its thriving agricultural and industrial economy, nascent public school system, and impressive transportation network, and the South, which they saw as a depressed, backwater region, increasing numbers of Northerners viewed slavery as a drag on the nation's economy and culture. Traveling through Virginia, Seward saw that "exhausted soil, old and decaying towns, wretchedly-neglected roads, and, in every respect, an absence of enterprise and improvement, distinguish the region through which we have come, in contrast to that in which we live. Such has been the effect of slavery."

Northerners like Seward believed that workers in a free-labor system were naturally industrious, inventive, and ambitious and that these virtues led inexorably to material and cultural progress. By contrast, in a slave system there was little incentive for work, industry, and development. Black slaves had little motivation to work hard or work smart ("Enslave a man and you destroy his ambition, his enterprise, and his capacity," Horace Greeley explained), while Southern whites often equated manual labor with "slave work" and therefore grew both complacent and idle. "Slavery always degrades labor," Thaddeus Stevens argued. "The white people who work with their hands are ranked with the other laborers—the slaves . . . They feel that they are degraded and despised." As a result, claimed Seward, "Go ask Virginia—go ask even noble Maryland . . . to show you her people, canals, railroads, universities, schools, charities, commerce cities, and cultivated areas." More than sixty years after the fact, Henry Adams, the grandson and great-grandson of American presidents, remembered traveling with his father along a rough, potholed strip of highway near Mount Vernon, Virginia. "To the New England mind," Adams wrote, "roads, schools, clothes, and a clean face were connected as part of the law of order or divine system. Bad roads meant bad morals. The moral of this Virginia road was clear, and the boy fully learned it. Slavery was wicked, and slavery was the cause of this road's badness which amounted to [a] social crime."

Southerners responded that slavery was integral to the preservation of white liberty and civilization. James Hammond, the South Carolina senator who declared that "Cotton is king," argued that "in

all social systems there must be a class to do the menial duties, to per-
form the drudgery of life . . . It constitutes the very mud sill of soci-
ety . . . Such a class you must have, or you would not have the other
class which leads progress, civilization, and refinement." Hammond
noted that slaves performed that function in the South, whereas in the
North a growing population of landless day laborers and factory
workers—most of them white—were "essentially slaves. The differ-
ence between us is, that our slaves are hired for life and well compen-
sated . . . [Y]ours are hired by the day, not cared for, and scantily
compensated." George Fitzhugh, a Southern polemicist of wide re-
pute, went a step further. "Free society!" he barked. "We sicken at the
name. What is it but a conglomeration of greasy mechanics, filthy op-
eratives, small-fisted farmers, and moon-struck theorists . . . The pre-
vailing class one meets with [in the North] is that of mechanics
struggling to be genteel, and small farmers who do their own drudg-
ery, and yet are hardly fit for association with a Southern gentleman's
body servant." Many Southerners believed that slavery placed all
whites on a plane of social and political equality, while the North's
free-labor system essentially made slaves of white working-class men.

For Southerners who set their eyes westward, the freedom to carry
slavery into the territories was a prerequisite for maintaining their
region's peculiar understanding of equality. For those Northerners
who harbored thoughts of picking up stakes and starting anew in the
West, slavery posed a very tangible threat. A white farmer from New
York or Ohio, relying only on his own sweat, and perhaps that of his
sons, could not hope to compete materially with his slaveholding
neighbor. That Northern farmer also hoped to see his community
thrive and flourish, and slavery, according to prevailing regional wis-
dom, inhibited physical and cultural progress in any territory where it
was permitted to sink roots.

To the generation of Americans who came of age in the antebellum
era, the western frontier represented more than just the promise
of cheap land and economic opportunity. The West embodied the
nation's popular imagination of its collective future. Writing in 1839,
John L. O'Sullivan, a New York newspaperman, announced that it

was America's "manifest destiny to overspread the continent allotted by Providence for the free development of our yearly multiplying millions." When Americans gazed toward the Pacific, they saw their country in thirty or forty years' time. Would that country look like the free-labor North or the slaveholding South?

The Compromise of 1850 effectively contained this simmering conflict until 1854. That year, Congress passed a new law, the Kansas-Nebraska Act, which organized the Kansas and Nebraska territories in preparation for the construction of a midwestern link to a planned transcontinental railroad. At the insistence of Southern senators who initially balked at supporting the bill, Stephen Douglas, the chairman of the Committee on Territories and chief author of the bill, inserted a "popular sovereignty" provision allowing the residents of the two territories to decide for themselves whether to permit slavery. Douglas privately admitted that this one detail would "raise a hell of a storm," but he underestimated just how quickly that storm would gather force. Kansas and Nebraska were part of the Louisiana Purchase, and as such they fell under the provisions of the Missouri Compromise, which prohibited slavery above the 36°30′ parallel. In one quick motion, Douglas and his Democratic colleagues obliterated a long-standing arrangement between the North and the South and reintroduced the slavery question into American politics. William Pitt Fessenden, a Whig senator from Maine, spoke for many Northerners when he called the Kansas-Nebraska Act "a terrible outrage . . . The more I look at it the more enraged I become. It needs but little to make me an out & out abolitionist."

In one fell swoop, the Kansas-Nebraska Act snapped the cords that bound many Northern voters to the two political parties and introduced a period of extreme volatility and excitement. At hundreds of political meetings around the country, antislavery activists abandoned their political bases for new "fusion" tickets. These activists cut a wide swath across the American political spectrum. Some were members of the moribund Free-Soil Party, which formed in 1848 to oppose the extension of slavery into the western territories. Others were "Conscience" Whigs who were committed to the Whig Party's economic

platform but shared the Free-Soilers' distaste for slavery. Still others were "anti-Nebraska" Democrats, who opposed the Whigs on most policy questions but thought slavery was a dangerous social and political system. In some states, these fusion tickets were called Anti-Nebraska, Democrat-Republican, or Free-Soil. In Ripon, Wisconsin, on February 28, 1854, several dozen residents of the surrounding county converged on the town's simple one-room wood-frame schoolhouse to forge a new political party. They called themselves Republicans, and the name soon stuck.

The Kansas-Nebraska Act created "a deep-seated, intense, and ineradicable hatred" of slavery, observed the editor of the *New York Times*. In its wake, "the North had got its back up," added Robert Winthrop, a prominent Cotton Whig from Massachusetts, "and I am pretty afraid that it will stay up, even after the question is settled."

CHAPTER 3

It Was My Privilege to Witness

Years later, John George Nicolay still remembered in vivid detail his passage to America. The youngest of four children born to John Jacob and Helena Nicolay, George—as he was known to family and friends—spent the first several years of his life in Essingen, "a hamlet too small to be found on even a large map of Bavaria," his daughter later remarked. There, his earliest days were spent wandering the cobblestoned streets that wound past rows of small, drab houses and led to the lush vineyards and farms that circled the town. Like millions of central Europeans in the mid-nineteenth century, the Nicolays made the decision to emigrate "primarily, but not solely, in the hope of bettering the family fortune." In 1837, "having disposed of their house and plot of land," they "set off on the long dusty road to Le Havre and took passage on a sailing ship bound for New Orleans. The stay [there] was short, yet long enough to afford my father, who was then five, a poignant sensation. He found himself the center of a group of chattering urchins, of whose talk he could not understand a syllable. He never forgot his feelings at the moment our American speech burst upon his consciousness."

Settling first in Cincinnati, which was already home to a sizable German immigrant population, the Nicolays moved successively to Indiana and Missouri and finally to Pike County, Illinois, where George's father bought and repaired a run-down gristmill and scratched out a living by helping local farmers grind their corn and wheat into meal

and flour. A small and sickly boy, George "found little companionship at home," his daughter later explained, "and being physically frail and of different mental caliber from the other lads at the log schoolhouse, he had few friends his own age. But he was quite happy. With the green woods for a playground, he made friends with the birds and animals there." Young Nicolay also found solace in the written word, though his family's financial straits made books a scarce luxury. "When I first felt the impulse to read," he said many years later, the "family Bible was my only resource. Like any other healthy child, I did not search it for doctrines of theology, precepts of moral philosophy, or beauties of poetry, but for its stirring, active, realistic pictures of life—its history, which to me had all the charms of romance." The boy who would later visit great battlefields at the side of a wartime president was transfixed by "the Books of the Kings with their record of war, siege, battle, conquest, captivity," the book of the Maccabees, and the stories of Samson, David, and Goliath. "Afterward, among the few books which fell into my hands were two of Shakespeare's plays, each bound in a single small volume—the first, the *Comedy of Errors,* the second, the tragedy of *Macbeth.* I must confess that I liked the Dromios better than the ghosts and witches. In both dramas I was deeply absorbed in the movement, but still too young to appreciate their literary beauty and power."

Tragedy cut short Nicolay's childhood. His mother died before the family left Cincinnati, and when he was just fourteen years old, his father passed away. Left to fend for himself, George became a clerk in Aaron Reno's general store in White Hall, where for a salary of $4 a month he worked the counter, stocked shelves, cleaned the floors, and kept the books for his employer. After two years, Reno informed George that although he was a good clerk, his nephew had recently been orphaned, and he felt obliged to offer the position to his own kin. "I fancy my father was not sorry to leave," Helen Nicolay wrote. "His duties did not particularly interest him, and some of them were too heavy for his strength." Writing to his former Sunday school teacher, Joel Pennington, Nicolay asked how one might go about seeking employment in the newspaper field. As luck would have it, Pennington

knew of a position. With little ceremony and few people to bid farewell, Nicolay threw his meager belongings into a bag, walked thirty-five miles to Pittsfield, and spent his first night sleeping on wool sacks in the town carding mill. The next day, he took up work as a "printer's devil" at the *Pike County Free Press,* a weekly paper with Whig leanings and a countywide circulation.

Part errand boy, part janitor, Nicolay was principally responsible for setting the paper's type in preparation for its weekly run. Many decades later, he delivered a lecture titled "Franklin the Printer," in which he traced Benjamin Franklin's "liberal and tolerant philosophy" to the "time when, slowly setting the type for his own pamphlet on the doctrine of Fate, his active thought, playing lightning-like around, over, and under his own arguments . . . showed him that he could construct as good or even a better argument on the other side." He might just as well have been reflecting on his own education as a newspaperman. Privately, he guessed that "next to typesetting, I derived more benefit from the effort to write (which in a newspaper office becomes irresistible) than from reading even the best books . . . [T]o learn to write is like learning to swim; everyone must teach himself. And, as in swimming, perhaps the most important thing to learn is when to stop."

The early years in Pittsfield were hardscrabble. Living in a half-story room above the newspaper office, Nicolay bought bread from the local bakery and counted on the proprietor's wife to bring him freshly brewed coffee. He worked long hours and knew few physical comforts. But Pittsfield adopted him as one of its own. Within two years, he began writing and editing for the paper. By 1852, his name appeared on the masthead. In 1854, at age twenty-two, he became the sole proprietor, editor, and publisher of the *Pike County Free Press.* In his spare time, George worked through a rude course of study with the local schoolmaster, John Thomson, and in that way came to befriend John Hay, who arrived in town only a few months after Nicolay.

For young men of Nicolay's generation, politics and journalism offered a well-trod path from poverty to middle-class respectability. The nation's mail system, which Alexis de Tocqueville called the "great

link between minds," underwent a massive expansion between 1815 and 1830, with the number of rural and small-town post offices more than doubling. Because Congress set postage rates for periodicals at one cent per hundred-mile radius, newspapers enjoyed an invisible subsidy and soon came to constitute 90 percent of all mail. Farmers on the distant frontier, who were increasingly being drawn into market relationships with people in other parts of the country, could now subscribe to a wide variety of newspapers and magazines. Alongside the development of new printing techniques like the cylinder press, which made it possible to churn out more copy in less time, and the steady expansion of railroads, canals, and macadamized roads, which sped the transmission of news, the growth of the postal system inspired a boom in periodical circulation. In 1835 there were 1,200 newspapers in America, most of them local weeklies. A decade and a half later, that number had risen to 2,526, of which 10 percent were dailies. The invention of the telegraph in the late 1840s further catalyzed this trend. By the 1850s the nation had laid over ten thousand miles of wire. People increasingly expected their news to arrive in real time.

At least since the early Federalist era, when supporters of Alexander Hamilton and Thomas Jefferson founded dueling national newspapers, American periodicals tended to assume avowedly partisan positions, drawing little distinction between news and editorials. The rise of America's modern, two-party system in the 1830s inspired Democrats and Whigs to establish local organs, which in turn derived a significant portion of their revenue from lucrative government advertising and printing contracts. By midcentury, 95 percent of daily and weekly newspapers were affiliated with one party or another, leading a contemporary to claim that "no political paper in the United States can be independent and live. It may, in some cases, be independent of persons, but never of party principles and party fealty." Beman Brockway, a journalist who apprenticed under Horace Greeley, later remarked that a typical newspaper in this period "was not a newspaper at all. It contained little news of a general character, and almost no local intelligence. It was simply the organ of a party."

For reasons both ideological and pecuniary, editors increasingly

played leading roles in partisan politics. They served on their local and state party committees, gave speeches, organized rallies, and often held office. Stepping into this growing profession required mastery of language, keen political sensibility, thick skin, and sharp elbows. But it did not require much in the way of family pedigree or formal education. It was the perfect career choice for Nicolay.

Pittsfield offered George his first real home. Though not formally religious, he enjoyed attending Pastor Carter's services on Sundays, where his self-taught music skills were sufficient to secure a position as church organist, at a nominal salary of $5 per year. But it was not money that motivated him to take the job. On his first day in town, as he walked down the street in his "funny snuff-colored suit," Nicolay's eye wandered in the direction of Therena Bates, the slim, dark-haired daughter of the village blacksmith. She smiled at him, and he was instantly smitten. His daughter later assumed that "the mere money value" of his church position paled in comparison to the "opportunity of looking down from the organ loft, on Sunday mornings, on an olive cheek and a knot of blue-black hair."

Nicolay's editorial control of the *Pike County Free Press* coincided with the Kansas-Nebraska controversy and the birth of the Republican Party. Unlike his friend John Hay, George was passionate about the politics of slavery, in part because his work required that he live, eat, and breathe current affairs, but also out of sincere hatred for the peculiar institution. As sole author of the paper's editorials, he issued sharp takedowns of the "slaveocracy" and beseeched his readers to "VOTE AGAINST THE EXTENSION OF SLAVERY" and "redeem Illinois from the thralldom of dough-faced demagogues." Though sometimes blunt to the point of being incendiary, Nicolay staked out a fairly centrist and conventional viewpoint. Like most anti-Nebraska men, but unlike most abolitionists, he believed that "the Compromise of 1850 had stilled the angry waters of the great political sea . . . allayed the turbulent sectional strife, which had excited the fears and apprehensions of our greatest statesmen . . . restored harmony and union [and] established terms of peace and amity between the North and South."

It was the introduction of the Kansas-Nebraska bill that had "renewed
the agitation," Nicolay maintained, by negating the principles of both
the Missouri Compromise and the more recent Compromise of 1850.
"Let it then be remembered, that the slavery question had remained
settled, quieted and adjusted until STEPHEN ARNOLD DOUGLAS
introduced it into Congress [and] *repealed* this time-honored law of
thirty-years standing."

Nicolay frequently described slavery as a "great evil" and echoed
conventional antislavery wisdom in characterizing African Americans
as human beings, not chattel. At the same time, like many antislavery
advocates, he was deeply prejudiced toward African Americans and
seemed unable to entertain the possibility that they might be his social
or intellectual equals. In his personal correspondence, and occasion-
ally in his published work, he referred casually to slaves and free black
persons as "niggers" and believed that "free negroes are often annoy-
ing and sometimes a nuisance." Nevertheless, he opposed an Illinois
state law that barred free African Americans from moving in state and
offered that they were "often a useful part of the community." While
conceding the need for laws to govern their scope of movement, he
asserted that if people were "free and have committed no crime, but
that of being born with a dark skin, we think they ought to be allowed
a little of God's earth to stand on."

Under Nicolay's editorial direction, the *Free Press* ran stirring re-
ports of a fugitive slave case in Milwaukee, where the local U.S. mar-
shal had joined forces with a plantation owner from Mississippi to
arrest Joshua Glover, a local free man of color whom the slave owner
claimed was a runaway. "Without showing legal authority," the *Free
Press* informed readers, "they broke open his house, entered, and pre-
sented a pistol to his head. Upon attempting to thrust it aside, he was
knocked down and badly injured, then gagged, and without coat or
hat thrown into a wagon, brought 25 miles in the middle of the night,
and lodged in a Milwaukee jail." The *Free Press* reported with approval
that a local vigilance committee had broken Glover out of prison, spir-
ited him north, and placed "the Slave catcher"—that is, the U.S.
marshal—under arrest.

Though he demonstrated liberal regard for the humanity and basic rights of black Americans, both free and slave, Nicolay was essentially a moderate, more focused on the social, economic, and political differences between free-labor and slave societies than on the injustice of holding human beings in bondage. During a trip to Washington, D.C., in 1852, two years before the Kansas-Nebraska Act rekindled the sectional conflict, he reported on the stark physical differences that he experienced upon crossing from southern Illinois into the upper South. The slave states offered no sign of "life or progress—age and decay is strongly marked upon everything. On the contrary, the free states exhibit every evidence of prosperity, improvement and go-ahead-ativeness . . . showing that they contain by far the greater portion of talent and industry, and that they must . . . attain preeminence in point of greatness and power." Slavery's principal evil, in Nicolay's mind, was its corrosive effect on labor, industry, and ambition—the engines that drove progress and civilization. Racially tolerant by contemporary standards, he shared the widespread and conventional belief that the United States was a white man's country. The "Far West" was America's safety valve, where "the rich inheritance of Freedom" was reserved for those who "live by their honest toil, free from the degrading competition of slave labor."

Passage of the Kansas-Nebraska Act threw Northern politics into a state of extreme confusion and resulted in a widespread rout of pro-slavery Democrats in the 1854 elections. In Illinois, anti-Nebraska forces gained slim control of the state legislature. Because state legislators were responsible for choosing U.S. senators, antislavery activists could reasonably expect to elect one of their own to replace the Democratic incumbent, James Shields, whose term was set to expire the following year. But in Illinois, as throughout the North, there was as yet no Republican Party. State by state, anti-Nebraska coalitions brought erstwhile Whigs, Democrats, and Free-Soilers into an unsteady alliance. Many of these new political allies scarcely trusted one another and often did not think of themselves as long-term partners. Adding to the confusion, the new, anti-immigrant American Party—popularly called the Know-Nothings—also won scores of state

legislative and congressional seats in the fall elections. Most Know-Nothings opposed the extension of slavery and therefore fell under the banner of the anti-Nebraska fusion coalition. In the wake of this incomplete electoral realignment, it was unclear who belonged to which party. When a close friend inquired as to his political allegiance, Abraham Lincoln replied, "This is a disputed point. I think I am a whig; but others say there are no whigs, and that I am an abolitionist. When I was in Washington I voted for the Wilmot Proviso as good as forty times, and I never heard of any one attempting to unwhig me for that. I now do no more than oppose the *extension* of slavery."

Lincoln quickly emerged as the favored candidate of the anti-Nebraska coalition forces for Shields's seat in the U.S. Senate. But there was a snag. On the first ballot, he won 45 votes to Shields's 41—just shy of the requisite number of votes needed to secure election. Five votes went to Lyman Trumbull, an anti-Nebraska Democrat who had served alongside Lincoln in the state legislature fifteen years earlier and whose wife, the former Julia Jayne, was a close friend of Mary Todd Lincoln's. Lincoln understood that these five holdouts were "men who *never could* vote for a whig; and without the votes of two of whom I *never could* reach the requisite number to make an election." Over the course of several roll calls, Lincoln bled support to Trumbull, while the Democrats swapped Shields out for the popular incumbent governor, Joel Matteson. Fearing that some of the anti-Nebraska Democrats might reunite with their party and send Matteson to the Senate, Lincoln instructed his Whig supporters to fall in line with Trumbull. It was a bitter pill to swallow, and it left Lincoln feeling "disappointed and mortified." Mary Todd Lincoln angrily cut off all relations with Julia Trumbull. For her husband, the sting was profound. "A less good humored man than I, perhaps, would not have consented to it," he remarked.

Though many of Lincoln's close supporters were deeply embittered by the triumph of five anti-Nebraska Democrats over forty-five anti-Nebraska Whigs, George Nicolay was pleased. "We have the pleasure of informing our readers, this week, of the utter and final overthrow

of Nebraskaism in Illinois," he crowed. "Mr. Trumbull is an uncom-
promising anti-Nebraska Democrat . . . We would have been much
more gratified by the election of a good Whig to that office; but as that
was impossible, we heartily rejoice at the result as it was." Nicolay made
no mention of the defeated Whig candidate, Abraham Lincoln.

Over the course of Nicolay's two-year tenure as editor and publisher of
the *Free Press,* practical application of the Kansas-Nebraska Act turned
the Great Plains into a tinderbox, as thousands of homesteaders poured
into the Kansas and Nebraska territories. Most went in search of cheap
land and opportunity, but the inevitable clash between slavery and
free labor quickly turned violent. Neither side was willing to shirk
away from the bitter "competition for the virgin soil of Kansas," as
William Seward framed the problem. Subsidized by a group of Mas-
sachusetts businessmen, the New England Emigrant Aid Company
offered material assistance to Northern homesteaders, while Missouri
"border ruffians," led by that state's Democratic senator, David Atchi-
son, determined that "the game must be played boldly." "If we win,"
Atchison promised, "we can carry slavery to the Pacific Ocean. If we
fail we lose Missouri, Arkansas, Texas, and all the territories."

By 1856, Kansas had spiraled into a well of violence and chaos. The
Missouri border ruffians rode roughshod through the territory, em-
ploying violence and fraud to rig a series of legislative elections. Egged
on by Atchison, who warned that Northerners planned to "take up
those fertile prairies, run off your negroes, and depreciate the value of
your slaves here," the pro-slavery forces undertook a campaign of ex-
treme terror and intimidation. "You know how to protect your own
interests," Atchison declared. "Your rifles will free you from such
neighbors . . . You will go there, if necessary, with the *bayonet* and with
blood." When they were not stuffing ballot boxes, the Missourians
were assaulting Free-Soil men. As a result, Free-Soilers, who probably
made up a healthy majority of the population, armed themselves to
the teeth and refused to acknowledge the authority of the official ter-
ritorial government in Lecompton. Instead, they established their

own shadow government in the town of Lawrence. Fighting between Free-Soilers and pro-slavery settlers grew so violent that the territory became widely known as "Bleeding Kansas."

Tensions had already started to boil over when pro-slavery forces pillaged the free-state capital city of Lawrence, destroying the local Free-Soil newspaper office and laying ruin to the Free State Hotel, which housed the shadow territorial government. Days later, on May 19, 1856, Charles Sumner rose on the Senate floor to denounce the "crime against Kansas." Ironically, neither Sumner nor his colleagues knew about the "sack of Lawrence," as news of the event had not yet reached Washington, D.C. The subject of his speech was the more general disruption of law and order. A tall, good-looking man, Sumner was as imperious as he was radical, and in his three-day speech, which he privately described as "the most thorough philippic" ever delivered in the Senate chamber, he managed to offend not only those Southern colleagues who perpetrated the "crime" but also many of his Northern colleagues who offered "apologies for the crime." The dramatic moment came when Sumner launched a sharp attack against Andrew Butler, a South Carolina senator and staunch defender of slavery. Employing highly sexual imagery—the "rape of a virgin territory," the "depraved longing for a new slave State," the "wench" that was slavery—Sumner denounced Butler for choosing "a mistress to whom he has made his vows, and who, though ugly to others, is always lovely to him; though polluted in the sight of the world, is chaste in his sight—I mean the harlot, Slavery." Sumner's attack touched a raw nerve among slaveholders who chafed at the suggestion (often true) that they engaged in consensual and nonconsensual sex with their female slaves. The day after his speech, as Sumner attended to routine paperwork on the Senate floor, Butler's cousin Congressman Preston Brooks entered the chamber and set upon him with a metal-tipped cane. The senators' desks were bolted to the floor, making it impossible for Sumner to escape from his seat. Writhing in pain, he wrenched the desk up with his knees and collapsed on the bloodstained carpet. His injuries nearly killed him, and it would be four years before he could return to normal duties in the Capitol.

The incident soon came to be known as "Bleeding Sumner," and it created a political firestorm throughout the North. The symbolic importance of the crime was arresting. Southerners no longer seemed content to employ violence and terrorism in Kansas. Now they had brought their war of aggression into the halls of Congress. "No meaner exhibition of Southern cowardice—generally miscalled Southern chivalry—was ever witnessed," the New-York Tribune intoned. "The South has taken the oligarchic ground that Slavery ought to exist, irrespective of color . . . that Democracy is an illusion and a lie." Writing for the Free Press, Nicolay joined the chorus of outrage, denouncing the attack as a "cowardly and atrocious" act. "Things have truly come to a pretty pass when a Senator of the United States is to be cruelly beaten by a cowardly ruffian for exercising his right of free speech in the council hall of his country." The slaveholders were now "determined to carry their points by foul means if not by fair. Unable to cope with such men as Sumner in open debate, they resort to weapons of the ruffian, and the robber's mode of assault."

Like that of other Free-Soil activists, Nicolay's opposition to slavery evolved as 1856 wore on. Slavery, it now seemed, was more than a bad social or economic system. It represented the absolute antithesis of democracy. Unless they met the challenge head-on, free white people stood to be enslaved themselves—and not just rhetorically. "In the coming campaign," he wrote that summer, "we shall fight for Freedom, and against Slavery. We shall fight for free suffrage, for the right of the people to bear arms, for their right to choose their own rulers, for liberty of speech and the freedom of the Press and for the protection of life and property. All these rights and privileges, which are the glory and pride of American citizens, have been violated and usurped by . . . an unscrupulous slave power."

The events of May 1856 electrified the Northern electorate and fused the anti-Nebraska coalition into a permanent political organization. That summer, delegates from every free state in the Union converged on Philadelphia to select the Republican Party's first presidential and vice presidential candidates. The convention adopted a strong anti-slavery platform (David Wilmot, whose proviso foreshadowed the

crisis of the 1850s, chaired the platform committee). Calling for a ban on slavery in the western territories, the Republicans forged a middle ground between radical antislavery activists and conservative supporters of law and order and union. On the second day of the proceedings, the convention tapped John C. Frémont, the famous army explorer whose movements in California during the Bear Flag Revolt had earned him national acclaim. A son-in-law of the mercurial Missouri senator Thomas Hart Benton, Frémont had served a brief term in the Senate, where he joined other Northern Democrats in opposing the westward spread of slavery. For the vice presidential spot, Abraham Lincoln enjoyed early support. But delegates ultimately selected William Dayton, a former Whig senator from New Jersey.

Hoisting banners that read "Free Soil, Free Labor, Free Speech, Free Men, Frémont," the delegates closed the convention's business and marched onward to the fall canvass. Frémont lost the election—in which a stunning 83 percent of eligible voters participated—to the Democrat James Buchanan, but the new party performed exceptionally well and won strong representation in both houses of Congress.

In Illinois, Lincoln emerged as the de facto leader of the new Republican organization. At some point that year, he and Trumbull staged a joint campaign appearance in Pittsfield, where a local Republican activist introduced him to Nicolay. By that time, the young editor had become a regular speaker on the Pike County campaign circuit and a prominent enough leader in the local antislavery movement to earn election as a delegate to the first statewide Republican convention, held in Bloomington. There, according to William Herndon, Lincoln's law partner at the time, the future president delivered a speech "full of fire and energy and force . . . It was logic; it was pathos; it was enthusiasm; it was justice, equity, truth, and right set ablaze by the divine fires of a soul maddened by the wrong; it was hard, heavy, knotty, gnarly, backed with wrath."

From his seat in the rafters, Nicolay watched as Lincoln "held the audience in such rapt attention that the news reporters dropped their pencils and forgot their work." Known thereafter as Lincoln's "lost speech," as no record of it exists, it was looked back on by many as the

best of his career. Decades later, reflecting on his "good fortune" to have been in the hall that day, Nicolay marveled at the string of

> momentous and related events it was my privilege to witness in the stirring years that succeeded. In the Representatives Hall at Springfield, I heard him deliver the famous address in which he quoted the Scriptural maxim that a house divided against itself cannot stand . . . In the Wigwam at Chicago I heard the roll-call and the thunderous applause that decided and greeted his first nomination for President. On the East Portico of the Capitol in Washington I heard him read his First Inaugural in which he announced the Union to be perpetual. On the battlefield at Gettysburg I heard him pronounce the immortal Gettysburg Address. I saw him sign the Joint Resolution of Congress which authorized the XIII Amendment to the Constitution of the United States. And once more, on the East Portico, I heard from his lips the sublime words of the Second Inaugural.

Though at the time he did not know it, for the rest of his life, Nicolay would be tied to Abraham Lincoln.

The Prairies Are on Fire

For a new political party not yet two years old, Illinois Republicans performed strongly in the 1856 elections, managing to hold four of the state's nine seats in the U.S. House of Representatives and winning a string of important statewide offices, including the governorship. One of the victors that year was Ozias M. Hatch, a former legislator from Pike County who won election as the first Republican secretary of state. John Nicolay had stumped hard for Hatch. He threw the full weight of the *Free Press* behind his candidacy and took to the hustings to speak at Republican campaign rallies throughout the county. In recognition of his hard work and talent, Hatch offered Nicolay the post of chief clerk on his government staff. The young man jumped at the opportunity. Just shy of his twenty-fifth birthday, Nicolay could learn little more from editing a weekly newspaper. In Springfield—relative to Pittsfield, a city of refinement and culture—he would find himself at the nerve center of statewide Republican politics and enjoy an opportunity to study the law in his spare time. It proved a fateful choice. Years later, he remembered that Hatch's office, "a large and well-appointed room in the old State House," functioned "in effect [as] the State political headquarters . . . Mr. Lincoln was of course a frequent visitor, and when he came he was always the centre of an animated and interested group. It was there during these years . . . that I made his acquaintance." Over the next four years, Nicolay became a trusted aide to the party's leading men, chief among them Lincoln. An

"assiduous student of election tables," Lincoln spent long hours poring over local returns with Nicolay, plotting another race for the Senate. This time, he would be the consensus candidate of the Republican Party. As animated as the political climate was in 1854, it was red-hot by the time of his second campaign in 1858.

Two days after President James Buchanan took the oath of office in March 1857, the U.S. Supreme Court delivered a shock to the nation's political system with its historic decision in the case of *Dred Scott v. Sandford*. Scott was a sixty-two-year-old slave who in the 1830s had accompanied his owner on extended sojourns in Illinois and Minnesota—the latter still a territory and part of the original Louisiana Purchase. With support from white abolitionists, he sued for freedom on the premise that his enslavement effectively ended the moment he stepped on free soil—an argument with which many antislavery activists would readily have agreed. Local courts in Missouri ruled against Scott, but over the years he persisted in appealing his case up the judicial ladder until it reached the Supreme Court. There, his fate lay largely in the hands of Chief Justice Roger Taney, a Maryland slave owner whom Andrew Jackson had elevated to the high court over twenty years earlier. Unflinching in his support of states' rights, Taney could very well have crafted a narrow decision rejecting either the court's jurisdiction in the case or Scott's standing to sue. Instead, he ruled expansively that U.S. citizens had a right to bring their property, including slaves, into federal territories. With one stroke of the pen, Taney declared both the Missouri Compromise and popular sovereignty null and void. According to the court, neither Congress nor a territorial government could prevent citizens from bringing slaves into federal territories. All federal land was now open to the peculiar institution.

Southern Democrats were elated. The *Dred Scott* decision, they believed, was the "funeral sermon of Black Republicanism . . . crushing and annihilating . . . the anti-slavery platform . . . at a single blow." Northern Democrats, particularly Stephen Douglas, were boxed into a corner. They had promised their constituents that popular sovereignty represented a reasonable compromise with the South. Now a

Southern chief justice, writing for a majority that principally comprised Southern jurists, had swept the rug out from under their feet by declaring it an unconstitutional principle. Republicans were enraged. Declaring that the *Dred Scott* decision held as much "moral weight [as] the judgment of a majority of those congregated in any Washington bar-room," the *New-York Tribune* viewed the court's latest dictum as yet another in a long string of betrayals. William Cullen Bryant, a former Democrat turned Republican, lamented that "if this decision shall stand for law, slavery, instead of being what the people of the slave states have hitherto called it, their peculiar institution, is a Federal institution, the common patrimony and shame of all the States." Above all, Republicans raised an inescapable question: If citizens were entitled to bring their "property" into federal territories, could they not also bring their slaves into free *states*? As Hay and Nicolay explained several decades later, although the *Dred Scott* decision technically applied only to territories, many Republicans genuinely wondered whether "if under the 'property' theory the Constitution carries slavery to the Territories, it would by the same inevitable logic carry it into free-States."

Heading into his reelection year, Douglas would have found himself in a bind on account of the *Dred Scott* decision alone. But the Buchanan administration added to his pain when it endorsed the so-called Lecompton Constitution—the work of a territorial convention elected by outright fraud and violence that comprised, in the words of one critic, "broken-down political hacks, demagogues, fire-eaters, perjurers, ruffians, ballot-box stuffers and loafers." Though the majority of Kansas settlers were antislavery, the Lecompton convention, acting as the territory's legitimate governing body, drafted a proposed state constitution that recognized slavery and placed enormous obstacles to any future legislative action to abolish it. Adopted by a popular referendum that was equally fraudulent, the constitution formed the territorial government's official application for statehood. Northerners were stunned when Buchanan gave the constitution his official endorsement and urged Congress to admit Kansas to the Union under its provisions. The administration's decision to sanction a profoundly tainted

political process caused a deep fissure in the Democratic Party. Many Northern Democrats agreed with Stephen Douglas, who saw only "treachery and juggling" in this latest betrayal of popular sovereignty. It was one thing to allow the South to run roughshod over long-standing territorial compromises. It was another matter entirely to allow the South so brazenly to rig and steal popular referenda. "We must stand on the popular sovereignty issue," Douglas declared, "and go wherever the logical consequences may carry us, and defend it against *all assaults* from whatever quarter." Privately, he promised friends, "I will show you that I will do what I promised. By God, sir, I made Mr. James Buchanan, and by God, I will unmake him!"

For Douglas, the stakes of the 1858 election were high. Illinois was trending Republican. The state's population was in the process of doubling, from 850,000 in 1850 to 1.7 million by 1860, as hundreds of thousands of settlers from New York, Pennsylvania, and New England flooded the state's northernmost counties and sharply reduced the electoral pull of the downstate, Southern-facing region, popularly known in those years as Egypt. With the regional divide so sharply pronounced, there was fierce competition for swing voters in central Illinois. "Talk of 'sectionalism' in the Republic!" quipped a newspaper correspondent. "There is not between South Carolina and Massachusetts . . . a more deadly hostility than between the ninth and first Congressional districts in this State."

Widely regarded as presidential timber for 1860, Douglas was now fighting for survival against both his Republican opponents and his own party's administration. For Lincoln, the race was an opportunity not only to win a much-coveted seat in the U.S. Senate but also to emerge as a giant killer. All eyes were on the race between these two long-standing rivals. For once, North and South agreed. The *Richmond Enquirer* noted that "the great battle of the next Presidential election is being fought in Illinois"; the *New York Times* called Illinois "the most interesting political battle-ground in the Union." One of Lincoln's correspondents told the candidate, "You are like Byron, who woke up one morning and found himself famous."

By agreement, the two candidates squared off against each other in

seven towns, one for each of the state's nine congressional districts, minus two, where they had already delivered well-attended speeches and rebuttals. Over the course of several autumn weeks, Lincoln and Douglas traveled more than ten thousand miles by boat, rail, and coach, drawing enormous crowds wherever they went. When not debating each other, they rallied the faithful. Lincoln estimated that he delivered 63 speeches—Douglas, 130. They were met by dramatic torchlight parades, men waving banners and women towing babies and toddlers. "The prairies are on fire," marveled one of the many New York newspaper correspondents who were dispatched to Illinois that fall. "It is astonishing how deep an interest in politics this people take."

From his perch in the state capitol building, where state Republican leaders plotted strategy before the great hickory fire in Ozias Hatch's office, Nicolay enjoyed an insider's view of the Lincoln-Douglas Senate race. The line between partisan operative and journalist was blurry in the antebellum era. Though he served as the de facto director of the state Republican Party, George also wrote anonymously for the *Pike County Free Press* and the *Chicago Tribune,* under the pseudonym Sangamon. His articles and editorials promoted the standard Republican argument: slavery was an evil and cancerous institution that should be restricted to the states where it already existed; the Kansas-Nebraska Act and its popular sovereignty provision posed a stark betrayal of an agreement on which good men had long ago shaken hands; the *Dred Scott* decision had rendered popular sovereignty a dead letter and threatened to introduce slavery into the free states; and Stephen Douglas had either knowingly colluded in the "slave power conspiracy" or been duped by his friends in the "slaveocracy." Nicolay carefully insisted that the Republican Party's platform began and ended with preventing the extension of slavery into new territories—no more, no less. Reporting from Pittsfield, where Douglas spoke before a rowdy audience in late August, he noted that the Little Giant (as Douglas was popularly known) indulged in "his favorite misrepresentations—stating, for instance, that Lincoln was in favor of negro equality—of a war on the South—of abolishing slavery in the States &c." The crowd

was wise to Douglas, Nicolay boasted, and heckled the incumbent senator with cries of "That's a lie!" and "We know better!"

To Nicolay, the "nub" of Douglas's stump speech was "'the nigger equality' dodge." Douglas was between a rock and a hard place. He had introduced the bill that overturned the Missouri Compromise and had appeased his Illinois constituents by promising that "popular sovereignty" would provide a democratic mechanism to keep slavery out of the new territories. Now his popular sovereignty proviso lay in tatters, flouted by border ruffians in Kansas and gutted by Southern Democrats in Washington. With nothing else to run on, he played the race card, charging repeatedly that Lincoln believed that "the negro was made his equal." For his part, Lincoln had long been on record as insisting that "the negro is a *man*," a position fully in accordance with the standard Republican argument that slavery was an aberration of natural law. While denying that African Americans were his "social equal," he saw "no reason in the world why the negro is not entitled to all the natural rights enumerated in the Declaration of Independence— the right to life, liberty, and the pursuit of happiness . . . [I]n the right to eat the bread, without leave of anyone else, which his own hand earns, *he is my equal, and the equal of Judge Douglas, and the equal of every living man.*" In that specific time (1858) and place (Illinois), Lincoln's position was sufficiently progressive to invite a backlash. Seeking to whip up racial animosities among conservative voters in the central and southern parts of the state, Douglas repeatedly warned that "black Republicans" would allow African Americans to "ride in a carriage with your wife, whilst you drive the team." At the debate in Charleston, his supporters hoisted a banner that read "Negro Equality," showing a white man, his black wife, and their mulatto child standing together. Many Republicans were no more accepting of racial equality than Douglas. When Douglas called Lincoln a "black Republican," Lincoln supporters heckled him with cries of "White, white!" There was no mistaking their position: to oppose slavery's extension— even to oppose the practice of holding other human beings in bondage—was not to favor black equality. If Lincoln's and Douglas's supporters agreed on nothing else, most held black Americans in

contempt. Lincoln carefully walked a tightrope, assuring conservative voters that he believed in the separation and social inequality of the races while still earnestly defending the natural rights of black Americans and decrying the spread of slavery.

Nicolay was present at Lincoln's campaign kickoff speech in Springfield, in which the nominee famously declared that "a house divided against itself cannot stand," and was also in attendance at Douglas's rebuttal, the following day. He was in the audience when Douglas visited Pittsfield later that summer, and he may also have witnessed some of their other debates and solo appearances. He also worked behind the scenes as a party lieutenant. Given his facility for research and writing, state leaders tasked George with preparing and publishing a campaign pamphlet, *The Political Record of Stephen A. Douglas*. He organized campaign rallies and lined up out-of-state surrogate speakers to stump on behalf of the candidate. Though it is possible that Nicolay took to the hustings to campaign for the Republican ticket in Pike County, as he had done in 1856, he left little public record of his sentiment during the fall canvass. What survive instead are several pages of notes that he scribbled out in a pocket journal. "In 1854, when the Dem. Party had repealed Mo. Compromise," he noted in neat, angular script, "they started with the assumption: Slavery & Freedom equal. 50,000 Niggers equal 50,000 white settlers. Equal in Abstract Right." Nicolay was turning Douglas's "nigger equality dodge" on its head. Republicans would preserve the western frontier for white farmers; Democrats would place slaves in a position of equality with whites. They had, in fact, "blockaded" the "border of Kansas . . . against free emigration . . . Lincoln would never have made white men compete with niggers." "Go it nigger, go it 'mudsill,'" Democrats cried. "Every act of the Dem Party—legislative, executive or judicial has been against the White man and for the Nigger . . . Could say everything in favor of Niggers—but nothing for white men." Playing on the familiar Republican charge that Buchanan, Douglas, and Taney had hatched a plot as early as 1854 to introduce slavery into the territories and possibly even the free states, Nicolay privately denounced the "Dred Scott decision—which says that niggers must go there [the territories]

anyhow—that no power can keep it out. So that White men, after running their race according to Democratic terms, and winning it under all these difficulties, are cheated out of the prize by three Democratic judges, who give it to the niggers."

It is unclear whether Nicolay's notes reflected his personal sentiment or were intended as an outline for a stump speech. He was certainly in a position to offer talking points to Lincoln and, from the many hours he spent poring over election returns with the candidate, understood as well as anyone the urgent need to neutralize Douglas's advantage with conservative voters in central and southern Illinois. In his personal correspondence, Nicolay made occasional use of the term "nigger," but in his newspaper articles and official letters he usually referred to African Americans as "negroes." Neither in private nor in public did he speak as venomously about black people as he did in the pages of his 1858 journal. Yet the line between personal belief and political rhetoric was thin. Two years earlier, as a newspaper editor, Nicolay proved willing to tap the reserve of popular racism to further the Republican cause, as when he denounced the "Pro-Slavery Black Democracy" or lambasted a Democratic rally as a "slavery-defending nigger-democratic Border-Ruffian pow-wow." In his private notes, he echoed Lincoln in calling slavery a form of "despotism" and wrote disapprovingly of the Democratic Party's insistence that "slaves are property." "Free society," he wrote, was "right & good. Slave society—wrong & evil." But he also drew a sharp line between Douglas, who "wants Kansas for white men *with* niggers," and Republicans, who "want it for white men *without* niggers."

Whether Nicolay's journal entries reflected his personal beliefs or were notes for a political speech or pamphlet, he gave expression to sentiments that his candidate, Abraham Lincoln, would never have indulged. While Lincoln told debate audiences that he wanted to preserve the West as "an outlet for *free white people everywhere* . . . in which [they] may find new homes and better their conditions in life," he also affirmed that what was at stake was no less than "the eternal struggle between these two principles—right and wrong—throughout the world. They are the two principles that have stood face to face from

the beginning of time; and will ever continue to struggle. The one is the common right of humanity and the other the divine right of kings."

By contrast, Nicolay hung his argument on a stated belief that the "territories [were] for free white men. [Republicans] want it for free white labor—want it for the strong arm and the willing heart—want it for farms and cities—for railroads & telegraphs . . . and engines—for enterprise and prosperity—for free schools and free children." As Henry Adams aptly summarized the Republican argument more than a half century later, bad roads meant bad morals, and slavery—the root of all immorality—was the antithesis of a prosperous and healthy society.

The Lincoln-Douglas debates attracted enormous attention that fall. Both the *Chicago Times,* a Democratic publication, and the *Chicago Tribune,* a Republican paper, assigned stenographers to take down each and every word that the candidates uttered. Eastern papers also sent correspondents to Illinois to follow the events. Everywhere Lincoln and Douglas debated, enormous crowds assembled, traveling by rail, riverboat, and wagon, their horses kicking up dirt and mud so that "the streets and avenues leading from the country were so engulfed with dust that the town resembled a vast smoke house," according to a contemporary account of the first debate, at Ottawa, where fifteen thousand spectators flooded a village that normally housed a population of just six thousand. Weeks later, in Charleston, a newspaper correspondent marveled that "over long, weary miles of hot, dusty prairie, the processions of eager partisans come on foot, on horseback, in wagons drawn by horses or mules; men, women, and children, old and young; the half-sick just out of the last shake, children in arms, infants . . . pushing on in clouds of dust under a blazing sun . . . talking, discussing, litigious, vociferous, while the roar of artillery, the music of bands, the waving of banners, the huzza of crowds . . . combine to render the scene one of commotion and confusion." In Galesburg, a charming college town with a strong antislavery bent, the Macomb Lincoln Club let James Hammond know what they thought of him when they raised an enormous placard that read "Small-Fisted Farmers, Mud Sills of Society, Greasy Mechanics for A. Lincoln."

Decades later, people still remembered those electrifying weeks as though they had been yesterday. Carl Schurz, the German American political leader, reminisced of his train journey to Quincy the evening before the penultimate debate. Riding in a packed railroad car, "all at once . . . I observed a great commotion among my fellow-passengers, many of whom jumped from their seats and pressed eagerly around a tall man who had just entered the car. They addressed him in the most familiar style. 'Hello, Abe!' they shouted, as they pressed his hand. 'How are you?' and so on. And he responded in the same manner: Good-evening, Ben! How are you, Joe? Glad to see you, Dick!" Schurz described his first encounter with "that swarthy face"—sunburned from the grueling early autumn campaign—"with its strong features, its deep furrows, and its benignant, melancholy eyes, now familiar to every American by numberless pictures." Clad in a black dress coat with sleeves too short for his arms, black trousers that barely reached his boots, white shirt, and thin black necktie, Lincoln doffed his "battered 'stove-top' hat" and worked the crowd. Schurz remembered that "on his left arm he carried a gray woolen shawl . . . a cotton umbrella of the bulging kind, and also a black satchel that bore the marks of long and hard usage. His right he had kept free for hand-shaking, of which there was no end until everybody in the car seemed to be satisfied." What struck Schurz so many years later was Lincoln's skill as a candidate. "When, in a tone of perfect ingenuousness, he asked me—a young beginner in politics—what I thought about this and that," he put Schurz at such ease that "I soon felt as if I had known him all my life and we had long been close friends."

Lincoln's political acumen, the product of a quarter century of experience, was on full display during his great campaign against Douglas, but the result proved a bitter disappointment to the Republicans. Taken in sum, Republican legislative candidates polled 125,430 votes; pro-Douglas Democrats, 121,609; and anti-Douglas/pro-Buchanan Democrats, 5,071—a slim Republican plurality (or a narrow loss, if the votes of the two Democratic factions were combined), but a meaningless one. Because seats in the state legislature were still apportioned according to the 1850 census, which had not yet taken into account the

enormous tide of population growth in the northern, Republican-leaning counties, Douglas carried the Senate election by a vote of 54 to 46. "After a hundred consecutive days of excitement, of intense mental strain, and of unremitting bodily exertion," Hay wrote many years later, "after speech-making and parades, music and bonfires, it must be something of a trial to face at once the mortification of defeat, the weariness of intellectual and physical reaction, and the dull common-place of daily routine." But that he did. Writing to a friend just two weeks after his defeat, Lincoln admitted that he "wished, but . . . did not much expect, a better result . . . I am glad that I made the late race. It gave me a hearing on the great and durable question of the age, which I could have had in no other way; and though I now sink out of view, and shall be forgotten, I believe I have made some marks which will tell for the cause of civil liberty long after I am gone."

In fact, the Senate campaign proved the launching point of Lincoln's presidential candidacy. He had squared off against the Little Giant and earned a national reputation for it. Enjoying political celebrity from coverage of his unsuccessful race, Lincoln agreed to deliver a string of political speeches in the fall of 1859 in Columbus, Dayton, Hamilton, Cincinnati, and Indianapolis, where his piercing censure of the slave power met with wide acclaim among Republican audiences. Responding to Douglas's recent declaration that "he was for the negro against the crocodile, but for the white man against the negro," Lincoln lamented that Douglas had encouraged supporters to suppose "that the negro is no longer a man but a brute . . . Public opinion in this country is everything," and Douglas was manipulating it in a vicious and highly immoral way.

It was around this time that John Hay first came to know the future president. "He came into the law office where I was reading, which adjoined his own, with a copy of *Harper's Magazine* in hand, containing Senator Douglas's famous article on Popular Sovereignty," Hay remembered. "Lincoln seemed greatly roused by what he had read. Entering the office without a salutation, he said: 'This will never do. He puts the moral element out of this question. It won't stay out.'"

The following February, with rumors swirling of his possible

presidential candidacy, Lincoln visited New York City at the invitation of leading Republican boosters, where he defied the expectations of his eastern audience, many of whom expected "something weird, rough, and uncultivated," by delivering a powerful antislavery broadside. "Let us stand by our duty, fearlessly and effectively," he implored listeners in his dramatic conclusion. "Let us have faith that right makes might, and in that faith, let us, to the end, dare to do our duty, as we understand it." On the heels of his success, Lincoln worked a speaking circuit through New England—ostensibly to visit his oldest son, Robert, who was attending prep school at Phillips Exeter Academy. He was again received by enthusiastic crowds who were intrigued by the rough-hewn Illinois politician who spoke so mightily yet in a strange Kentucky-Indiana tongue.

To win the presidency, the Republican Party would need to carry all of the states where Frémont prevailed in 1856 and any combination of two states among Pennsylvania, Illinois, and Indiana. Though its candidate lacked the stature and experience of top-tier aspirants like William H. Seward and Salmon P. Chase, Illinois Republicans could credibly argue that the party needed to nominate a midwestern moderate to pull off a regional hat trick. Lincoln seemed to fit that bill better than any other man. Certainly some of his Illinois friends thought so. Early in 1860, they dispatched John Nicolay to Ohio to oversee logistical arrangements for the publication of *Political Debates Between Hon. Abraham Lincoln and Hon. Stephen A. Douglas, in the Celebrated Campaign of 1858, in Illinois.* The 268-page transcript became an instant bestseller. That spring, as the two parties began preparing for their nominating conventions, mention of his name became more frequent alongside those of more long-standing repute.

As early as 1858, Nicolay had the audacity to suggest in his private journal that "when we get him to the Senate—& the White House," Lincoln would prove a steady and fearless leader. It was a bold prediction at a time when few people yet knew his name. Now circumstances had changed. "I will be entirely frank," Lincoln wrote to Lyman Trumbull in early 1860. "The taste *is* in my mouth a little."

CHAPTER 5

Wide Awake

I n May 1859, shortly after arriving in "the dreary wastes of Springfield—a city combining the meanness of the North with the barbarism of the South"—John Hay fired off a letter to his college friend William Leete Stone reporting on the "life of listless apathy which I [have] been leading ever since we parted" and apologizing for his long delay in writing. "Let the cry of your mourning go up continually for your brother of old time," he pleaded, only half in jest, "for he hath fallen on evil days. There is no land so sad as this. The sky is forever leaden with gloomy clouds, or glowing with torrid fervors . . . Yet such as it is, Springfield is my home. I am settled here—a student of the law an't please you—& here shall I abide for many days to come."

Though Springfield was not where he wanted to be, Hay indeed settled in quickly enough. His days given over to obedient study of the law, he spent evenings and weekends running the full circuit of church fairs, "sociables," lyceum lectures, and political rallies. He also became a fixture in the home of Nicholas Ridgely, a wealthy banker whose teenage daughters, Anna and Mary, staged elaborate "soirees" where attendees spoke to one another only in French. Caroline Owsley Brown, who knew Hay well in these years, remembered his "bright, dark eyes that wrought havoc in the hearts of susceptible maidens, and a tongue that could have talked the traditional bird off the bush—fortunately he was of an age when a few soft words, and a few softer looks, did not

count. So he flitted from flower to flower, with a sonnet to this one's sweet eyes, and to that damsel's rosy lips, with no worse result than a fleeting pang which was speedily soothed by the flash of brass buttons." At first meeting, Anna Ridgely privately sized him up as "a very pleasant young fellow & very intelligent," "a bright, handsome fellow of medium height and slight build, with good features, especially the eyes, which were dark, lustrous brown [*sic*]; red cheeks and clear dark complexion." Springfield was a small town and, for a young man of Hay's intellect and good looks, an easy one to conquer. In this pursuit, he had a partner.

It was in these late days of 1859 that Hay rekindled his friendship with George Nicolay. A lively dancer and talented musician, Nicolay was an accomplished autodidact who held his own at the Ridgely girls' French-language soirees. Holding a position that in modern terms might be analogous to executive director of the state Republican Party, he was a close confidant to the capital city's leading elected officials and boosters and a rising talent in his own right. Photographs from that era show a man of twenty-seven or twenty-eight, his youthful features masked ever so slightly by a carefully trimmed, and not especially full, mustache and beard. With thick black hair that he brushed straight back and clipped just a few inches above his shoulders, and piercing, dark eyes, he looked the part of a no-nonsense political operator. Nicolay was by then either engaged to Therena Bates or in a serious, though long-distance, relationship with her. Now twenty-three years of age, Therena had grown into a pretty woman with jet-black hair, strong features, and a warm smile. Like most of his closest friends, she called him George, after his middle name; he called her Maggie, after hers.

From their letters, it is clear that Nicolay and Therena made frequent trips to see each other, taking turns in traveling the seventy miles that separated Pittsfield and Springfield, by rail and coach. In each city they shared common friends and built a common life. "I scarcely know what I shall do with myself tonight," he wrote to her, in a plea for a visit. "Miss Ella Irwin is in New York, Miss Ridgely and Miss Latham are visiting in Quincy, and down at Mr. Chatterton's,

where Miss Stack is staying, they have a very cold parlor, and which can scarcely be kept comfortable. So you need not think it strange that I should be especially wishing that I could spend the evening with you, where I could have a voice in regulating the temperature of the room. Don't you pity me?"

Friends and colleagues who knew him for his stiff, businesslike demeanor would have been surprised by how freely and frequently Nicolay expressed his affection for Therena. "It's been raining all day," he wrote on an overcast winter afternoon, "and as night approaches it is becoming particularly gloomy and disagreeable outdoors. I sit here and, shutting my eyes to the murkiness of the clouds, and my ears to the patter of the rain, vainly imagine how pleasant it would be to sit beside you for the evening. I would be willing to give you a dozen warm kisses to have the vision made real." As his workload inevitably increased during the 1860 campaign, visits between the couple grew less frequent—intervals of two or three months, rather than weeks— and "the sixty or seventy miles of intervening space" between Springfield and Pittsfield began to feel like the span of a continent. Without reservation, George regarded Therena as the love of his life, though expressions of personal affection did not come easily to him. "I have rarely ever either delighted or disgusted you (which would it be?), with sentimentalism of any sort," he admitted, "—because I happen to think that words are empty things." However clumsy his love letters sometimes were, he genuinely missed her when they were apart. "I repeat my wish that I could be with you," he told her. "I think the mood would last me long enough to sit by you and talk you weary of it."

For Nicolay, the year 1860 proved a turning point. He witnessed "something genuine, elemental, uncontrollable in the moods and manifestations" of the Republican National Convention in Chicago, where between thirty thousand and forty thousand party loyalists, many of them traveling from northern Illinois by specially chartered trains, converged on the city to select the party's presidential and vice presidential candidates. Decades later, he could still recall the view from inside the "wigwam," the temporary structure built to house the gathering. "Seats and standing-room were always packed in advance,

and, as the delegates entered by their own separate doors, the crowd easily distinguished the chief actors." Lincoln's strategy going in was to make a respectable showing on the first ballot against the top-tier contenders, William Seward and Salmon Chase. "I am not the *first* choice of a very great many," he conceded. "Our policy, then, is to give no offense to others—leave them in a mood to come to us, if they shall be compelled to give up their first love."

Nicolay would never forget the exhilarating moments before the first roll call—the "united voice of a great crowd." As the chairman began to call the roll, "the tumult gradually died away," leaving hushed delegates and spectators in eager suspense as the states called out their votes, one by one. On the first ballot, Seward won 173½ votes to Lincoln's 102, with Chase and other candidates trailing far behind. No candidate came close to the magic number—233. Nicolay remembered the "groundswell of suppressed excitement which pervaded the hall" as Lincoln supporters, sensing that momentum was on their side, cried out, "Call the roll!" On the next ballot, Seward saw his lead evaporate, as he won 184½ votes to Lincoln's 181. "When the vote of Lincoln was announced," reported Nicolay, "there was a tremendous burst of applause, which the chairman prudently but with difficulty controlled and silenced. The third ballot was begun amid a breathless suspense; hundreds of pencils kept pace with the roll-call, and nervously marked the changes on their tally sheets." When the chairman announced the totals, Lincoln was ahead with 231½ votes—just one and a half shy of the nomination—with Seward trailing far behind at 180.

> A profound silence suddenly fell upon the wigwam; the men ceased to talk and the ladies to flutter their fans; one could distinctly hear the scratching of pencils and the ticking of telegraph instruments on the reporters' tables . . . While every one was leaning forward in intense expectancy, David K. Cartter sprang upon his chair and reported a change of four Ohio votes from Chase to Lincoln. There was a moment's pause,—a teller waved his tally-sheet towards the skylight and shouted a name,—and then the

boom of a cannon on the roof of the wigwam announced
the nomination to the crowds in the streets, where shouts
and salutes took up and spread the news. In the convention
the Lincoln river now became an inundation. Amid the
wildest hurrahs, delegation after delegation changed its
vote to the victor.

Lincoln never saw any of it and would have to rely on Nicolay and
others for their firsthand accounts. Adhering to tradition, he remained
in Springfield, nervously awaiting results. The candidate tried to dis-
tract himself by playing a game of fives—a variant on handball—in a
vacant lot adjacent to the offices of the *Illinois State Journal* before mak-
ing his way to the paper's telegraph room. "I knew this would come
when I saw the second ballot," he said, upon learning of his nomina-
tion. After accepting the congratulations of friends and colleagues
who joined him in the cramped room, he took his leave. "Well Gentle-
men," he said, "there is a little woman at our house who is probably
more interested in this dispatch than I am."

John Hay was also in Springfield that day, and though he still main-
tained a deliberate skepticism toward all things political, he could not
help but note with pride that his hometown had become "the central
city of the north." Prior to the convention, Hay had agreed to write a
series of dispatches for the *Providence Journal,* now edited by his former
college professor James Angell—brother of his college sweetheart,
Hannah. With the town in a state of pitched excitement, he freely
joined in the moment. "When the lightning came down from Chi-
cago, on Friday," he wrote, "to tell us that the nation had honored the
honest man whom we have so long delighted to honor, the deep and
earnest enthusiasm of the hearty western populace burst forth in the
wildest manifestations of joy." Hay described enormous bursts of can-
non fire from the lawn of the state capitol, "Lincoln banners, decked
in every style of rude splendor, fluttered in the high west wind, and the
very church bells signaled the triumph of stainless honor." That eve-
ning, hundreds of loyal Republicans gathered by candlelight in the
rotunda of the statehouse and then marched to the Lincoln residence,

with thousands more joining the procession along the way. Hay was on the scene when "the tall, gaunt form of the future anchor of the republic appeared in his doorway, and in a few good-humored and dignified words he thanked them for their kind manifestations of regard." The next morning, when the official delegation arrived from Chicago to inform Lincoln of his nomination, it was met with "round after round of rousing, electrifying western cheers." The city brimmed over with popular enthusiasm. "Until nearly midnight the rejoicings continued. The principal streets were ablaze with illuminations. Bonfires flamed and roared in public places, and bursting rockets paled the splendor of the calm May star-light."

A few weeks later, on June 7, Nicolay mustered up the courage to ask Lincoln's key campaign managers for the one and only perquisite he had ever sought in his years of loyal service to the antislavery cause. He was "filled with an ambitious desire to write a campaign biography of the Republican candidate for President, and was greatly disappointed and chagrined to learn that that honor had already been promised to a young Ohioan, then little known . . . [William] D. Howells." Nearly choked up with tears, Nicolay spoke privately with his boss, Ozias Hatch, who placed a hand on his shoulder and said, "Never mind. You are to be private secretary." Later that afternoon, at five o'clock, following another day of rallies, parades, and marching music, George informed Therena of his good fortune. "I can now definitively answer your question as to what I am going to do, for a while at any rate. Mr. Lincoln has engaged me to act as his private secretary during the campaign, and pays me at the rate of $75 per month for the service . . . He has a room here in the State House, and so I go right along without any change of quarters or arrangements of any kind other than indicated." From that day forward, until the day that Lincoln died, Nicolay would remain in his service.

From the moment that it began, the presidential race of 1860 emerged as one of the most dramatic moments then or since in American political life. In the weeks after his unexpected nomination, Lincoln benefited from what soon proved an irrevocable split in the Democratic

Party. With his longtime foe Stephen Douglas closing in on the nomi-
nation, Southern Democrats conditioned their fealty on his support of
new constitutional protections for slavery. In response, Northern
Democrats insisted that *"never, never, never,* so help us God," would
they abandon their popular sovereignty platform. For the first and
only time in American history, a major political party rent itself in
two, with Northern Democrats nominating Douglas and Southern
Democrats running John C. Breckinridge of Kentucky, the young,
dashing vice president and a stalwart defender of slavery. Adding to
the year's confusion, a coalition of conservative ex-Whigs and Know-
Nothings ran its own slate of electors in favor of John Bell, a former
Tennessee senator and advocate of sectional compromise. To win the
election, Republicans needed to pick off any combination of two states
among Pennsylvania, Illinois, and Indiana, a task made easier by the
divided opposition.

As summer gave way to fall, the canvass reached a fever pitch. Iron-
ically, Abraham Lincoln, the consummate political animal, was bound
by tradition to sit out the most electrifying campaign of his life. Pre-
vailing convention, stretching back to the earliest days of the Republic,
held that public men should make themselves available for office but
that it was unseemly for them to work for it. The logic behind this
display of disinterestedness flowed from classical republican fears of
tyrannical leaders who aggressively sought and protected power. Dur-
ing the Jacksonian era, this form of reserve largely fell by the wayside
in congressional, state, and local races, as Americans came to embrace
a more vibrant and earthy form of popular democracy. But many peo-
ple still expected their presidents to demonstrate republican virtue.
Under pressure to smooth over his rough image and to prove his fit-
ness for high office, Lincoln was in no position to test tradition. Doug-
las, however, felt that he was. The senator broke with custom and
barnstormed the country, as would later become the norm among
presidential contenders, while Lincoln remained in careful seclusion,
leaving it to others to deliver speeches, pen broadsides, and work the
enormous crowds that gathered at Republican campaign rallies. With
Nicolay as his sole aide, he managed the enormous influx of correspon-

dence, much of it political in nature and requiring delicate attention, and tried to satisfy the numerous party operators who traveled to Springfield to confer with the candidate. He made no public appearances and said nothing that might clarify his position on the central issues, beyond his allegiance to the Chicago platform. Upon visiting Lincoln at his temporary office in the statehouse, Herndon found him "bored—*bored badly*. I would not have his place and be bored as he is."

The electorate was anything but bored. Across the country, Republicans held enormous political rallies that tapped into the imagination and fervor of an electorate that was larger and younger than ever before. In almost every small town and large city throughout the North, young men joined Wide-Awake Clubs, donned oilcloth capes, and staged dramatic torchlight parades meant to stir the passions of the faithful. None of these practices were new, though the intensity of the canvass was in many ways unprecedented. Politics in the antebellum era was a deeply polarized affair. The object of a campaign was not so much to persuade the small sliver of undecided voters as to drive turnout among the party faithful. "Party lines were as strictly drawn as were the lines of religious sects," the *Philadelphia Inquirer* observed several years later. "A man belonged to either the Democratic or the Whig party, to the Republican or the Democratic. He did not merely entertain opinions, he had convictions." The steady expansion of the franchise in the first decades of the nineteenth century had inspired new mechanisms to stir popular passions, including party clubs, rallies, campaign songs, pole raisings (a throwback to England's Maypole rituals), and torchlight processions meant to inspire awe and fervor among ordinary voters. Democrats were first to adopt these practices, but the Whig campaign of 1840, in which young men flocked to the banner of the war hero and everyman William Henry Harrison, set a new standard for democratic electioneering. By 1860, most Northerners likely knew where their political sympathies lay. It was incumbent upon the parties to use public spectacles in order to socialize their nominees (some of whom, like Lincoln, might be unknown outside their regions) among the party base and run up the numbers in the fall. The

fireworks displays and martial parades were, in some respects, an early
form of popular entertainment, in an age before professional sports and
cinema. But "people did not go to the stands for amusement," one jour-
nalist claimed. "Everybody was intensely excited" by the issues at stake.
Whereas only 48 percent of eligible voters cast ballots as late as 1836, by
the Civil War turnout in presidential elections averaged 69 percent, a
testament to the success of democratic campaign practices.

Though the fires burned bright throughout the North, naturally
they were the most intense in Springfield. Writing in the twilight
hours of a massive rally in Springfield, which he judged "the greatest
political demonstration that our State has ever seen," Hay marveled
that "veteran stumpers, who have mingled in every fight since Jack-
son's time, fail of comparisons to describe it. Editors and reporters
who have haunted for years the mass meetings of the nation, say they
have seen nothing to compare it to. Grey-haired Whigs, who shouted
and drank hard cider on the Tippecanoe battle field, at the monster
meeting of twenty years ago, and have lived ever since in the confident
belief that no other meeting ever would be held like it, shake their
heads since yesterday, and mourn over a broken idol, an ideal eclipsed."
In a dispatch for the *Providence Journal,* Hay described the bright illu-
minations of the nighttime sky that met the tens of thousands of party
loyalists who had flocked to the capital city to support its native son.
"If you are a man of lively imagination," he advised, "take a dose of
Hasheesh and turn your mind to some such brilliant subjects as the
Feast of Lanterns, the Vale of Cashmere, Bengal lights, and Choate's
oratory, and you will drift into a kaleidoscope of fantastic design and
gorgeous colors, which may realize to your perceptions the show that
yesterday's parade gave us." Everywhere one turned, there were rep-
licas of log cabins, "monster flatboats, and big Indians, and allegorical
representations of all the trades, and beautiful young women clothed
in innocence and tarlatan, personating the Union-loving States, and
every conceivable variety of mottoes, inscriptions, and devices on ban-
ners, globes and transparencies that swayed and floated and revolved
along a seemingly interminable line of eight miles of procession."
The state's leading Republicans were on hand to deliver the expected

oratory, and as the afternoon sky began to tinge with the reddish yellow of sunset, "Mr. Lincoln appeared upon the grounds, to see for a moment, and be seen by the eager thousands who had come so many miles with that one purpose and hope." The candidate said nothing, but his mere presence satisfied the throngs of Republican loyalists, many of them first-time voters who had only just come of age.

"Night came at last," Hay continued, "and the enthusiasm rekindled under the stars. The torch-light parade of the Wide-Awakes . . . was the most magnificent thing that could have been devised to close worthily a demonstration like this. Viewed from an elevated position, it wound its sinuous track over the length of two miles, seeming, in its blazing lights and glittering uniforms, like a beautiful serpent of fire." As the procession turned at Fifth and Adams streets, in the center of town, its young members set off hundreds of Roman candles that covered the statehouse in a "hissing and bursting blaze of fiery splendor, that cast a lurid glare on the upturned faces of the excited thousands, [and] the enthusiasm of the people broke out in wild cheerings, that came back in redoubled echoes from the four sides of the square." For Hay, it caused the first stirrings of political awakening.

The first harbinger of good news came in October, when Republicans won state elections in Pennsylvania, Ohio, and Indiana. If the same pattern carried in November, Lincoln would command enough electoral votes to win the presidency. Nicolay reported that the "effect of the glorious news . . . was signally illustrated in the splendid demonstrations of the Republicans of this city last night, in honor of these victories." By now, the city had grown so accustomed to massive party demonstrations that local partisans erected a temporary meeting hall, to impose order where chaos otherwise prevailed. "Darkness had scarcely set in," Nicolay noted, "when the Republican Wigwam was lighted up, and soon filled with an eager crowd of Republicans. Soon the 'Wide Awake' torches dashed out, and the organized and uniformed Lincolnites ranged themselves shoulder to shoulder for a march . . . From different points in the city rockets and other fireworks were filling the air with light, the windows of the Head Quarters of the Lincoln Club, and numerous business houses were beautifully

illuminated. Passing once around the square they took their way toward the residence of Mr. Lincoln." Standing near the candidate, Nicolay heard the crowd give "three cheers for Lincoln—three cheers for Trumbull—three cheers for Pennsylvania—three for Indiana, and three for Ohio."

For Nicolay, these were heady times. Almost always at Lincoln's side, he worked out of the governor's office in the statehouse, reading and answering mail, managing the multitude of visitors who jockeyed for the candidate's attention, conducting the flow of information between Springfield and key battleground states, and, on occasion, performing delicate political tasks. Mary Ridgely later noted that "if ever there was a man who worked, John Nicolay was that man." In July, Nicolay traveled to Indiana to meet with a prominent Know-Nothing leader who commanded a key block of nativist voters. "Ascertain what he wants," Lincoln instructed. "On what subjects he would converse with me. And the particulars if he will give them. Is an interview indispensable? Tell him my motto is 'Fairness to all.' But commit me to nothing."

Throughout the fall, Republicans enjoyed what political commentators one hundred years later might call "the big momentum," while Democrats suffered an enormous enthusiasm gap, particularly in the North. Writing just two weeks before the election, Nicolay dismissed a Douglas rally in Springfield as a "miserable . . . mortifying failure." There were "some feeble fireworks," but "public faith was shaken when the trains came in and brought only some little squads of fifties and hundreds—not making in the aggregate a thousand, all told . . . To the crown dismay of the Douglasites, fully one-half of the crowd on the sidewalks wore Lincoln badges, and every shout for Douglas was met by an answering shout from the enthusiastic Lincolnites." Compared with the Wide-Awake revelry of several weeks before, the Douglas rally did not " 'shine' any better at night. The torch bearers again patched up a ragged single file procession . . . shot off some straggling Roman candles, and the whole affair 'blowed out' at about nine o'clock, leaving the city in darkness, and almost as total quiet as if there were no squatters in the land." Even in the southernmost

counties, known colloquially as Egypt, or Africa, and usually a reliable source of Democratic support, Hay found that the "watchfires of liberty are lighting."

Election Day fell on a crisp autumn day. At 3:30 in the afternoon, Lincoln—accompanied by fellow attorney Ward Hill Lamon, the law student Elmer Ellsworth, Ozias Hatch, William Herndon, and John Nicolay—made his way to the courthouse to vote. John Hay was there, too, and bore witness as "the dense crowd immediately began to shout with the wild abandon that characterizes the impulsive heart of the west." To emphasize his availability for, but nonpursuit of, office, Lincoln made a show of clipping his name—and that of his designated electors—off the preprinted Republican ballot. That night, as returns began to roll in from around the country, he and Nicolay set up camp in the headquarters of the Illinois & Mississippi Telegraph Company, on the north end of the town square, to keep tally. "Here in this little room," Nicolay remembered years later, "in the company of two or three silent operators moving about their mysteriously clicking instruments, and recording with imperturbable gravity the swift-throbbing messages from near and far, Mr. Lincoln read the reports as they came, first in fragmentary dribblets, and later in the rising and swelling stream of cheering news." Outside, Hay recorded, "the crowd had speeches and songs. They grew uproarious over some telegraphic dispatches that Mr. Nicolay read to them . . . It seems absurd to write about the good time here, when the whole continent is aglow with the same good feeling. But the peculiar warmth that lives on the rejoicing here seems to me worthy of especial note. It is not so much the return of purity and the triumph of freedom that the people here hail, as it is the recognition by the world of the great soul that they have honored and loved for many years."

Lincoln won the presidential election with over 1.8 million votes— a plurality that came just an inch shy of 40 percent of all votes cast, but a commanding majority of 180 votes in the Electoral College. Even when combined, the popular votes of his three opponents would not have been sufficient to defeat him in the Electoral College, a testimony to the yawning gap in population between the North, where Lincoln

carried every state but New Jersey, and the South, where his name appeared on the ballot in just a handful of states.

Nicolay stayed up until four o'clock, taking in the "shouting, yelling, singing, dancing" and celebratory firing of guns and Roman candles. "I can scarcely realize that, after having fought this slavery question for six years past, and suffered so many defeats, I am at last rejoicing in a triumph which only two years ago we hardly dared dream about," he crowed to Therena. "Though I was fighting then as something more than a private, I should have thought it a wild dream to imagine that six years after I should find victory so near the Commander-in-Chief."

In the coming weeks, the pace of work accelerated, as would-be office seekers, party leaders, and veterans of past presidential administrations flocked to Springfield in search of patronage appointments or to make general introductions to the president-elect. From the governor's office in the statehouse, measuring just fifteen feet by twenty-five feet, Nicolay controlled access to Lincoln and labored alone at reading and answering anywhere between fifty and a hundred letters each day. When *Frank Leslie's Illustrated Newspaper* ran a sketch of their working space, Nicolay smiled at "the marvelous truthfulness of the representation of Mr. Lincoln, and his elegant and accomplished private secretary who sits writing at the desk." He jokingly advised Therena not to spend more than "say $75" on the frame.

When the influx of mail and visitors grew unmanageable for just one staff member, John Hay began showing up at the statehouse and assisting his friend on an informal basis. It was still not clear that either man would accompany the president-elect to Washington. As late as December 9, Nicolay told Therena that Lincoln had not yet offered him the position of secretary to the president, though he was "gratified to tell you that I have . . . evidence that Mr. Lincoln reposes entire confidence in me, which I deem sufficient gauranty [sic] that my present confidential relation to him will be continued." Presidential staffs were then very small, and the job of secretary traditionally carried more authority and importance than its title would suggest. By custom, presidential secretaries lived in the White House and served as the

primary interface between members of Congress, the press, and the public, on the one hand, and the commander in chief, on the other. Without prior political experience in Washington, or even outside the Midwest, and still unknown to the men who ran the Republican Party in large states like New York and Pennsylvania, Nicolay struck some critics as loyal but dramatically underqualified to be appointed to head the president's office. But Lincoln valued loyalty. By the end of December, it was understood that Nicolay would be awarded the coveted position, at a princely salary of $2,500 per year—almost three times what he presently earned as Lincoln's campaign secretary. Not long after, Nicolay suggested that Hay be appointed assistant secretary. "We can't take all Illinois down with us to Washington," Lincoln replied. When Milton offered to pay his nephew's salary for six months, the president-elect relented. "Well, let Hay come," he agreed. He would be appointed a clerk in the Interior Department, at an annual salary of $1,500, and detailed to the White House.

Throughout the long interregnum between Lincoln's election in November and his inauguration the following March (it was not until 1937 that the Twentieth Amendment, which was ratified in 1933, moved the start of presidential terms to January), Nicolay enjoyed greater exposure and insight into the president-elect's thinking than anyone, except perhaps Mary Todd Lincoln. His role was not consultative, but in managing Lincoln's relationships with national Republican officeholders and in communicating his instructions to members of the House and Senate, many of whom were in a state of panic at the prospect of disunion, George spent many hours in private discussion with the president-elect and came to know his point of view. In early December he told Therena that the Deep South states were likely to pass secession ordinances, but he believed that Tennessee, Arkansas, Missouri, Delaware, and Maryland would show "a decided disposition to remain *in* the Union." Quite likely echoing Lincoln's own thinking, he saw "no single reason why they should secede now, more than there was four years ago when Buchanan was chosen. True the Republican party have succeeded in electing their president. But neither Lincoln nor the

party have ever avowed any purpose to interfere with, or deprive them of any recognized right, and as both Houses of Congress have a Democratic majority they could not do so if they wanted . . . The truth is that the State of South Carolina is a nest of traitors—disunionists *per se* who make Lincoln's election the *mere pretext* not the *cause* of dissolution." Nicolay also doubted very seriously that the seceding states could effectuate a break with the United States, as it was "easy enough for a State or States to *resolve* themselves out of the Union. But a State or nation cannot do without a government." How would they re-create from scratch the elaborate web of institutions and services that the federal government had established gradually over the course of almost seventy-five years? "To maintain an independent government requires a lot of Executive officers, which must be paid," he observed, "an army, which must be paid—a navy, which must be paid— ambassadors at foreign courts, which must be paid—a postal service, which must be paid—and a thousand other things which cost money. Where is the money to come from?" By and large, he did not regard secession fever as a particularly serious threat, and in holding this position, he very likely imitated the views of his employer.

If Nicolay gave voice to Lincoln's cool state of mind, many Republicans who should have been basking in victory quickly turned to jelly at the first threat of disunion. As early as the day before the election, a prominent New England merchant and politician beseeched Lincoln to stake out a compromise—"to reassure the men honestly alarmed." Nicolay would long remember that his boss "bluntly replied" that there "are no such men . . . This is the same old trick by which the South breaks down every Northern victory. Even if I were personally willing to barter away the moral principle involved in this contest, for the commercial gain of a new submission to the South, I would go to Washington without the countenance of the men who supported me and were my friends before the election." Throughout the winter, special House and Senate committees convened to explore potential compromises. Simultaneously, a group of aging political leaders gathered in Washington as an unofficial "peace convention" to consider a range

of measures intended to mollify the Deep South. One proposal, of-
fered by the Kentucky senator John Crittenden, would extend the Mis-
souri Compromise line across the whole continent and forever protect
the institution of slavery through the passage of an irrevocable consti-
tutional amendment; another would require the Northern states to
abrogate their "personal liberty laws," meant to protect free black
Americans from capture under the provisions of the Fugitive Slave
Act. On all of these proffers, Lincoln held firm. "The tug has to come,"
he privately told several congressmen, "& better now, than any time
hereafter." Even if the seceding states were in earnest, he advised wa-
vering Republicans to hold firm, for there were moral and political
considerations at stake. "We have just carried an election on principles
fairly stated to the people. Now we are told in advance, the govern-
ment shall be broken up, unless we surrender to those we have beaten,
before we take the offices. In this they are attempting to play upon us,
or they are in dead earnest. Either way, if we surrender, it is the very
end of us, and of the government." It was a refrain that he sounded for
anyone who would listen. "Give them personal liberty bills, and they
will pull in the slack, hold on, and insist on the border-state compro-
mise," he told Senator Charles Sumner. "Give them that, they'll again
pull in the slack and demand Crittenden's compromise. That pulled in,
they will want all that South Carolina asks . . . By no act or complicity
of mine shall the Republican party become a mere sucked egg, all shell
and no principle in it."

Events took a decisive turn on December 20, when South Carolina
officially seceded from the Union. Two days later, when Lincoln ar-
rived at his office to begin his morning meetings, Nicolay asked if he
had read the latest telegraph reports. When Lincoln replied no, the
secretary informed him of rumors that Buchanan intended to abandon
federal forts in South Carolina, rather than risk armed conflict. "If that
is true they ought to hang him!" the president-elect snapped, in a mo-
ment of uncharacteristic anger. As it became clear that the outgoing
president would do nothing to protect federal property and installa-
tions, even allowing his secretary of war to transfer guns to Southern

outposts, where they would surely fall into secessionist hands, Lincoln's distrust of Buchanan hardened. Privately, Nicolay relayed his boss's ire. "Just think of it!" he told Therena, in terms that very likely echoed his privileged conversations with Lincoln.

> The President of the United States—the Commander-in-Chief of the Army and Navy—the man to whom thirty millions of people have confided their interests—sits in the capitol [sic] of the country, and regardless of the protestations and entreaties of twenty millions of his subjects to do his duty . . . whines and weeps and prays, entirely unmanned and unnerved by a remote and worse than babyish fear . . . Truly the country is in great danger—but it is from the traitors and *imbeciles* who are at the head of national affairs, and not from the beggarly mutinous crew down South.

Hay, too, thought the lame-duck president a "weak, pottering old man" who would leave only a "dark footprint upon our history, one which a century will hardly obliterate."

Throughout it all, the president-elect maintained his official silence. Even as he privately beseeched his party brethren to hold firm, Lincoln hewed carefully to a policy that his friend Congressman Elihu Washburne dubbed "masterly inactivity." Declining almost every opportunity for public comment, he studiously avoided the appearance that efforts at compromise bore his sanction or endorsement. Which was not to say that the months between his election and his inauguration were idle ones. With Nicolay at his side, joined later by John Hay, he received what the journalist Henry Villard dismissed as a "motley" array of office seekers, advice offerers, and hangers-on. "Muddy boots and hickory shirts are just as frequent as broadcloth, fine linen, etc.," Villard snorted. The incoming correspondence started as a trickle but soon became a flood. Hay watched as the president-elect "dived into his capacious coat pocket, and bringing up a handful of letters began

to look over them." With the secretaries sifting the wheat from the chaff, Lincoln carefully considered the most important dispatches, many dealing with the portentous issues of war and disunion, others dedicated to more pedestrian but highly consequential matters of patronage. "He reads letters constantly," Hay observed sympathetically. "At home—in the street—among his friends. I believe he is strongly tempted in church."

With the president-elect maintaining his deliberate public silence, newspapermen struggled to find something to write about. Lincoln's decision to grow a beard in the months before his inauguration offered Americans temporary refuge from the more sobering intelligence coming in from all points southward. "The President's whiskers continue to flourish vigorously," Hay told readers of the *Providence Journal.* "Some assume to say that he is putting on 'airs, and the following is a frantic distich that I rescued to-day on its way to the stove":

> Election news Abe's hirsute fancy warrant—
> Apparent hair becomes heir apparent.

By January, with the new governor about to be sworn into office and the state legislature poised to begin its session, Lincoln left his quarters in the statehouse and set up temporary shop in Johnson's Building, an office complex on the square. It was a "good room, about twenty feet square, newly painted, papered and carpeted, and pretty well furnished," Nicolay reported. The president-elect had gone "to his own house where he will stay most of the time . . . I shall be here all the time at work . . . Mr. Lincoln will come here occasionally, when I need his advice or he my immediate assistance." Soon enough, the throng of visitors threatened to overtake Lincoln in his own home. February found the president-elect taking refuge in the attic above his brother-in-law's dry-goods store, on the south side of the square, where he was able to cull together the fragments of the address that he had been drafting over the preceding weeks. Occasionally walking finished pages to Nicolay, for review and copying, he found much-needed

solace in what Herndon later described as an "unromantic," "claustro-phobic . . . dingy, dusty, and neglected back room . . . [T]hen and there he wrote his first inaugural."

Monday, February 11, was gray and cold. The Lincolns had already emptied and rented out their house at Eighth and Jackson streets and were staying at a downtown hotel. After breakfast, the president-elect made his way to the Great Western depot and prepared for his journey to Washington. The plan called for a whistle-stop tour lasting ten days and winding through Illinois, Ohio, Pennsylvania, New York, New Jersey, and Maryland, allowing Lincoln to introduce himself to the citizens of the North and to build popular support for the decisions that lay in the immediate weeks ahead. It was to be a grueling trip. On the first day alone, there would be more than twenty stops, most lasting just minutes. William Wood, the official advance man, stipulated that at every overnight destination local organizers should arrange hotel accommodations for Nicolay and Hay, "contiguous to the President elect." In a sign of how far he had risen from his days as a Senate candidate in 1858, when he rode coach, Lincoln now occupied a specially outfitted railcar that afforded him and his family all of the comforts then available in train travel. Nicolay was assigned a place in the third carriage, and Hay, the fourth, though as a matter of necessity they spent most of the journey beside the president-elect. "The scene at the depot before starting was impressive and touching in the last degree," Hay recorded. "Upward of a thousand people were assembled, and Mr. Lincoln, taking his place in one of the rooms at the station, bade farewell to his friends and neighbors, to the number of several hundreds, with an affectionate grasp of the hand. As the time approached for the departure of the train, he mounted the platform, and, in a brief and touching speech, which left hardly a dry eye in the assemblage, bade them farewell." Years later, Hay and Nicolay still remembered the scene, as "Lincoln appeared on the platform of the car, and raised his hand to command attention. The bystanders bared their heads to the falling snowflakes, and standing thus, his neighbors heard his voice for the last time."

The speech in question would go down in the annals of history as

one of Lincoln's finest, and certainly the most personal ever delivered by a singularly private man. "To this place, and the kindness of these people, I owe every thing," he told the crowd.

> Here I have lived a quarter of a century, and have passed from a young to an old man. Here my children have been born, and one is buried. I now leave, not knowing when, or whether ever, I may return, with a task before me greater than that which rested upon Washington. Without the assistance of that Divine Being, who ever attended him, I cannot succeed. With that assistance, I cannot fail. Trusting in Him, who can go with me, and remain with you and be every where for good, let us confidently hope that all will yet be well. To His care commending you, as I hope in your prayers you will commend me, I bid you an affectionate farewell.

Moments after retiring to his railcar, Lincoln began transcribing to the best of his recollection—and with some edits for the sake of posterity—the words that he had uttered moments before. Nicolay helped him reconstruct the speech. The surviving manuscript copy shows the opening lines in the president-elect's hand, at first steady, but then faltering as the train began rocking into motion. Midway through, the handwriting becomes Nicolay's. The closing lines are again in Lincoln's script.

Though it was certainly not his first time on the rails, Hay found the first day of travel exhilarating. He noted that Lincoln seemed to betray "something of the gloom of parting with neighbors and friends, bidding farewell to the community in the midst of which he has lived for a quarter of a century," and found the president-elect to be "abstracted, sad, [and] thoughtful . . . [he] spent much of his time in the private car appropriated to his use." But at every small depot, "Mr. Lincoln left the car, moving rapidly through the crowd, shaking hands vigorously, and incurring embraces and blessings to an extent that must have given him a slight premonition of what was in store for

him." Nicolay took note of the "crowds of people at every station" and
the large welcoming party at the first overnight stop in Indianapolis
("if it were during a campaign," he quipped, "it would be called fifty
thousand"). Hay admired the "President's coolness under the terrific
infliction of several thousand hand-shakings . . . I have made some
amateur studies of the art of hand-shaking at the West, and I think I
may say that the rack, the thumb screw, King James's boot, the cap of
silence, with all the other dark and recondite paraphernalia of torture,
become instruments of cheerful and enlivening pastime, beside the
ferocious grip and the demonic wrench of the muscular citizen of the
West." From their quarters at the Bates House hotel in Indianapolis
("don't I feel at home?" Nicolay kidded his fiancée, Therena Bates), the
secretaries revealed something of their polar dispositions. Nicolay
thought the horde of onlookers a "severe ordeal." "The House is per-
fectly jammed full of people," he complained. "Three or four ladies
and as many gentlemen, have even invaded the room assigned to Mr.
Lincoln, while outside the door I hear the crowd pushing and grum-
bling and shouting in almost frantic endeavors to get to another parlor
in the door of which Mr. Lincoln stands shaking hands with the mul-
titude." Hay, on the other hand, fully enjoyed himself. "Men embrace
each other wildly without provocation," he remarked with wry be-
musement. "Shorthand reporters, with the great speech in phonetic
characters, resembling flys' legs, are surrounded and smothered. The
bar-room throbs with patriotic sentiments and calls for drinks. 'Lin-
coln and Union forever' is intoned with subdued emphasis in every
direction. Indianapolis is not one of the great western towns, but a
stranger, visiting it to-day for the first time, would have suspected its
population numbering several millions." Their reverse attitudes to-
ward the trip hinted at the roles they would soon play in Washington,
with Nicolay assuming the part of grim enforcer and Hay the smiling
emissary to cabinet members and congressmen.

Over the next ten days, Lincoln and his entourage traveled nine-
teen hundred miles, visiting seven states and making brief—sometimes
just momentary—appearances in hundreds of small towns and vil-
lages. The president-elect delivered at least 101 speeches—in state

capitol buildings, from the back of his railcar, in crowded streets, hotel lobbies, and restaurants. He appeared in no fewer than twenty-four parades and shook tens of thousands of hands—a punishing schedule for even the most ardent politician. By one account, three-quarters of a million people got to see Lincoln in person during his swing through the Northern states, making his inaugural journey an unprecedented show of political muscle. Everywhere they went, Hay noted, there were "crowds, cannon, and cheers." "Such crowds—surging through long arches, cursing the military and blessing Old Abe; swinging hats, banners, handkerchiefs, and every possible variety of festive bunting, and standing with open mouths as the train, relentlessly punctual, moved away." Nicolay enjoyed the stopover in Cleveland, where "for the first time we found the crowd tolerably well controlled by the police and military" and "were assigned to comfortable quarters, treated to a good dinner, and altogether about as well taken care of as was possible." Buffalo was a different matter. The crowd was so aggressive that Lincoln's military escort suffered a dislocated shoulder, and once the presidential party "arrived at the hotel all was confusion—the [local] committee not only did nothing but didn't know and didn't seem to care what to do." As usual, Hay found more light than darkness, agreeing that the arrangements in the city were "utterly inadequate" but finding much to admire in the streets "densely thronged, the cheers unremitting, the stars and stripes wav[ing] everywhere, from roofs, from windows, from balconies," where "all the traditionary accessories of popular demonstration were copiously distributed throughout the entire route."

In New York City, Lincoln stared down a group of Wall Street financiers who urged compromise for the sake of keeping the wheels of commerce well greased. When one of his breakfast hosts remarked that he would "not meet so many millionaires together at any other table in New York," the president-elect responded tartly, "I'm a millionaire myself. I got a minority of a million in the votes last November." At Trenton, the "official display was embarrassingly elaborate," Hay reported. Official marshals bearing white satin badges escorted the presidential party to the gold-domed statehouse, where Lincoln

delivered separate speeches to each chamber of the legislature. In a dramatic display of resolve, the president-elect pledged every effort at peace but also promised that "we shall have to put the foot down firmly." At that moment, he "lifted his foot lightly," according to Hay, "and pressed it with a quick, but not violent gesture upon the floor. He evidently meant it. The hall rang long and loud with acclamations." In Philadelphia, the next day, Lincoln swore to a crowd at Independence Hall that he would sooner be assassinated than betray his constitutional duty to defend the integrity of the Union, and at Harrisburg— where even Hay, normally good-natured to the extreme, admitted that the crowds were "uniformly rough, unruly, and ill bred," and the accommodations "unprecedentedly bad"—the presidential party made its final stop on free soil. "This trip of ours has been very laborious and exciting," Hay wrote to a friend. "I have had no time to think calmly since we left Springfield. There is one reason why I write tonight. Tomorrow we enter slave territory . . . There may be trouble in Baltimore. If so, we will not go to Washington, unless in long, narrow boxes."

Unbeknownst to Nicolay and Hay, the president-elect had already agreed to a plan that would spirit him secretly through Baltimore and into Washington. Acting on intelligence from multiple sources, Lincoln begrudgingly agreed to bypass a rumored assassination plot in Maryland by splitting off from his party and traveling overnight with an armed guard. Early that evening, the secretaries began to suspect that something was afoot. "[T]here is something *up*," Nicolay told Norman Judd, who was among the very few who knew of the plan. "George," Judd replied, "there is no necessity fore your Knowing & one man can keep a secret better than two." The next morning, with Lincoln safely installed in the nation's capital, the rest of the presidential entourage, including Mary Todd Lincoln, her three sons, and the two secretaries, completed their long journey to Washington.

For the nine days preceding his inauguration, the president-elect opted to use Willard's Hotel as his temporary home and base of operations. Filling most of a city block on Fourteenth Street, between F Street and Pennsylvania Avenue, Willard's was a modern wonder,

with 150 guest rooms, lecture and meeting halls, and a massive bar and dining room where hundreds of patrons gorged themselves daily on fish, oysters, venison, and good champagne. Nathaniel Hawthorne said that it was "much more justly called the center of Washington and the Union than either the Capitol, the White House, or the State Department," and with the Lincolns now occupying the best suite in the house, the hotel struggled to keep up with the crush of visitors. Dignitaries were forced to double and triple up in rooms—and sometimes in beds—as overworked hotel staff moved hundreds of mattresses into the hallways to house the multitudes who converged on Washington for the inaugural festivities. Nicolay grumbled that "all of the party except Mr. & Mrs. Lincoln have but sorry accommodations" but offered as an aside that "next week we hope to be in the White House, where perhaps it may be better."

Walking from the hotel to the Mall, Hay observed the steps on the east end of the Capitol, where carpenters had already constructed "a platform, in the midst of which a canopy is to be arranged, beneath which the President will stand while delivering his inaugural." Several blocks away, by the old post office, workmen erected a temporary structure for the inaugural ball, "capable of accommodating six thousand people." Back at Willard's, he noted with bemusement that "the number of western politicians here is beginning to tell with fearful effect upon the market for alcoholic beverages." Writing for the *Providence Journal,* he reported that "Mrs. Lincoln received nightly at her parlors at Willard's. She has won all hearts by her frank, unaffected cordiality of manner." The president's oldest son, Robert Todd Lincoln, known popularly as the Prince of Rails for his famous, rail-splitting father, "has been extensively lionized, and a good deal of regret is expressed by the ladies at his approaching departure for Harvard." Finally, "the private secretaries of the President, Nicolay and Hay, are toiling early and late with a mass of correspondence, of the extent of which I can convey no adequate idea." Most of the incoming mail was from office seekers, leading Hay to conclude that "the number of people in the United States who find it impossible to earn an honest living must be appalling."

Monday, March 4, was Inauguration Day. From his suite at Willard's, Lincoln listened calmly as Robert read aloud the final draft of his father's address. Outside, the weather was "cold and bracing" as the outgoing president arrived at the hotel in a splendid carriage. A bystander reported that "the streets adjacent to . . . the Capitol were nearly impassable by the crowds of people . . . Every available spot was black with human beings; boys and men clinging to rails and mounting on fences and climbing trees until they bent beneath the weight." Donning a "low-crowned, broad-brimmed silk hat," James Buchanan stepped into the Willard's lobby to meet his successor. Moments later, the two men exited the hotel together and took their places in the open carriage. Arriving a short while later at the Capitol, they attended the swearing in of Vice President Hannibal Hamlin in the Senate chamber and strode out to the east portico. The Lincoln family was already seated beneath the canopy; Hay and Nicolay were assigned chairs just next to Robert Todd Lincoln. They were only a few feet away when Lincoln delivered his inaugural address and Chief Justice Roger Taney administered the oath of office.

Years later, Hay recounted the moments following Lincoln's swearing in. Back inside the Capitol, Buchanan pulled the new president aside for "some parting words in the corner where I was standing. I waited with boyish wonder and credulity to see what momentous counsels were to come from that gray and weathered head. Every word must have its value at such an instant. The ex-president said: 'I think you will find the water on the right-hand well at the White House better than the left,' and went on with many intimate details of the kitchen and pantry." Hay recalled that Lincoln stood politely at attention, "with that weary, introverted look of his, not answering, and the next day, when I recalled the conversation, admitted he had not heard a word of it. Through every chamber of his heart and brain were resounding those solemn strains of long-suffering warning which he had that day addressed to the South. 'With you, not me, rests the awful issue. Shall it be peace or the sword?'"

PART II

CHAPTER 6

A Young Man of His Age

As you see from the heading of my letter, I am fairly installed in the 'White House,'" John Nicolay reported proudly to Therena on March 5. The orphan boy who just ten years earlier earned his keep as a printer's devil now worked and resided in the Executive Mansion. He was pleased with his station in life and eager that Therena appreciate his newfound importance. "Since I commenced writing this I have again been called away to appease visitors who are importuning to see Mr. Lincoln," he wrote, "so don't be surprised if I break off anywhere and fold it up and mail it to you—for I am going to send you something to-night if it is only an envelope. The first official act of Mr. Lincoln—after the inauguration—was to sign my appointment as Private Sec'y, and I have been busy enough since . . . I assure you. As the work is now, it will be a very severe tax on both my physical and mental energies, although so far I have borne it remarkably well."

Washington was the largest city in which either Nicolay or Hay had ever lived. Encompassing Washington City, Georgetown, and outlying rural areas, the district numbered seventy-five thousand people, including eleven thousand free black residents and three thousand slaves. Though cosmopolitan in the extreme when compared with Springfield—to say nothing of Warsaw or Pittsfield—it was nevertheless a poor cousin to New York, Boston, or Philadelphia. Seventy years earlier, its founders resolved to turn swampland and tobacco fields into a capital city. By 1861 the city was still an incomplete mix of crude mud

streets lined with two- and three-story brick row houses, ramshackle wood slums and boardinghouses, and roughly one dozen federal government buildings, which stood out in these rough environs for their aspirational grandeur. The Capitol, where workmen had recently completed north and south wings to house the new Senate and House chambers, was surrounded by unsightly scaffolding and toolsheds, as engineers and laborers awaited the new cast-iron dome that would soon replace the decades-old wood roof. In the vast spaces between buildings, city residents let their pigs and cattle graze freely. "To make a Washington street," an English visitor scoffed, "take one marble temple, or public office, a dozen good houses of brick and a dozen of wood and fill in with sheds and fields."

Nicolay had visited Washington once before. John Hay, who had not, agreed with critics that "the town is a congeries of hovels, inharmoniously sown with temples . . . Why did they attempt to build a city where no city was meant to be reared?" Still, the young presidential aide, not yet twenty-three years old, found his first few days in "this sprawling, chaotic town" electrifying. A city with strong Southern leanings, Washington had long been in the social and political grip of the Democratic establishment. Now it was overrun with Republicans. Incumbent officeholders, all Democrats, grimly steeled themselves for dismissal, while thousands of Lincoln loyalists swarmed the White House in search of favor, fortune, and patronage. To get to the president, they had first to get past Nicolay and Hay.

A British journalist visiting Washington described the Executive Mansion as "beautiful on a moonlight night, when its snowy walls stand out in contrast to the deep blue sky, but not otherwise." William Stoddard, an Illinois journalist who later joined Lincoln's staff as an assistant secretary, found the White House a "dirty rickety concern," its rooms in disrepair, its carpets threadbare, its walls badly in need of a new paint job, its china and crystal half-broken and mismatched after decades of neglect. By and large, it had the look of "an old and unsuccessful hotel." On the first floor were the family and state dining rooms; the East Room, where past occupants (and now Lincoln) staged large receptions, or "levees"; and several parlors—the Blue, Red, and

Green rooms—where the president and first lady entertained visitors. Upstairs, on the west side of the building, were the family quarters, including an oval-shaped library that the Lincolns used as a family room and separate bedrooms for the president and Mrs. Lincoln, their sons Tad and Willie, and Robert, who was away at Harvard.

On the east side of the second floor, accessible through a central corridor that ran past the library, were the presidential offices. Adjacent to the reception room was the president's office (known today as the Lincoln Bedroom), with an adjoining door to Nicolay's office (known today as the Lincoln Sitting Room). The journalist Noah Brooks found the suite "very meagerly furnished, and old-fashioned in appearance as, in fact, is all of the upper part of the mansion—the dark mahogany doors, old style mantels and paneled wainscoting being more suggestive of the days of the Madisons and Van Burens than of the present." All three rooms had windows facing the south lawn, though midway through the term Nicolay and Hay ordered a slice of the reception hall cordoned off, to create a private passageway through which the president could access the family quarters unmolested. Across the narrow corridor were Hay's office (known today as the Queens' Sitting Room) and a large bedroom that the two secretaries shared for the next four years (now called the Queens' Bedroom). Nicolay was happy with the "very pleasant offices" and the "nice large bed room, though all of them sadly need new furniture and carpets. That too we expect to be remedied after a while."

Both the secretaries and the Lincoln family soon learned that the White House would afford them very little privacy. Though the gates and doors were under military guard—later, as the war progressed, plainclothes detectives mingled among the household staff for added security—the public was perfectly at liberty to enter the mansion during regular business hours. As a general rule, visiting hours "began at ten o'clock in the morning," Hay later explained to William Herndon, "but in reality the anterooms and halls were full before that hour—people anxious to get the first axe ground." After rising at dawn and eating a sparse breakfast of one egg, toast, and black coffee, the president read

over the morning dispatches from his generals, reviewed paperwork
with his secretaries, and when necessary conferred with members of
his cabinet. He was "extremely unmethodical," Hay noted. "It was a
four-years struggle on Nicolay's part and mine to get him to adopt
some systematic rules. He would break through every regulation as
fast as it was approved—although they"—the congressmen, the office
seekers, the widows seeking pensions, and the mothers begging clem-
ency for their deserter sons—"nearly annoyed the life out of him by
unrealistic complaints & requests." Breaking at noon for a solitary
lunch—"a biscuit, a glass of milk in the winter, some fruit or grapes in
the summer—he returned to his office and received visitors until 5 or
6 in the evening, though when possible he indulged in a late afternoon
carriage ride on the wooded edges of town, often with his wife." Din-
ner was served at six, when Lincoln "ate sparingly of one or two
courses," preferring simple country fare like corn pone, cabbage, and
chicken fricassee to more extravagant dishes. "Before dinner was over
members [of Congress] would come back up & take up the whole eve-
ning. Sometimes though rarely he shut himself up & would see no
one. Sometimes he would run away to a lecture or concert or theatre
for the sake of a little rest." Most days, Lincoln worked until 11:00 p.m.;
during critical battles, he stayed up until the early daylight hours, re-
viewing telegraphic dispatches from the War Department. Unlike
modern presidents, Lincoln never took a vacation. He worked seven
days each week, fifty-two weeks of the year, and generally left Wash-
ington only to visit the field or, on one occasion, to dedicate a battle-
ground cemetery in Gettysburg, Pennsylvania. Faced with the
demands of governing a divided nation in times of war, Lincoln
worked harder than any president before him and arguably harder
than most who succeeded him in office.

For the secretaries, too, the work was punishing. When their boss
was in the office, often fourteen hours each day, they remained on call.
In late March, Nicolay reported to Therena that he and Hay "took
quite a stroll this afternoon, and I feel much rested and refreshed by it.
So far we have been out very little, but we shall not neglect the oppor-
tunities we *expect* to have by and by. I have not yet spent a single hour

in sight-seeing although there is much about the city that is well worth
seeing." They were astonished to find themselves devoting the better
part of their days to negotiating the swarm of office seekers who be-
sieged the president from morning to night. Especially in the first
weeks of the new administration, before the war effort consumed his
attention, the portion of time given over to filling patronage positions
was disproportionate. Nicolay frequently complained of "being con-
tinually haunted by some one who 'wants to see the President *for only
five minutes.'* At present this request meets me from almost every man
woman and child I meet—whether it be by day or night—in the house
or on the street." William Seward, the newly confirmed secretary of
state, was no stranger to the ways of Washington. A veteran member
of the Senate and protégé of New York's Thurlow Weed, arguably the
most powerful political boss in the country, he understood the game.
But even he was astonished to find the White House "grounds, halls,
stairways, closets . . . filled with applicants, who render ingress and
egress difficult." Hay told his college roommate that "the throng of
office-seekers is something absolutely fearful. They come at daybreak
and are still coming at midnight."

Many seasoned political professionals faulted the president for his
inordinate attention to patronage. The *New York Times,* a moderate
Republican organ, groused that "Mr. Lincoln owes a higher duty to the
country, to the world, to his own fame, than to fritter away the price-
less opportunities of the Presidency in listening to the appeals of com-
peting office-hunters, in whose eyes the loss of a thousand-dollar
clerkship would be a catastrophe little inferior to the downfall of the
Republic!" But the president's strategy was not without rhyme or rea-
son. In 1861 the federal government employed roughly forty thousand
civilians either directly or as third-party contractors. The jobs ranged
from highly lucrative (customs collectors, port inspectors, govern-
ment printers) to respectably middle-class (lighthouse superinten-
dents, government clerks, consulate employees) to painfully modest
(the postmaster of New Salem, Illinois, who earned $74.10 per year).
Over the next four years, the Union war effort vastly enlarged the
number of military commissions, civilian posts, and government

contracts under the direct control of the administration. Patronage was the glue that held the Republican Party together. State and federal officeholders derived much of their local prestige from their ability to command influence in the assignment of government perquisites. For the Republican Party—still a shotgun marriage of former Democrats, Whigs, and Know-Nothings, many of whom instinctively distrusted one another—the challenge was all the greater. "It is morally impossible for any man, even of transcendent ability, to so distribute his patronage and shape the policy of his administration as to gratify and keep together such a heterogeneous compound of discordant materials as that of which the 'Republican' party is composed," observed an editor from Ohio. Lincoln's ability to command congressional and gubernatorial support for his war program hinged on his success at rewarding friends and punishing enemies. Estimates suggest that in the course of his administration, the president replaced upward of 78 percent of federal officeholders—most of them beneficiaries of the Democratic Party, which had controlled the White House for twenty-four of the preceding thirty-two years—with Republican loyalists. In hindsight, his attention to the power of federal appointments proved critical in cementing a temporary coalition into an institutional, ruling party.

As gatekeepers to the president, the secretaries made enemies as well as friends. Claiming no prior tenure in Washington and lacking a strong understanding of the city's political habits and power structures, they were outsiders trying to learn an insider's game. Their quick ascendance raised more than a few eyebrows among more experienced hands. Noah Brooks, a reporter with close ties to the president and first lady who coveted the secretaries' jobs and schemed to replace them, wrote them off as "snobby and unpopular." His was probably a minority opinion, though even their admirers sometimes wondered whether they were up to the task at hand.

Technically speaking, the position of secretary to the president was relatively new. Though every president since Washington had used personal funds to employ a private secretary, it was not until 1857 that Congress made the job official and appropriated government money to cover the salary and expenses of the incumbent officeholder. Many

of Nicolay's predecessors played important roles both during and after their tenure in the executive branch. Washington's first secretary, Tobias Lear, went on to serve as an American envoy during the first and second Barbary wars. He was succeeded by William Jackson, former secretary to the Constitutional Convention and combat veteran of the Revolutionary War. Meriwether Lewis, who earned fame as an explorer, was private secretary to Thomas Jefferson, as was William Burwell, who held the post until his election to Congress in 1806. Edward Coles, secretary to James Madison, went on to serve as governor of Illinois, while Nicholas Trist followed his stint under Andrew Jackson with a controversial diplomatic career. Some presidential secretaries played consultative roles and managed congressional and political affairs for the White House; others were little more than clerks. In later years, the role would grow exponentially in power and influence, as men like George Cortelyou (William McKinley and Theodore Roosevelt), William Loeb (Theodore Roosevelt), Joseph Tumulty (Woodrow Wilson), and Louis Howe (Franklin Roosevelt) assumed the prerogatives and responsibilities of a modern-day chief of staff. Nicolay and Hay occupied the middle ground. Lincoln preferred to keep his own counsel, but he relied on his secretaries to execute his decisions. They played no role in developing strategy for the administration, but when they issued directives or orders, it was widely understood that they spoke for the president. As time wore on, Lincoln entrusted them with more sensitive political tasks. They learned how to anticipate his thought process, and he increasingly granted them leeway in managing access and work flow.

Washington soon learned that the secretaries, though the closest of friends, were very different sorts of men. Nicolay quickly developed a reputation as "the bull-dog in the anteroom"—a "grim Cerberus of Teutonic descent," often "very disagreeable and uncivil," who bristled at the "impatient demands of the gathering, growing crowd of applicants which obstructs passage, hall and ante-room." The journalist John Russell Young took a different view, admiring Nicolay's "close, methodical, silent German way" and judging him "scrupulous, polite, calm, obliging, with the gift of hearing other people talk; coming and

going about the Capitol like a shadow; with the soft, sad smile that seemed to come only from the eyes; prompt as lightning to take a hint or an idea; one upon whom a suggestion was never lost, and if it meant a personal service, sure of the prompt, spontaneous return." Prone to frequent bouts of illness, George stood five feet ten but rarely weighed much more than 125 pounds, leading Young to remark on "the thin, frail body upon which disease seemed to be doing its work." But much like another White House visitor, who found the secretary "a man of more ability than his appearance indicates," Young was impressed by Nicolay's discretion, loyalty, and talent. William Stoddard, the "third secretary" who filled in when the workload grew heavy, acknowledged that people often found Nicolay "sour and crusty," but he added that it took "a steady fellow like Nicolay, or somebody as quick-witted as John Hay" to perform what was otherwise an impossible job. "The President showed his good judgment of men when he put Mr. Nicolay where he is, with a kind and amount of authority which is not easy to describe." Thanks to his "dyspeptic tendency," Nicolay developed "an artificial manner the reverse of 'popular' . . . That, however, for which we all respected him, was his devotion to the President and his incorruptible honesty Lincoln-ward. He measured all things and all men by their relations to the President."

If Nicolay played the part of the stern gatekeeper, Hay was quick with a quip and more apt to wear a smile, even as he explained that, no, the president was not available to take a meeting. Like many Washington observers, John Russell Young found him "brilliant and chivalrous," "independent, with opinions on most questions." The young secretary had a "genius for romance and politics as no one . . . since Disraeli" and was eminently "suited for his place in the President's family." A close friend later noted that Hay "loved to talk, and his keen joy in it was so genuine and so obvious that it infected his listeners. He was as good a listener as he was a talker, never monopolizing the conversation . . . He talked without the slightest sign of effort or premeditation, said his good things as if he owed their inspiration to the listener, and never exhibited a shadow of consciousness of his own brilliancy . . . Every person who spent a half-hour or

more with him was sure to go away, not only charmed with Hay, but uncommonly well pleased with himself."

Despite being a bon vivant, Hay attracted his share of resentment and jealousy. A reporter who visited Washington in the early months of 1861 found him "a young, good-looking fellow, well, almost foppishly dressed, with by no means a low down opinion of himself, either physically or mentally, with plenty of self-confidence for anybody's use, a brain active and intellectual, with a full budget of small talk for the ladies or anybody else, and both eyes keeping a steady lookout for the interests of 'number one.'" The abolitionist Thomas Wentworth Higginson thought him "a nice young fellow, who unfortunately looks about seventeen and is oppressed with the necessity of behaving like seventy." He was a "nice, beardless boy," a newspaperman wrote condescendingly, but his proximity to the president underscored a very real problem—that "Mr. Lincoln has no private secretary that fits the bill."

In those heady first days, the secretaries struggled to conceal their self-satisfaction. George informed his fiancée that "in my position I necessarily hear something new almost every day, that would be of infinite interest sometime to one and sometimes to another, but about which my duty is to say nothing." When the editors of the *Chicago Tribune,* a staunchly Republican paper with a robust circulation throughout the Midwest, asked if the president was still reading his paper, Nicolay replied tartly that it was "received very regularly, opened and kept with the other papers on the newspaper table in my offices . . . [T]he President rarely ever looks at any papers, simply for want of leisure to do so . . . I can assure you . . . that the President's task here is no child's play." In a job that called for unconditional loyalty and unrelenting toughness, Nicolay provided both, often at the expense of his own popularity.

Hay was equally prone to demonstrations of braggadocio. Just prior to the departure for Washington, he confided to Hannah Angell that he had "showed part of your last letter (so long ago) to Mr. Lincoln at a little musical soiree, whereat he grinned his majestic delight. I am beginning to respect him more than formerly." In his next dispatch,

written on Executive Mansion stationery, he instructed, "If you do write to me I will get your letter addressed 'Care of the President,' Washington, DC." The envelope was handsomely "franked: John Hay, *Acting Private Secy.*" At Willard's, where he and Nicolay dined most evenings, Hay enjoyed the knowing stares of "office-seekers, wire pullers, inventors, artists, poets, prosers (including editors, army correspondents, attachés of foreign journals, and long-winded talkers), clerks, diplomatists, mail contractors, railway directors," and politicians whom Nathaniel Hawthorne scorned. In his first few weeks in Washington, one of his classmates from Brown, Frederick Augustus Mitchell, happened across him at the hotel, where Hay was leaning casually against a cigar stand, taking in the scene. When Mitchell congratulated him on his appointment, Hay gave a wry smile and replied, "Yes. I'm Keeper of the President's Conscience."

Living down the hall from the president and spending nearly every waking hour in his presence, "the boys," as Lincoln called them, soon came to know him intimately. He often took carriage rides with the boys, and when the first lady was out of town or indisposed, they accompanied him to the theater. To distinguish between the two Johns, the president referred to Hay by his first name and to Nicolay by his last. In good humor, they referred to him privately as "the Tycoon" and "the Ancient," though they always addressed him directly as "Mr. President" ("it still seems queer" to call him that, Nicolay admitted to Therena in early 1861). Charles G. Halpine, an Irish-born writer who came to know Hay during the war, later judged that "Lincoln loved him as a son," a sentiment shared by Galusha Grow, the House Speaker, who remembered that "Lincoln was very much attached to him, and often spoke to me in high terms of his ability and trustworthiness. I know of no person in whom the great President reposed more confidence and to whom he confided secrets of State as well as his own personal affairs with such great freedom." Sharing a love for witty verse and wordplay, the president and Hay developed a close bond. Nicolay's rapport with Lincoln was more formal but still close. The president trusted him to manage delicate political relationships and to act as his political gatekeeper. Nicolay decided which visitors

would enjoy a presidential audience and which dispatches would fall under Lincoln's gaze. In many cases, he issued orders and responses without consulting the president, whose policies and priorities he came instinctively to understand and anticipate. Even his detractors did not second-guess his standing.

As the responsibilities of war bore down hard on Lincoln, the president's sleep became more fitful. Many evenings, he wandered down the hall in his nightclothes, seeking out the company of his secretaries. Hay took note of a typical occasion when he and Nicolay were finishing the day's business "a little after midnight [and] the President came into the office laughing," clutching a volume of verse by the English humorist Thomas Hood.

> "An unfortunate Bee-ing," seemingly utterly unconscious that he with his short shirt hanging about his long legs & setting out behind like the tail feathers of an enormous ostrich was infinitely funnier than anything in the book he was laughing at. What a man it is! Occupied all days with matters of vast moment, deeply anxious about the fate of the greatest army of the world, with his own fame & future hanging on the events of the passing hour, yet he has such a wealth of simple bonhomie & good fellow ship that he gets out of bed & perambulates the house in his shirt to find us that we may share with him the fun of one of poor Hood's queer little conceits.

The door swung both ways, as the secretaries enjoyed access to the family quarters. Early in 1861, Hay received a late-night call from Jean Davenport Lander, a famous stage actress now married to a Union officer. Lander shared news of an improbable plot to kill or kidnap the president. Though he thought nothing of the story, Hay nevertheless enjoyed meeting "the Mona Lisa of my stage struck days." After seeing her out of the mansion, he walked to the private quarters and "went to the bedside of the Chief *couché*. I told him the yarn; he quietly grinned."

Hay later claimed that there "was little gaiety in the Executive house" during the Civil War. "It was an epoch, if not of gloom, at least of a seriousness too intense to leave room for much mirth." But Lincoln had a sharp sense of humor and told his secretaries that "he must laugh sometimes, or he would surely die." William Stoddard recorded the events of a typical Sunday afternoon, when he was finishing a batch of correspondence in the president's office. Lincoln was in the family quarters, and "the whole floor [was] as silent as a graveyard or a hospital," when "in came John Hay, all one bubble. He is sober enough most of the time, but he had heard something funny, and he was good-natured about dividing it." In repeating the joke for Stoddard, Hay broke down in laughter "before he got well into it. The door was open and so was Nicolay's, and he heard the peal of laughter when the story proved too much for its narrator, and over he came, with a pen in one hand and a long paper in the other, and he sat right down to listen. Hay began at the beginning, and went on very well until the first good point was reached," but all three men again "exploded as one" before reaching the punch line. In their fit of laughter, none of the secretaries noticed Lincoln slip through the office door. "Down he sank into Andrew Jackson's chair, facing the table, with Nicolay seated by him, and Hay still standing by the mantel." From behind his gentle grin, the president said, "Now, John, just tell that thing again." As Hay reached the end of the joke, "down came the President's foot from across his knee, with a heavy stamp on the floor, and out through the hall went an uproarious peal of fun." Moments later, the secretary of war appeared in the doorway bearing bad news, and "the shadow came back to Lincoln's face, and he arose, slowly, painfully, like a man lifting some enormous burden."

Those who were jealous of the secretaries sneered at their familiarity with the president. Those who understood the art of politics took them under their wings, regardless of ideology or party. Hay and Nicolay were frequent dinner guests of the increasingly conservative cabinet secretary William Seward, whose son Frederick, serving as his father's assistant secretary of state, also struck up a warm friendship with the White House aides. Gideon Welles, the moderate secretary

of the navy, invited them into his home, as did the Treasury secretary, Salmon P. Chase, and Lyman Trumbull, radicals who grew estranged from the president over the course of his first term. These men appreciated the utility of remaining on good terms with Lincoln's gatekeepers.

As Washington, D.C., swelled with tens of thousands of soldiers, journalists, petitioners, and hangers-on, the city became "as gay, as jolly and as dissolute as in the flush times that are gone," Hay wrote. He and Nicolay spent their evenings at Willard's, "the most crowded, extortionate and uncomfortable of caravansaries," but a place to see and be seen. They strolled Pennsylvania Avenue, with its "flood of uniforms" and parade of "Northern beauty and fashion." They frequented the "brilliant succession of reviews" on offer at the city's playhouses and theaters. They haunted the salons of leading socialites like the Eames family, whose parlor, Nicolay assured his fiancée, "is really a sort of focal point in Washington society, where one meets the best people that come here." Charles Hay, who had only recently despaired of John's aimlessness, proudly boasted that his son had "obtained a position, in a social and political point of view, never before reached by a young man of his age in this generation . . . The guest of Cabinet Ministers [and] foreign ambassadors, and occupying a position in the public mind, which causes a day's illness to be flashed across the Continent as a matter in which the nation felt an interest. His arrival in a city noticed in the dailies as much as General Jackson's would have been thirty years ago." The secretaries later developed a deep appreciation of their good fortune. But they did not always grasp the significance of events as they lived them. In no small way, they were living in "stirring times," Nicolay told Therena, though he confessed to "hardly realize that they are so, even as I write them."

Despite the secession of seven Deep South states, the first month of Lincoln's presidential tenure saw no formal declaration of hostilities. As late as April 1861, Nicolay still dismissed "all the excitement . . . over the prospect of a war with the South." There might be "a little brush

at Charleston or Pensacola," but no one expected a full-blown military engagement. These predictions faded away with the Confederate attack on Fort Sumter on April 12, the secession of four states in the upper South, and the president's order calling up seventy-five thousand militiamen to quash the insurrection. With the administration intent on keeping the border states of Maryland, Kentucky, Delaware, and Missouri squarely in the Union ranks—together, they would have added 45 percent to the Confederacy's white population and 80 percent to its manufacturing capacity—the city of Baltimore, already a hotbed of secessionist conviction, fell into a state of armed chaos. On April 19, as the Sixth Massachusetts attempted to pass through the city en route to Washington, an armed mob attacked the soldiers, who returned fire, killing twelve local citizens. To prop up the faltering unionist governor, Lincoln agreed that troops arriving from Northern states would travel around, not through, Baltimore.

From his office in the White House, Nicolay privately believed that the skirmish in Baltimore, more so than the attack on Fort Sumter, was "likely to become historic in the nation's annals." It was, he told Therena, "the first bloodshed in this civil war, and singularly enough," it fell on the "anniversary of the first bloodshed in the Revolution. We are expecting more troops here . . . but are also fearful that secessionists may at any hour cut the telegraph wires, tear up the railroad track, or burn bridges, and thus prevent their reaching us, and cut off all communications." In fact, that is precisely what happened, when the mayor and the governor ordered the detonation of railroad bridges that connected Baltimore to Philadelphia and Harrisburg, as well as telegraph lines that serviced Washington, D.C. For days, the capital lay in siege, with no effective means of sending or receiving news. No one knew when Northern troops would complete their circuitous route to defend Washington, which lay vulnerable to an attack from the South.

For Lincoln, these were dark days. The president stared out at the Potomac, wondering repeatedly, "Why don't they come!" While Lincoln was visiting wounded soldiers from the Sixth Massachusetts, Hay heard him offer, darkly, "I don't believe there is any North. The Seventh Regiment is a myth. R. Island is not known in our geography any

longer. *You* are the only Northern realities." To buck up the capital's defenses, Senator James Lane of Kansas recruited a company of fellow Jayhawkers (veterans of the border wars of the 1850s) who happened to be in town seeking government employment. His so-called Frontier Guards camped out in the East Room at the White House, lending an almost carnival atmosphere to the mansion. Hay found them "a splendid company." Over at the Capitol, the Sixth Massachusetts took refuge in the new House and Senate chambers. Nicolay and Hay ventured over to inspect the "novel" scene. "The contrast was very painful between the grey haired dignity that filled the Senate Chamber when I saw it last and the present throng of bright-looking Yankee boys," Hay noted, "the most of them bearing the signs of New England rusticity in voice and manner, scattered over the desks, chairs and galleries, some loafing, many writing letters, slowly and with plough hardened hands," while Speaker of the House Galusha Grow "stood patient by the desk and franked" mail for the line of soldiers. Hay lay down on a leather sofa toward the rear of the chamber and stared at the "wide-spreading skylights over arching the vast hall like heaven blushed and blazed with gold" and thought it a fitting place to quarter the troops.

The capital lay under siege until April 25, when the Seventh New York arrived. Nicolay later explained to Therena that Washington remained susceptible to a Southern assault, as there were only three thousand members of the local Washington, D.C., militia, and "with the city perfectly demoralized with secession feeling, no man could *know* whom of the residents to trust . . . We were not only surrounded by the enemy, but in the midst of traitors." In a dispatch to his former boss Ozias Hatch, Nicolay passed on orders from the president that officials raising the Illinois regiments pay close attention to "*efficiency*—to perfection in drill, equipment, &c. Have them ready for *work* and not for show."

In the coming months, the population of Washington swelled with tens of thousands of federal troops who would soon be drilled into a proper army. In the early days, they camped out on the Mall, in hotels, in the Capitol rotunda, and in the lobbies of federal buildings. By

midyear, when Lincoln called up 500,000 men, they manned protective forts from Georgetown to Alexandria and bunked in carefully aligned encampments spread throughout the city. Under the direction of General George McClellan, the troops staged elaborate reviews that were intended to instill confidence among the elected officials who had appropriated the funds to amass such enormous armies, as well as the troops, most of them farm boys who had never soldiered a day in their lives. The high-water mark of military splendor came that November, when 100,000 troops staged a grand review over an eight-mile stretch, enveloping the city in a pageantry of banners, marching bands, cavalry, and finely appointed citizen-soldiers in crisp blue uniforms. "Went out to-day to see the grand review at Munson's Hill," Nicolay recorded in a private memorandum. "President and others in his carriage—Hay and I in coupe. Clear track and good road going out." After greeting McClellan and General Irvin McDowell, the president mounted a steed and, flanked by his generals, "rode several horses' lengths ahead while a cavalcade of perhaps a hundred officers (myself among them) followed at a swift hard gallop." By the end of the day, he told Therena, "I had tired myself out, lost my dinner, spoiled my pantaloons . . . but I had seen the largest and most magnificent military review ever held on the continent."

The rhythms of life in wartime Washington quickly assumed a martial spirit. There were twice-weekly performances by the marine band on the White House lawn and concerts at the navy yard, where the secretaries and their boss hobnobbed with military officers and "an elegant audience of some two or three hundred invited guests." Nicolay reported that he, along with Hay and the president, toured a battleship and witnessed a display of a Dahlgren gun that was mounted on the nearby shore. "We could hear the explosion and as quick as thought afterwards see the ball . . . flying through the air," he marveled. "I had not thought before that the flight of a cannon-ball could be seen so distinctly."

Though these were exhilarating times for the two secretaries, the first year of the Lincoln administration was overshadowed by a string of military and political defeats that left the president badly bruised.

Nicolay and Hay were at the White House on July 21 when McDow-ell's forces attacked the Confederates at Manassas Junction in Virginia. Huddled with the president, who received dispatches from the field at intervals of roughly fifteen minutes, they waited for decisive news. To break the tension, Lincoln left the White House for a carriage ride. At six o'clock that evening, Seward burst into Nicolay's office looking for the president. "The battle is lost," he informed the secretaries. "Find the President and tell him to go immediately to Gen. Scott's." "Thus go the fortunes of war," Nicolay continued in his letter to Therena. "Our worst fears are confirmed. The victory which seemed in our grasp at four o'clock yesterday afternoon, is changed to an overwhelming defeat."

The next day, Hay watched as

> with the ushering in of daylight there came pouring into the city crowds of soldiers, some with muskets, some with-out muskets, some with knapsacks, and some without knapsack, or canteen, or belt, or anything but their soiled and dirty uniform, burned faces and eyes, that looked as they had seen no sleep for days . . . One by one came wag-ons filled with the dead and wounded. Most horrible were the sights presented to view, and never to be forgotten by those who witnessed them. The bodies of the dead were piled on top of one another; the pallid faces and blood-stained garments telling a fearfully mute but sad story of the horrors of war.

He believed that "there was never such a day here before—it is to be hoped that there will never be such another."

Though the last six months of 1861 saw critical battles at Port Royal, South Carolina, and in the western theater, the bulk of this period was given over to a massive reorganization and training of Union forces, now wholly under McClellan's command.

In Missouri, General John C. Frémont reported to Lincoln that divi-sions between unionists and Confederates had created vast "disorder, nearly every county in an insurrectionary condition." In an effort to

put his boot on the neck of Confederate guerrillas, Frémont placed the entire state under martial law, threatened active disunionists with summary execution, and announced the immediate emancipation of all slaves owned by Confederate sympathizers. The last order placed the president in a difficult bind. With friends warning him that military emancipation would "crush out every vestige of a union party" in the border states—particularly in Kentucky, a state of central geographic importance to the Union—Lincoln asked Frémont to withdraw his directive. When the general refused, Lincoln canceled the order himself. "I think to lose Kentucky is nearly the same as to lose the whole game," he said. "Kentucky gone, we cannot hold Missouri, nor, as I think, Maryland. These all against us, and the job on our hands is too large for us."

Lincoln's action met with the stern disapproval of radical and even some moderate Republicans. Frémont enjoyed the backing of the *Chicago Tribune,* New York *Evening Post, Springfield Republican, New York Times,* and *National Intelligencer*—the most influential Republican newspapers in the country, running a full gamut from radical to conservative. For many years, antislavery politicians had warned that the law of nations permitted the emancipation of slaves—their return to a natural state of liberty—in times of war or insurrection. Most free-state Republicans regarded Frémont's directive as perfectly lawful, if politically ill-timed. In passing through St. Louis on a trip to visit his family, Hay took time to visit with Frémont and his wife. He found the general "quiet earnest industrious, imperious," and his wife, Jessie Benton Frémont—daughter of the late Missouri senator Thomas Hart Benton—"much like him, tough talking more and louder." Even the president's assistant secretary found much to admire in the general.

In late September, Nicolay privately assessed the Frémont imbroglio "one of the most troublesome affairs which the Govt has yet had upon its hands." Acknowledging that "high hopes had been entertained of [Frémont] by the admin and the country," he blamed the general for refusing the president's initial instructions to reverse his emancipation edict. In October, Nicolay left the White House for Springfield. The ostensible purpose of his trip was to visit Therena, but

at Lincoln's behest he also met with military and political officials in Missouri. Since his emancipation edict, Frémont had tangled with the powerful Blair family of St. Louis, going so far as to order the arrest of Congressman Frank Blair, the brother of Lincoln's postmaster general. On October 17, Nicolay informed Lincoln that "neither [General John] Pope nor [Major David] Hunter have any faith that Fremont will or can accomplish anything whatever on the contrary are quite convinced that he will not." Four days later, he elaborated, explaining that he had "taken some pains to learn the feeling here as to Fremont. The universal opinion is that he has entirely failed, *and that he ought to be removed*— that any change will be for the better." Nicolay's confidential assessment may have confirmed what the president had already concluded from other sources. He soon dismissed Frémont from command.

More incommodious than the Frémont affair was the president's increasingly strained relationship with McClellan, whom he had appointed general in chief of the Union army. Initially hailed as a hero who had forged a professional fighting force out of the ramshackle volunteer army that staggered back to Washington after the Battle of Bull Run at Manassas Junction, McClellan had sorely tried the patience of Congress by refusing to advance on the Confederate capital that fall. Time and again, he incorrectly insisted that the Confederate army outsized his own and delayed action. With Nicolay dispatched to the western theater to gather intelligence on the political and military situation in Missouri, Hay accompanied Lincoln to McClellan's headquarters. "I intend to be careful," McClellan told Lincoln, "and do as well as possible. Don't let [Congress] hurry me, is all I ask." "You shall have your own way in the matter I assure you," Hay heard the president respond. Ever loyal to Lincoln, Hay privately deprecated Lincoln's radical critics as the "Jacobin club" and scorned their entreaties to move harder against the South. In his diary, the secretary noted a conversation with McClellan in late October at the White House, in which the general suggested that radical Republicans "preferred an unsuccessful battle to delay." The president reminded McClellan that public opinion could not be discounted forever but agreed that "you must not fight till you are ready."

At the time, Hay knew nothing of the extreme derision with which

McClellan spoke of the president, in private as well as in the company of other officers. He had little concept that the general referred to Lincoln as an "idiot," "baboon," and "gorilla"; to the secretary of state as a "meddling, officious, incompetent little puppy"; or to the secretary of the navy, Gideon Welles, as a "garrulous old woman." He could not have known that McClellan professed to "find myself in a strange position here: President, Cabinet, Genl. Scott & all deferring to me. By some strange operation of magic I seem to have become *the* power of the land."

On November 13, Hay confided to his diary a "portent of evil to come. The President, Governor Seward and I went over to McClellan's house tonight." When a servant explained that McClellan was still out attending the wedding of an army colleague, the presidential party sat down in the parlor to await his return.

> After we had waited about an hour McC. came in and without paying any particular attention to the porter who told him the President was waiting to see him, went up stairs, passing the door of the room where the President and Secretary of State were seated. They waited about half an hour, and sent once more a servant to tell the General that they were there, and the answer came that the General had gone to bed. I record this unparalleled insolence of epaulettes without comment. It is the first indication I have yet seen, of the threatened supremacy of the military authorities. Coming home I spoke to the President about the matter but he seemed not to have noticed it especially, saying it was better at this time not to be making points of etiquette & personal dignity.

With trouble brewing along the border, the Union army stuck in first gear outside Washington, and the president's relationship with McClellan souring by the minute, the new administration had trouble finding its footing. Most Republicans had given up all hope in Secretary Simon Cameron, whose administration of the War Department

veered between ineptitude and outright corruption. Salmon Chase warned the president that the Treasury was teetering on the verge of bankruptcy. Radicals grew impatient at the slow progress of the military campaign and the president's reluctance to make abolition a tactic and an aim of the war.

That fall, before Lincoln took the decision to dismiss Frémont, Nicolay had a long conversation with the president about his political, financial, and military troubles. His notes reveal a new president back on his heels.

Political
Fremont ready to rebel.

Chase despairing.

Cameron utterly ignorant and regardless of the course of
 things, and the probable result.

Cameron
 Selfish and openly discourteous to the President.
 Obnoxious to the Country
 Incapable either of organizing details or conceiving and
 advising general plans.

Financial
Credit gone at St. Louis

" Cincinnati

" Springfield

Over-draft today Oct. 2, 1861. = 12,000,000

Chase says the new loan will be exhausted in 11 days.

Immense claims left for Congress to audit.

Military
Kentucky successfully invaded

Missouri virtually seized

October here, and instead of having a force ready to
 descend the Mississippi, the probability is that the
 army of the West will be compelled to defend St. Louis

The year ended badly. With McClellan on indefinite sick leave, the army stalled in its tracks, and his political fortunes at a nadir, Lincoln told his quartermaster general, "The people are impatient; Chase has no money and he tells me he can raise no more; the General of the Army has typhoid fever. The bottom is out of the tub. What shall I do?" Writing to Therena on Christmas Day, Nicolay betrayed the dark mood that had befallen the White House in recent weeks. "John and I are moping the day away here in our offices like a couple of great owls in their holes," he wrote, "and expect in an hour or two to go down to Willards and get our 'daily bread,' just as we do on each of the other three hundred and sixty four days of the year, without anything special to remind us that there are ever any things as Christmas dinners." In those cheerless hours, Nicolay thought back on his orphan childhood, admitting in a rare moment of introspection that in his "fifteen years' straying about the world alone, I have gotten pretty well 'used to it.' It is only now and then that I think of this being any other than my normal condition. But sometimes—as to-day—far back across the sea—I remember a scene of childish pleasure amid Christmas enjoyments, which makes me wonder if it is not the part of wisdom to treasure up such recollections with an industrious care for the after-days, when our eyes become too keen to be cheated by the illusions of their tinsel and gilding." As the calendar gave way to 1862, he shook off his holiday blues and looked forward to a quick, decisive Union victory.

CHAPTER 7

Despotic Act in the Cause of Union

J anuary found Nicolay in better spirits and seemingly reinvigorated by the whirlwind schedule of social events that beckoned for his attention. On December 31 he attended a New Year's Eve party that was not, he admitted, "the best preparation in the world for a hard day's work." The next day, "the reception at the Executive Mansion began at 11 A.M., at which time the Cabinet and their families and the Diplomatic Corps in all their stars and crosses and gold lace appeared and were presented to the President. At 11:25 came the Judges of the Supreme Court, at 11:30 the officers of the army and navy in uniform, and at 12 N., the public. This lasted until 2 P.M. when the doors were closed. Of course there was a great jam." By midafternoon, Nicolay and Hay had summoned a carriage and had begun paying calls on the members of the cabinet, who were also expected to host public receptions at their homes. The festivities lasted well into the evening, beginning with a "little gentleman's party" at the home of John Forney, an influential Republican newspaper editor now serving as secretary of the Senate, and ending, as they often did, at the Eames residence. "I was as tired as I would ever wish to be when we got to bed," Nicolay told Therena.

Thanks to the careful ministrations of the first lady, the White House had regained something of its lost luster by early 1862. Vastly overspending the official budget for refurbishment and upkeep of the Executive Mansion, Mary Todd Lincoln adorned weatherworn rooms

with handsomely embroidered French wallpaper, plush draperies and
curtains, and new furniture. The trim work was newly painted. Tables
were regularly decorated with fresh-cut flowers from the White House
gardens. Matching china and service sets replaced the hodgepodge of
heirloom items left behind by prior administrations. Little by little, the
mansion's thirty-one rooms came to life. When the president learned
that his wife had exceeded the standard appropriation, he responded
with uncharacteristic rage and threatened to pay the difference out of
his own pocket, but Mary was savvy enough to balance the books at
state expense. She understood that the president's annual salary of
$25,000 was nowhere near the princely sum that it seemed. There was
at the time no official entertainment budget, and first families were
expected to host weekly levees, seasonal receptions and parties, and
state dinners for visiting diplomats and dignitaries. Most of Lincoln's
predecessors had left Washington poorer than when they arrived. For
the Lincolns, the pressure would be double. With so many army offi-
cers, contractors, and diplomats swelling the population of wartime
Washington, they would be expected to receive overflow crowds at all
times. Mary found ways to plug the hole. At her behest, Benjamin
French, the commissioner of public buildings, quietly convinced Con-
gress to issue supplemental appropriations for the White House, as it
had done for prior administrations. Mary fired the steward and as-
sumed personal supervision of the cooks and servants. Under the in-
fluence of the unscrupulous White House gardener, John Watt, she
learned how to pad official expenses and kick back the difference to
fund household necessities. By the eve of his assassination, the presi-
dent, perhaps unknowingly, had managed to save $70,000 of his official
salary.

 None of these maneuvers sat well with Nicolay and Hay. At the
beginning of the term, their relationship with Mary was cordial,
though not particularly friendly. Hay accompanied the first lady and
Robert Todd Lincoln to the seaside resort town of Long Branch, New
Jersey, in August 1861. It was "hideously dull," he told a friend, "the
crowd a sort of queer half-baked New Jersey confectionery." Inventing
a reason to depart early, he took the train to New York and then

returned to Washington, bypassing the Jersey shore altogether. "If you see Mrs. Lincoln," he implored, "don't hint to her that anything but inexorable necessity called me from Long Branch. I impressed her with the belief that the delay of another day, would break the blockade, recognize Davisdom, impeach the Cabinet and lose the Capital. Like a Roman matron she sacrificed her feelings to save the Republic."

By November 1861, with the first lady attempting to siphon off the White House stationery fund, relations between Mary and the secretaries deteriorated rapidly. Having long been a partner in building her husband's political career, she resented her relegation to the lesser status of presidential spouse and coveted the professional relationship that Hay and Nicolay had built with Lincoln. She also needed their complicity in jiggering various White House funds, a service that they consistently refused to supply. Conflict was almost inevitable. The secretaries privately took to calling Mary "the Hellcat." In March 1862, Hay warned Nicolay, who was traveling in the West, that "the 'enemy' is still planning Campaigns in quiet." When Mary asked Hay to pay her the salary of the White House steward, whom she had recently fired, the young secretary refused. "I told her to kiss mine," he told Nicolay. "Was I right?" Mary would not let the matter drop. "The devil is abroad," he moaned a few days later, "having great wrath. His daughter, the Hell-Cat . . . is in 'a state of mind' about the Steward's salary. There is no Steward . . . She thinks she will blackguard your angelic representative into giving it to her 'which I don't think she'll do it, Hallelujah!'" Days later, the trouble was still not settled. "The Hellcat is getting more Hellcattical, day by day," he complained to Nicolay.

Mary grew tougher to manage when personal tragedy was visited upon the first family. In early February, the Lincolns' young boys, Willie and Tad, fell grievously ill. The White House drew its water from the Potomac River; with tens of thousands of soldiers camped along its banks and their latrines in a constant state of overflow, contamination was inevitable. Stricken by typhoid, the older boy, Willie, aged eleven, endured weeks of agonizing cramps, diarrhea, and spasms before slipping into a coma. For the Lincolns, who adored their sons, it

was pure hell to see Willie suffer so long and without relief. Late in the afternoon on Thursday, February 20, Nicolay was half-asleep on his office sofa when the president walked in. " 'Well, Nicolay,' said he choking with emotion, 'my boy is gone—he is actually gone!' and bursting into tears, turned and went into his own office." Some time later, George walked over to the family quarters to speak with the president, who had "lain down to quiet [Tad]," the younger son, who, though very sick himself, was beside himself with grief. "[I] asked him if I should charge Browning with the direction of the funeral," Nicolay noted, in reference to Lincoln's longtime friend Senator Orville Browning of Illinois. "Consult with Browning," the president agreed.

In the months that followed, the president and first lady dealt with their heartache in different ways. Mary was too inconsolable to attend Willie's funeral or burial, though it was not altogether unusual for women to absent themselves from such public rites. For the rest of her days in the White House, she never again set foot in the Green Room, where Willie's body had been laid out for mourning. Mary later turned to spiritualists in a desperate effort to speak with her son from beyond the grave. This practice, too, was not unheard of in its time. Queen Victoria was said to have consulted spiritualists who enabled her to communicate with her late husband, Prince Albert, and no lesser figures than Secretary of the Navy Gideon Welles, Senator Ira Harris of New York, and Mrs. James Gordon Bennett, wife of a prominent Democratic newspaper publisher, dabbled in the movement after their children died. Even so, more than a few of Mary's enemies scoffed at her efforts, demonstrating little sympathy for a mother's loss. "Our home is very beautiful," she confided to a friend. "The grounds are very enchanting, the world still smiles and pays homage and we are left desolate—the world has lost its charm." Neither Hay nor Nicolay made mention in letters or diaries of the private anguish to which the secretaries bore intimate witness. But they knew how deeply affected the president was by Willie's death. Every Thursday, the president locked himself in the boy's bedroom, leaving the secretaries to fend off congressmen and office seekers while their boss mourned in silence.

"He was too good for this earth," Lincoln said of Willie, with tears in his eyes, "but then we loved him so."

Willie's death came at a time of great military and political strain. In 1862, Lincoln's war plan could fairly be described as two-pronged: in the East, the great army under George McClellan's command was tasked with invading the Confederate capital of Richmond; in the West, armies under the command of Henry Halleck were systematically choking off Southern commerce and communications by securing a long perimeter along the Ohio, Tennessee, Cumberland, and Mississippi rivers. With the Union navy successfully blocking Southern access to the Atlantic and the Gulf of Mexico, the loss of major river arteries would deal a significant blow to the fledgling Southern nation.

The western campaign at first proved a qualified success. On February 6, General Ulysses S. Grant's forces overtook a small Confederate outpost at Fort Henry in just three hours, thereby securing for the Union control of the Tennessee River. Several miles to the east, it took slightly longer for Grant's men to wrest Fort Donelson from Confederate hands, but after a three-day pitched battle the Union controlled the fort—and thus, the Cumberland River—and effectively cordoned off Confederate access to the key border state of Kentucky. Over the next month, Grant marched his men down the Tennessee River, allowing the Union to occupy the western half of Tennessee. These efforts culminated in a bloody confrontation with Confederate forces at Pittsburg Landing, near the border of Tennessee, Mississippi, and Alabama. Known thereafter as Shiloh, the two-day battle exacted a fearsome toll, with thirteen thousand Union soldiers—and ten thousand Confederates—dead, wounded, or missing in action. Nicolay may have echoed the president's thinking when he told Therena that Shiloh "*finishes* the rebellion in the West—they can never recover . . . It may take us some time yet to secure and make fast all we have gained, but the work is substantially done." In fact, just one month later, Union forces captured New Orleans, thus cutting off Confederate access to the lower Mississippi and the Gulf of Mexico. Later that fall, the Union

army dislodged Confederate forces from Corinth, a key railroad junction in Mississippi that connected east–west and south–north trunk lines. On balance, the western campaign had been a success. But the intensity of the fighting and the full extent of the carnage at Shiloh came as a shock to the Northern public. By the year's end, with Grant's army stalled outside the vital river outpost of Vicksburg, many Northerners despaired of the quick victory they had hoped—and expected—to achieve.

Matters were worse in the East. In late March, after months of delay, McClellan, whom Lincoln had replaced as general in chief but who retained command of the Army of the Potomac, finally began moving on the Confederate capital. Rather than a confrontation with Southern forces by land, his plan called for a complicated amphibious approach down the Chesapeake Bay. Union soldiers would land at the mouth of the Rappahannock River, flank the Confederate army, and conquer Richmond. The elaborate scheme left Washington with only a thin line of defense and opened McClellan to criticism by radical Republican opponents that he was either averse to fighting a real battle or somehow in quiet collusion with the rebels. Over the course of the spring and summer, the Peninsula Campaign proved a spectacular disappointment, as time and again McClellan advanced, fought, and stalled, allowing the Confederates to gather their forces and hold their line. By midsummer, Lincoln was sufficiently worried about the lack of progress that he visited McClellan in the field. After inspecting the troops at Harrison's Landing, the president retired into private conference with his general.

Seemingly oblivious to his own tenuous position, McClellan handed a letter to Lincoln, in which he laid out his view of the sectional conflict. He instructed the president to conduct the war "upon the highest principles known to Christian civilization. It should not be a war looking to the subjugation of the people of any State in any event. It should not be at all a war upon population, but against armed forces and political organization. Neither confiscation of property, political executions of persons, territorial organization of States, or forcible abolition of slavery should be contemplated for a moment." Lincoln ignored the

advice and soon began redeploying McClellan's troops in northern Virginia. The Peninsula Campaign was effectively over.

Though a troubling show of insubordination, McClellan's letter spoke to the intense pressure that Lincoln faced to broaden the scope of the conflict. As the war dragged on, many Northerners came to believe that abolition should be a goal, or at least a tool, of battle. For some, it seemed a just way to punish traitors and to deprive the Confederates of a vital economic resource. For others, the war prompted a change in thinking about the morality of slavery. Determined to keep the border states in the Union, Lincoln walked a tightrope. Privately, he agreed with many Republicans that the war could and should open new opportunities to attack slavery. Publicly, he insisted that he had no intention of expanding the scope of the war. When, in May 1862, General David Hunter declared all slaves in his portion of the Department of the South "forever free," Lincoln reversed the decree, just as he had when Frémont issued his directive a year earlier. Yet in his statement countermanding Hunter, Lincoln also urged the border states to initiate their own programs of compensated, gradual emancipation. "You cannot if you would, be blind to the signs of the times," he warned them.

The signs were many. Throughout the South, slaves were walking off farms and plantations by the tens of thousands, flooding Union army camps and forcing military commanders to create ad hoc solutions to an unprecedented race problem. Faced with the prospect of a long and costly war, many Northerners grew averse to protecting an institution that they abhorred but that their enemies seemed to cherish more than the Union itself. The year 1862 saw Congress pass, and Lincoln sign, a series of laws abolishing slavery in Washington, D.C. (with government-funded compensation for slaveholders); barring slavery in the territories; and providing for the confiscation of all rebel property, including slaves. "Only the damnedest of 'damned abolitionists' dreamed of such a thing a year ago," marveled the New York financier George Templeton Strong.

Antislavery activists had long maintained that the federal government had the legal right to attack the institution in the service of

suppressing a rebellion. Now they seized every opportunity to put that theory into practice. When Charles Sumner urged the president to issue a general emancipation order on July 4, the president replied that he would do it, if he did not think that "half the army would lay down their arms and three other states would join the rebellion." When Horace Greeley called publicly for abolition, Lincoln responded that his "paramount object in this struggle *is* to save the Union, and is *not* either to save or to destroy slavery. If I could save the Union without freeing *any* slave I would do it, and if I could save it by freeing *all* the slaves I would do it; and if I could save it by freeing some and leaving others alone I would also do that." Careful observers took note of the president's closing lines, in which he promised that he would "correct errors when shown to be errors; and I shall adopt new views so fast as they shall appear to be true views. I have here stated my purpose according to my view of *official* duty; and I intend no modification of my oft-expressed *personal* wish that all men every where could be free."

This was no hollow warning. In recent months, Lincoln had consistently pleaded with border-state elected officials to enact gradual emancipation schemes and even proposed a bill that would provide federal bonds to enable such states to compensate slave owners for their loss of property. Every day that the war dragged on, Lincoln privately argued, the peculiar institution dissolved "by mere friction and abrasion." He reminded border-state congressmen that his reversal of Hunter's emancipation edict gave "dissatisfaction, if not offense, to many whose support the country cannot afford to lose" and warned that "pressure, in this direction, is still upon me, and increasing." Was it not better for the border states to reach "a *decision* at once to emancipate *gradually*," and with compensation, rather than risk losing their slaves immediately, and with no recompense?

The stubborn resolve of border-state leaders convinced Lincoln that the time had come to change course. In mid-July, while en route to the funeral of Secretary of War Edwin Stanton's infant child, the president confided to Welles and Seward that he was prepared to embrace emancipation as a "military necessity absolutely essential for the salvation of the Union." The next week, he assembled his cabinet and read aloud

the draft of a proclamation emancipating all slaves behind enemy lines on January 1, 1863, unless the rebels in those states laid down their arms and pledged allegiance to the United States. The cabinet members, except Welles and Seward, were stunned. After heated debate, Seward convinced the president to shelve his proclamation until the Union achieved a decisive victory on the battlefield. To act before such time would convey the appearance of desperation. Nevertheless, word of the meeting soon leaked. "Broken eggs cannot be mended," Lincoln told the New York financier August Belmont in late July. "The government cannot much longer play a game in which it stakes all, and its enemies stake nothing."

Prior to his service as Lincoln's secretary, John Hay left little record of his thinking on race relations. In 1856 he calmly applauded the election of the first Republican Speaker of the U.S. House of Representatives and related his disgust in hearing a Southern acquaintance "flaying the Abolitionists alive. Southern Chivalry is in the ashes at present. '*Sic semper Tyrannis*' says the North." Born into an antislavery family, he held the peculiar institution in low repute, even if he did not share the ardor of more committed abolitionists. Like Nicolay, and even Lincoln, Hay trafficked casually in racial slurs, though seldom if ever in public. In his first weeks in the White House, he wrote in his diary of "a jolly-hearted old Shaker from N.H." who came to see the president. "He said they were late getting here, as their driver who was a constable had to stop to whip a nigger. It was a rich and novel idea to the broadbrimmed Northerner." He also wrote frequent, anonymous dispatches for several Missouri newspapers in which he spoke indifferently of "the nigger question." Cotton from the South was "nigger wool." Confederate sympathizers in England had "a natural inclination for rebellion and niggers." The nation had been "dragged into this bloody strife by traitors North and South"—by abolitionists and secessionists alike—"and now that the life of the nation, and not the condition of the nigger, is at stake, we must fight through it." During a visit to Yorktown in June 1862, Hay described a wasteland of "old houses and old darkies—big guns and little niggers—dull skies and bright

mulattos—complex uniforms and complexions not uniform—
piccaninnies and *Enfans Perdus*—and a general flavor of colored per-
son." Repeating the well-worn logic of the free-labor critique of slavery,
he marveled at the

> pall of densest indolence and sloth [that rested] palpably
> on the face of this unparalleled richness of nature. Any-
> where but here the fields would be opulent with grain;
> those hill sides would be fragrant with fruit and pictur-
> esque with vineyards . . . What good reason is there why
> this region should not be as rich, inch for inch, as Rhode
> Island?
>
> There may be many answers to this question, but only
> one suggests itself to me. It will suggest itself to you, if you
> sail down this river. There it stands now in the front door
> of the negro quarters with no shoes on its feet—its white
> tow breeches held up by one suspender—its black face agrin
> with childish delight—its shock head bare, while it waves
> its old wool hat as a banner in welcome to what it considers
> the Abolition invasion. It is the oppressed type, as Brother
> [Wendell] Phillips calls it—the man and brother as Exeter
> Hall hails it—the impending crisis as Helper names it—the
> contraband as General Butler styles it—the image of God
> cut in ebony as Fuller phrased it—the *what-will-we-do-with-it*
> as the earnest spirit of American patriotism must regard it.

In his unsigned articles, Hay took special care to lay blame for the
war at the foot of "fanatics and fire-eaters . . . Both equally mad and
equally criminal." Carefully positioning Lincoln as a good-faith broker
for the loyal slaveholders of the border states, he affirmed that "this
bloody revolution was brought upon the country by the slavery propa-
gandists of the South and the radical abolitionists of the North. They
can divide the honor and responsibility of the matter in such propor-
tions as they like."

There was a wide divergence between what Hay wrote for public

consumption (though never under his own byline) and what he wrote and said in private company. As early as May 1861 he told Carl Schurz that the army ought not return fugitive slaves who fled behind Union lines. "Their owners are in an open state of rebellion against the government & nothing would bring them to their senses more readily than a gentle reminder that they are dependent on the good will of the Government for the security of their lives and property. The action would be entirely just and eminently practicable." In the pages of his private diary, he noted with approval Schurz's assessment that "slavery offers itself more vulnerable to our attack than at any point in any century and the wild malignity of the South is excusing us, before God & the World."

In 1862, while visiting for several weeks with General Hunter in South Carolina, Hay informed Nicolay that "the General says he is going to announce me tomorrow as a Volunteer Aide, without rank." His mind clearly straying to the possibility of a political career, Hay was "glad of it, as the thing stands . . . I want my abolition record clearly defined," and serving under Hunter would "do it better than anything else, in my own mind and the minds of the few dozen people who know me."

The discordance between Hay's private utterances and his public newspaper work was a matter of politics. In a day before there was such an institution as the White House communications office, and long before such conventions as the press release and the press conference came into wide use, presidents communicated at large through various means. They issued public letters and proclamations, as Lincoln did in his response to Greeley. They raised money for, or steered government advertising to, friendly editors, who repaid the kindness by toeing the administration line. Though Hay took up midnight journalism on his own initiative and in part to supplement his government salary, he did so with Lincoln's knowledge and at every turn crafted his articles to appeal to the particular prejudices and concerns of a key readership—Republicans and War Democrats in the border states.

In April 1862, he told Missouri newspaper readers that "one thing we have certainly gained by the fierce convulsions of the past year . . .

is the power of discussing the question of slavery in a practical, common-sense way, without any of the former captiousness and irritability that has marked all disputations upon this delicate subject . . . The people of the North are discussing it, not with the heat and fervor of former fanaticism, but with the practical perception of economic and political influence." Hay maintained that "conservative citizens and presses of the Border States" were moving toward an embrace of gradual, compensated emancipation. They saw the writing on the wall: the war had weakened the institution of slavery beyond repair, and better to come to terms with this truth now than to let the vagaries of battle settle terms. Writing at a time when the president was urgently pressing such a scheme on border-state congressmen, he framed the administration's policy as a conservative middle ground between fire-eaters and abolitionists. "It is true," he wrote, "that the philosophers of the Hub of the Universe"—Boston—"still talk of the Oppressed Type as a Man and a Brother, and call down Heaven's vengeance on his wrongs, but the mass of the people are beginning to talk and think of slavery as an ugly question, to be discussed and settled coolly, and not, as in all former years, to be shelved quietly out of sight."

Hay and Nicolay were among the handful of people who first knew that Lincoln was contemplating emancipation as a war measure. Days after the president announced his intentions to Welles and Seward, Hay wrote to Mary Jay, the daughter of a prominent New York abolitionist. "How gloriously General Hunter has justified my statement that the future would prove his soundness in hatred of slavery," he wrote.

> He has done the greatest thing of the war even though unfruitful of results. Although the President repudiated his order he regards him none the less kindly, and so told the Border State Slaveholders the other day. The President himself has been, out of pure devotion to what he considers the best interests of humanity, the bulwark of the institution he abhors, for a year. But he will not conserve slavery much

longer. When next he speaks in relation to this defiant and ungrateful villainy it will be with no uncertain sound. Even now he speaks more boldly to slaveholders than to the world. If I have sometimes been impatient of his delay I am so no longer.

While Hay genuinely resented the sharp censure that his boss endured from the radical wing of his own party, he freely acknowledged in print that they "far more nearly sympathize[d] with the President on all questions of National concern" than conservative Republicans and Democrats. He was bothered less by their politics than by their constant attempts to undermine their own president. A year later, he took note in his diary of a private conversation with Lincoln. Speaking of the radicals, Lincoln said, "They are nearer to me than the other side, in thought and sentiment, though bitterly hostile personally. They are utterly lawless—the unhandiest devils in the world to deal with—but after all their faces are set Zionwards."

Like his friend and colleague, Nicolay exhibited many of the contradictions of his age. Personally opposed to slavery, he viewed himself as a moderate of the Lincoln persuasion, and like that of many moderates his thinking evolved as the war dragged on into its second and third years. "I walked up this morning to the Senate Chamber to hear a sermon by [Moncure] Conway, an Abolitionist, but one of the most eloquent men of the country," he told Therena in early 1863. "I should be willing to go to Church every Sunday, if I could hear a sermon of equal power."

However much his position on abolition had evolved, Nicolay struggled like many Americans to make sense of a post-emancipation world in which black Americans operated on nominally equal footing with whites. Writing to Therena, he related details of "a party at Mrs. Hoopers, where the new Haytian [sic] charge d'Affaires (Col. Ernest Romaine he calls himself) made his social debut. I suppose he is a negro, although he does not look like one, having straight black hair, and a very brown, Spanish looking face. His secretary of legation, who was with him had more unmistakable African features. They were quiet

and well-behaved, and said to be quite intelligent; but on the whole it was rather difficult to disassociate them in one's mind from the other colored waiters in the room." Unable to distinguish physical difference from social inequality, Nicolay puzzled at the sight of a black diplomat from a sovereign black nation. His opposition to slavery notwithstanding, he was more accustomed to meeting black servants or slaves. Early during their White House tenure, Nicolay, Hay, and Robert Todd Lincoln mounted horses and rode over the Long Bridge connecting Washington with occupied northern Virginia. There, they visited the stately Custis mansion at Arlington, where Robert E. Lee and his wife made their home before abandoning it at the start of the war. "In the garden we found an old negro at work, who was born at Mt. Vernon before General Washington's death," he explained to Therena. "We asked him many questions—delighted him in introducing Bob the President's son, in whom the old darkey expressed a lively interest—and further pleased him with a gift of small change. Altogether I don't know when I have passed so satisfactory and pleasant an afternoon." For Nicolay, as for many Northerners, wishing for the destruction of slavery was not the same as believing in the social equality of black and white Americans.

In the early weeks of the war, John Hay found Lincoln reclining on a chair by his office window, "calmly looking out of the window at the smoke of the two Navy steamers puffing up the way, resting the end of the telescope on his toes sublime." Nicolay followed, carrying a batch of paperwork, and the conversation soon turned to the cause and scope of the conflict. "Some of our northerners seem bewildered and dazzled by the excitement of the hour" and seem "inclined to think that this war is to result in the entire abolition of Slavery," the president noted. At this stage in his presidency, Lincoln still believed that the war would test the strength of popular democracy, not the institution of slavery. "We must settle this question now," he told his secretaries, "whether in a free government the minority have the right to break up the government whenever they choose. If we fail it will go far to prove the incapability of the people to govern themselves."

By late 1862, Lincoln understood that it was no longer possible to preserve "the government as we found it." As he explained to Congress in his annual message in December, "The dogmas of the quiet past, are inadequate to the stormy present . . . As our case is new, so we must think anew, and act anew. We must disenthrall ourselves, and then we shall save our country." The country understood what he meant. Just over ten weeks earlier, George McClellan, newly reinstated to command, had pursued Robert E. Lee's Army of Northern Virginia across the Maryland border, where the two forces fought a bloody, one-day battle alongside Antietam Creek. It proved the deadliest day of the war, with twenty-three thousand Union and Confederate troops left dead, wounded, or missing in action. Though the battle resulted in a technical loss for Lee, whose army limped back into Virginia badly depleted in manpower and supplies, McClellan characteristically failed to give chase, resulting in his second, and final, dismissal. Still, the day provided Lincoln with enough cause to issue his edict.

On Tuesday, September 22, Hay sat in the president's office as Lincoln informed his cabinet that he had resolved to issue his edict. "It is a despotic act in the cause of the Union," noted Gideon Welles, "and I may add of freedom."

The preliminary Emancipation Proclamation declared that on January 1, 1863, all slaves behind rebel lines would be "then, thenceforward, and forever free." Rebel states still had until New Year's Day to lay down their arms, in which case they would be permitted to keep their slaves. The edict exempted roughly 800,000 of the nation's 3.9 million bondsmen who lived in the loyal border states and in areas of the Confederacy already under Union control. It also disappointed some abolitionists and radicals, who regretted its dispassionate, legalistic tone. Nevertheless, the moment was greeted with tremendous excitement. The nature and stakes of the war had changed with the single stroke of a pen. "I told the President of the Serenade that was coming," Hay recorded in his diary, "and asked if he would make any remarks. He said no, but he did say half a dozen words, & said them with great grace and dignity." Later that evening, Hay went to Chase's house, where several of the cabinet secretaries addressed the revelers

still animating the streets with torchlight and song. "They all seemed to feel a sort of new and exhilarated life," Hay remarked of the cabinet members and congressmen who "staid at the Governors [Chase's] and drank wine." "They breathed freer; the Prest. Procn. had freed them as well as the slaves. They gleefully and merrily called each other and themselves abolitionists, and seemed to enjoy the novel sensation of appropriating that horrible name."

Writing that week for the *Missouri Republican,* Hay took care once again to position the president between Southern fire-eaters and "extremists from the North." Appropriating the rallying cry of the Democratic representative Clement Vallandigham—a slavery apologist from Ohio and the most outspoken war critic in Congress—he asserted that Lincoln had begun the war seeking to preserve "the Union as it was and . . . the Constitution as it is." At all times the president "stood between slavery and those who would destroy it, as a strong and steadfast bulwark, waiting, hoping, praying to God that the Border States would read the signs of the times." Now, Lincoln had extended to the "murderous traitors" of the South "but one more opportunity for repentance and safety. If they reject this, let their ruin rest upon their own heads." Writing as always with an eye on the critical swing states of the Midwest and the border region, Hay claimed the middle ground for the administration.

That fall, Republicans braced for steep losses in congressional and statewide elections. The preliminary Emancipation Proclamation armed Democrats with a powerful rhetorical cudgel. Denouncing the measure as "an act of Revolution," Democratic newspapers complained that it made "the restoration of the old Constitution and Union impossible." One of Chase's political allies placed the matter in sharp relief when he explained that Democrats could now look moderate and conservative voters in the eye and say, "I told you so; can't you see this is an Abolition war and nothing else?" Lincoln expected losses, and he expected to be blamed for them. His armies were bogged down. The human toll of the war had become shocking even to the most sanguine of observers. Emancipation was a deeply controversial measure. And the government was incurring piles of inflationary debt

to fund the military. But to the president's surprise, Democrats profited less from his emancipation edict than from popular opposition to his heavy-handed censure of public debate. Lincoln had suspended the writ of habeas corpus, and under the stern direction of Secretary of War Edwin Stanton the administration had imprisoned multiple newspaper editors, small-time politicians, and opponents of the war effort. On a visit to Springfield in late October, Hay told Nicolay that he was "astonished to hear so little objection to the proclamation. Republicans all like it and every Democrat who does not swear by Vallandigham comes up to it." Nevertheless, "things look badly around here politically. The inaction of the Army & the ill success of our arms have a bad effect and worse than that, all our energetic and working Republicans are in the Army . . . This state is in great danger."

Republicans were routed in the fall elections. The party lost key legislative and statewide contests in the battleground states of New York, Pennsylvania, Ohio, Indiana, and Illinois and saw more than twenty congressmen, including Speaker of the House Galusha Grow, ousted from their seats. Though they retained control of both chambers of Congress, they now had to contend with an enlarged and emboldened Democratic minority.

The year 1862 ended as it had begun for Lincoln: badly. Disgruntled Republicans blamed him for the party's electoral defeat and for the slow pace of the war. Newspaper editors scored him for political and military ineptitude. A restive citizenry began to chafe against the privations and costs of war. And no one could be sure if the final Emancipation Proclamation would foster solidarity or dissent among the rank-and-file soldiers in the field.

On New Year's Day 1863, Lincoln and his wife opened the doors of the White House to the same throng of visitors who overtook the Executive Mansion a year before: senators, congressmen, the Supreme Court, the diplomatic corps, and, finally, the public. Later that afternoon, the president retreated to his upstairs office. Sitting before the final copy of the Emancipation Proclamation, he lifted his pen and prepared to affix his signature. But then he stopped. His hand was sore and spasmodic from hours of hand shaking. "I do not want it to appear

as if I hesitated," he said, knowing that the document would define his legacy for all time. Then, with a steady hand, he signed it. "This temple of our idolatry is cast down," wrote Nicolay in an unsigned newspaper column. "This Baal of our wickedness is destroyed . . . To-day, the principle of right and justice and liberty has dealt its antagonist the mortal wound from which it can never recover."

Nicolay had revered Abraham Lincoln from the moment they first met. The year 1863 marked a turning point in Hay's perception. The junior secretary had served the president loyally but came gradually to perceive his mastery of people and politics. "We shall never agree on some points," he told a friend later that year. "You must pardon me for saying that if the Tycoon had kept his fingers from meddling with the war, we should now have had neither war nor government I think." The manner and timing with which Lincoln unleashed the blunt instrument of emancipation convinced Hay of his superior skills as a statesman and leader. "I have to a great extent stopped questioning where I don't agree with him, content with trusting to his instinct of the necessities of the time and the wants of the people. I hardly ever speak of him to others than you, because people generally would say, 'Yes! of course: that's how he gets his daily bread!' I believe he will fill a bigger place in history than he even dreams of himself."

CHAPTER 8

God Placed Him Where He Is

I t was not long into their White House tenure that the grind of eighty-hour workweeks began to exact a severe physical toll on the president's secretaries. Especially when Congress was in session, the pace and intensity were grueling. Slight of frame and prone to frequent bouts of illness, both Hay and Nicolay worried constantly about their health. "I had a sore mouth, and it has troubled me considerably ever since until today," Nicolay told Therena in a typical dispatch. "It seems to have resulted from my being 'bilious,' to remove which I have been taking medicine for a couple of days and as a consequence have been moping around the house, playing 'sick.'" The doctor's prescription for bile, he explained, was "to wake up my liver from its torpidity," a task that required frequent ministrations of "calomel pills, seidlitz powder, coffee, tea, and chicken-soup." For days, he had felt nothing but

> nausea and weakness . . . I am feeling a personified anomaly, being in a state, at the same time of great *muscular* lassitude, and great nervous vigor and excitement. I can't possibly lie still, and yet the muscular effort of even raising a finger. The consequence is that I lie down on the bed, turn over, change my pillow, throw out my arm, get up again, go to the window and look out, walk across the room, stop in the middle of the floor, whistle half a bar of Yankee

Doodle, take two steps of an extempore and original *pas sent,* and instantly becoming disgusted, with the whole matter go lie down again, and so repeat ad infinitum.

Months later, Hay, too, was "flat of my back with bilious fever." Writing to Nicolay, who was visiting New England, he reported that he "had a gray old delirium yesterday, but am somewhat better to-day . . . The air here is stifling. You had better stay as long as you like for there is nothing but idleness here. As soon as I get on my pins I shall shab."

The primitive discomforts of Washington scarcely helped matters. In the summer, the White House was stiflingly hot. Leaving the windows shut was not an option, but opening them—for there were no screens—invited "all bugdom outside . . . to have organized a storming party," Nicolay complained. "The air is swarming with them, they are on the ceiling, the walls and the furniture in countless numbers, they are buzzing about the room, and butting their heads against the window panes, they are on my clothes, in my hair, and on the sheet I am writing on." The heat also intensified the noxious and disease-ridden fumes from a marsh adjacent to the White House grounds, where local residents discarded their dead animals. "I am all alone in the White pest-house," Hay quipped one summer. "The ghosts of twenty thousand drowned cats come in nights through the South Windows." In the winter, the Executive Mansion was damp and drafty, so much so that Nicolay's hand was "almost too numb to write, sitting here in my own office." It was in these months that the secretaries often came down with debilitating colds and fevers. "So Washington weather goes," Nicolay wrote. "Rain or dust—cold or heat—always a disagreeable extreme, that adds to the annoyance of its people, and increases their ill-temper."

Unlike their boss, who rarely left Washington and never once traveled for pleasure during his presidential term, the secretaries began alternating vacations in search of health and recreation. Both men took frequent trips back to Illinois—Nicolay to visit Therena in Pittsfield, and Hay to visit his parents in Warsaw. They also made occa-

sional journeys to New York, the Jersey shore, and even, in Nicolay's case, to the Rocky Mountains. Late summer of 1861 found George in Newport, Rhode Island—"a very quaint and old place," he told Therena, where "the streets are narrow and irregular, but the cottages and grounds very pretty and inviting." He had "left Washington because of the overpowering heat" and found Newport a cool and pleasant seventy-five degrees during the day and sixty degrees at night. "I have hardly yet learned the fashionable routine," he admitted. "It is substantially, to go and bathe in the surf at any time before 12 o'clock (fashionable people do not get up a great while before that). Then the ladies do their calling until dinner which occurs at 3. Then there is music and promenading at the hotels until 4 to 5, at which time everybody goes driving (in carriages and vehicles of all sorts) along Bellevue Avenue . . . When the tide is out, people ride and drive on the beach, which is then as smooth and hard as the floor, making the most agreeable and splendid road in the world."

From early in his tenure as presidential secretary, Nicolay also traveled at Lincoln's behest on government and political business. In August 1862, an undeclared war broke out in southern Minnesota between white settlers and Sioux (Dakota) Indians. Upon surrendering their land several years earlier, the Sioux had been promised annuities from the federal government. The government had not delivered on its pledge, and now the Sioux faced the very real prospect of starvation. In August, several young Sioux men broke into a local farm in search of food; in the ensuing fight, five people were killed, triggering a wave of violence that ultimately claimed the lives of 350 white settlers. The president, who could scarcely afford to lose the allegiance of Minnesotans, ordered General John Pope to the state to break the back of the Sioux rebellion. It so happened that earlier Lincoln had dispatched Nicolay to join the federal Indian commissioner in St. Paul to observe negotiations for a land-cession treaty with Chippewa (Ojibwe) Indian bands living far to the northwest. After visiting with Therena and friends in Pittsfield, Nicolay embarked on a two-day steamboat ride up the Mississippi. "The trip is truly delightful," he told Hay, "and the Mississippi scenery magnificent." Upon arriving in St. Paul, he installed himself in the International Hotel, a

"primitive . . . building of considerable size [that] smells strongly of pine and kerosene." There, he spent several pleasant days fishing, horseback riding, and picnicking, before heading north to St. Cloud. The official party forged a path along the Mississippi River bank, passing through "fine rolling prairies, with very sandy soil." "Our point of destination is the junction of the river which runs into Red Lake with the Red River of the North," he explained to his fiancée. "We cannot tell certainly, but think it will take twelve or fifteen days to go there. I think we will strike another Post Office or two above this. If we do I will write again."

But before Nicolay could leave St. Cloud, trouble erupted with a much nearer band of Chippewa in ominous coincidence with the outbreak of Sioux hostilities in the south. Nicolay's party had to change plans, and he was soon involved in a different kind of negotiation. He wrote that "the mess with Hole-in-the-Day, the Chippewa Chief, is a complicated affair— involving official frauds on the one hand, and Indian depredations on the other. The Indians are in bad temper and the young braves want to fight; but they are poorly armed and have but little ammunition . . . Hole-in-the-day is a shrewd and intelligent and able diplomatist, and has the counsel and assistance of interested whites." From their garrison at Fort Ripley, Nicolay and his associates alternated between peace talks, which seemed to lead nowhere, and recreation. "Since I wrote you last there has been the usual dilly-dallying by the Indians," he told Therena in early September. "I am getting tired of staying here and doing nothing, but must stay and go down with the crowd. We had a fine ride to the lake on our fishing excursion and good sport spearing pickerel at night with boat and torch. The lake is the most beautiful one I have yet seen here or elsewhere."

While Nicolay and the official Indian commissioners worked to maintain the peace with the Chippewa, Hay reported from Washington that "there is positively nothing of the slightest interest since you left. The abomination of desolation has fallen upon this town." Envious of his companion, who was hunting and fishing in the cool woods of Minnesota, Hay complained that it was "horribly hot—all but me who have gone to shaking again. Your infernal South windows always give me the chills . . . If in the wild woods, you scrounge an Indian damsel,

steal her moccasins while she sleeps and bring them to me. The Ty-coon has just received a pair, gorgeously quilled, from an Indian Agent who is accused of stealing. He put them on & grinned."

"Where is your scalp?" Hay joked toward summer's end. "If any-body believes you don't wish you were at home, he can get a pretty lovely bet out of me. I write this letter firing into the air. If it hits you, well. It will not hurt as much as a Yancton's rifle. If in God's good Providence your long locks adorn the lodge of an aboriginal warrior and the festive tomtom is made of your stretched hide, I will not grudge the time thus spent, for auld lang syne."

The excursion reached its high point on September 10, when Nicolay and his colleagues "went to Crow Wing to hold a council with the red chief. Before we knew it, he had over a hundred Indians in front of us and nearly a hundred behind us. We were surrounded. We put a bold face on the matter and went into council, spent perhaps an hour in preliminary talk after which ye gentle savage proposed to adjourn the council till next morning." Ultimately, peace prevailed in northern Minnesota, while the army put down the insurrection in the south. Of the 303 Sioux men whom a military commission condemned to death, all but 38 were par-doned after the president carefully reviewed their records. The uprising hurt Lincoln in Minnesota. When a Republican senator suggested that the administration could have bolstered its support by executing more Sioux, the president replied, "I could not afford to hang men for votes."

Nicolay assured Hay that his "scalp was yet safe . . . I shall make but a short stay in Springfield and Pittsfield and then hasten to Washing-ton to relieve you—that is Stonewall Jackson willing."

In April 1863, Hay embarked on a two-month sojourn in South Caro-lina and Florida, ostensibly to carry presidential dispatches to naval officers who were then preparing an offensive campaign in Charleston Harbor. At the president's arrangement, he would spend several weeks as a volunteer adjunct to General David Hunter, whose broader cam-paign in the coastal South was key to Union victory. Though Hay was to function as Lincoln's eyes and ears on the ground, the voyage south would also allow him a respite from the punishing demands of his

White House duties, as well as a visit with his brother Charlie, then serving as an officer on Hunter's general staff.

On April 2, with the president and first lady bound for Virginia to review the troops, he began his journey, leaving Nicolay alone to manage affairs at the White House. ("The President and Mrs. L. went to Falmouth last Saturday, and are there yet," Nicolay wrote in jest. "I guess the Tycoon has concluded to follow your example and go on [General] Hooker's staff.") Still recovering from his illness and unaccustomed to ocean journeys, Hay suffered in "solitary agony" through several days of seasickness. He arrived in South Carolina a day after the Union navy's failure to take Charleston Harbor. Following a forty-minute pitched battle, Rear Admiral Samuel Du Pont had determined that his ironclad fleet faced destruction or capture by the well-positioned Confederate artillery. Rather than risk the loss of so valuable a resource, he pulled his ships back, enraging Hunter, who criticized the decision as yet another example of Union trepidation and overcaution. Hay interviewed Du Pont and wrote sympathetic reports to Nicolay and the president. From his exchange with Nicolay, Hay learned that the White House was largely in disagreement with Du Pont's version of events, and after several weeks at Hunter's side Hay too came around to this position. Despite the initial divergence of first-hand accounts, his dispatches were valuable to the president, who ordered Du Pont to devise another attack.

Over the next seven weeks, Hay traveled with Hunter's army as it snaked its way up and down the South Carolina and Florida coastline. Though he was not yet formally commissioned an army officer (that would come the following year), he received an honorary rank that seemed both to please and to embarrass him. "I am a Colonel s'il vous plait," he told Nicolay. "Col. John Hay Vol. A.D.C. &c." "Write to me when you have nothing else to do & be good enough to remember that I have a pretty extensive handle to my name."

Having escaped a late spring snowstorm in Washington, he was "getting browned by equitation" and could now manage to "digest an enormous quantity of beef and sleep." He assured his mother that he "never felt better in my life than I do now. I ride a good deal, eat in proportion,

and sleep enormously. I hope to weigh about a ton when I return." To his grandfather, Hay sent an enthusiastic hello from "the land of the rebels" and gave a glowing report of the natural beauty of the Southern landscape, a theme he revisited in his frequent letters to the White House. "I wish you could be down here," he told Nicolay. "You would enjoy it beyond measure. The air is like June at noon & like May at morning and evening. The scenery is tropical. The sunset unlike anything I ever saw before. They are not gorgeous like ours but singularly quiet and solemn. The sun goes down over the pines through a sky like ashes-of-roses and hangs for an instant on the horizon like a bubble of blood. Then there is a twilight, such as you dream about." Florida seemed to Hay "the Original Eden on the Continent," its unsculpted beauty unlike anything he had ever before seen. "As we sat in the shade of St. Augustine & watched the picanninnies catching crabs in the lazy sunshine on the seawall, the quaint old town lying sleepy and still before us & the orange groves filling the background with the vivid green of the tropics, while a sky without blemish of cloud hung like a visible benediction over all, I felt as useless and irresponsible as the lizards in the grass or the porpoises that leaped in the liquid basin of the bay."

Hay's diary entries for April and May 1863 reveal an outsider's fascination with the dying remnants of the antebellum South. All around him were foreign landscapes, strange vegetation and wildlife, abandoned plantations, and a bewildering dissipation of racial and social boundaries. In a series of brief, highly impressionistic entries, he captured the first eerie aftershocks of civil war: "The sunset scene. The wild tropical splendor of the dying day. The weirdlike mist that hangs over the woods. The gathering shadows of water, & the lights glimmering up one by one from the black bulks of the fleet. A splendid harbor going to waste. A great country aroused & filling it with hostile power." He remarked on the "weird effect of the uninhabited village" and the "picturesque scenery of the circling shores. White cottages nestling by the shores. Village to be burned." Once-opulent homes, now derelict and abandoned, placed in sharp relief the terrific wager that white slave owners had been willing to place on disunion. Wandering one evening through an empty plantation house—"the finest place I have ever seen"—he was awestruck by the

sprawling "grounds well kept. The wharf with steps for boats. The boat house. The Sea entrance. The business office. The Aloe about to bloom. The conservatory. The summer houses." It all made him shake his head in wonder at "what this man wanted & what he got."

The Union-occupied coastal landscape that Hay traveled in 1863 afforded him a first intimate gaze at American slavery. Though he had encountered African Americans, both free and slave, during boyhood sojourns in St. Louis, in Springfield, and, more recently, in Washington, his time with Hunter's army offered a stark introduction to the system of plantation slavery that most Northerners knew only through the prism of *Uncle Tom's Cabin*. What's more, that system was crumbling under the pressure of war and occupation. Hay had been present when Lincoln signed the Emancipation Proclamation. Now he was on hand to view its profound aftershocks. Everywhere he went, he took note of the unfamiliar surroundings, both animate and inanimate. The palm trees and "pomegranate at Major Dormans" were as foreign to him as "the darkey girls" who "delight in his return." He encountered soldiers from the First South Carolina, one of the first all-black regiments in the Union army, and spoke with Thomas Wentworth Higginson, the white Cambridge-born abolitionist who commanded their unit. He marveled at the lowly appearance of war-weary "Secesh women" and recorded, without commentary, seeing thirteen hundred contrabands—slaves who fled behind Union lines—working under the watchful eye of white Union soldiers.

In Charleston, Hay conferred with Robert Smalls, a slave who earned wide acclaim when he commandeered a Confederate vessel and sailed himself to freedom and who was now a pilot for the Union navy. He also recorded details of a conversation with "Eugene, an intelligent contraband. His story. The condition of the rebels in Georgia. The secret understanding among the negroes. More wd come but they are afraid of being caught & sent back, and not until lately were they sure in reception." In Beaufort, Hay noted with fascination the intense religious sentiment that the president inspired among former slaves. "Talk about Linkum!" he heard one man say. "Linkum walk as Jes. walk! no man see L."

Emancipation was technically in full effect, but no one yet

understood how freedmen would fit into a post-slavery world. Later in
the decade, Americans would fiercely contest the meaning of free la-
bor. Would ex-slaves become self-sufficient yeoman farmers, working
their own plots of land? Or would they be compelled to work the cot-
ton fields for wages? As a direct observer of these first "rehearsals for
Reconstruction," Hay gained an early understanding of the terms of
the debate. "The plantations neat and well tilled, people"—meaning
Negroes—"apparently contented and happy," he noted on a visit to
Lady's Island, near Hilton Head. "Williams says they work better on
their own grain crops than on Govt cotton crops."

Hay also visited freedmen's schools that were staffed principally by
white abolitionists from the North. The students, young and old,
burned a lasting impression in his mind. "Song by a Florida slavegirl,"
he noted. "We will fight for liberty. The children join. Sergeant Proc-
tor delighted. 'Roll Jording [sic] Roll.'" With a poet's ear for dialect,
Hay recorded the unfamiliar accents and cadences of the young chil-
dren whom he encountered. Though he left little commentary or anal-
ysis, the episodes and snippets he chose to preserve suggest a growing
understanding, even approval, of the social revolution that the war had
unleashed. "Went to the colored Schools," he recorded on April 27.
"Miss Harris and Miss Smith"—white abolitionists from Massachusetts
and New Hampshire, respectively—"in charge of the Abcdarians . . .
Light mulatto girls and white children. All singing together."

> *Say my brother aint you ready*
> *Get ready to go home*
> *For I hear de word of promise*
> *At de breaking of the day*
> *Ill take de wings of de morning*
> *& fly away to Jesus*
> *Ill take de wing of de morning*
> *& Sound de Jubilee.*

On Paris Island, Hay and his party "went to the Plantation house . . .
to see darkies. Genl. Saxton made a little speech about their relatives

in the Army. Revd. Moore followed and talked freedom & general politics & Littlefield was very characteristic in the same groove. I said ½ dozen words in behalf of the Tycoon. Then sang some strange & wild songs."

Like hundreds of thousands of Union soldiers who confronted Southern slavery head-on, Hay left South Carolina and Florida less hardened in his thinking about African Americans. He did not walk away from the experience an out-and-out egalitarian. He still viewed African Americans as unequal to whites in many respects. But their hymns struck a resonant chord. More than most people, Hay appreciated verse. He studied it and took it seriously. Speaking to him in the language of gospel, the ex-slaves of the South Carolina and Florida coastline forced the young man's attention. "They swayed to & fro as they sang with great feeling," he observed. "An old woman who came over fr. Africa. Says she was grown when she came."

> *Genl. Hunter sitting on the tree of life*
> *To hear the wind of the Jordan roll*
> *Roll J.R.R. J. Roll*
> *(Ch.)*
> *March de Angel March*
> *March de Angel March*
> *My soul is rising heavenward*
> *To hear the wind of the Jording roll.*
> *I ax old Satan why follow me so?*
> *Satan aint got nothing to do with me.*
> *Hold yr. light (Bis) on Canaan's shore.*
> *Oh Sister Ketchum dont you want to get religion*
> *Down in the lonesome valley, (my lord).*
> *And meet my Jesus there—*

By the end of his Southern travels, Hay had seen and heard enough to become an ardent convert to the cause of black enlistment in the army. His experience among white officers and black freedmen led him to understand that ex-slaves were strongly motivated to fight.

"Why is not authority given to Genl. Hunter to organize Negro Regiments?" he asked Nicolay. "He very much needs it. He has written twice for it, and has gotten no answer. I wish you would, simply *pro bono publico,* have some resurrection made of the matter. Negroes are coming in, slowly as yet. But when our expeditions get on the Main he will be very much embarrassed for authority to do this."

Hay returned from his trip in early June, just as the war began to take a dramatic turn. On June 21, Nicolay informed Therena that "Pennsylvania and Maryland have had another 'invasion' fright, and not without some reason, though I believe it is turning out to be only a raid." Nine days later, his assessment changed radically. "Stirring times seem to be upon us again," he wrote. "It appears pretty evident that Lee has taken the most of his army into Maryland and Pennsylvania, with perhaps the design of taking Baltimore or Washington . . . At present the rebel army is scattered about over Pennsylvania gathering up forage and stealing supplies. The State is almost completely paralyzed by fear or entirely apathetic, and is moving in a very feeble way to help herself. Whether as the danger presses her she will arouse herself to more vigorous action is yet a problem."

The events of July 1863 in many ways signaled a turning point in the Union's fortunes, as well as Lincoln's. The Northern victory at Gettysburg in early July, followed a day later by the Confederate surrender of Vicksburg, dealt a major blow to Robert E. Lee's Army of Northern Virginia and deprived the Confederacy of free navigation along the Mississippi. For Lincoln, the twin events supplied a much-needed jolt of enthusiasm to the Northern public. As was the case so often, hope turned to disappointment when the Union commander, George Meade, failed to give chase to Lee's rebels. "The Prest was deeply grieved," Hay privately noted on July 14. " 'We had them within our grasp,' he said. 'We had only to stretch forth our hands & they were ours. And nothing I could say or do could make the Army move.' " Neither in his letters nor in his diary did Hay make note of the fearsome riots then engulfing New York City, where angry working-class mobs lynched scores of black residents and menaced the lives and

property of leading white Republicans, ostensibly to protest the government's new military draft. The violence stemmed from multiple sources, the draft certainly among them, but also including the ruinous effects of wartime inflation on workingmen, popular working-class opposition to the Emancipation Proclamation, and ethnic resentments that had long been simmering in the cauldron of New York's local politics. It would ultimately require thousands of federal troops, some fresh from the fields of Gettysburg, to put down the draft riots. The conflagration was evidence of the deep political divisions and social discord that the war had wrought. What should have been a crowning month for the administration ended inconclusively and with strong portents of future trouble.

Late summer and early fall found Nicolay traveling in the Colorado Territory, where Lincoln sent him to carry out negotiations with local Indian tribes. A lifelong outdoorsman, Nicolay jumped at the chance to visit the Rocky Mountains. Upon reaching Denver, he fired off a note to Therena, relating the details of a seventy-eight-hour trip through the western desert ("in a coach with a load of six inside passengers and a nigger baby to say nothing of several tons of express matter") and marveling at the scenery. "Off to the west the mountains lie wrapped up in a most alluring cool blue haze," he reported, "and occasionally send down a whiff of cold air, pure and refreshing as the breezes of paradise. I am anxious for a closer acquaintance with them . . . as soon as I can get the soreness out of my bones." Over the next several weeks, he shared the vivid imagery of his sojourn with Hay and Therena: The vibrant commercial spirit of Central City, a rough-hewn mining town forty miles west of Denver, "frailly built of knotty pinelumber, sawed here in the mountains . . . chock full with some kind or other of business . . . trade, banking, hotels, restaurants, grogshops, courts, schools—vending every imaginable thing from a hoop-skirt to a quartz mill." The quartz mines and "cool clear" mountain air of the Rockies. The wildlife and unfamiliar vegetation. "I have not experienced the exhilaration that I felt at Newport and in Minnesota," he admitted, "but I am in perfect health (so far as feeling goes) and have an enormous appetite which I am able to gratify with impunity."

In Nicolay's absence, Hay managed affairs in Washington. "It would do you good to see how daily I hold the Tycoon's nose to the Court Martial grindstone," he told Nicolay, in knowing reference to the hundreds of military criminal judgments that Lincoln personally reviewed each week. ("Today we spent 6 hours deciding on Courtmartials, the President Judge Holt & I," he noted in his diary. "I was amused at the eagerness with which the President caught at any fact which would justify him in saving the life of a condemned soldier. He was only merciless in cases when meanness or cruelty were shown. Cases of cowardice he was specially averse to punishing with death. He said it would frighten the poor devils too terrible, to shoot them.") Though Washington in summertime was "dull . . . as an obsolete almanac," Hay found a steady companion in Robert Todd Lincoln—"le dauphin Bob," who had returned from Harvard to visit his parents. "Bob & I had a fearful orgy here last night on whiskey and cheese," he reported in mid-July. "The house is gradually going to the bad since you left." By early August, with Bob and his mother departed for a vacation in New Hampshire's White Mountains, Hay was left alone with the president. "The newspapers say the Tycoon will join them after a while," he noted with amusement. "If so, he does not know it."

Unlike Nicolay, Hay had not chosen politics as a career. Politics chose him. Those who knew him three years earlier, when he was an aspiring poet with a diffident outlook on affairs of state, might have been surprised by his swift professional conversion. To all outward appearances, he never took himself too seriously. "You are a fortunate man," John Forney, a longtime Washington insider, told him. "You have kept yourself aloof from your office. I know an old fellow now seventy who was Private Secretary to Madison. He has lived ever since on its recollection. He thought there was something solemn and memorable in it. [But] Hay has laughed through his term." Yet by 1863, Hay had developed a deep reverence for the president and a newfound appreciation of the transformational power of politics. "The Tycoon is in fine whack," he told Nicolay, who was still in Colorado. "I have rarely seen him more serene & busy. He is managing the war, the draft, foreign relations, and planning a reconstruction of the Union, all at once.

I never knew with what tyrannous authority he rules the Cabinet, till now. The most important things he decides & there is no cavil. I am growing more and more firmly convinced that the good of our country absolutely demands that he should be kept where he is till this thing is over. There is no man in the country, so wise so gentle and so firm. I believe that God placed him where he is." Weeks later, he marveled at the president's equanimity and control under pressure. "The old man sits here and wields like a backwoods Jupiter the bolts of war and the machinery of government with a hand equally steady & equally firm," he wrote to Nicolay. "I do not know whether the nation is worthy of him for another term. I know the people want him. There is no mistaking that fact. But politicians are strong yet & he is not their 'kind of cat.' I hope God wont see fit to scourge us for our sins by any one of the two or three prominent candidates on the ground."

No president had won a second term since Andrew Jackson in 1832. Now in his third year in office, presiding over a war that many Northerners believed should have been won a year before, and still regarded by many leaders of his own party as unequal to the task at hand, Lincoln set his sights on renomination. "I hope you are getting well and hearty," Hay wrote to Nicolay, who was then finishing his stay out west. "Next winter will be the most exciting and laborious of all our lives. It will be worth any other ten."

New Birth of Freedom

B y November 1863, the citizens of Gettysburg, Pennsylvania, had succeeded in restoring a modicum of order and tranquillity to their small town. The great military battle that temporarily swelled the city's population from 2,400 to over 150,000 left a terrible scar on the sleepy college town. The poisonous stench from the corpses of several thousand dead men and thousands more horses and mules, left lying in roads and cornfields under a burning midsummer sun. The flies and gnats. The tons of human and animal excrement left unburied. The bloodstained walls of private homes and businesses. The massive applications of lime, meant to ward off disease and pestilence, which dusted the streets in fine white powder. It was "a scene of horror and desolation which humanity, in all the centuries of its history has seldom witnessed," claimed the U.S. Christian Commission. In the aftermath of the battle, farmers emerged from their homes to find their livestock stolen or destroyed, their orchards picked clean by fleeing rebels, their crops in tatters, and their trees shot full with bullets. Gettysburg stood as a stark testament to the physical ruin of modern war.

For several weeks, local townspeople lightly buried as many bodies as they could manage, marking the dead with crude wooden posts. David Wills, a prominent businessman and civic leader, reported to Governor Andrew Curtin that a more permanent solution was needed. Heeding the advice, Curtin named Wills to head an interstate

commission charged with creating a permanent resting place for the
Union dead. States would contribute to the costs of exhuming and
reburying the dead; the federal government would furnish the caskets.
With single-minded purpose and dispatch, Wills hired a contractor to
exhume and reinter the bodies (at $1.59 per grave) and secured the
services of William Saunders, a noted horticulturalist and landscape
architect, to design the cemetery. Saunders's plan called for a semi-
circular arrangement of graves, organized by state, with officers and
enlisted men commingled without regard for rank.

Eventually, a date was selected in late November for the dedication
of the Gettysburg cemetery. Curtin extended invitations to the gover-
nors of each state whose servicemen had fought at Gettysburg; six ulti-
mately accepted. The former Massachusetts governor and U.S. senator
Edward Everett was chosen to deliver the principal oration. Also ex-
pected were dozens of ranking military officers, mayors, congressmen,
and political leaders, as well as journalists representing most of the ma-
jor Northern newspapers. At the last minute, Lincoln accepted Wills's
invitation to offer "a few appropriate remarks." He would travel by
train the day before, along with Secretary of State William Seward,
Nicolay, Hay, and a delegation consisting of leading congressmen, for-
eign diplomats, and Washington-based newspapermen. For Lincoln,
the trip served political as well as official purposes. With an eye toward
securing renomination the following summer, he would use his ap-
pearance at Gettysburg to lock down the support of key state delega-
tions and broadcast his interpretation of the war to a national audience.

On November 8, three days after Nicolay returned from his west-
ern trip and ten days before their departure for Pennsylvania, the sec-
retaries joined Lincoln at Alexander Gardner's studio in Washington,
where, as Hay recorded, "we had a great many pictures taken. Some
of the Presdt. the best I have seen. Nico & I immortalized ourselves by
having done in group with the Presdt." It was the only photograph in
which Lincoln, Nicolay, and Hay appeared together. (The following
year, the president posed for several pictures in his White House of-
fice. One surviving photograph shows Lincoln seated at his desk. Nico-
lay's legs are visible to his left.)

"Spent the evening at the theatre with the President Mrs. Lincoln, Mrs. Hunter, Cameron and Nicolay," Hay recorded on November 9. "J. Wilkes Booth was doing the 'Marble Heart.' Rather tame than otherwise." Two days later, Hay returned to "see Wilkes Booth in Romeo. Wheatly took all the honors away as Mercutio." A week later, they left for Gettysburg.

Years later, Nicolay remembered that Wills's invitation arrived only two weeks before the dedication of the national cemetery at Gettysburg. "It was a time when [the president] was extremely busy, not alone with the important and complicated military affairs in the various armies, but also with the consideration of his annual message to Congress, which was to meet early in December. There was even great uncertainty whether he could take enough time from his pressing official duties to go to Gettysburg at all. Up to the 17th of November, only two days before the ceremonies, no definite arrangements for the journey had been made." The plan originally called for the presidential party to depart Washington early on Thursday, November 19, but the president, appreciating the political importance of the trip and anticipating the usual train mishaps, insisted on arriving the evening before the dedication. "I do not wish to so go that by the slightest accident we fail entirely," he told the secretaries, "and, at the best, the whole to be a mere breathless running of the gantlet." In later years, much speculation would surround the timing and location of Lincoln's formulation of the Gettysburg Address. Nicolay, who helped transcribe the final copy on the morning of November 19, admitted that he had no idea when the president began preparing his remarks. "He probably followed his usual habit in such matters, using great deliberation in arranging his thoughts, and molding his phrases mentally, waiting to reduce them to writing until they had taken satisfactory form," he speculated more than three decades after the fact. Based on his analysis of the different pieces of stationery on which the president composed his first draft, Nicolay agreed with James Speed, Lincoln's future attorney general, who claimed "that the President told him that the day before he left Washington he found time to write

about half of his speech." Contrary to popular myth, Nicolay believed that Lincoln did not work on the draft during the train ride from Washington. Doing so would have been impossible "amid all the movement, the noise, the conversation, the greetings and the questionings which ordinary courtesy required him to undergo." He completed his remarks later that evening in Gettysburg.

"We started from Washington to go to the Consecration of the Soldiers' Cemetery at Gettysburg," Hay scribbled in his diary on Wednesday evening. "We had a pleasant sort of trip." Arriving just after sunset under a damp, overcast sky, Lincoln and Seward proceeded directly to David Wills's house for a large welcome dinner in the president's honor. Curtin and his fellow governors were expected to attend, but train troubles delayed them until almost midnight. Lincoln nevertheless had an opportunity to confer that evening with dozens of leading politicians whose support would prove critical to his renomination efforts. As Nicolay later recalled, "Except during its days of battle, the little town of Gettysburg had never been so full of people . . . [T]he streets literally swarmed with visitors, and the stirring music of regimental bands and patriotic glee-clubs sounded in many directions." A journalist on hand remembered that the presidential party appeared "a straggled, hungry set. Lincoln, with that weary smile, which a poet might have read as a forecast of destiny; Seward, with an essentially bad hat; John Hay, in attendance upon the president, and much to be troubled by the correspondents, handsome as a peach, the countenance of extreme youth." While the president dined with the reception committee and honored guests, Hay "foraged around for a while—walked out to the College got a chafing dish of oysters then some supper," and strolled over to the courthouse, where he found John Forney, the influential Republican newspaperman, who "had been drinking a good deal during the day and was getting to feel a little ugly and dangerous."

A veteran of Pennsylvania's internecine political wars, Forney was critical to the president's renomination efforts; accordingly, Hay suffered his drunken ramblings with sportsmanlike demeanor. "We went out after a while following the music to hear the serenades," he

continued in his diary. From inside the Wills house, "the President appeared at the door and said half a dozen words meaning nothing & went in. Seward who was staying around the corner at Harper's was called out and spoke so indistinctly that I did not hear a word of what he was saying . . . We went back to Forney's room having picked up Nicolay and drank more whiskey. Nicolay sung his little song of the 'Three Thieves' and we then sung John Brown. At last we proposed that Forney should make a speech and two or three started out . . . to get a band to serenade him."

The secretaries cannot be faulted for missing the full weight of the moment. Living events in real time, they had little way of knowing that they were witnessing history. They were also drinking copious amounts of whiskey. Back at the Wills house, Lincoln was quietly at work in his upstairs guest room, completing his speech. A block away, Seward delivered impromptu remarks to the serenaders that John Hay strained to hear and that presaged the president's speech. The war, Seward proclaimed, would invariably result in the destruction of slavery, and "when that cause is removed, simply by the operation of abolishing it, as the origin and agent of the treason that is without justification and without parallel, we shall henceforth be reunited, be only one country, having only one hope, one ambition, and one destiny." A Detroit newspaper described Seward as "taking more decided anti-slavery grounds, more bold than in any previous utterance of his since the war commenced." Days later the *Chicago Tribune* pointed out the symmetry between the two speeches when it noted that the president "means that this nation shall have 'a new birth of freedom,'" while Seward "is still more emphatic. He denounces slavery." Both men identified the destruction of slavery as a turning point in the nation's destiny, a point that was not lost on contemporary observers.

Without fanfare, the administration was about to confirm what many Americans already perceived: that the war was no longer about restoring the "Union as it was, and the Constitution as it is," as many Democrats insisted. Instead, it had evolved into a struggle to elevate the principles of the American Revolution above the embarrassing series of compromises of human liberty that lay so deeply embedded

in the Constitution. In the opening line of his address, "Four score and seven years ago our fathers brought forth, upon this continent, a new nation, conceived in liberty, and dedicated to the proposition that all men are created equal," Lincoln would date the founding of America to 1776, not 1787. To the modern ear, this phraseology is unremarkable, but for its time it was freighted with great meaning. For two decades, antislavery radicals had publicly venerated the Declaration of Independence and scorned the Constitution, with its two-thirds compromise and recognition of the international slave trade, as a sordid, morally tainted document. Frederick Douglass called on Americans to unleash the "great doctrines" of their founding article from the "narrow bounds of races or nations," while his fellow abolitionists rechristened Pennsylvania's "Old State House Bell" the "Liberty Bell," claimed it as their symbol, and turned a once-obscure historical relic into a national icon. Borrowing from this legacy, Lincoln would soon recast the meaning of the Civil War, and that evening Seward had sent up the first test balloon.

Hay and Nicolay were focused elsewhere. They were tasked with handling the president's politics, and in that service they were drunk. Late evening found them mingling among a "large and clamorous" crowd of reporters and onlookers as Forney stumbled his way through an emotional philippic. Hay noted that the much-inebriated speaker delighted the equally impaired crowd with "the eulogy of the President, that great, wonderful mysterious inexplicable man . . . And very much of this." Sometime between late evening and early morning, Forney retired to his bedroom to pass out, and the secretaries went to sleep.

The next morning at roughly nine o'clock, Nicolay managed to present himself at Lincoln's room, where the two men spent an hour creating a clean copy of the final draft. This was probably the first time that Nicolay read the speech; Hay, who took longer to stir from the night's revelries, had not yet seen a draft—a point that he apparently pressed to no avail with reporters, who did not believe him and bothered him relentlessly for an advance copy. At ten o'clock, Nicolay and Lincoln left the Wills house to join the procession to the cemetery. "In

the morning I got a beast and rode out with the President's suite to the Cemetery in the procession," Hay noted in his diary. "The procession formed itself in an orphanly sort of way & moved out with very little help from anybody & after a little delay Mr. Everett took his place on the stand—And Mr. Stockton made a prayer which thought it was an oration—and Mr. Everett spoke as he always does perfectly—and the President in a firm free way, with more grace than is his wont said his half dozen lines of consecration and the music wailed and we went home through crowded and cheering streets. And all the particulars are in the daily papers."

That was that. Neither Nicolay nor Hay made any further mention of the Gettysburg Address at the time. Initial reviews were mixed. Democratic newspapers faulted the president for mixing partisanship with the solemnity of the moment and for identifying 1776—not 1787—as the birth of the American nation. The New York *World*, a Democratic organ, thought it "questionable" to date the nation's founding to the "stages of conception and parturition." An Ohio Democrat denounced the address as a "mawkish harangue about this 'was for freedom' of the negro." The *Chicago Times,* no friend of the administration's, complained that "Lincoln did most foully traduce the motives of the men who were slain at Gettysburg." They had not died to give the nation a "new birth of freedom." Rather, "they gave their lives to maintain the old government, and the old constitution and Union." Predictably, Republicans praised the speech. One paper called it "the right thing, in the right place, and a perfect thing in every respect." The *Chicago Tribune* averred that it would "live among the annals of man," and two years later Ralph Waldo Emerson predicted that it would "not easily be surpassed by words on any recorded occasion," a prophecy that later proved true enough.

But Emerson's assessment was still mere prophecy. In its immediate aftermath, the Gettysburg Address was received neither as a great failure (as historical myth would later hold) nor as a landmark document (as we tend to assume today). It was an important political oration, carefully calculated and successfully delivered. Only in later years would Hay and Nicolay come to regard the Gettysburg Address as an

"immortal" document, as they undertook the work of securing Lincoln's place in history.

The Gettysburg Address came at a key moment for Lincoln. As would prove the case throughout the war, the president's political fortunes, and those of his party, moved in almost perfect concert with the Union army's battlefield success. Buoyed by victories at Gettysburg and Vicksburg, the Republicans performed strongly in key off-year gubernatorial and legislative elections, most notably in several large battleground states. Lincoln and his allies also found help in an unlikely quarter: the opposition Democratic Party undermined much of its own credibility by seeming too close in alignment with the rebels. In Ohio, Democrats nominated the former congressman Clement Vallandigham for governor; an outspoken Copperhead of dubious loyalty to his country, he was forced to campaign from Canada, having been banished by government decree from the United States. In Indiana, the Democratic-controlled legislature had refused to appropriate funds for the military effort, compelling the Republican governor to assume extralegal executive powers to secure funding outside the ordinary channels. These public offenses, as well as the antiwar stridency of the Democratic press, struck many Northern voters as borderline seditious and produced a groundswell of support for the Republican Party that fall, particularly in Ohio and Pennsylvania, two powerhouses in the Electoral College. In early October, Hay traveled to Columbus to debrief John Brough, the Republican gubernatorial candidate. "He says they will carry Ohio by at least 25,000 votes, independent of the soldiers who will indefinitely increase it," Hay reported to the president. "Brough is much more anxious about [Pennsylvania governor Andrew] Curtin than himself.

> Brough thinks that as yet in the Keystone State
> The prospect is rather uncertain—
> The fifth act is near, and we only can wait
> Impatient, the rise of the *Curtain*.

A hazy joke, with which I close."

Lincoln was by no means a passive observer in these struggles. Behind the scenes, he actively raised money for state Republican parties, furloughed thousands of Ohio soldiers so that they could return home to vote, and, in the final days of the canvass, issued a robust campaign speech that was read on his behalf before a massive rally in Illinois and disseminated nationally through the Republican press. These efforts paid handsome dividends. Standing alongside Curtin, who was handily reelected, and Brough, who trounced Vallandigham at the polls, Lincoln used his appearance at Gettysburg to solidify his position in advance of the 1864 nomination fight.

Lincoln faced certain obstacles in his effort to earn renomination, chief among them the unrelenting ambition of his Treasury secretary, Salmon P. Chase. It was the worst-kept secret in Washington that Chase was conspiring to depose Lincoln at the next year's Republican convention. As early as the summer of 1863, Hay noted with bemusement the observations of an Ohio Republican who thought Chase "a good man, but his theology is unsound. He thinks there is a fourth Person in the Trinity, *S.P.C.*" Lincoln understood that Chase's head was "full of *Presidential* maggots" but struck the secretaries as more amused than concerned by his "mad hunt for the Presidency." Yet Chase was a formidable opponent. His "head is turned by his eagerness in pursuit of the presidency," a rival cabinet member privately observed. "For a long time he has been filling all the offices in his own vast patronage, with extreme partisans, and contrives to fill many vacancies, properly belonging to other departments." When Hay warned the president about Chase's political use of federal patronage, Lincoln "laughed on & said he was sorry the thing had begun, for though the matter did not annoy him his friends insisted that it ought to . . . He prefers letting Chase have his own way in these sneaking tricks than getting into a snarl with him by refusing him what he asks."

Above all, the president understood that his success would hinge on the progress of the war effort. Eager to expedite matters, in late 1863 Lincoln announced his Ten Percent Plan, which offered amnesty to all

Southerners who would pledge allegiance to the United States and invited any Confederate state that could muster up enough such loyal men, equal to 10 percent of those who had voted in 1860, to form a new state constitution without slavery. The Ten Percent Plan was more about prosecuting the war than reconstructing the South. Its intent was to establish rival state governments in the South, undermine the Confederacy's hold on its own people and territory, and encourage desertion in the rebel army. As an added bonus, reconstructed Southern governments might be able to send delegates to the 1864 Republican convention and participate in the presidential election. By definition, most of those re-swearing allegiance to the United States would support the president and the Republican ticket.

In late December, with Nicolay away on a visit to Philadelphia, Hay spent "a lonesome sort of Christmas. I breakfasted, dined, and supped alone. Went to the Theatre & saw Macbeth alone. Came home and slept alone." Three days later, Lincoln spoke with his secretary "about the matter of reconstruction in Florida. He wants me to take one of his Oath books down to Pt. Lookout and get the matter going there and after that he will appoint me a Commissioner to go to Florida and engineer the business there." In practical terms, Hay's challenge was to convince approximately thirteen hundred residents of occupied Florida (10 percent of those who had voted in the 1860 presidential election) to swear allegiance to the United States. For Lincoln, the mission was critical: reconstructing Southern states would allow him to sow discord in the Confederacy and rack up an important political win ahead of the presidential election. For Hay, it was an opportunity to step into a larger role. Recognizing the stakes at hand, key Republicans wondered aloud why the president would tap his twenty-five-year-old secretary to perform so sensitive a mission. Hay was "young, almost beardless," complained one Republican editor, and unprepared for the "official responsibilities and the tumult of action in time of pressure." The Washington correspondent for a midwestern newspaper wrote him off as "that fellow five feet tall, that walks like lightning down the street" in his "turtle-backed hat, just the shape of his cranium, with well oiled locks, and handsome kid gloves," speaking "in the choice

and expressive language which prevails at 'Chebang,' as he pleasantly terms the White House. Inquire affectionately after the health of the President of the mightiest nation on earth, and John will inform you that the 'old Tycoon is in high feather.'"

Perhaps recognizing that a young man in a turtle-backed hat would not be taken seriously, on January 13 the president commissioned Hay a major in the army and sent him with a presidential letter of introduction to the commander of the Department of the South. Still detailed to the White House, Hay would remain a soldier for the duration of the war, serving in effect as a presidential military aide. "Great good luck and God's blessing go with you John," Lincoln said affectionately.

Following roughly the same coastal route that he had traveled the year before, Hay contended once again with bouts of seasickness along the way. He noted with interest the "embarkation of the 54th boys"— the celebrated colored soldiers of the Massachusetts Fifty-fourth who had fought valiantly and suffered enormous losses at Charleston in 1863. "Variety of complexions," he observed, "redheads—filing into their places on deck—singing whistling smoking and dancing—eating candy & chewing tobacco. Jolly little cuss round rosy and halfwhite, singing

> Oh John Brown dey hung him
> Were gwine to jine de Union Army
> Oh John Brown dey hung him,
> We're gwine Dixie's land."

Arriving in South Carolina, Hay reported to General Quincy Gill-more, commander of the Department of the South, who "held the President's letter in a helpless sort of way, like a bachelor with a baby: he didn't know what he was to do with it or me: had a vague idea that he was to split his army up into squads and watch the polls while I carried on the election . . . But was comforted when I told him I wanted no soldaten—only orders." Gillmore found himself in an unusual position; he outranked Hay by several grades, but the young major was also a senior presidential aide. The general gladly drafted

official orders and sent Hay on his way. After awaiting arrival of his
army uniform and personal effects, which traveled on a separate ship,
Hay set sail for Florida, where, according to plan, he began the work
of securing the allegiance of vanquished Confederates. After several
days at work, he was optimistic. "The people are ignorant and apa-
thetic," he informed Lincoln. "They seem to know nothing and care
nothing about the matter. They have a vague objection to being shot
and having their houses burned, but don't know why it is done. They
will be very glad to see a government strong enough to protect them
against these everyday incidents of the last two years. I have the best
assurances that we will get the tenth required."

As was the case on his earlier Southern journey, Hay was charmed
and haunted by his unfamiliar surroundings, particularly by the bio-
luminescent bays that dotted the Florida coastline in the era before
commercial shipping killed off the microorganisms that created this
unusual lighting effect. "I came down the St. John's River last night,"
he told Nicolay. "There was no moon and the stars glistened in the
warm wintry air with a steady softness. The harbor as I entered it lay
in a charmed quiet. I saw for the first time in its glory the wonder of
the southern seas—the phosphorescent light of the waves. As I rowed
across every stroke of the oars splashed melted silver. This is abso-
lutely true. I floated in a vast reservoir of molten metal, white and lu-
minous."

Setting up shop at a general store, Hay distributed leaflets and
waited as "a few men straggled in and swore. One hesitating cuss who
evidently feared he was going to be tricked into the army swore, but
dallied so on the signing that I shut the book & told him to make up
his mind before calling again." Moving down toward Jacksonville, he
addressed a motley band of prisoners of war. Decked out in his blue
army uniform, he rose to inform them "of the Executive act [the Ten
Percent Plan] & extend to you its benefits . . . If you sign you will be
released & allowed to return to your homes if they are not &c. If not
you will be sent north as prisoners of war, for exchange . . . It is a mat-
ter for yr. own choice. There is to be neither force or persuasion used
in the matter." When Hay finished his lecture, several of the men

posed questions. Then they approached, "a dirty swarm of grey coats &
filed into the room, escorted by a negro guard. Fate had done its
worst for the poor devils. Even a nigger guard didnt seem to excite a
feeling of resentment." This late in the war, Hay had met many black
soldiers and was impressed by their valor and ability. He no longer
traded as freely in racial epithets as in earlier years. It is unclear
whether he was imagining the internal monologue of the vanquished
Confederate prisoners or still derogated African Americans in his pri-
vate conversations and writings.

Hay was repulsed, but not surprised, by the abject poverty and ig-
norance of his wards. "Some wrote [in] good hands," he observed, "but
most bad. Nearly half made their mark." As a solid antislavery man, he
expected exactly this paucity of intellectual achievement among
Southern whites. Neither did he harbor any illusions about their mo-
tives. "The fact that more than 50 per cent of the prisoners of war were
eager to desert & get out of the service shows how the spirit of the
common people is broken," he noted. They might not have had a
change of heart about secession and slavery. But they were "tired of the
war. Peace on any terms was what they wanted. They have no care for
the political questions involved. Most of them had not read the oath &
when I insisted on their learning what it was they would say listlessly,
'Yes I guess I'll take it.'"

Despite his early enthusiasm, Hay soon concluded that his mission
would likely fail. Only thirteen thousand Floridians had cast ballots in
1860, setting the bar low under the terms of the Ten Percent Plan. But
with tens of thousands of white men serving in uniform, and large
portions of the state still under rebel control and beyond his reach, he
concluded that there were not enough voters in the occupied portion
of Florida to achieve his target number. He could not enroll black men,
nor women. "I find nearly everybody willing to take the oath of alle-
giance," he privately concluded, "but I find scarcely anyone left in the
country. Whole counties seem almost thoroughly depopulated."
When Gillmore's forces suffered defeat at the Battle of Olustee in late
February, Hay's mission effectively came to an end. In a veiled swipe
at Hay, one Union officer wrote the entire project off as "a gigantic

humbug. Besides the Floridians who were already with the Union forces at St. Augustine, Fernandina, Key West, etc., we have scarcely met a man who would be allowed to vote in Connecticut,—that is with sufficient intelligence and education. Not enough white men have we picked up to make one good country school district in the north."

Others agreed. The *New York Herald* suggested that the president had ordered Gillmore to tie up precious resources in Florida, a state of low strategic priority, "simply . . . for the purpose of securing the election of three Lincoln delegates to the National Nominating Convention, and that of John Hay to Congress." Hay took the criticism personally, flatly denying any ambition to run for office in reconstructed Florida. He pointed out that plans for a military offensive predated his own mission. Several weeks later, after his return to Washington, he was ready to laugh the matter off. "The original lie in the *Herald* was dirty enough," he conceded, "& the subsequent commentaries were more than usually nasty. But the Tycoon never minded it in the least and as for me, at my age, the more abuse I get in the newspapers, the better for me. I shall run for Constable some day on the strength of my gory exploits in Florida."

As for "gory exploits," Hay did have the opportunity to witness some. Serving as a staff officer, he was near but not engaged directly in combat. "I have seen some rather rough incidents since I came here," he told Nicolay. "But am pretty nearly emancipated from the nerves." He also observed the performance of black soldiers and was impressed by what he saw. "The fighting on both sides was very fine," he wrote. "The conduct of our troops was superb. The negro Regiments, 54th, 55th Mass. 8th U.S. and 3rd S.C. under Montgomery behaved like veterans, standing like rocks in a fire that decimated their ranks. The commanding officers of two regiments fell in the fight but they fought on without flinching."

Like many Northerners who spent time in the Southern theater and observed the valor of black troops, Hay experienced a modest personal conversion on the issue of race relations. The lyricism of the black spirituals that he heard during both of his sojourns also struck a

deep chord with Hay, who could not help but be moved by the stark way in which so many ex-slaves interpreted the Civil War as a liberation struggle. Later that summer, he privately noted in his diary that he was "glad the President has sloughed off that idea of colonization. I have always thought it a hideous & barbarous humbug." In fact, he had not always thought so, or at least he had not always said so. Early in the war, Hay penned anonymous editorials that touted the president's support of voluntary colonization. As was often the case, he may have been promoting administration policy even when it was not in accordance with his own beliefs. But his views on race had become noticeably more liberal. By no means did he shake off the prejudices of his age, but he privately acknowledged doubts about some of his earlier preconceptions. "There was a pic-nic yesterday, in the Presidents grounds, of the negroes of Washington," he recorded just after Independence Day. It surprised him that "they were neatly & very carefully dressed very quietly & decently behaved . . . There were many of both sexes," he observed with curiosity, "perfectly white and blue-eyed."

Shortly after Hay returned from his unsuccessful mission to Florida, the president sent Nicolay on the first of two critical trips to New York, where he was tasked with assuaging the enormous ego of the political boss Thurlow Weed and sorting out a tangled mess at the New York Custom House. The most lucrative of all patronage mills in the federal government's care, the customhouse technically fell under the aegis of the Treasury Department. To Weed's great consternation, Chase had filled most of the coveted positions there with his own political supporters, willfully denying Weed—and by extension, Weed's political partner Seward—the spoils of office. In early 1864, Weed warned the president that unless changes were made, he could not assure him that New York would remain in the Republican column. The customhouse dilemma was made easier when Chase's candidacy petered out. Most of his allies came to the unhappy realization that Lincoln enjoyed too strong a base of support at the state and local levels. That summer, the Treasury secretary offered his resignation—for the fourth time in three years—over a matter of small consequence. This

time, Lincoln stunned Chase by accepting the resignation. Hay privately thought that the president had "made a mistake" by allowing Chase to depart at so critical a time. The markets reacted unsteadily to the news, and it was by no means clear that the government could expect to continue raising funds with turmoil at the Treasury. But the president no longer felt the need to humor his chief administration antagonist.

Lincoln's confidence in Nicolay had grown steadily since 1860. Though the secretary never played a consultative or strategic role in formulating administration policy, the president trusted him to manage key political relationships and gave him wide leeway in enforcing orders and directives. He sent Nicolay to Baltimore in June to be his eyes and ears at the Republican convention. He then sent him back to New York with a broad mandate to hear out influential members of the state party elite and hammer out a solution that would unite the different factions. The timing was critical. Lincoln's new general in chief, Ulysses S. Grant, had launched a massive, coordinated assault on the Confederacy but had suffered a series of costly setbacks that spring and summer. Many Republican leaders were urging Lincoln to withdraw from the race, leading Nicolay to complain privately of "weak-kneed d——d fools" who conspired to "supplant the Tycoon. Everything is darkness and doubt and discouragement." Writing to Therena, he admitted that the chairman of the national party, Henry Raymond, believed that "unless *something* was done, (and he thought that 'something' should be the sending [of] Commissioners to Richmond to propose terms of peace to the Rebels, on the basis of their returning to the Union) that we might as well quit and give up the contest." Even the president conceded that "unless some great change takes place" on the battlefield, he would be *"badly beaten"* in the November election. Upon arriving in New York, Nicolay held a series of meetings with both Weed and Raymond. After a whirlwind round of conferences, the secretary secured the resignation of top customhouse appointees, doled out their positions to men favorable to the local party bosses, and left the city with its principal Republican leaders once again on the Lincoln bandwagon.

Lincoln's confidence also grew in Hay. Though unsuccessful in Florida, the junior secretary moved with ease among Washington's opinion makers, collecting intelligence without ever betraying the president's confidence. In a city where discretion counted for every-thing, Lincoln trusted him for his good judgment and loyalty. That summer, he deputized Hay for a critical political mission. In an extreme case of gullibility, Horace Greeley allowed himself to be taken in by two men purporting to bear authorization from Jefferson Davis to negotiate an armistice. Lincoln suspected a trick but felt compelled to hear Greeley out. Though exasperatingly fickle, the editor wielded considerable power through his newspaper's vast circulation. Lincoln could not afford to slight him, even if he had no intention of empowering him to negotiate on behalf of the federal government. He also could not afford to seem inhospitable to peace talks. Boxed in by circumstances, the president dispatched Hay to deal with Greeley. Sitting across from the famous editor at the *Tribune*'s offices in Manhattan, Hay personally wrote out two safe-conduct passes for the Confederate commissioners and instructed Greeley to shepherd them from the Canadian side of Niagara Falls to Washington. Arriving back at the White House, he received a telegram from Greeley, who had gone to Niagara as instructed. In fact, Greeley explained, the two envoys bore no official relationship to Jefferson Davis but believed that they had the ability to place a credible peace before the Confederate president. Suspecting that Greeley had walked into a trap, Lincoln sent Hay to Niagara Falls with a letter. "To Whom It May Concern," the president's message began. "Any proposition which embraces the restoration of peace, the integrity of the whole Union, and the abandonment of slavery, and which comes by and with an authority that can control the armies now at war against the United States will be received and considered by the Executive Government of the United States." Greeley resisted predicating peace talks on abolitionist terms, fearing that such a hard line would shut down the negotiations. Hay, who was skeptical that there were even peace talks to be had, was present to ensure that he held the line. After meeting at the International Hotel, the two men crossed the suspension bridge to the Canadian side of the falls and

delivered Lincoln's letter to the self-styled Confederate commission-
ers, who were taking tea at the Clifton House. In fact, it soon emerged
that the entire affair was a political ruse meant to embarrass the pres-
ident with the Northern electorate, by making him appear unwilling
to negotiate an end to the war. When the fake Southern envoys leaked
details of Lincoln's letter to the press, it proved a great embarrassment
for Greeley, who had clearly been duped. It also caused the president
grief from conservatives in his own party. But by and large, the inci-
dent bolstered Lincoln's position with the antislavery Republican base.
When Hay told the president that conservative Republicans wanted
him to repudiate his "Niagara manifesto," Lincoln replied tersely,
"Lose ten times as much on the other side."

Hay also worked with Nicolay to collect and disburse party funds.
In the era before modern campaign finance law, this exercise usually
involved soliciting tithes from federal officeholders and distributing
the proceeds to central party committees in important swing states.

Military developments soon turned the political tide. On Septem-
ber 1, Atlanta surrendered to General William Tecumseh Sherman,
delivering a massive blow to the Confederacy and a major military and
political win to the president. Days later, Ulysses Grant lent aid to the
Republican cause by issuing a highly acclaimed public letter that
promised (in Nicolay's words) "an encouraging view of the military
situation" and that told the country "the true road to peace is through
hard fighting till the rebellion is put down." Revered by most of the
country for his merciless pursuit of victory, Grant lent something of
his own prestige to the party's cause.

What the Republicans could not accomplish politically, their op-
ponents did for them. Meeting in Chicago in late August, the Demo-
cratic convention nominated George McClellan for the presidency but
saddled him with a peace platform that all but promised to end the war
on terms favorable to the Confederacy. McClellan did not explicitly
endorse the plank, but as Nicolay explained to his fiancée, "having at-
tempted in [his acceptance letter] to ignore and dodge the question
presented by the platform whether he was for war or peace," the nom-
inee found himself in the political crosshairs: Republicans would taint

him with the charge of Copperheadism, while many Peace Democrats would doubt his reliability on the core question of the campaign. Writing again from Warsaw, Hay told Nicolay that "the Republicans here are talking better and *sassier* since the nomination of McClellan." Writing to an influential New York newspaperman, Hay sharply observed that "this nation may have sinned grievously, but neither you nor I believe it deserves that the murrain of McClellan should fall upon it." Many erstwhile dissenters in the Republican ranks agreed.

The fall campaign proved an unusually brutal affair. At Lincoln's behest, the Republicans had adopted a convention platform calling for the abolition of slavery by constitutional amendment. In turn, Democrats took race-baiting to a new extreme, unprecedented in American politics. Democratic newspaper editors coined a new term, "miscegenation," and accused the president of fighting a war of race amalgamation. They claimed that Lincoln was in fact "the outcrop of a remote African in his ancestry" and mocked the Republican Party's agenda as

> Hurrah for the nigger
> The sweet-scented nigger,
> And the paradise for the undertaker!
> Hurrah for Old Abe!

The president knew enough of popular opinion to understand that this line of attack could be devastatingly effective. On Election Day he ruefully told Hay, "It is a little singular that I who am not a vindictive man should have always been before the people for election in canvasses marked for their bitterness; always but once: When I came to Congress it was a quiet time. But always besides that the contests in which I have been prominent have been marked with great rancor." Even after Republicans swept state elections in October, racked up wide margins in Indiana and Ohio, and scored a smaller but still-definitive win in Pennsylvania, Lincoln predicted that he would lose New York and Illinois the following month and squeak by with a bare Electoral College majority of 117 to 114—assuming that none of his electors abandoned him.

Events proved him wrong. Lincoln carried every state except

Kentucky, Delaware, and New Jersey, defeating McClellan in the popular vote by a margin of 55 percent to 45 percent and in the Electoral College by a whopping 212 votes to 21. Most gratifying to the president was the soldier vote, which broke for Lincoln by a margin of 78 percent to 22 percent. John Hay was proven correct in judging that "the people"—or at least a strong majority of them—wanted Lincoln, even if the politicians did not view him as "their 'kind of cat.'"

Less than two weeks after the election, the president received an unusual request from Governor John Andrew of Massachusetts. Lydia Bixby, a widow and resident of the Bay State, had lost five sons in the Union cause. In a country that had grown too accustomed to the death of its young men on the battlefield, her sacrifice stood out as tragically exceptional. Andrew asked the president to send a personal tribute to Mrs. Bixby. Though no original copy of Lincoln's message survives, his letter was widely disseminated in the Northern press later that month.

> Dear Madam—
>
> I have been shown in the files of the War Department a statement of the Adjutant General of Massachusetts that you are the mother of five sons who have died gloriously on the field of battle.
>
> I feel how weak and fruitless must be any word of mine which should attempt to beguile you from the grief of a loss so overwhelming. But I cannot refrain from tendering you the consolation that may be found in the thanks of the Republic they died to save.
>
> I pray that our Heavenly Father may assuage the anguish of your bereavement, and leave you only the cherished memory of the loved and lost, and the solemn pride that must be yours to have laid so costly a sacrifice upon the altar of freedom.
>
> Yours, very sincerely and respectfully,
> A. Lincoln

In the aftermath of Lincoln's own martyrdom, the Bixby letter quickly ascended to the highest echelons of American letters. The poet Carl Sandburg later called it a "piece of the American Bible." Other scholars revered its "haunting strain of poetry" and compared it to the Gettysburg Address and the second inaugural. It was, in the estimation of a journalist in 1925, "one of the finest specimens of pure English extant." So enduring was its influence that more than 125 years later a film set in World War II (*Saving Private Ryan*) based its plot on the story of Lincoln's famous communication.

Few Americans in 1864 knew that Lydia Bixby was not what she appeared. A Southern sympathizer, she "had 'little good to say of President Lincoln,'" according to her granddaughter, and destroyed the original letter immediately upon receipt. She lost two sons, not five. Few Americans knew as well that the Bixby letter was probably the work of John Hay, not Abraham Lincoln, though it gave subtle and dignified voice to the sentiment of a president who was himself no stranger to a parent's grief. In the middle decades of the twentieth century, historians debated the letter's origin. Most refused to believe that a sometimes glib twenty-six-year-old political aide, accomplished though his later career may have been, could have captured so perfectly the voice of a great American statesman. But as Hay later told William Herndon, Lincoln "wrote very few letters. He did not read one in fifty that he received. At first we tried to bring them to his notice, but at last he gave the whole thing over to me, and signed without reading them the letters I wrote in his name. He wrote perhaps half-a-dozen a week himself—not more." Several of Hay's associates, including his private secretary, claimed after his death that he privately admitted to authorship of the Bixby letter, though he swore them to secrecy. A subsequent analysis of its wording persuasively suggests that it was a strong literary imitation of Lincoln that could only have been written by John Hay.

Unlike many men of their generation, Hay and Nicolay avoided direct experience with combat by virtue of their political positions. But some of their closest friends and family members lost lives and limbs in battle. As residents of the White House, they witnessed

firsthand the profound toll that the war took on grieving widows and parents, and indeed on the president himself. In future years, both men would work to ensure that the sacrifice of those who had fought in the Civil War would not be stripped of its meaning and purpose. Particularly for Hay, who would one day occupy a seat at the cabinet table, the violence of armed conflict held little allure. It was a terrible reality to be avoided at almost all costs.

His Heart Was Too Sad

In the weeks following Lincoln's reelection, the presidential secretaries quietly contemplated their own futures. Though their devotion to the president was steadfast and their proximity to power difficult to relinquish, they were physically drained and also increasingly uneasy about their personal and professional destinies beyond the White House. In early February, Nicolay assured Therena that just "because I have written nothing of it," she should not assume that he had "not been engaged in considering the question as to where I shall stay and what I shall do after next fourth of March. I have thought about the matter almost constantly ever since we talked it over in Delphina's parlor last fall; but I have not as yet reached any definite conclusion."

Left unsaid, but probably not unbeknownst to Therena, was the possibility that Lincoln might effect a change in White House personnel. For one, the relationship between the secretaries and the first lady (whom they privately dubbed Her Satanic Majesty) had grown poisonous. The year before, Mary had exploded in anger when Nicolay included the Rhode Island senator William Sprague and his wife, Kate Chase, on the guest list for a major state dinner. Mary was not without cause for complaint. Much younger and exceedingly popular among the city's political barons, Kate had shown the first lady little courtesy over the previous three years and had, with limited success, even managed to displace her from her rightful position as hostess in chief of the capital city. Kate was also an effective political agent for her father,

who was then plotting openly to remove the Lincolns from the White House altogether. But where Mary let personal (albeit legitimate) grudges trump political consideration, the president understood the value of keeping his friends close and his enemies closer. "When it came time to direct the cards for the dinner," Nicolay informed Hay, "I referred the question of [the] snub to the Tycoon who after a short conference with the powers at the other end of the hall came back and ordered Rhode Island and Ohio to be included in the list. Whereat soon arose such a rampage as the House hasn't seen for a year, and I am again taboo. How the thing is to end is yet as dark a problem as the Schleswig-Holstein difficulty. Stod[dard] fairly cowered at the violence of the storm, and I think for the first time begins to appreciate the awful sublimities of nature." In the aftermath of the tempest, Mary took control of the dinner arrangements and banned Nicolay from even attending. "She fished around with Stod to try to get posted about managing the affair," Nicolay continued, "but I instructed Stod to tell her, 1st that there was no way of his obtaining the requisite information, and 2ndly that if there were, yet as it was exclusively my business he *could* and *would not* do anything in the premises." The standoff continued, according to Nicolay, until "the afternoon of the dinner, when Edward," the White House doorman, "came up to tell me that she had backed down, requested my presence and assistance—apologizing, and explaining that the affair had worried her so that she hadn't slept for a night or two. I think she has felt happier since she cast out that devil of stubbornness."

Mary waited patiently to settle scores. Early 1865 found her lobbying the president behind closed doors for a new presidential staff. Noah Brooks, a newspaper correspondent from California, emerged as the most likely candidate for the secretary's post. One of the very few Washingtonians who bothered to befriend and publicly defend Mary, Brooks had also developed a close relationship with the president. A year and a half older than Nicolay, Brooks held the secretaries in ill regard and hoped to replace them. Apart from the first lady, he claimed powerful backers, including Speaker of the House Schuyler Colfax and Anson Henry, a longtime friend of the Lincoln family's.

The possibility of a switch was not far from Nicolay's mind. "As the case now stands," he told Therena, "I am pretty well resolved not to remain here in my present relation" after March, "and I think the chances are also against my remaining in Washington. This feeling does not result from any talk with the President about the matter, although I have once or twice alluded to the subject in our conversation, but from other causes and considerations. I think he does not now wish to be troubled with the question in any way, and therefore I do not repeat it to him. After his inauguration, however, other changes will necessarily take place, and after which I will probably be able to determine my own course. So I remain as patient as I can, three or four weeks longer."

George could wait patiently for three or four weeks, but Therena could not. Nicolay had met the love of his life when he was sixteen and she twelve or thirteen years old. They had grown up together but for the better part of a decade had to settle on a long-distance relationship. Therena was now twenty-eight years old, going on twenty-nine— older than most brides in her day. She had waited loyally but was at the end of her rope. Nicolay visited her in Pittsfield several times each year; they met occasionally in Springfield, when he was there on business; and from Nicolay's letters, it is clear that Therena traveled to Washington several times over the course of the war. Their letters to each other were filled with local gossip about relatives and mutual friends, concern for each other's health, discussions about religion and art, professions of love and admiration. It was not necessarily unusual that they put marriage on hold during the war. As it was customary for presidential secretaries to reside in the White House, it would have been impracticable for Nicolay to wed and establish an independent household with Therena during his term in office. But as the years wound on, she grew restive. George did not always pick up on the cues. In May 1864, he sent her a long letter full of war news and political prognostications. As an afterthought, he asked, "What did you mean when in your letter before the last you wrote that you thought we were slowly but surely drifting apart?" He was living on borrowed time, and in the weeks before the inauguration he seemed finally to know it.

Days before Lincoln was to be sworn in for his second term, Nico-

lay informed Therena that the president had named him to a diplomatic post in Europe, and the Senate had approved the nomination. "You have probably seen from the dispatches that I was yesterday appointed and confirmed as Consul to Paris," he wrote. "The salary is $5000 per annum. I have not yet fully matured my future movements. The probability however is that I will not start there for two or three months yet, and that meanwhile I shall see you and ask you to be ready to go with me. While I have not yet fully decided this point, it will be well for you to be quietly getting your wardrobe ready for the trip."

Some observers incorrectly concluded that Lincoln moved Nicolay out of his position in Noah Brooks's favor. The evidence establishes otherwise. In late February or early March, Lincoln offered Nicolay a diplomatic post and the job of private secretary to Brooks. When it first seemed that Nicolay preferred to remain in the White House, Lincoln offered Brooks a well-paying patronage position at the customhouse in San Francisco as a consolation prize. Only when Nicolay changed his mind and accepted the consular position was the path clear for Brooks.

In Paris, George would not be alone. Two days before Lincoln's assassination, Hay wrote to a friend that he planned to "sail as soon as the President can spare me . . . I am to be Secretary of the Legation of the United States at Paris. I think it will be a pleasant place for study and observation. I shall no doubt enjoy it for a year or so—not very long, as I do not wish to exile myself in these important and interesting times." For some time, Hay had hungered for a larger role. An army major, he had done a brief turn as a staff officer in the field. He had gone to Florida in vain hopes of reconstructing its citizenry. He was now ready for a year abroad. A former presidential secretary and diplomat could surely return to a promising public or private career. Confiding to his brother Charles that the appointment presented a "pleasant and honorable way of leaving my present post which I should have left in any event very soon," Hay admitted that he had grown "thoroughly sick of certain aspects of life here." The plan was to remain in Washington to help effect a smooth transition. In early April, Nicolay embarked on a short trip to Cuba, to restore his health. Upon

his return, the two men would train a new White House staff, return to Pittsfield for Nicolay's wedding, and sail for Paris. "Every young man has work to do at home, in this age," Hay affirmed. "I go away only to fit myself for more serious work when I return."

John Hay would later remember April 14 as "a day of deep and tranquil happiness throughout the United States. It was Good Friday, observed by a portion of the people as an occasion of fasting and religious meditation . . . The thanksgiving of the nation found its principal expression at Charleston Harbor, where . . . at noon General Robert Anderson raised over Fort Sumter the identical flag lowered and saluted by him four years before; the surrender of Lee giving a more transcendent importance to this ceremony, made stately with orations, music, and military display." The Union victory at Appomattox Court House just days earlier sounded the final death knell for the Confederacy, and though the war was not yet formally concluded, most Americans understood that they were living in its final hours. Hay, who spent the afternoon at the White House, testified that

> the day was one of unusual enjoyment to Mr. Lincoln. His son Robert had returned from the field with General Grant, and the President spent an hour with the young captain in delighted conversation over the campaign. He denied himself generally to the throng of visitors, admitting only a few friends. In the afternoon he went for a long drive with Mrs. Lincoln. His mood, as it had been all day, was singularly happy and tender. He talked much of the past and future; after four years of trouble and tumult he looked forward to four years of comparative quiet and normal work; after that he expected to go back to Illinois and practice law again. He was never simpler or gentler than on this day of unprecedented triumph.

Hay spent that evening drinking whiskey and talking with Bob Lincoln at the White House. Shortly before 11:00 p.m., Tad Lincoln

burst through the front door of the mansion, crying to the door-keeper Thomas Pendel, "They've killed Papa dead!" The young boy had been attending an evening performance of *Aladdin* in the company of his tutor when the management of Grover's National Theatre interrupted the show to announce that the president had been shot. His chaperone returned the grief-stricken boy home just minutes later. Upon learning the news, Hay and Robert rushed by carriage to Tenth Street, where the mortally wounded president had been transferred to the Petersen House, a boardinghouse across from Ford's Theatre. Upon their arrival, a doctor informed them that the president would not survive his wounds.

With John Hay at his side, Robert Todd Lincoln walked into the room where his father lay stretched out on a narrow bed. Unconscious from the moment of his shooting, the president "breathed with slow and regular respiration throughout the night," Hay later recalled. A hodgepodge of family friends and government officials filed in and out of the chamber: Secretary of the Navy Gideon Welles; Elizabeth Dixon, the wife of Senator James Dixon of Connecticut and a close friend of the first lady's; Secretary of War Edwin Stanton, who had all but assumed the reins of power in the wake of the shooting; Generals Henry Halleck and Montgomery Meigs; and Vice President Johnson, who briefly paid his respects but left at the urging of Stanton, who knew that Mary thought poorly of him. Robert maintained his composure throughout most of the ordeal but broke down several times in tears, leaning on Charles Sumner for support. "As the dawn came and the lamplight grew pale," Hay remembered, the president's "pulse began to fail; but his face, even then, was scarcely more haggard than those of the sorrowing men around him. His automatic moaning ceased, a look of unspeakable peace came upon his worn features, and at twenty-two minutes after seven he died. Stanton broke the silence by saying: Now he belongs to the ages." Hay was at the president's side when he passed.

The day after Lincoln's death, Nicolay was aboard a navy warship, returning from a brief excursion to Cuba. As his party entered Chesapeake Bay, they

took a pilot on board to enter Hampton Roads [and] heard from him the first news of the terrible loss the country had suffered . . . It was so unexpected, so sudden and so horrible even to think of, much less to realize that we *couldn't* believe it, and therefore remained in hope that it would prove one of the thousand groundless exaggerations which the war has brought forth during the past four years. Alas, when we reached Point Lookout at daylight this morning, the mournful reports of the minute guns that were being fired, and the flags at half-mast left us no ground for further hope.

In his sorrow, Nicolay admitted to Therena that he was "so much overwhelmed by this catastrophe that I scarcely know what to think or write . . . It would seem that Providence had exacted from him the last and only additional service and sacrifice he could give his country—that of dying for her sake. Those of us who knew him will certainly interpret his death as a sign that Heaven deemed him worthy of martyrdom."

Nicolay arrived back in Washington on Monday, April 17. Writing to Therena, he struggled to "describe the air of gloom which seems to hang over the city. As I drove up here from the Navy Yard almost every house was draped and closed, and men stood idle and listless in groups on the street corners. The Executive Mansion was dark and still as almost the grave itself." At the White House, he paid his first respects to Lincoln's corpse, which was displayed in the East Room, where "crowds are taking their last look at the President's kind face, mild and benignant as becomes the father of a mourning nation, even in death."

Hay, who was seldom at a loss for words, left little record of his feelings in the days and weeks following Lincoln's assassination. Of the two men, uncharacteristically, it was Nicolay who opened up. "After the funeral of the President on Wednesday last I felt entirely too depressed in spirits to write you a letter," he told Therena. "Words seemed so inadequate to describe my own personal sorrow at the loss

of such a friend as the President has been to me . . . that I could not bring myself up to the task of attempting to portray them in language. I think that I do not yet, and probably shall not for a long while realize what a change his death has wrought in my own personal relations, and the personal relations of almost everyone connected with the government in this city, who stood near to him."

On April 21, a week after the president's assassination, Hay and Nicolay traveled directly to Illinois, declining to join the nine-car funeral train that would transport the slain president to his final resting place in Springfield. The procession retraced the route that the presidential party had followed in 1861 to Washington, with only a few minor deviations. In every small town and city along the way, mourners lined the railways and crowded the train depots. As the train passed through Lancaster, the town's most prominent citizens, Thaddeus Stevens and James Buchanan, lifted their hats solemnly. In New York City, young Theodore Roosevelt watched the procession from the second floor of his parents' Gramercy area town house, as two hundred African American soldiers joined the official cortege; though the city had attempted to bar them from the proceedings, Secretary of War Edwin Stanton sternly interceded. Ultimately, some five million Americans paid their respects, either at public viewings of the president's casket or in somber funeral trains along packed city streets.

Hay and Nicolay were present in Springfield, where thousands of old friends and neighbors—veterans of the great political battles of the prior decade—walked somberly past the president's coffin as it lay in state at the old capitol building, where Lincoln once prophesied that the nation could not endure half slave and half free. The next day, May 4, they accompanied the procession to Oak Ridge Cemetery, where the Great Emancipator was laid to final rest. Later that evening, Anna Ridgely happened across Nicolay at a small gathering of friends. "He looked very much fatigued and his face was the picture of despair," she observed. "He did not stay very long. I suppose his heart was too sad."

The secretaries returned to Washington, where they worked at a feverish pace to box up Lincoln's papers and effects, remove their

personal belongings from the White House, and prepare themselves for the trip to Europe. They were present for the grand review of the Union army, as its columns marched by the tens of thousands through Washington. Nicolay found it an impressive affair, though left unsaid was his obvious heartache at knowing that Abraham Lincoln, not Andrew Johnson, should have been present on the grandstand. In early May, he told Therena that he was "sorry to say that I think I shall not be able to take you to Paris with me this time—but this I will talk over fully with you while at Pittsfield. I am still trying to get ready to sail about the first of June." Therena left no record of her disappointment, but she evidently presented George with a stark choice when he reached Illinois. And he took heed. Upon returning to Washington several days later, he sent instructions for their wedding:

> We will have the ceremony performed either at your house in the presence of a few friends, or at the Congregational Church by Mr. Carter, at six or seven o'clock in the evening, and then go out to Mrs. Garbutt's and have a party or reception from eight to ten o'clock as you may decide. Major Hay will be groomsman, and you must select a bridesmaid for him . . . Tell Mrs. Garbutt not to worry herself about any elaborate preparations, and we will save her what trouble and expense we can by bringing cakes, confections and berries from St. Louis . . . Make a list of Pittsfield people to be invited—only let it be large enough. Let the house be filled to overflowing—a perfect jam—and everybody will be entertained and delighted.

Nicolay asked Hay, who was in Springfield tying up loose ends, to meet him in St. Louis in early June, from which they would journey "to Pike so as to be there certainly on the evening of the 15th, when (if my plans don't fail), I shall need your services." After the wedding, Hay would have sufficient time to take a few meetings in New York and pay a last visit to the White House, "which I think you had better do, as there are still lots of your little traps lying around that I don't know

what to do with." Secretary of War Edwin Stanton had offered to send their personal boxes home to Illinois, sparing them any further trouble. In closing, Nicolay relayed more good news. "You may sport eagles the first time you wear shoulder straps. The President yesterday signed the order giving you indefinite leave of absence, without pay, but with a brevet colonelcy."

On June 15, with John Hay at his side, George was married to Therena in her parents' front parlor in Pittsfield. The ceremony was delayed a half hour by a ferocious thunderstorm, "such as Illinois can manufacture very suddenly on a June evening," their daughter later wrote. "The storm passed; the minister at last arrived. The reception at Mrs. Garbutt's was as much of a 'jam' as the bridegroom desired and proved a great success. It went down in local history as the first time ice cream was served in Pittsfield to a large evening party."

After the wedding, Hay paid a brief visit to Washington to clear his belongings out of the Executive Mansion and "found the shadow of recent experiences resting on everything." "The White House was full of new faces," he mournfully told Robert, "a swarm of orderlies at doors and windows—the offices filled with new clerks, the anterooms crowded with hungry visitors. It was worse than a nightmare. I got away as soon as I could from the place. I think it will never be again anything less than the evil days in which we left it." He walked away expecting never to set foot in the building again.

On June 24, John Hay, George Nicolay, and Therena Bates Nicolay boarded the *City of London* in New York, bound for Paris.

PART III

CHAPTER 11

Europe

S hortly before Abraham Lincoln's assassination, a letter arrived at the White House bearing the signature of John Bigelow, the outgoing American consul in Paris. A respected newspaperman with close ties to Seward and Weed, Bigelow served with distinction alongside William Dayton, the U.S. minister to France. When Dayton passed away in late 1864, Lincoln appointed Bigelow to the ministerial post. In effect, he was to be Nicolay and Hay's new boss.

"I learned yesterday with unmixed pleasure that you were to succeed me in the Paris Consulate," Bigelow wrote to Nicolay. "I only regret that your departure from the U.S. is to be so long deferred. The Spring months in Paris are the most pleasant, and the summer the most favorable for establishing yourself in an apartment." Unaware of his successor's impending nuptials, Bigelow assured him that "all things considered for the four years to come, there is not a pleasanter office in the gift of the govt. for a bachelor, in my opinion, than that to which you are appointed." Based on his personal experience, Bigelow estimated that Nicolay could "satisfactorily live here as a bachelor for from $2500 to $3000" and, for that amount, "have a nice apartment, keep a man servant, entertain when necessary at a club, and enjoy all the rational pleasures of the Metropolis," with enough wiggle room to save $2,500 each year. "Let me beg you to come without delay," he implored. "It would be a pity to lose the spring in Paris, independent of which, the sooner there is a more mature head in the Consulate the better."

From Thurlow Weed, Bigelow received assurances that Nicolay was "an intelligent, honorable man, with a bilious temperament. I *think* you will like him. Hay is a bright, gifted young man, with agreeable manners and refined tastes. I don't believe that he has been spoiled, though he has been exposed. If he remains the modest young man he was, I am *sure* you will like him." Time proved Weed right. In Nicolay, Bigelow found a smart, capable diplomat with keen political sensibilities and workmanlike efficiency, and in Hay, a charming bon vivant who quickly ingratiated himself with all members of the minister's household—not least among them his wife, Jane, of whom Hay gushed in his diary, *"Mon Dieu! qu'elle est vive, qu'elle est vive."* Long after they left Paris, the Bigelows and Hay would remain close friends and frequent correspondents.

The Nicolays spent their first years of marriage in "Paris of the Second Empire—gorgeous, perhaps a little tawdry," as their daughter later observed, "and seething with political undercurrents, for Napoleon III was already beginning to find himself embarrassed by the forces that later brought about his downfall." Though the emperor's regime was in many ways despotic and antidemocratic, it succeeded in modernizing France's public infrastructure. By the time George and Therena arrived, many of the city's narrow, winding neighborhoods, historically susceptible to insurrection and disease, had been flattened, replaced by wide, tree-lined boulevards and modern apartment houses and public buildings. Paris was still very much under construction during their tenure there, leading Hay to warn his brother that he ought to visit "the old city before the rest of it is gone." Strangers in a strange place, the Nicolays arrived armed with a letter from Horace Greeley to his sister Esther Cleveland, a resident of Paris. "I wish you to know and to advise my friend Mrs. J. G. Nicolay," he began, "who will make her first experiments in housekeeping in your city, and who will greatly profit by your experience and thrift . . . I pray you be as wise and good to her as you possibly can." During their first year in Paris, the Nicolays installed themselves temporarily at the Hôtel Chateaubriand, a middling establishment where they occupied a large, comfortable room and took their meals with the other guests. They

acclimated to communal living with good cheer, amusing themselves with gossip about the eclectic group of residents who constituted their "'monde' at the Hotel Chateaubriand." With Therena away on a summer sojourn, George reported that "the literary lady and her daughter (or relative or whatever she is—I have not had the curiosity to ask) are still there. Col. Travers is back, and our numbers have also been swelled by the addition of an elderly English lady and a daughter . . . Two little dogs are at the present the most stirring, noisy and important personages in the house. It is way far from being 'gay,' I can assure you."

The hotel was roughly two and a half miles from 79, rue de Richelieu, where the American consulate was then located. It was a twenty-minute ride by carriage, or an hour's walk, depending on the time of year. "During the winter weather in Paris the day is a myth," Nicolay complained to a friend. "I am not exaggerating when I say that the sun sets every morning at seven o'clock, and that the rest of the twenty-four hours is a night of clouds and fog." Arriving in late summer and settling in by early fall, the couple eagerly awaited the Parisian spring, which they understood to be "bright and lovely." Weather aside, Nicolay sized up Paris as "a great city, having much to admire and more to condemn; a sort of delta in a stream of human life; rather an aggregation of *debris* than a fresh healthy organic structure of vital and intelligent forces. As study, social, political and historical, it is infinitely curious and interesting. As a station of travel it is central and amusing. But as a place to live in, or to die in—well, it may do for Frenchmen."

Sometime in their second year, the family moved to a spacious apartment, their first private home together. While he attended his share of requisite diplomatic functions, the charms of Paris took a second seat to the call of fatherhood when in 1866 Therena gave birth to a baby girl. They named her Helen, after George's mother. Therena evidently enjoyed her four years in Europe. She and her husband vacationed in Italy, Switzerland, and Austria; and Paris, once they settled in, proved a charming city in which to raise a young daughter. "I wish you could take a look at the Champs-Elysées on a pleasant afternoon now," she wrote to her sister. "The costumes are so pretty. Short satin

skirts and short velvet over-dresses, in all colors. Of course the black ones are the prettiest. The upper skirts are all puffed and *puckered* in a wonderful manner, and as you inwardly think, in a shameful waste of nice velvet: but for all that they are *awfully* pretty." Though "George makes fun of everything French, from their language, their poets, their authors, down to their cooking," she found a great deal to admire. Therena admitted to having been "pretty extravagant" during their second year abroad, ordering a wardrobe of new clothing from local couture shops. "I have been wearing old dresses ever since," she explained, though before the end of her husband's tenure she commissioned several more. Though she still suffered the same headaches and eyestrain that had plagued her since childhood, she happily acceded to a French doctor's prescription of red wine and iron tablets and was consuming enough of both to "make me strong as a giant again." "Dr. tells me that I only need to 'eat and drink and be merry,' to be well."

Therena shared her husband's love of travel, though the demands of motherhood made it difficult to indulge that yearning as often as she wished. In late 1867 she wrote to her mother, "George has been gone a week on the trip [to] Vienna, Munich, Prague and Dresden. I wanted to go most awfully, but not bad enough to take Helen, and not enough to leave her. If she was only through teething I wouldn't be a bit afraid to leave her . . . I wish you could take a peep at her now," she continued. "She is sitting in her little chair, sewing away for dear life with a worsted needle on a mitten which I have just finished for her, and which she thinks is wonderfully nice. She only stops talking when she is asleep. Strange to say, although she was so dark when she was a little baby, she is a regular blonde now—so much so that she don't look pretty at all in a red dress." Though she was proficient in French, Therena gravitated to a community of American expatriates, finding companionship with a number of young women approximately her age.

Compared with the weighty responsibilities that they shouldered at the White House, Nicolay's and Hay's jobs in Paris were workaday and mostly ceremonial. Though the United States and France were involved in tense discussions surrounding the emperor's installation

of a puppet regime in Mexico, which Americans regarded as a violation of the Monroe Doctrine, neither man was engaged in any meaningful way in these bilateral talks. As first secretary, Hay performed mostly clerical and administrative duties, leaving him ample time to explore the city, take in healthy doses of French theater and museums, and run the circuit of diplomatic receptions and dinners. As consul, Nicolay devoted the better part of his day to fielding requests, large and small, from American expatriates and travelers and managing the routine affairs of a government office. "Business is dull at the Consulate," he remarked some time into his tenure.

George found great satisfaction in domestic life. During the summer of 1866, he took his wife and daughter to Switzerland, where they could better hope to avoid the cholera epidemic then sweeping through Paris and other large European cities. With Therena and Helen safely installed in a comfortable resort town, he returned to the consulate, only to realize how much he missed his family. "I won't flatter you by writing how I find every hour and at every turn, that a wife is an almost indispensable necessity in a household," he told Therena. "I look around our room, and counting the merely visible objects in it, I fancy it ought to be about the same in appearance as before you went away. Chairs, table, curtains and furniture are all in their places, and ever reinforced by your large trunk, which is still where you left it. I find there is something gone—something wanting which makes it look and feel . . . cheerless and . . . desolate." When Therena sent a picture of baby Helen, George all but gushed at "how still she must have sat. All the ladies at the house were very much pleased with it and pronounced it a great success." "Kiss Helen for me," he instructed, "for being so good when her picture was taken." When a second photograph arrived, Nicolay wryly observed that Helen "appears like [Dickens's] Major Bagstock, 'wide awake and staring,' as though she were trying to fathom the meaning of all this shooting at her through a bright brass tube without powder."

"I received your letter of Monday last," he wrote on another occasion, "in which you tell me that Helen is taking to bread and milk. Is she not too young yet to begin eating solid food? Are you sure it is

good for her?" In 1868, Nicolay installed his family for several weeks at a shore house in Normandy, to spare them the discomfort and dangers of the summer heat. Toward the end of July, he planned to join them for a family reunion. "There is a little tot who has been gathering shells on the beach at Houlgate for me today," he boasted to Hay, "whose embrace tomorrow evening at half past six will make me forget everything except the happy consciousness of again hearing her gleeful prattle." It had taken little time to transform the "the bull-dog in the anteroom" into a proud, doting father.

John Hay was not long in Paris before he began to sour on the call of diplomatic ceremony, with its endless cycle of introductions and flummery. "One torment of diplomatic life," he noted in his diary, "is that you never know the names of these agreeable fellows. They lose all identity in their violet coats and Imperial moustaches. You do not hear their names when you are presented to them, and if you look upon the official list of the officers of the Emperor's household you only find that you may take your choice of a dozen names for the man you are looking after." Though office work and diplomatic functions only punctuated the many hours that he spent exploring the city, Hay was intrigued, and in no small measure repulsed, by the opulence and antidemocratic spirit of empire. Invited to a Christmas reception at the palace, he reluctantly "hired a carriage and two servants . . . It was a highly respectable looking affair, not fresh enough to look hired, with a couple of solemn flunkies that seemed to have been in the family for at least a generation." Arriving at the home of General John Dix, who succeeded Bigelow in November 1866, Hay observed the new American minister approach the "court carriage, the Imperial arms blazing on the panels and the harness, drawn by four horses and accompanied by two mounted outriders. Everything covered with tawdry, tarnished gold lace. It seemed like the Triumphal Car in a flourishing circus. Into this vehicle mounted the General and the Chamberlain, Hoffman and I following in our sham-private *remise;* and we had all the honors of a stare from the *badauds* on the asphalt of the Champs Elysées as the party lumbered down to the Tuileries. We were all in our Army uniform."

Upon reaching their destination, the American party was escorted by the emperor's "violet people" to a large anteroom, where they "were presented to the Duc de Cambacérès, a jaunty old gentleman, lean and shaven and wigged—long also. He bowed lavishly and seemed distressed that nobody would sit down." When finally an adjoining door opened and the Americans were "ushered into The Presence," Hay was amused by Dix, who "looked anxiously around for the Emperor, advancing undecidedly, until a little man, who was standing in front of the Throne, stepped forward to meet him. Everybody bowed profoundly as the Duc de Cambacérès gave the name and the title of the General. The little man bowed, and the General, beginning to recognize in him a dim likeness to the Emperor's portrait, made his speech to him."

Accustomed to the democratic ethos of the United States, where, for better or worse, ordinary citizens could rush the public rooms at the Executive Mansion during presidential levees, helping themselves to snippets of drapery and carpeting or making souvenirs of the White House silver, Hay scorned the "rich lights and soft shadows" that contrived to enlarge "the little man who is listening or seeming to listen to the General's address." Compared with his slain idol, who had twice earned a popular mandate to govern, Napoleon III seemed a second-rate pretender. Hay could scarcely conceal his disgust. "If our Republican eyes can stand such a dazzling show, let us look at him," he scribbled in his diary.

> Short and stocky, he moved with a queer, sidelong gait, like a gouty crab; a man so wooden looking that you would expect his voice to come rasping out like a watchman's rattle. A complexion like crude tallow—marked for Death, whenever death wants him—to be taken sometime in half an hour, or left, neglected by the Skeleton King, for years, perhaps, if properly coddled . . . He stands there as still and impassive as if carved in oak for a ship's figurehead. He looks not unlike one of those rude inartistic statues. His legs are too short—his body too long. He never looks well but on a throne or on a horse, as kings ought.

When at last Hay was presented, the emperor, "clearly wishing to
be very civil, as it is most rare that a monarch addresses a Secretary of
Legation, said, 'But you are very young to be a Col-o-nel. Did you
make the war in America?' I wanted to insist that older and wickeder
men than I were responsible for that crime, but I thought it best to
answer the intention rather than the grammar, and said I had a hum-
ble part in the war.

" 'Infanterie or cavalerie?'

" 'The general staff!' "

The emperor, unimpressed, turned to his next guest.

With the Bigelows bound for home, Hay decided he had seen
enough of Paris. Now twenty-eight years old, he had little material
wealth to show for his years of work but an orange grove in Florida
and a vineyard in Illinois, neither of which brought steady investment
income, and a modest sum in cash and war bonds. "I must begin to
occupy myself seriously in earning a livelihood," he told Seward, "and
the first step in my preparations is necessarily the resignation of my
present position." To his uncle Milton, Hay was more candid, acknowl-
edging that he had "got as much out of this place as there is to be got
by one. I have lived within my means & have learned French and the
machinery and mechanisms of the Diplomatic service." In the short
term, Hay was certain that he could move to Washington or New York
and earn a decent living by writing for a magazine or newspaper, but
he was "getting too old to be drifting about much longer. I want some
steady employment. I could get anything reasonable I asked for in
Washington but I would rather not hold any more offices if I can help
it." Instead, he asked whether he might join Milton's law firm. "I have
forgotten most of the law I read with you," he admitted, "& would
have to learn it all over again. I am not even a good clerk as I know
very little about money or business. It is nearly an even chance whether
I would ever get to be worth my salt at the bar, but I feel like trying it
on." Milton's reply must have been disheartening. There was no room
for John in his small but thriving practice.

Early 1867 found Hay in Washington, D.C., where he made the
rounds of his old acquaintances and announced his availability

for employment. Only two years earlier he had scorned the unwashed office seekers who banged daily on the president's door in search of patronage and favor. Now he was one of them, and he hated it. Everything about Washington seemed tawdry. "I drove to Willard's," he privately noted, "saw the same dead beats hanging around the office, the same listless loafers moving gloomily up and down, pensively expectorating." After paying his respects to Ward Hill Lamon, Hay made his way to the State Department, where Seward greeted him warmly.

"Well, John Hay," he said with a grin, "so you got tired of it and came home."

"Yes," replied Hay, "I had enough of the place and the place had enough of me."

Seward approved of the move, launching a "clever disposition on the dangers of a man holding office—the desiccation and fossilizing process . . . and saying he feared Nicolay was getting into that way. I assured him Nicolay was not; that he was single-heartedly pursuing 10,000 dollars, and that when he got it he would come home and go to his ranch. He was glad to hear it, he said." Seward nevertheless asked whether he wanted or needed a job, and Hay, sensing that it would be wise to hedge his bets, answered that he would "like anything worth having, if it could be given to me without embarrassment to him or the President at the present time." Several days later, Seward offered him the post of private secretary in his own office, but Hay declined, assuring him that "if he wished my personal services in the Department that of course they were entirely at his service; but that if he had done this out of his own usual kindness for me, that I thought it best to decline; that I had better go home and see my parents for the present." Seward assured him that the job was there for the taking if he changed his mind and, for good measure, had even proposed Hay "to the President . . . as Minister to Sweden." It was a kind gesture, though Hay knew very well that he was unqualified for the post, and in any event Johnson "had another man for it."

Much had changed in the year and a half since Hay's departure for Europe. American politics had descended into a blood feud between the Republican-controlled Congress and the Tennessee Democrat who

succeeded Lincoln as president. Though a committed wartime union-
ist, Johnson preferred a swift and lenient approach to Reconstruc-
tion that would invariably deprive freed slaves of full citizenship and
protection. Early in his tenure, he summarily readmitted Southern
states to the Union and issued a general amnesty proclamation that
applied to all but a small number of former Confederate civilian and
military officials and large landholders. (Soon thereafter, he issued per-
sonal pardons to many of these powerful Southern elites.) The presi-
dent turned a blind eye when multiple Southern legislatures passed
"black codes"—restrictive legislation that denied freedmen the right
to free assembly, movement, and speech and that pressed African
Americans, including children, into long terms of compulsory servi-
tude if they refused to enter into coercive labor contracts with planta-
tion owners. When Congress assembled in December 1865, the
Republican majority defied Johnson by refusing to seat newly elected
members from Southern states, many of whom had doffed their gray
uniforms only six months earlier. The House and the Senate then
passed expansive civil rights legislation over the president's veto, ne-
gating the effects of the black codes, as well as the Fourteenth Amend-
ment to the Constitution, guaranteeing full citizenship to all
Americans, regardless of race. With the relationship between Con-
gress and the president at a nadir, in March 1867 the Republican su-
permajority enacted new legislation dividing the South into military
districts and placing most of it under military rule.

Though most Republican congressmen opposed Johnson's Recon-
struction policy and voted in favor of both civil rights and military
occupation, wartime divisions between radical, moderate, and conser-
vative Republicans had grown more pronounced by the time Hay re-
turned to the United States. Radicals believed that the rebel states had
effectively committed "state suicide," leaving them outside the Union;
the citizens of these "conquered territories" enjoyed no claim to the
protections guaranteed by the U.S. Constitution. Some radicals, like
Charles Sumner, pushed for restoration on terms of full enfranchise-
ment for ex-slaves, while others, like Thaddeus Stevens, proposed seiz-
ing the plantations of wealthy white landowners and dividing them

"Nico & I immortalized ourselves by having [a photo] done in group
with the Presdt." John G. Nicolay, Abraham Lincoln, and John Hay,
November 1863

"I'm Keeper of the President's Conscience." John Hay in 1861, as a new presidential secretary

John Hay, summer 1862, in a photograph taken at the Treasury Department

"All these things will make stirring times, and I hardly realize that they are so, even as I write them." John G. Nicolay as presidential secretary

"To learn to write is like learning to swim; everyone must teach himself." John G. Nicolay as a young editor, 1850s

Robert Todd Lincoln, circa 1865

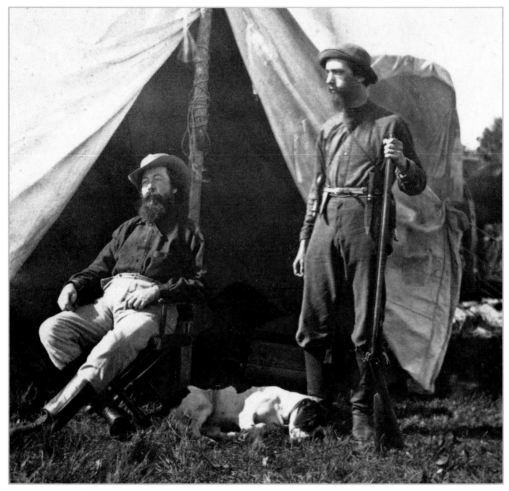

John G. Nicolay with Indian Commissioner William P. Dole, Minnesota, 1862

"She has kept me young and allowed one to smile complacently at my grey hairs." Therena Bates Nicolay in later years

"The mere money value was greatly enhanced by the . . . opportunity of looking down from the organ loft, on Sunday mornings, on an olive cheek and a knot of blue-black hair." Therena Bates, 1860s

John G. Nicolay in his study; his daughter, Helen Nicolay, seated on the sofa

"I do not let any unsatisfied ambitions worry me." John G. Nicolay in later years

John Hay signing a treaty with Spain in the president's office, 1899

"I have had success beyond all the dreams of my boyhood."
Secretary of State John Hay, 1905

into small plots for freedmen and loyal white yeomen farmers. Moderates tended to recoil at the notion that Southern whites be stripped of their citizenship or suffer wholesale expropriation, but they supported the notion of equal rights, including universal male enfranchisement. Competing with the radicals and moderates were a small but influential number of conservative Republicans who rejected plans for a wholesale reconstruction of Southern society.

These intra-party divisions were very much on display when Hay returned from Europe. During his brief stay in Washington, he determined that the "Copperheads and Democrats who now form almost the entire support of the President, are continually boring him for offices and accusing Mr. Seward of wickedly keeping in their places the old radical Lincoln appointees." When he stopped to take a meal at Willard's, a number of radicals stepped up to shake his hand. They assumed that he had been made a "martyr"—displaced in favor of a conservative Johnson loyalist—and were "a little disappointed when they found I was none." Hay remained a great personal admirer of Seward, who occupied a lonely ideological space somewhere between the president and his erstwhile Republican allies. At the same time, he agreed with a radical friend who was "disgusted with Johnson. His first words to me were, 'Everything has changed—You find us all Copperheads . . . You will find the home of virtue has become the haunt of vice.' [Henry] Adams said, 'A man asked me the other day if I had been at the White House lately, and I told him no. I want to remember that house as Lincoln left it.' Everyone I met uttered some such expression. It is startling to see how utterly without friends the President is." Privately, Hay lamented that Johnson "would ruin the best cause a man ever fought for."

Like the vast majority of Republicans, Hay found himself in accordance with ideas that only five years earlier would have been unthinkable: black suffrage, equality under the law, and the subordination of states' rights to a strong central state. Visiting the Capitol as the House of Representatives debated the military Reconstruction bill, Hay spoke with a conservative congressman who "was really despondent about the course things were taking—deprecating most earnestly the

abdication of civil power in favor of the irresponsible military. I thought the case was not hopeless—bad as it was—as Congress could at any time resume the powers it now delegates for a temporary purpose." Hay acknowledged that it was "un-Anglo-Saxon to perpetuate" martial law on a civilian population and acknowledged the "miserable situation of the South," but he concluded that military Reconstruction was a "necessary" instrument to secure the hard-fought gains of the Civil War.

If Hay had learned anything during his tenure as a presidential aide, it was the virtue of cultivating friends in all camps. During his stopover in Washington he accepted two invitations to the White House, finding it "more richly and carefully furnished than in my time." "The President was very cordial to me," he noted, but the "crowd not choice . . . scarcely any distinguished people and none squalid. We used to have plenty of both."

In Paris, Hay had kept a happy distance from the political wars consuming his native country. In Washington, he found them impossible to escape. Back in Warsaw, he welcomed the opportunity to drop out of the world and took simple delight in "digging some, planting, pruning . . . I find a singular love for that kind of work in myself. It is the sense of justification it gives me for now doing nothing." To Nicolay, he confided that he was once again "a little at sea about what I shall do. The law has been a magnificent business for the past two years—a little duller now . . . I may go at law after I have rested a while. Everybody, without exception, tells me I am looking very ill. It has discouraged me a little." There was "poverty everywhere," he warned. Perhaps regretting his premature abandonment of a well-paid government post, Hay advised Nicolay to "stay where you are for the present . . . You had better not come home till you are kicked out, and our crazy friends in the Senate have legislated all the dead-beats now in office into an eternity of bread and butter."

By late summer, Hay was short on money and out of options. When Seward offered him the post of chargé d'affaires in Vienna, at a princely sum of $6,000 per year, he readily snapped up the opportunity. Sep-

tember found him in the seat of the Hapsburg Empire, where he installed himself in "an apartment of three good rooms, kitchen & servants' room for which I pay 500 florins [approximately $200 per month]" and set immediately upon exploring the city's music and café scene. "You ought to come see this town," he told Nicolay. "The asses say, as the asses say everywhere, that it is only unpleasant in summer . . . But if a man be not an ass he knows there never was a town north of the tropics that was not [more] pleasant in summer than in winter."

Hay used his central European sinecure as a platform for travel. He traveled west to visit the Nicolays in Paris, then back east, where he "poked around Poland lonesomely enough, but fully compensated by the unusual and peculiar towns I passed through." In Warsaw, he attended the Polish opera. In Cracow, "the quaintest and most entirely satisfactory little town I ever saw," he toured the local cathedral and walked through "a regular medieval Jews' quarter." In November he was bound for Constantinople, stopping along the way to tour small towns on the Danube, where the weather was "perfect . . . June at its prettiest in Illinois." "I hate the water worse than any cat," he reminded Nicolay. "It will be hard to get me on the Mediterranean again. But I feel very anxious to make that Nile trip with you. When do you think of starting? I shall try to take a flight into Italy this winter—I shall never have time to do it thoroughly & then, if I can, next spring, after I leave here, take a rapid run through Spain." Returning to Vienna, Hay attended an imperial wedding where he "had a small confab with the Kaiser." With bemusement he reported to John Bigelow that the "Emperor is a great admirer of President Johnson! Or else he thought it would be flattering to tell me so. I grinned horribly a ghastly smile." Hay remained unimpressed by the trappings and excesses of empire and encouraged by the stirrings of democratic reform that he observed in Austria. "It is curious & instructive to see this people starting off on the awkward walk of political babyhood," he told Bigelow. "The aristocracy are furious and the Kaiser a little bewildered at every new triumph of the democratic and liberal principle. But I don't think they

can stop the machine now—though they may get their fingers mashed in the cogs . . . If ever, in my green and salad days, I sometimes vaguely doubted, I am safe now. I am a Republican till I die. When we get to Heaven, we can try a monarchy, perhaps."

In the coming months there was more travel. Nicolay paid Hay a visit in September 1867, then returned the following January with Therena and Helen on a circuitous route back from their family holiday in Italy. Vienna made for a pleasant sojourn, but by mid-1868 Hay once again found himself drifting. He feared that he would become just another civil servant "of prime talents and ambition, sinking year after year into the baleful quicksand of routine."

In theory, Hay could easily have remained in his post until the new administration took office the following year. Nicolay also expected his tenure to end at that time. Both men thought poorly of the president, but their fortunes were hitched to Seward, who was due to retire from public life at the close of Johnson's term. "I have been hoping all along that the *status quo* would be maintained a while longer," Nicolay wrote to Hay that summer, "so that we might take that boat ride up the Nile next winter. Now I suppose we shall have to rub off the slate." By late summer, Hay had resigned his post, stopping only to take a last whirl through Paris and London, where he attended a public reading by Charles Dickens, before sailing home. Once again, he set his sights on a lucrative career in law or business.

Matters did not go as well as planned. By December he was back in Washington, in "peaceful pursuit of a fat office." Seward, now a lame duck, agreed to keep an eye out for another suitable post and "will wrestle with Andy for anything that turns up." Hay advised Nicolay to "stick it out at Paris as late as possible . . . [D]on't you come home before the 1st of March or so. It takes a month to do anything here and you can't afford to get stale before the inauguration." President-elect Ulysses S. Grant, though a Republican, was "as close-mouthed as ever," and it was impossible to say whether their friends would be in a position to help them attain meaningful and remunerative government posts, if they opted to remain in public service. To pick up extra money,

Hay began selling poems and sketches to mass-market magazines. He also tried his hand on the lecture circuit, giving a paid talk in Buffalo titled "The Progress of Democracy in Europe." Reviewing the slow but steady march of anti-imperial politics, from the French Revolution through the Austro-Prussian War, he was "severe upon Louis Napoleon," according to a reviewer. "He doesn't like Bismarck." But he was, on balance, "hopeful for Democracy in Europe."

In the fall of 1869, Hay set sail for Madrid, where his friends managed to secure his appointment as secretary of the legation. The timing was near perfect. A year earlier, Queen Isabella II had been deposed in Spain's Glorious Revolution, an event soon followed by the establishment of a new constitution granting universal male suffrage and broader civil liberties. "I have determined, *malgré* my better judgment, to go to Spain for a little while," he informed Bigelow. "I have read and thought a good deal about revolutions, and I cannot resist an opportunity so favorable of lifting the very pot lid and seeing the 'hellbroth seethe and bubble.'" From his perch in Madrid, Hay contributed a series of articles to the *Atlantic Monthly,* chronicling the folkways and habits of Spanish society. Later bundled into a book titled *Castilian Days,* his essays also ruminated on the many structural challenges to Spanish democracy, including the "twin despotism of the Church and the king" and, more generally, the country's "blind reverence for things that have been." Despite these historical obstacles, Hay detected a "new and beneficent spirit" in Spanish politics. "The day that is coming is not to be tranquil and cloudless. The transformations of systems are not accomplished like those of the pantomimes. There will be bloodshed and treasons and failures enough to discourage and appall the faint-hearted. But the current cannot be turned backward." In a final chapter titled "Necessity of the Republic," Hay concluded that "the condition of the world has changed greatly. We are nearing the close of the nineteenth century. The whole world, bound together . . . by telegraphs and railways, is moving forward along the line of nations to larger and ampler liberty. No junta of prominent gentlemen can come together and amiably arrange a programme for a nation, in

opposition to this universal tendency." Democratic republics would ebb and flow, but their general progress "cannot well be checked. The people have the right to govern themselves, even if they do it ill."

Helen Nicolay later claimed that "every month that my father and John Hay spent in Europe increased their belief that, whatever its faults, the American system of government was the best yet devised." Their intense chauvinism was a product of experience. Years earlier, as he peered out his office window, gazing through a spyglass at the navy ships steaming up the Potomac, Abraham Lincoln told them that the "central idea pervading" the Civil War was "the necessity of proving that popular government is not an absurdity." In 1863 they stood near his side in Gettysburg when he promised a grieving nation that "government of the people, by the people, for the people, shall not perish from the earth." They saw young men willingly lay down their lives and fortunes in defense of that same proposition, and former slaves don army uniforms to achieve their right to personhood and citizenship. The contrast between America and Europe was too sharp to go unobserved. Ever more the pessimist, Nicolay did not share Hay's faith in the steady, forward progress of European democracy. "The heap will smoulder for perhaps a quarter of a century longer," he predicted, "and allied King-craft and Priestcraft is still the 'worm that dieth not.'" Upon returning to the United States, he went so far as to secure proof of his American citizenship from a federal court in Illinois. "After four years in Paris," Helen later explained, "he had reached the conclusion that American citizenship was something very precious, to be surrounded by every possible safeguard."

Hay remained in Spain for less than a year. "I am glad I committed the folly of coming," he admitted to Nicolay. "I have seen a great deal and learned something. I speak the language well enough to be understood and not well enough to be taken for a . . . Spaniard—a Dieu ne plaise." Three plum assignments in the diplomatic corps in five years had afforded Hay opportunities that few Americans of his generation could claim. He had mastered three languages, traveled widely throughout Europe, and established relationships with leading men on

the Continent. His grasp of foreign affairs was first-class. But he felt at sea. "I was never so thoroughly out of the world before," he told John Bigelow.

That fall, John Hay came home. He was thirty-two years old, with more than half a lifetime still ahead of him.

CHAPTER 12

Pike County Balladeer

The Nicolays understood that their tenure in Paris would likely draw to a close with William Seward's departure from the State Department. Though George made lukewarm overtures to friends in the Senate, it became clear in the months between Ulysses S. Grant's election and his inauguration that the new administration intended to redistribute plum jobs to a growing list of friends and petitioners. The Paris consulate was one such prize. Shortly before Lincoln's death, George had bought a small farm in Kansas; his brother Jacob had tended the land in his absence. "Should the worse come to the worst," he told Hay, "and my *caput officium* (Is that good Latin?) roll in the dust, I would retire with dignity to Dragoon Creek, and inscribe myself for the horticultural prize at the State Fair." George never did settle there, though his daughter was convinced that "during the years the deed remained in my father's name, its ownership gave him a comfortable assurance that if all other plans went awry, he could settle down on Dragoon Creek and live in comfort, if not in luxury."

Returning to the United States in the spring of 1869, George and Therena lived a peripatetic existence for the next three years. They passed their winters at a rickety old mansion in Florida, where both husband and wife could hope to restore their chronically unsteady health. Most summers they sojourned in New Hampshire, riding horses, visiting the seashore with their daughter, and hiking through the White Mountains. Missing home, in 1871 they bought a small farm

outside Springfield, where they passed the autumn and spring months. George let the productive parts of the land to a neighbor and focused on restoring and landscaping the gardens.

For a time, it seemed that George would assume the editorship of the *Chicago Republican,* but upon inspecting the paper's books, he determined that the venture was financially untenable. Instead, he continued to wander with the seasons. For the first time in over two decades, he had no career, no job, no goals. Years later, Helen recalled the delight that her father took in sitting by the side of a stream that ran through their rented farmhouse in New England. "Small water lilies floated on its surface. Little pools along its edge reflected the gorgeous red of cardinal flowers, and there were shade trees near by. My father enjoyed such small beautiful things more keenly than any other man I have known." Helen remembered that "when he needed all the courage and patience he could find, he found both on the banks of that little river."

Absent from Washington for five years, George had not been present for the political mayhem of the early Reconstruction era. He remained on close terms with most Republican members of Congress, but Lincoln's death and Seward's retirement left him without power or standing. He tried his hand at poetry but was disappointed when his old acquaintance William Dean Howells politely declined his submission for the *Atlantic*. He attempted to start a newspaper in St. Louis, a growing border-state city with a sizable German population and a vibrant Republican Party. That, too, proved a nonstarter. During the winter of 1870–71, he wrote a series of dispatches from Florida for the *New York Times*. Focusing raptly on the same exotic landscape that John Hay had found so beguiling during his journeys in 1863 and 1864, Nicolay described in vivid terms the half-finished regeneration of a tropical paradise laid to ruin not so much by battle as by abandonment during the war. Otherwise silent on the political issues of the Reconstruction era, George betrayed an unforgiving political bias when he praised the "Northern men" who "restored business, reorganized society, reestablished political order. They re-built the burned piers and warehouses of Jacksonville, they started anew its dilapidated sawmills, they

repaired its railroad, they freighted its boats and schooners with
Northern goods. They reconstructed the state and provided it with a
new Constitution." He likened Northern-born "carpetbaggers" to the
"Daniel Boones and the Davy Crocketts of our Western history"—
storied pioneers who tamed and democratized an unruly land. In a
revealing aside, Nicolay regretted that the war failed to eradicate
Florida's plantation system and instead "kept the ownership of large
tracts in single hands." Though he did not elaborate on how Congress
might otherwise have remedied the concentration of economic and
political power in the postbellum South, Nicolay surely understood
that his position aligned neatly with the land redistribution policies
recently advocated by radical Republicans.

On the strength of his Florida articles, Nicolay explored the possi-
bility of a permanent position at the *Times* but learned that the only
open spot was for an evening editor, an unsuitable arrangement for a
husband and father. The publishers invited him to contribute more
freelance work, but at $10 per column the offer was nowhere near lu-
crative enough. When the American minister to Bogotá resigned in
1872 to run for Congress, George appealed to anyone who would hear
him out—Senators James Harlan and Zachariah Chandler, Vice Presi-
dent Schuyler Colfax, Secretary of the Treasury George Boutwell—for
an endorsement. That all pledged their support spoke to the enduring
strength of Nicolay's relationships. That the president gave the job to
another man spoke to the limits of his influence. Later that year, at the
prodding of Robert Todd Lincoln, who was married to Harlan's daugh-
ter, Nicolay was appointed marshal of the U.S. Supreme Court. With
relatively easy duties when the court was in session, and virtually none
at all when it was not, the post came with a comfortable salary, a plum
office in the U.S. Capitol, and renewed proximity to Washington's
power center. From Springfield, Milton Hay sent hearty congratula-
tions. He could name "few more desirable" assignments and would
not, if he were Nicolay, trade it for one paying twice the salary. Milton
was being kind. It had been many years since Lincoln's secretaries
rolled their eyes at the hordes of office seekers banging down their
doors for favors. Now, as they approached middle age, their perspec-

tive on political patronage had changed markedly. "M. Hay told me you might have been Secretary of State if you had made any push for it: or Clerk of the Supreme Court," John Hay wrote in jest. "A man's friends have excellent memories for these things after the thing has gone by. But you ought to keep your eyes peeled, and ask without reserve for anything you want. Modesty is the most fatal . . . of vices."

Shortly before leaving his post in Madrid, Hay assured his former boss John Bigelow that he would not be without wherewithal upon his return to the United States. "I have a sure income of two or three hundred dollars in ordinary times," he figured, taking into account his freelance writing and interest in government bonds, "and that is opulence in Warsaw—where living costs nothing and where I have all the comforts of a home, within five minutes walk of the station. If I go away from that bower of innocent repose, I shall spend more and make more." Though Hay genuinely hoped to spend time tending to his vineyard and visiting with family, his friends hoped that he would put his talents to more productive work. He initially agreed to join George as assistant editor at the *Chicago Republican,* but, as he explained to William Dean Howells, the paper was "hopelessly" mired in financial trouble. "Nicolay and I agreed in advising the proprietors to sell out on any terms, and they have done it." From Warsaw, where his "shy little vineyard made its debut with 240" gallons of "good wine," Hay told Nicolay that he had been in conversation with their friend Whitelaw Reid, then deputy editor of the *New-York Tribune.* On the strength of Hay's foreign contacts, Reid was interested in offering him a position as the newspaper's Paris correspondent, but after five years abroad the prospect of returning to Europe was unappealing. "I will try to shin around and keep afloat until spring," he decided, and would be "tempted to follow you to Florida—a position which will probably increase as the mercury sinks."

Hay soon resumed talks *"au sérieux"* with Reid and joined the *Tribune*'s New York staff at a salary of $50 per week, a generous sum for that time. If he felt strange being in the employ of a man whom he had once chaperoned at Niagara Falls, Hay said nothing about it. Almost

instantly, he became one of "Greeley's young men," a group of thirty-somethings to whom the venerable old editor gradually relinquished control of his newspaper. Reid was first among equals and de facto editor in chief. Among the other wunderkinder was Noah Brooks, who had conspired years before to replace the secretaries during Lincoln's second term. Hay explained to Nicolay that his principal responsibility involved writing editorials—mostly, but not exclusively, on foreign and diplomatic affairs. The first few weeks proved difficult, as he was unaccustomed to churning out regular copy. Having held three diplomatic posts in five years, on the heels of his White House tenure, he was uniquely qualified to comment on a range of topics. "I cannot regard it as a successful experiment as yet," he admitted, "though Reid and the rest seem satisfied." In fact, only weeks after his arrival, Reid raised his weekly salary to $65. A year later he was earning $100. "I have seen now enough of your capacity in sudden emergencies and in a wide scope to be ready to repeat the assurance which I gave you at the beginning," Reid told Hay, "that journalism is sure to prove your true field." Once again, Hay accidentally found himself in a position of real influence. Though the paper was undergoing a generational change in leadership, what Ralph Waldo Emerson once told Thomas Carlyle—that "Greeley does the thinking for the whole West at $2 per year for his paper"—was essentially still true.

In October 1871, just a year into his tenure at the *Tribune*, Hay hastily packed his bags and made the arduous, thirty-eight-hour journey by rail to Chicago, where a great fire lasting three days ultimately consumed the whole of downtown. Finding that the telegraph lines were backlogged by many thousands of messages, he managed to talk the Associated Press into transmitting one of his columns; he sent the others back to New York by mail. Enjoying front-page placement in the *Tribune,* as well as national distribution in other papers, Hay described for millions of readers "six miles, more or less, of the finest conflagration ever seen. I have here before me smoking ruins and ruins that have broken themselves of smoking; churches as grand in their dilapidation as Melrose by moonlight; mountains of brick and mortar and forests of springing chimneys; but I turned to them all this

morning to hunt for the spot where the fire started." Venturing through the smoke and rubble to that "mean little street of shabby wooden houses" where Mrs. O'Leary (soon of lasting fame) lived, he managed to find the "warped and weather-beaten shanty" where "last Saturday night, came a woman with a lamp to the barn behind the house, to milk the cow with the crumpled temper, that kicked the lamp, that spilled the kerosene, that fired the straw that burned Chicago." Walking around the rear of the house, Hay spied "Our Lady of the Lamp" knitting by the window. Her husband was talking with two neighbors and greeted the inquiring newspaperman with "sleepy, furtive eyes. I asked him what he knew about the origin of the fire. He glanced up at his friends and said, civilly, he knew very little; he was waked up at about 9 o'clock by the alarm, and fought from that time to save his house . . . He seemed fearful that all Chicago was coming down upon him for prompt and integral payment of that $200,000,000 his cow had kicked over." His work done, Hay left Chicago for Springfield, assuring Reid that he had "done as well as I could. I have a clean conscience, [having] given the Great Moral Organ 16 hours a day ever since I arrived."

Hay kept late hours at the paper, often working until two o'clock in the morning to shepherd his copy through editorial review and layout, though he admitted to John Bigelow that he "waste[d] two-thirds of my time trying to think of something to write about." For hours at a time, he sat "staring at the City Hall in blank imbecility." At his best, Hay churned out as many as four columns each day, on topics as diverse as European diplomacy, the dissolution of liberty, the secretary of the Treasury, and the defects of the jury system. The *Tribune* offices were a flurry of activity at almost all hours, with some of the brightest men of their generation jockeying for chairs and desks, of which there seemed to be a chronic shortage. When Greeley left the paper in 1872 to run for president, Reid inherited his mantle. Without formal title, Hay became his second-in-command. Among his peers, he was greatly admired. Widely read and traveled, formally educated, and a veteran of the Lincoln White House, he struck his fellow journalists as several cuts above ordinary. "It was a liberal education in the delights of intellectual life," observed one of his colleagues, "to sit in intimate

companionship with John Hay and watch the play of that well-stored and brilliant mind . . . the wide knowledge of men and nations, of peoples and governments; the familiar and ever-ready knowledge of all that is best in literature, and over it all the play of a humor which was next-door neighbor to melancholy and all the finer for that close association." It was around this time that friends saw Hay and Reid playing a game of leapfrog over the ash cans outside the Century Club, after shutting down its bar in the twilight hours of morning. After years of wandering, he had regained his "rocking walk" and stride.

Hay's growing influence at the *New-York Tribune* dovetailed with his emerging renown as a poet, essayist, and short-story writer. Though he contributed occasional poems to Northern newspapers and magazines during the war, his breakthrough moment came in 1871, when his work appeared five times in the *Atlantic,* six times in *Harper's Weekly,* and once in *Harper's Monthly.* Finally abandoning his trademark mimicry of romantic English verse, Hay returned to the dialect and setting that he knew most intimately. His Pike County ballads, cast in the vernacular of southern Illinois, were first published and then republished in dozens of newspapers and magazines in 1870. A pamphlet edition sold as quickly as it came off the presses, followed shortly thereafter by a 167-page book. Hay initially played down the value of his poems. He professed to have dashed them off mostly for sport, as well as for easy money (*Harper's* paid him as much as $50 per contribution). He told Nicolay that he was amazed to find that his "ridiculous rhyme" was having a "ridiculous run." "Little Breeches," the first of his efforts, "has been published in nearly the whole country press from here to the Rockies. As my initials are not known . . . I have not been disgraced by it."

Hay's volume opened with "Jim Bludso," a poem that he privately judged "more widely liked and denounced than Little Breeches." Like all of the verse in *Pike County Ballads*, it spoke the vernacular that Hay knew as a young boy living in a river town along the Mississippi.

> Wall, no! I can't tell whar he lives,
> Becase he don't live you see;

Leastways, he's got out of the habit
Of livin' like you and me.
Whar have you been for the last three year
That you haven't heard folks tell
How Jimmy Bludso passed in his checks
The night of the Prairie Bell?

The story of a steamboat engineer who sacrifices his life to hold off a
boiler-room fire long enough for the crew and passengers to debark to
safety, "Jim Bludso" revealed Hay's evolving relationship with the
West. As a college student, he apologized awkwardly for his coarse
upbringing; now in his thirties, with a decade of political and diplo-
matic experience under his belt, he saw something valuable in the small
river towns and prairie villages he had known so intimately in his
youth. Also evident in the Pike County ballads is a strong democratic
spirit, nurtured during his White House tenure. In his younger days, as
in his later years, after he married into considerable wealth, it was easy
for Hay's detractors to write him off as a snob. It was true that he did
not suffer fools (or, more accurately, that he suffered them all too
gladly). But his lifelong devotion to Lincoln fostered in Hay a theoreti-
cal reverence for common men and common places. His wartime dia-
ries and letters often compared the Washington cognoscenti in terms
sharply unflattering with the collective wisdom of Northern soldiers
and voters. His regard for hardworking, honest, common people—
people with whom Hay grew up but now rarely mingled—was on full
display in his tale of the riverboat engineer. Jim, his title character,

... weren't no saint,—but at jedgment
I'd run my chance with Jim,
'Longside of some pious gentlemen
That wouldn't shook hands with him.
He seen his duty, a dead-sure thing,—
And went for it thar and then;
And Christ ain't a going to be too hard
On a man that died for men.

In its day, *Pike County Ballads* won wide acclaim and placed its young author squarely within the early ranks of the American literary realist movement. Though unromantic, the poems were sentimental, as was the case with "Little Breeches," the adventure of a toddler who goes missing in the snowy woods when the team harnessed to his carriage scares at a foreign sound and bolts off, leaving his helpless father to give chase by foot. Just four years old, young Gabe is a salty character:

> Peart and chipper and sassy,
> Always ready to swear and fight,—
> And I'd larnt him to chaw terbacker
> Jest to keep his milk-teeth white.

After hours of vain pursuit, and despairing of ever finding his son, his father stumbles upon Gabe in a small wooden shed, buried deep in the snow-covered forest.

> How did he git thar? Angels.
> He could never have walked in that storm.
> They jest scooped down and toted him
> To whar it was safe and warm.
> And I think that saving a little child,
> And fotching him to his own,
> Is a derned sight better business
> Than loafing around The Throne.

Among the many American literary types who admired Hay's new departure was Mark Twain. Just a few years Hay's senior, Twain grew up in Hannibal, Missouri, six hundred yards across the Mississippi River from Pike County. Largely populated by the same transplants from Virginia and Kentucky, Hannibal shared almost every cultural trait with Warsaw and Pittsfield, except slavery. Fourteen years after Hay's collection appeared in print, Twain explained that in his new work, *Huckleberry Finn,* "a number of dialects are used, to wit: the

Missouri negro dialect; . . . the ordinary 'Pike-County' dialect; and four modified varieties of this last. The shadings have not been done in a hap-hazard fashion, or by guess-work; but pains-takingly, and with the trustworthy guidance and support of personal familiarity with these several forms of speech. I make this explanation for the reason that without it many readers would suppose that all these characters were trying to talk alike and not succeeding." After Hay's death in 1905, Twain recalled that *Pike County Ballads* was the first literary incarnation of the dialect now so intimately associated with heroes of his own work. In fact, Hay's good friend Bret Harte had beaten him to the punch by two months. Harte's immensely popular poem, "Plain Language from Truthful James" (known alternatively as "The Heathen Chinee"), delighted readers of the *Overland Monthly* in September 1870, just a few weeks before the first of Hay's ballads appeared in print. Inspired by native Pike County migrants whom he met in the gold mines of California, Harte technically pioneered the use of regional vernacular in realist poetry. But to both men went the credit for making American characters speak in authentic American accents. Hay's "sense of the backwoods" and "knowledge of the frontier . . . loom large and rude" in these poems, Howells told readers of the *North American Review*. "They belong to the very few results in any of the arts which have been absolutely of the Western cause." Only someone with Hay's "scope and penetration" could have written so vivid a portrait of "that bygone West." The college sophomore who had once been so thoroughly embarrassed by the return address on his trunk had made it safe for a generation of authors to extol the virtues of the ascendant West.

Hay's friends and admirers would not likely have been surprised by the political principles sharply on display in his poem "Remarks of Sergeant Tilmon Joy to the White Man's Committee of Spunky Point, Illinois." First published in 1871, as the federal government was employing military and civil means to root out Klan violence in the former Confederate states, his polemic revealed the lasting effect of the war on his outlook on race and slavery, as well as the political prejudices of one who would never entirely disassociate the Democratic

Party from disunion and disloyalty. In an address before a white vigilante mob, his title character, a Civil War veteran, begins:

> I reckon I git your drift, gents,—
> You 'low the boy sha'n't stay:
> This is a white man's country;
> You're Dimocrats, you say;
> And whereas, and seein', and wherefore,
> The times bein' all out o' j'int,
> The nigger has got to mosey
> From the limits o' Spunky P'int!
>
> Le's reason the thing a minute:
> I'm an old-fashioned Dimocrat too,
> Though I laid my politics out o' the way
> For to keep till the war was through.
> But I come back here, allowin'
> To vote as I used to do,
> Though it gravels me like the devil to train
> Along o' sich fools as you.

At the Battle of Vicksburg, the speaker was left for dead on the battlefield, his leg and rib cage shattered by a rebel bullet. As he lay wounded in the hot sun—"and br'iled and blistered and burned!"—and waited to die, suddenly "I seen a thing/I couldn't believe for a spell." Tim, a "contraband," was wounded multiple times in saving the narrator.

> So, my gentle gazelles, thar's my answer,
> And here stays Banty Tim:
> He trumped Death's ace for me that day,
> And I'm not goin' back on him!
> You may rezoloot till the cows come home,
> But ef one of you tetches the boy,
> He'll wrastle his hash to-night in hell,
> Or my name's not Tilmon Joy!

By the early 1870s, many erstwhile supporters of black civil rights had
turned against the Reconstruction project. Some looked askance at
biracial, reconstructed state governments in the South, some of which
shared in the general corruption that pervaded politics in the late 1860s
and the 1870s. Others grew tired of rehashing a decades-long debate
over race relations and expected freedmen to fend for themselves, now
that the work of emancipation and constitutional revision had theo-
retically been accomplished. Tilmon Joy continued to stand by Tim,
just as John Hay continued to stand by the Southern Negro. In his
mind, black soldiers earned their citizenship on the battlefield; white
Democrats remained a suspect breed—disloyal in war, a mobocracy
in peace.

"Remarks of Sergeant Tilmon Joy" (known in some editions as
"Banty Tim") was not Hay's first literary treatment of race and slavery.
In 1869, not long before the first of the Pike County ballads appeared
in print, *Harper's Monthly* published one of his short stories, "The
Foster-Brothers." Hay's tale was set in two fictive Mississippi River
towns (Thebes, Missouri, and Moscow, Illinois—perfect stand-ins for
Hannibal and Warsaw, or countless other border villages), in a time
"not many years ago," before America had been "dipped in blood
and . . . arisen from the red baptism cleansed of its deadliest sin." A
young Southern gentleman, Clarence Brydges, pays a visit to his col-
lege friend in Moscow. There, he falls madly in love with his friend's
comely, dark-haired neighbor, the enchanting Marie Des Ponts, who
lives just across the river with her father. Mr. Des Ponts, Marie's father,
is a "lawyer by profession, gentleman by practice," "the richest man in
Thebes, and the best bred man in Missouri." A French Creole, he has
"the good taste to speak English without lisping . . . good books and
good wine . . . The most curious thing about him is that every body
owes him money and nobody hates him." Des Pont's late wife—
Marie's mother—was an "enthusiastic Southern woman," according to
their neighbor, and an inveterate white supremacist who "thought a
free State the abomination of desolation . . . and she did not see how
one could be a Christian and not own slaves, when their means per-
mitted; and I believe honestly doubted whether negroes had souls."

Des Ponts honored his wife's wish that he not bring Marie to dwell in the North, though in choosing Thebes for his home, he resided in the "extreme corner of a slave territory, in sight of free sky and soil."

Matters come to a head when Marie accepts Clarence's marriage proposal. With the river rising to dangerous heights, Des Ponts watches from the banks as a steamboat engine explodes, leaving the water filled with "struggling and drowning passengers." Des Ponts rows out to the scene and rescues one of the drowning men, who turns out to be not only Clarence's father—en route from Mobile to attend the wedding—but none other than his former master. Des Ponts, the reader now learns, is a runaway slave who has been passing for several decades as a white man. "Sam, you're a d——d lucky nigger!" his onetime owner says with a smirk. "You have saved your hide forty by picking me up to-night." Des Ponts—the former slave boy Sam—does not deny his identity. "I have no legal existence, you say; I have no child, no name," he concedes. "Granting that, your son is legally married to the natural daughter of Miss Julia Shelby of Glenarthur . . . Our children are married and happy. Let them alone. I have given my daughter a dowry of one hundred thousand dollars. I will give you the highest market-price for myself. In return, you will bind yourself by oath, in writing, to silence—that is all." In the ensuing argument, Victor Brydges counters with his own offer. "Consent to break up this marriage, pay me for yourself and the girl, and we will fix it up without scandal. I don't forget that we are foster-brothers. You have received much kindness from my family."

"Stop there!" Des Ponts cries.

> I was brought up with you to serve you. I learned to read, helping you. I learned French to be useful to you when you went abroad. I studied at the University to coach you through. I got my degree, and you failed. When at last I offered to buy myself and remain in France, you cursed me and struck me; and after that you were fool enough to trust me. You made me use my credit at the Prefecture of Police

to get you a passport under the name of Des Ponts, to assist you in some scandalous intrigue. I swear that until I had that passport in my hands I never dreamed of running away.

The two men come to blows as the boat drifts perilously near the fiery steamboat. Victor's "whole soul revolted against making any compromise with his slave." At the last instant, the "foster-brothers" go overboard and sink "to the bottom locked in each other's arms. They were found in the same posture two days later, lying on the shining sand." A neighbor comforts the grieving newlyweds with the assurance that "from their graves your beloved fathers—one of whom lost his precious life in this noble effort to rescue the other from the waves—exhort you continually to love one another." None would be any the wiser in seeing the tragedy for what it was: a metaphorical case of fratricide.

Hay's short story presaged a larger body of literature featuring African American characters who pass for white. From Charles Chesnutt and Mark Twain in the late nineteenth century to James Weldon Johnson, William Faulkner, Sinclair Lewis, Ralph Ellison, and Philip Roth in the twentieth century, authors made wide use of the "passing" trope to question the boundaries of race. Although the black author William Wells Brown may have pioneered this literary convention in 1853, with the publication of his novel, *Clotel,* Hay was one of its earliest practitioners. The arbitrary bifurcation between black and white had been on his mind at least since the war, when he wondered at the "perfectly white and blue-eyed" Negroes, "neatly & very carefully dressed very quietly & decently behaved," among the larger crowd of black picnickers on the White House lawn. Nicolay, too, had grappled with these questions after meeting the Haitian chargé d'affaires, a man whom he supposed was "a negro, although he does not look like one, having straight black hair, and a very brown, Spanish looking face." The war compelled both men to rethink many of their assumptions about the meaning of race, and if neither became an outright egalitarian, they

emerged with a greater respect for black Americans and a fundamen-
tal commitment to ensuring that they be treated equally under the law.

Widely known as "an immense favorite of the ladies," Hay was content
to lead a bachelor's life until 1872, when he met Clara Stone, the daugh-
ter of a wealthy railroad magnate from Ohio. The attraction was in-
stant. "I have been brought down," Hay admitted to a friend. "Mourn
for me. *La femme* has ceased to exist for me. There is only one—and
one is enough . . . I part from the old life without regret save for the
dear old reprobates whom I shall hereafter love in secret and remorse-
lessly cut in public . . . Believe me, I am not the thing I was." After
Clara returned to Cleveland, Hay struck up an intense correspondence
with her. He was smitten. Passing through Ohio, he made a stopover
to meet her parents, Amasa and Julia Stone. A self-made millionaire
many times over, Amasa was formally trained as an engineer and had
first made his mark by designing railroad bridges and trestles. He then
branched out into railroad management and later assumed a place on
the board of directors at both Western Union and Standard Oil. By the
time Hay made his acquaintance, the Stone family patriarch had built
an enormous mansion on Euclid Avenue, Cleveland's "Millionaires'
Row," where his neighbors included John D. Rockefeller. Amasa took
an instant liking to Hay and freely gave Clara his permission to return
to New York the following winter, where she stayed for three months
with her aunt and uncle and saw Hay almost daily. "I have sometimes
gazed at you until your eyes and mouth seemed radiant and glorified
with some divine beauty and promise," Hay wrote, "until it seems to
me that I could not live without falling at your feet and pouring out
my full heart in worship." Later that year, Hay asked Amasa for his
daughter's hand in marriage, a request to which Stone happily gave his
consent. Clara's mother proved a tougher nut to crack. "There will be
an internecine war before Mrs. Stone consents to give up her daugh-
ter," Hay informed Nicolay. "But before many centuries I shall win." It
was not lost upon his friends that marrying into the Stone family would
make Hay a millionaire by default. In a letter to Nicolay, Robert Todd

Lincoln observed that Amasa Stone would one day be "obliged to leave
to . . . J.H." somewhere between $6 million and $8 million, "which will
make John to write with a first class gold pen."

Hay's marriage to Clara in February 1874 profoundly changed his
material fortunes. On the occasion of the wedding, Amasa Stone
gifted his son-in-law $10,000 in railroad bonds, a portent of good
bounty to come. "Both my books got more praise than they deserved,"
John admitted with satisfaction to a friend, soon after moving with his
bride to a comfortable home at 111 East Twenty-fifth Street. "My work
in journalism is successful and well paid. And now my father-in-law
wishes me to go into a new line of business, which will bring me im-
mediate wealth." Sensitive to Clara's longing for the familiar home and
hearth of her childhood, Hay agreed the following year to leave the
New-York Tribune and move to Cleveland, where Amasa installed the
newlyweds in a handsome new mansion of their own on Euclid Ave-
nue. John entered the employ of his father-in-law, who, true to his
word, rewarded him with a handsome income. Privately, Hay con-
ceded that his work was "merely the care of investments which are so
safe that they require no care." Amasa had done the hard work in
creating the family's wealth; Hay was now responsible for managing
it. He joined the board of the Western Union Telegraph Company and
soon proved deft at protecting and growing his wife's fortune. As an
unsympathetic biographer later remarked, "Known best as a verse-
maker, John Hay became actually a better businessman." In truth, he
devoted the better part of his time to literary and political pursuits and
made a mere sideline of railroad management and bonds. Owing
mostly to the generosity and financial tutelage of his father-in-law,
within ten years John was worth at least $3 million, a sum equivalent
to well over $50 million in today's money.

When the couple's first daughter, Helen Julia Hay, was born, John
found to his great delight that domestic life suited him well. "My wife
keeps well and lovely," he told a friend, "and my daughter is . . . nine
months old and fat and rosy and her only defect is that she looks like
me to an extent which is absurd." Over the next decade, John and

Clara would have another daughter, Alice, and two sons, Adelbert (Del) and Clarence. After his death, his daughters would remember him as a kind and doting father. "He was so tender-hearted," remarked Alice, "that my mother always had to deal with our youthful injuries, illnesses & discipline. He couldn't bear to see us hurt or made unhappy even for our own good. He spoiled us shamefully." To Helen, her father was "the jolliest kind of pal" who taught the children "old war time songs & plantation melodies." When she was older and moved away to attend boarding school, "he used to come out & always arranged a program ahead which began with 'we will have a nice sandwich for lunch at the Station, we then will go & call on an old lady who wishes to see you & we will finish the day with a delightful & improving lecture on Astronomy'—which of course meant that we lunched at Delmonico's on whatever I wanted to order . . . & shopped & 'played' all afternoon & finished up with a musical comedy." John was less at ease with his sons, particularly Del, whom he privately ridiculed as "fat and dull." Father and son had great difficulty in connecting, though it pleased Hay to no end when, years later, President William McKinley appointed Del to an assistant secretary's position in the White House. Tragically, Del died in an accident in New Haven, just weeks before he was to take up his post.

When Governor Rutherford B. Hayes of Ohio won a sharply contested presidential election in 1876, John Hay, now a resident of the Buckeye State, sent him a gold ring that contained a strand of George Washington's hair, a souvenir that Alexander Hamilton's grandson had given him years before. The incoming president was deeply moved by the gesture and promised to "prize it [and] wear it on special occasions if not constantly." Over the next two years, Hay assumed an ever more active role in Republican Party politics, stumping for local and statewide candidates in Ohio and contributing funds to the national and state parties. Growing restless, he took an immediate interest when friends suggested that he run for Congress. Though he had not considered running for office since his abortive trip to Florida some fifteen

years earlier, the prospect of returning to Washington, where he now made periodic trips to visit Nicolay, was appealing. Still, the "Congress matter is not so simple as my high-toned friends think," he told Whitelaw Reid. "All Euclid Avenue says with one accord that I am the man, but E.A., with all its millions and its tone, does not influence a single primary." Washington beckoned in other ways. In late 1879, Frederick Seward resigned his post as assistant secretary of state, a position that he also held under his father during the Civil War. As a veteran of three diplomatic stations and a former foreign affairs columnist for the *New-York Tribune,* Hay was as good a candidate for the job as could be found. He first demurred when Secretary of State William Evarts asked him to serve but soon relented. Over the next year and a half, Clara would remain in Cleveland with the children, making occasional visits to the capital.

By November, Hay had taken up his office at the State Department, where he oversaw a staff of eighty employees, in addition to hundreds of diplomatic and consular appointees serving in foreign posts. On his first day of work, he wandered over to the White House. The president was not in, though Hay experienced an eerie sense of déjà vu upon being ushered into his secretary's office to leave his card. Two days later, Evarts announced that he was leaving town on personal business and that Hay would serve as acting *"Secretary of State* in his absence." "Think of that and hold up your head," Hay gushed to Clara. "Today was an important one in our history," he reported the following day. "I sat for the first time in Cabinet meeting, and took the place of highest rank in the room, at the President's right." His mind flashed back to the days when he sat against the wall during cabinet meetings and observed William Seward occupying the very place he now claimed. "I felt very odd and modest," he admitted, "sitting there among the grey-haired elders of the land." As a secretary, he had stayed silent through countless meetings. Now he was "entitled to speak first on matters of national importance. You may imagine I did not avail myself of the privilege. But I enjoyed listening to the discussions of the others very much indeed. It seems a much more important matter to

me now, to be so near the source of authority than it did when I was younger. I did not appreciate it in Lincoln's time."

Hay's tenure at the State Department also afforded him the opportunity to rekindle an old friendship with Henry Adams. The two men had first met in early 1861, when Henry, the grandson and great-grandson of American presidents, had been in Washington serving as private secretary to his father, Congressman Charles Francis Adams. Neither Adams thought much of Lincoln and hoped that more experienced political hands would steady the ship of state. But Henry quickly found much to admire in the president-elect's assistant secretary. "Friends are born, not made," Henry wrote. "From the first slight meeting in February and March 1861, [I] recognized Hay as a friend, and never lost sight of him at the future crossing of [our] paths." Shortly after taking office, Lincoln appointed Charles to the critical American ministry in Great Britain. Henry sailed with him, serving simultaneously as his father's secretary and as the anonymous London correspondent for the *New York Times*.

Though their paths occasionally crossed in the following years, Adams and Hay did not have occasion to revisit their friendship until two decades later. In the fall of 1880, Adams and his wife, Clover, rented a comfortable town house at 1607 H Street, adjacent to Lafayette Park and just a stone's throw from the White House. They quickly connected with Hay. Together with Clara, who joined him for most of the winter of 1880–81, and Clarence King, a dashing, Yale-educated geologist who earned fame for surveying the spans of the transcontinental railroad, Hay found fast and enduring fellowship among a self-selected set of wealthy, educated peers. Calling themselves the "Five of Hearts," the group went so far as to design its own emblem, which they then emblazed on stationery and dinner menus and even on custom-made china and tea sets and enamel breast pins. From the recesses of Clover and Henry's drawing room, the five "hearts" talked art, politics, literature, science, and gossip. Of the group, Clara was the least worldly and the most reticent. She "never speaks," Clover noticed, which was fine, since John "chats for two."

George Nicolay was Hay's oldest friend. Henry Adams became his closest. Over the next quarter century, they traveled together, dined together, and, when apart, wrote each other nearly every week. In later years they would even build adjacent mansions on Lafayette Square, with direct views to windows of the White House bedroom that Hay had once shared with Nicolay. But in 1880, Hay longed once again to break free from Washington. With Clara back in Ohio, he looked forward to March 1881, when the new president, James A. Garfield, would take office. "I cannot really say I regret having come here," he told his wife, "because it was a duty & the experience will be good to remember. But it is a hard business to live in a tavern, when one has a pretty house, and a pretty wife, and three pretty babies somewhere else." His workdays were long. He grew weary of the "clamorous greedy host that comes continually for offices that are not worth having." While the parties were exciting at first, it soon got "a little tiresome to meet the same diplomats every night." Even filling in at cabinet meetings grew routine. But Hay knew that he would be "glad all my life to have had the opportunity of serving" and "to have had my little share in the work of carrying on the government of a great nation."

Hay still entertained the notion of running for Congress in 1880, though his position would require that he skip the fall canvass and leave it to friends to present his case to the voters. If elected, he could bring his family to the capital. But Clara preferred Cleveland to Washington. Neither did she care for many of the dinners, teas, and salon parties that had sustained her husband for two decades and counting. Mark Twain later remembered a Sunday afternoon when he and Hay were "chatting and laughing and carrying on almost like our earlier selves of '67." In came "Mrs. Hay, gravely clad, gloved, bonneted, and just from church, and fragrant with the odors of Presbyterian sanctity." When Twain stood up to exchange pleasantries, Clara brushed right past him, offering a cool "Good morning, Mr. Clemens," before leaving the room. Embarrassed but not surprised, Hay offered feebly that his wife was "very strict about Sunday." If he were to convince her to move to Washington, life as a congressional spouse would not likely be the right inducement. For her sake, he assured Clara that he could

not be nominated if he did not work for it, and when another man was chosen to be the party's standard-bearer, he pretended to content himself with the knowledge that "I should have been nominated if I had stayed in—but I am glad I did not." "The more I see the life of a congressman here," he told her on another occasion, with uncertain conviction, "the less agreeable it appears."

In the months between Garfield's election and his inauguration, Hay prepared to close up shop at the State Department and go home. In December, the president-elect tendered an unexpected offer: he wanted Hay to return to the White House as presidential secretary. Technically, during the Lincoln administration Nicolay had been secretary and Hay, assistant secretary. But Garfield was sensitive to the appearance of asking Hay to take two steps back, to a job he had essentially occupied twenty years earlier. He meant for his chief aide to play a consultative role in developing administration policy, much as later presidential secretaries would do. He was also prepared to ask Congress to make the position equal in rank and pay to an assistant cabinet position. Hay waited a decent interval before politely declining the offer. "To do a thing well," he told Garfield, "a man must take some pleasure in it." He held the president-elect in the highest esteem, but he could not stomach the constant "envy, meanness, ignorance, and the swinish selfishness" that necessarily greeted the gatekeeper to the most powerful person in the land. "I am not going back on Democracy," he promised. "It is a good thing—the hope and salvation of the world. I mean simply that I am not fit for public office."

The Hays were in Washington for Garfield's inauguration and stayed for several weeks after so that John could be on hand to advise the new president on cabinet and diplomatic appointments. In late April, Clara returned to Cleveland with the children, while John headed north for New York. Whitelaw Reid was in Europe for six months on his honeymoon, and Hay reluctantly agreed to fill in as acting editor of the *Tribune*. It had been some twenty years since he arrived in the capital with Lincoln. He looked forward to the day when he could set aside all other pursuits and join Nicolay in the serious work of writing their authorized biography.

CHAPTER 13

Breadwinners

The house that Amasa Stone built for his daughter and son-in-law on Euclid Avenue was a lasting monument to his family's wealth. Fashioned out of sandstone, it boasted intricate, hand-carved woodwork made of black walnut, furnishings selected by the same interior designers who had refurbished the White House, "gilding and black dado," and a rolling front lawn tucked neatly behind a row of tall elm trees and flagstone sidewalks. Incredibly, the mansion served as John and Clara's primary residence for just a handful of years. Soon after returning to Cleveland in 1881, Hay began suffering from debilitating headaches, nausea, and dizzy spells that would bedevil him for the rest of his life. His friends privately judged him a hypochondriac, but they encouraged his frequent sojourns in Europe, where he ministered to his ailments at clinics and spas then regarded as the most advanced in the world. In 1883, when a large parcel of land on Lafayette Square went onto the market, Hay and Henry Adams decided to buy it and build adjacent homes. John and Clara took the larger, corner plot, at a price of $50,000, while Henry and Clover purchased the smaller plot for $25,000. Over the next two years, both families oversaw the construction of manors that put Euclid Avenue to shame. The Hay mansion ultimately cost $100,000 to construct. At twelve thousand square feet, it featured marble fireplaces in almost every room, an entire floor for servants, a sprawling parlor and library, five bedrooms, three bathrooms with modern plumbing, mahogany woodwork,

wainscoting, and a grand stairway "so wide that ten persons could walk abreast without jostling," according to one newspaper account. It was filled to the brim with ornate furnishings from what Hay sardonically referred to as a "$1,000 store," as no item could be bought for less. And yet the Hays barely lived there, either, until John's appointment as secretary of state in 1898. Despondent over the death of her father, Clover Adams committed suicide shortly before the twin houses were complete. Grief-stricken, Henry set out for years of travel, stopping only intermittently to visit his new house. With Clover dead and Henry gone, the entire rationale for living in Washington seemed obviated. The Hays spent only half of each year in Washington and no more than a few weeks in Cleveland. The rest of their months were spent traveling in Europe. Effectively, they had two mansions but no home.

Hay, who was raised solidly middle-class, soon learned by observation that wealth cannot necessarily buy happiness. In December 1876, shortly after John and Clara moved into their house on Euclid Avenue, a railroad bridge over Ohio's Ashtabula Creek snapped under the weight of a heavy snowfall, causing an engine and several passenger cars to fall into the ravine below. Ninety-two people perished in what was then the worst train accident in American history. Amasa Stone owned controlling interest in the Lake Shore Railway, which had built—and owned—the Ashtabula Creek bridge. In the ensuing months, he and his company withstood blistering attacks in the press for allegedly shoddy engineering work. His chief engineer, Charles Collins, committed suicide after withstanding hours of hostile questioning in front of a state legislative investigative committee. The Lake Shore Railway paid out fines and damages in the amount of half a million dollars, and though Amasa's personal fortune remained intact, his reputation lay in tatters. He never recovered from his psychological scars. In 1883, while John and Clara were in Europe, Stone shot himself to death in the upstairs bathroom of his Euclid Avenue estate.

In the aftermath of his death, Amasa's two daughters and sons-in-law split an estate valued at between $6 million and $20 million, equivalent in today's money to over $400 million. Effortlessly—by

no more than marrying the right bride—Hay acquired more wealth than he could have imagined in his youth. He was free to write books, play at politics, serve in high office, travel, or do nothing at all for long stretches at a time.

Affluence had an indelible influence on Hay's worldview. As he associated more exclusively with well-to-do peers, he grew more removed from the world he had known as a young man. In distance, his oldest friends, George and Therena Nicolay, lived just a quarter mile away, where they built a fine new house on Capitol Hill ("it is a new large roomy one," Hay reported to Clara, "and cost almost nothing, $5400"). But they might as well have lived a continent apart. After gentle prodding from Therena, Hay genially dropped by for an early evening meeting of a "literary society" that the Nicolays hosted regularly in their parlor. "It was not very gay," he told Clara. "Mr. Wordhoff read an essay on Darwin and a large artist, 7 feet high, with hair seven inches long, read a paper on art." Going forward, he would find a polite way to decline such invitations. In later years, Nicolay and Hay vacationed together in Colorado, followed each other's sicknesses and family crises attentively, and devoted the better part of two decades to their Lincoln biography, an endeavor that required close and constant collaboration. They spent countless hours in each other's studies and parlors and were the closest of friends until they died, but more and more it was history that formed their bond, rather than a commonality of lifestyles or interests. Their worlds were no longer quite the same.

Hay's critics would later criticize him as an elitist. A financial booster of the Republican Party, he came to be associated with its conservative, hard-money wing. He opposed labor unions and government regulation of the economy. He fraternized easily with the barons of industry and sympathized with their laissez-faire worldview. The onetime champion of European revolutionary movements now feared blood in the streets at every work slowdown or strike. It was easy to assume that Hay's social and economic conservatism sprang from his newfound wealth. But it was not money—which he acquired by accident more than anything else—that informed his social outlook. Hay

traveled the same ideological road as many men of his generation. In their youth, they cut their teeth on political reform; as older men, they settled comfortably into conservatism. As with so many other pieces of their lives, the Civil War had much to do with the trajectory of their thinking.

When he returned to the United States with his father in 1868, after serving for eight years as private secretary at the American embassy in London, Henry Adams had been astounded by the vast changes that the Civil War had wrought. "Had they been Tyrian traders of the year B.C. 1000," he later reflected, "landing from a galley fresh from Gibraltar, they could hardly have been stranger on the shore of a world, so changed from what it had been ten years before." In 1861, when he departed Washington for England, four million African American slaves lived in a state of perpetual, hereditary bondage. Thousands of these enslaved souls lived within a stone's throw of the Capitol. Now they were all legally free, invested with the rights and immunities of citizens and well on their way to enjoying the right of manhood suffrage—at least for a time, and in certain parts of the country. Within months of Adams's return, the first African American congressmen would take their seats in the U.S. House of Representatives, where his grandfather and father had served honorably in early times. The sweep of history had indeed been profound. But Henry was likely thinking of a larger and more encompassing change, best expressed that year by James Garfield. "In April 1861, there began in this country an industrial revolution . . . as far-reaching in its consequences as the political and military revolution through which we have passed," the young war hero turned congressman told the House. A country of small towns, small shops, and small farms was well on its way to becoming an urban, industrial behemoth, and to many Americans this transformation was owed at least in part to the modernizing influence of the war. It was little wonder that the historian George Ticknor, writing in 1869, perceived a "great gulf between what happened before in our century and what has happened since, or what is likely to happen hereafter. It does not seem to me as if I were living in the country in which I was born."

In truth, the change was not so complete, nor wholly a product of the war. But the challenges of paying, feeding, clothing, arming, and transporting two million soldiers and sailors dramatically accelerated economic transformations that were already evident by 1860. To fund the Union war effort, Congress borrowed heavily and passed a legal tender act, creating the nation's first uniform paper currency. The resulting expansion of the monetary supply spurred economic development throughout the North and the Northwest, while widespread bond sales cemented the attachment between ordinary citizens and the federal state. For those who invested their savings in 5-20 and 7-30 Civil War bonds, inflation likely ate away at many of the profits, but the financier Jay Cooke and his army of subscription agents earned a fortune, as did speculators who later gobbled the notes up at a discount. So, too, did a new industrial class grow rich off government contracts—men like Philip Armour, who revolutionized the canned-meat industry; John D. Rockefeller, who conceived new processes for oil refinement; and Thomas Scott, a wartime innovator in railroad management. The economic revolution did not stop there. With Democratic opposition sharply curtailed by the withdrawal of Southern congressmen, Republican congressional leaders enacted a sweeping legislative agenda that fundamentally transformed the country. They passed the Homestead Act, which bequeathed 160 acres of federal land to any western settler who lived for five years on his allotment and made requisite improvements to the land. They passed the Land-Grant College Act, which provided each state with 30,000 acres of federal land for each of its senators and congressmen; the states, in turn, were empowered to dispose of their grants and dedicate the sale proceeds to the establishment of state universities. Finally, Congress passed the Pacific Railroad Act, granting private railroad companies 6,400 acres of federal land, and between $16,000 and $48,000 in loans, per mile of track laid. One hundred and twenty million acres and thirty-five thousand track miles later came the realization of a long-deferred dream: a transcontinental rail system that opened the "vast, trackless spaces" of the West (in Walt Whitman's words) to settlement and economic development.

The results of this catalytic spurt of spending, monetary expansion, and railroad construction baffled the mind of young Henry Adams, who had been abroad for most of it. Between 1865 and 1873, industrial production increased by 75 percent, allowing the United States to leap-frog ahead of every other nation, save Britain, in manufacturing out-put. Giant trunk lines absorbed smaller railroad companies, while the rush for construction caused iron and steel demand to double. The burgeoning system unified the inhabitants of a sprawling continent and created new opportunities for farmers, ranchers, miners, and in-dustrialists to exploit, finish, and merchandise the vast resources of the trans-Mississippi West. Now connected to major centers of trade and commerce, cattle ranchers moved their herds into the flat plains of Kansas and Nebraska. Wheat fields flourished from the Dakotas down to Oklahoma. Timber flowed in from the Pacific Northwest, while miners tapped enormous deposits of gold, silver, and copper from California, Nevada, Colorado, and Arizona. These extractive and pro-ductive industries sparked an economic boom that lasted well into the early 1870s, and the boom created unprecedented opportunities for graft. In 1872, the Crédit Mobilier scandal implicated thirty sitting con-gressmen, as well as Vice President Schuyler Colfax, in an elaborate double-billing and securities fraud scheme associated with the con-struction of the Union Pacific Railroad line. The Republicans were ultimately forced to replace Colfax on the ticket, bringing the vice president's public career to an inglorious close. Three years later, the Whiskey Ring affair exposed dozens of federal revenue collectors in a massive kickback scheme. On the state and local levels, corruption was equally rampant, though nowhere more brazen than New York City, where William M. Tweed, the boss of the Tammany Hall Democratic organization, made an art form of public graft and fraud. Through the good offices of Thomas Nast, the staff cartoonist at *Harper's Weekly*, Tweed became an emblem for the excesses of the new age.

To many Americans, it seemed that trains were responsible for all that was good and bad about the new economic order. "The locomo-tive," argued the *Nation*, "is coming in contact with the framework of

our institutions." Railroad companies hired armies of lobbyists, placed state and federal legislators on "retainer," and extracted grants of money, tax rebates, land, and monopoly rights from every level of government. "Corruption belongs to no one party but has invaded all," claimed a Pennsylvania newspaper, an observation that was true but that sidestepped the inexorable bond the Republican Party forged with the emerging industrial and financial elite in the interest of prosecuting a war on slavery.

Many Republicans, particularly the generation of soldiers and officeholders who rose up the party ranks in the 1860s, easily reconciled their antislavery origins with their party's increasingly symbiotic relationship to the nation's economic titans. Businessmen who helped finance and furnish the army had proven themselves patriotic partners in blotting out the dual sins of slavery and disunion. As Carl Schurz noted, his friend the financier and bond broker Jay Cooke had "rendered very valuable service to the country during the Civil War, and I do not think anybody grudged him the fortune he gathered at the same time for himself." Many Republican elites recalled that during the New York City draft riots in 1863, working-class ruffians had shamelessly attacked defenseless black orphans, while the city's business and professional classes, joined under the auspices of the Union League, lent their wealth and prestige to the struggle against slavery and secession. The antislavery position was itself grounded in a laissez-faire economic worldview that understood economic progress as a noble goal, ipso facto. The free-labor synthesis held that men should be unrestricted in their ambition to work, thrive, and accumulate wealth. Left to their own devices and unencumbered by artificial barriers to progress—the most egregious barrier being chattel slavery—the intelligent, worthy, better citizens would prosper, while society as a whole would benefit from the cumulative effect of self-interested competition. The rise of a prosperous industrial and professional class in the postwar period, and the party's close association with its leading beneficiaries, did not strike most Republicans as a betrayal of their moral legacy. Most antebellum Republicans detested slavery because they

believed that it impeded material progress. That the economic boom
of the 1860s coincided with the destruction of the peculiar institution
seemed only natural to many party leaders and supporters.

Even on questions that bore no ostensible relationship to the old
issues of secession and slavery, public men often filtered their ideas
through the prism of the Civil War. While many Democrats sup-
ported an inflationary policy of redeeming war bonds with green-
backs, Republicans like Charles Sumner insisted on a hard-money
policy that benefited bondholders at the expense of indebted farmers
and workers. "Every greenback is red with the blood of fellow-
citizens," he intoned. It was the government's obligation to redeem the
bonds in gold, no matter the social consequences.

The boom proved lucrative to the small number of men who con-
trolled access to local resources, though much less profitable for the
hundreds of thousands of ranchers, farmers, factory workers, miners,
and railroad laborers who supplied the muscle. Rarely did it occur to
business and political elites that they had not prospered strictly by the
rules of the free-labor economy. Railroad companies profited heavily
from government land grants and financial subsidies. The Timber Cul-
ture Act (1873) and the Desert Land Act (1877) gave away millions of
acres of public land to those with the means to plant trees and irrigate
arid allotments in the Southwest. The Mineral Land Act of 1872 sold
access to valuable metal deposits at a song—no more than $5 per
acre—to mining companies, while cattle ranchers freely availed them-
selves of grazing rights on public land. At every turn, an activist state
born of necessity to prosecute the Civil War found new and increas-
ingly inventive ways to subsidize business concerns that had grown
out of the same armed struggle. Many of the primary recipients of this
public largesse remained oblivious to the role that the government
played in making them wealthy.

The postwar economic boom profoundly altered the political land-
scape. By the early 1870s, many Republicans had tired of the Southern
problem; twenty years of heated debate over slavery and the Civil War,
race and Reconstruction, had diminished their interest. The rampant
graft of the Grant years inspired many of the party's founding

stalwarts, including Charles Francis Adams Sr., to bolt and form a new Liberal movement founded on solid anticorruption and free-market ideas. When the Liberals nominated Horace Greeley for president in 1872, John Hay, as an employee of the *Tribune,* joined the reformist bandwagon and penned regular columns that lambasted the president's organization men. Later that year, when the Democrats formed a coalition with the Liberals and also nominated Greeley as their standard-bearer, Hay gravitated back to Grant. In his capacity as a *Tribune* editorial writer, he might have been compelled to contribute anonymous broadsides for his boss, but as he later remarked to Whitelaw Reid, "The Democratic party is our Evil—our virtue is developed by fighting it." Enough veterans of the antislavery political movement shared Hay's animus for the Democratic Party and helped Grant secure a landslide reelection victory.

For many onetime Republicans, the short-lived Liberal Party proved a temporary byway to the Democrats, as concern over political and economic corruption displaced race as a primary driver of political identification; those who traveled this migratory route included Charles senior and Henry Adams, Lyman Trumbull, George Julian, and John Andrew, many of whom believed that the Grand Old Party had lost its way and become a permanent governing fixture of industrial interests. Others, like John Hay, remained in the Republican fold, though they regarded themselves as friends of reform. Writing to William Dean Howells several months after Rutherford B. Hayes triumphed over the Democratic nominee, Samuel Tilden, Hay admitted that he "liked Tilden very much, I voted for him for Governor [of New York]—the only Democratic vote I ever cast—I did not vote for Greeley. But I never allowed myself to expect as much from any man as I feel forced now to hope from Hayes. We are in a bad way. That herd of wild asses' colts in Washington, braying and kicking up their heels, is an unsatisfactory result of a hundred years of democracy." Hay did not believe that the incoming president possessed sufficient political capital to achieve meaningful civil service reform, but he hoped that he could "chasten the outrageous indecency of the present system as much as any one could." Privately, Hay dismissed most congressmen

as "asses" but laid ultimate blame for the sorry state of politics on the voters themselves.

Political corruption was one part of the political debate in the 1870s. Economic justice was another. Most Republicans, be they reformers or "stalwarts," and even many Democrats (particularly those who had once been Liberal Republicans), were united in their hostile reception of so-called class legislation—laws intended to blunt capitalism's rougher edges. "I am utterly opposed to the idea of regulating hours of labor by law," declared Senator William Pitt Fessenden, who had served as Lincoln's Treasury secretary, following Salmon P. Chase's departure from the cabinet. Many Republicans similarly decried efforts to regulate labor and factory safety as akin to "subverting the right of individual property." "The government," wrote E. L. Godkin, the influential editor of the *Nation* and a leading liberal reformer, "must get out of the 'protective' business and the 'subsidy' business and the 'improvement' and 'development' business . . . It cannot touch them without breeding corruption." In theory, Republicans were equally offended by the "class" demands of organized laborers and industrial titans. Francis Parkman, a noted historian and author, spoke for many upwardly mobile professionals when he lamented the rise of an "ignorant proletariat and a half-taught plutocracy." Most liberals shared with their more conservative brethren an overriding fear of working-class excess. In their minds, as a threat to public institutions, it far outweighed the immoderation of the railroad or mining interests. Men who once used a strong central state to destroy slavery and promote economic development now lambasted the "fallacy of attempts to benefit humanity by legislation" and believed any such effort "by nature wasteful, corrupt, and dangerous." "Things must regulate themselves," one newspaper argued, in a pithy but powerful iteration of prevailing Republican wisdom.

If liberals were more offended than party stalwarts by public corruption, they shared with most Republicans a theoretical commitment to laissez-faire capitalism—except when their personal interests demanded state intervention. When times were good, it was easy to preserve the fiction that the free-labor society had created the same shared

prosperity and harmony of national interests that its theorists had long posited. With real wages up roughly 40 percent since the end of the war, there seemed to be something for everyone to enjoy in the new order, at least outside the South, a region that would struggle for decades to overcome staggering wartime losses—roughly one-third of its livestock, half the value of its land, and the expropriation of slave property worth at least $3 trillion in today's currency. But when the economy crashed in 1873, brought on by the failure of Jay Cooke to market $300 million in Northern Pacific Railroad bonds, increasing attention turned to the political corruption that had fed the cycle of overbuilding and overspeculation and to the class inequities that seemed to have deepened over the previous decade and a half. In the wake of the crash, various labor and reform movements took center stage, their partisans decrying the practical demise of the old free-labor dream in which each man owned his own farm or workshop, and where even the hired man could earn sufficient wages to become economically independent one day. This ideal was fast giving way to "the wages system," whereby most men, and now many single women, worked for someone else. Reflecting popular dismay at the rise of a permanent workforce of employees, one union cried that "the masses will never be completely free—until they have thrown off the system of working for hire."

Tensions boiled over in 1874 when a massive strike wave hit the nation's mines and railroads. The following year, thousands of miners brought operations in the anthracite coal region to a virtual standstill. Republican newspapers railed against the workers, deeming them "enemies of society" who believed that "the world owes them a living." Horace White, a veteran of the political antislavery movement who had traveled the rails with Lincoln during the 1858 Senate race, warned of a "communistic war upon vested rights and property" and bewailed the extent to which universal manhood suffrage had "cheapened the ballot." These concerns reached a crescendo in 1877 when workers on the Baltimore & Ohio Railroad staged a walkout over scheduled wage cuts, provoking a nationwide general strike that paralyzed commerce across the emerging industrial belt of the Midwest and mid-Atlantic

states. In Pittsburgh, working-class protesters clashed with the state militia, resulting in a fire that destroyed a hundred locomotives and two thousand railroad cars. General work stoppages quieted factories and mills in Chicago and St. Louis. In the coalfields of western and southern Pennsylvania, forty thousand workers walked off the job. Predictably, Republican organs, both reform and regular, bitterly condemned these actions. The *Nation*, once known for its strident support of civil rights for freedmen, now rebuked "the most extensive and deplorable workingmen's strike which ever took place in this, or indeed in any other country." In cities across the country, wealthy and middle-class professionals formed armed militia groups to protect private property against the "Great Strike." Many militiamen even donned tight-fitting army uniforms that had been gathering dust in their closets for over a decade. From Washington, President Hayes ordered the military to break the strike, which it did with overwhelming force, reopening clogged rail lines, busting up union meetings, and escorting strikebreakers through the line. "The strikers have been put down by *force*," noted Hayes, a Civil War combat veteran who had fought enthusiastically against slavery just a decade before. In their zeal for a free-labor economy free from state intervention, Republicans could be brutally inconsistent when their economic or political interests were on the line. Years after they left active duty, they continued to view themselves as citizen soldiers, now engaged in an armed struggle to protect private property rights.

Writing to a friend, Ulysses S. Grant, whose presidential administration, if corrupt, had nevertheless attempted to protect the rights and safety of Southern freedmen, found the entire episode "a little queer." "During my two terms of office the whole Democratic press, and the morbidly honest and 'reformatory' portion of the Republican press, thought it horrible to keep U.S. troops stationed in the Southern States, and when they were called upon to protect the lives of negroes . . . the country was scarcely large enough to hold the sound of indignation belched forth by them for some years. Now, however, there is no hesitation about exhausting the whole power of the government to suppress a strike on the slightest intimation that danger threatens." Grant

did not disapprove of his successor's actions. "All parties agree that this is right," he explained, "and so do I." Unlike most members of his party, he simply demanded that the forces of Confederate retrenchment be met with the same steady hand as the fomenters of labor unrest. Republicans continued to insist on the benefits of unfettered markets, free of government interference, even as they supported policies that converted public lands and resources to private wealth. By the same token, the experience of war made them comfortable with the existence of a strong central state, armed with a strong standing army that could be put to use in the protection of capital. It is hard to imagine such equanimity in the face of government coercion before the Civil War. But as a speaker at the Williams College commencement explained in 1864, "We at the North, all learned that there was in our . . . Government a power of which we never dreamed."

For John Hay, the Great Strike of 1877 was no mere abstraction. Following the collapse of the railroad bridge at Ashtabula, Amasa Stone left the country for a long sojourn in Europe, where he could close his ears to the widespread censure of his managerial and engineering skills. Left to manage the family's business affairs, Hay reported with disgust and alarm that "the country has been at the mercy of the mob, and on the whole the mob has behaved rather better than the country." With the city's businesses at a standstill and strikers preventing merchants from receiving their goods, Cleveland was a powder keg, vulnerable to the first spark of violence. "A few shots fired by our militia company would ensure their own destruction and that of the city," he wrote. His ideology still colored by memories of the Civil War, Hay condemned the "unarmed rebellion of foreign workingmen, mostly Irish," who at "any hour the mob chooses can destroy any city in the country." He assured his father-in-law that he would send Clara and the children away if the strikers grew violent. "There is a mob in every city ready to join with the strikers, and there is no means of enforcing the law in case of a sudden attack on private property. We are not Mexicans yet—but that is about the only advantage we have over Mexico." In the aftermath of the disturbances, Hay took spiritual refuge in

his partisan Republican temple, daring to hope that "the law-and-order men may rally to the party which is unquestionably the law-and-order party."

Like many of his party and class, Hay was profoundly unnerved by the labor strife of the mid-1870s. "The very devil seems to have entered into the lower classes of working men," he told Stone, "and there are plenty of scoundrels to encourage them to all lengths." He soon enough resumed the easy task of running Amasa's business concerns and researching the first chapter of the Lincoln biography. Two years later, he returned to Washington to take up the second chair at the State Department. But the strikes seared his political consciousness. During the winter of 1882–83, while traveling through Europe with his family, Hay dashed off a short novel that he titled *The Bread-Winners* and sent it off to his old friend William Dean Howells. Howells had by then departed the *Atlantic* but readily agreed to share the manuscript with the new editor, Thomas Bailey Aldrich. Upon reviewing Hay's work, Aldrich offered to serialize it in the magazine, provided that he be permitted to publish the author's name. Hay preferred to lob his brick through the enemy's window anonymously. He found another magazine, the *Century,* that was willing to safeguard his privacy. *The Bread-Winners* appeared chapter by chapter from August 1883 through January 1884 and was issued in book form by Harper & Brothers. It proved an instant success and provoked widespread speculation as to its authorship.

Set in the fictional city of Buffland—a medium-sized industrial town on Lake Erie, bearing an uncanny resemblance to Cleveland— *The Bread-Winners* told the story of Arthur Farnham, a wealthy former military officer who lives a refined life of leisure in his mansion on Algonquin Avenue. When an unscrupulous labor agitator, Sam Sleeny, calls a general strike and threatens the town's better citizens with several nights of violence and expropriation, Farnham organizes a militia company of army veterans to protect the city's homes and businesses. Other characters include Maud Matchin, a carpenter's daughter who imprudently fritters away her days dreaming of ascendance to the upper class, even at the expense of a marriage offer from a perfectly

respectable, if dim-witted, apprentice craftsman; Maud's father, who is wisely content with his place in the world; and Alice Belding, the fair-haired daughter of Farnham's next-door neighbor, and his eventual love interest. In the novel, as in life, the mob ultimately meets with swift justice, while Sleeny dies at the hands of a gullible young tradesman whom he had shamelessly manipulated. The London *Saturday Review* declared the novel "one of the strongest and most striking stories of the last ten years." Other critics were less effusive in their praise, arguing that "Thackeray and Dickens were powerful because they supported justice against prejudice . . . [T]he author of *The Bread-Winners* will never turn out permanently valuable work, so long as he misrepresents a legitimate force in the interest of a false political economy and an antiquated spirit of caste." Some readers took note of Hay's mocking treatment of Buffland's new-money arrivistes, judging the novel a "free-hand sketch in which the follies and fads of all classes are shown with marvelous impartiality." But most reviewers took it for what it was: a full-throated attack on organized labor and a defense of property rights.

Writing as the unnamed author of *The Bread-Winners*, Hay defended his novel's premise. His critics insisted "on the right of the working-man to sell his labor at the best price," but "trade-unionism is the very negation of that right. The inner circle of petty tyrants who govern the trade-unions expressly forbid the working-man to make his own bargain with his employer; his boys may become thieves and vagabonds, his girls may take to the streets, but they shall not learn his trade, or any other honest trade, without the consent of the union." Hay deplored the "murder, arson and rapine" that befell midwestern cities during the 1877 strike wave and, more recently, the "foolish" decision of several thousand telegraph operators to "give up their means of livelihood at the dictation of a few conspirators, whose vanity and arrogance had blinded them to the plainest considerations of common sense." The author of *The Bread-Winners* was no "aristocrat, or snob." He was himself a "working man, with a lineage of decent working men." He had "been accustomed to earning my own living all my life with rare and brief holidays. I have always been in intimate personal

relations with artisans and with men engaged in trade." Viewing his own success as the epitome of free labor—never mind that his father-in-law's industry enjoyed heavy public subsidies and favors—Hay bitterly resented the censure of opponents who would introduce into the political economy artificial controls and barriers to natural progress.

As he grew into middle age and wealth, Hay settled comfortably into a social and political conservatism that may seem at first blush inconsistent with his earlier politics. But for many men of his genera-tion, the road from antislavery conviction to anti-union, pro-business principles was linear and natural. He still spoke passionately in favor of the social and political revolution wrought by the Civil War. Stump-ing for the Republican state ticket in Royalton, Ohio, in 1879, he exco-riated Southern Democrats for trampling on the civil rights of black freedmen. "We think we have done all that men could be asked to do in the way of reconciliation," he intoned. "With not a traitor hanged or punished for his treason; with no restraints even upon the most persistent slack-jaw in the land . . . And now in addition they ask us to consent to sit by in silence and smile approval while they tear from the statute book every vestige of those righteous laws, by which we tried to secure the fruits of freedom and nationality after the terrible civil war into which the rebellion of Democrats had forced us." Almost fifteen years after the war ended, Republicans still perennially waved the bloody flag to rally their voters to their cause. But Hay's perora-tions were rooted in sincere belief. "Which party elected Abraham Lincoln?" he asked the Republican faithful. "Which party opposed, vilified and killed him? Which party freed the slaves? Which built the Pacific Railroad? Which saved the Union and the honor of the flag? Which sustained the financial integrity of the nation, and made its credit the best in the world?" Democrats were the party of Val-landigham and Buchanan. Theirs was a "discredited and soiled rec-ord." Republicans kept faith with the "patriots and martyrs of the great war." Their past was "luminous with the story of beneficent achievements," their "future . . . as bright with promise as the radi-ance of the morning stars." They had saved the country from slavery and disunion and built the framework for a century of prosperity. All

of which they did in the name of free labor. Over the next decade, Hay would celebrate Abraham Lincoln's common origins and mystical bond with millions of ordinary Northern farmers, soldiers, and citizens. He remained, in theory, a committed republican. For John Hay, as for so many men of his generation, the path from radicalism to conservatism was purely semantic. The world had changed; they had not.

PART IV

CHAPTER 14

A Model for All the Good Little Boys to Follow

Hours after his father's death on April 15, 1865, Robert Todd Lincoln sent an urgent telegram to David Davis, a longtime family friend whom the president had appointed associate justice of the U.S. Supreme Court. At the time of the assassination, Davis was in Chicago, presiding over a federal circuit court. "Please come to Washington at once to take charge of my father's affairs," Robert brusquely instructed. "Answer." Davis made haste for the capital, where he immediately began placing the slain president's financial and personal matters in order. Pausing only to accompany the funeral train to Baltimore, he circled back to Washington, where he was "busy getting [Lincoln's] papers ready to take to Illinois. They will be ready today, I hope, and I will return direct to Chicago tomorrow. I am tired, very tired and worn out with excitement, and I want to get with my loved ones for a day. I shall accompany the remains from Chicago to Springfield." Davis was too optimistic. Lincoln's official White House correspondence comprised more than eighteen thousand documents, sprawled across roughly forty-two thousand individual pieces of paper. Most of these items were letters and telegrams written by other people to the president, but dispersed among the dozens of boxes were copies of thousands of Lincoln's outgoing letters and telegrams, memorandums, congressional reports, and speeches. Organizing and transporting the papers proved a herculean task. Following the burial in Springfield, Nicolay and Hay returned to Washington, where they

spent several weeks arranging the papers for shipment to Illinois. The task delayed their arrival in Paris by well over a month. In Bloomington, Davis deposited the Lincoln archives in a bank vault. "At some time within the next three or four years," Robert informed a correspondent, "I propose, in conjunction with the secretaries and one or two friends of my Father on whose judgment I rely, to open the boxes and glean out what is useless and to classify the remainder in some sort. No one will have access to them before that time."

In the half dozen years that followed, the Lincoln papers remained sealed behind closed doors. When Charles Eliot Norton, the editor of the prestigious *North American Review,* inquired through an intermediary whether he might have use of the archive to write a definitive biography of Lincoln, Robert politely demurred. William Herndon, who was planning his own Lincoln biography, also asked for access. Robert insisted that he had "not any letters which could be of any interest whatever to you or anyone." With the son now single-mindedly devoted to his fledgling law practice in Chicago, and the secretaries away in Europe, the task of remembering Lincoln fell by default to individuals without access to the official recordings of his administration.

The first substantive attempt at memorializing Lincoln fell to George Bancroft, the unofficial dean of the American historical enterprise, whom Congress invited to deliver a commemorative tribute in early 1866. A Democrat who had served in James Polk's cabinet, Bancroft was an unusual choice to eulogize the first Republican president. The two men were not well acquainted, and though a unionist, Bancroft cast a critical eye on Lincoln's abilities. Speaking from the well of the House for more than two and a half hours, the gray-haired relic delivered a stem-winder packed with dense and often tangential references to American and British history. He offered little background beyond a stock biographical sketch of the sixteenth president, though he managed to issue a cool, outwardly polite rebuke of Lincoln's administrative skills and intellectual capacity for high office. The speech was well received by Bancroft's circle of literary friends, but most of Lincoln's close acquaintances, and a great many Republicans, were appalled. From Paris, John Hay fumed that "Bancroft's address was a

disgraceful exhibition of ignorance and prejudice. His effeminate nature shrinks instinctively from the contact of a great reality like Lincoln's character." The former secretary was particularly offended that Bancroft, who as a young man had followed up his Harvard degree with course work at the great German universities at Berlin, Heidelberg, and Göttingen, seemed fundamentally to underestimate Lincoln's native genius. It was an error he had seen committed time and again during the war, by better-educated but lesser men who remained stubbornly ignorant of the president's inner reserve of intelligence and strength. That same intellectual elite that he once aspired to join, Hay now scorned as unmanly and unknowing. "I believe Lincoln is well understood by the people," he told Herndon. "Miss Nancy Bancroft and the rest of that patent-leather kid-glove set know no more of him than an owl does of a comet blazing into his blinking eyes." A fervent partisan, he considered Lincoln to be "Republicanism incarnate, with all its faults and its virtues. As, in spite of some evidences, Republicanism is the sole hope of a sick world, so Lincoln, with all his foibles, is the greatest character since Christ."

Herndon likely shared Hay's contempt for George Bancroft, though for reasons of his own. Lincoln's friend and law partner of sixteen years, Herndon was a man of stark contradictions. Swept up by the reform wave that cut a path through much of the antebellum North, he was a committed abolitionist and temperance man, though also a lifelong alcoholic who fell off the wagon repeatedly and to great personal detriment. Better educated and more widely read than his famous partner, he prided himself on being Lincoln's intellectual mentor but deferred to the elder man on almost every matter concerning business and politics. Less distracted and more workmanlike than the slain president, he kept their partnership afloat during Lincoln's long absences on the campaign trail but proved inept at earning a living after his death. Yet for all of his faults and inconsistencies, Herndon understood Lincoln intimately and frowned upon the popular impulse to apotheosize the man whom he had known in the flesh and blood. He may have agreed with Hay that the "patent-leather kid-glove" crowd fundamentally misunderstood Lincoln, but he was equally

unforgiving of those who sought to make Lincoln larger in death than he was in life. "The age of blind hero worship, thank God, has gone," he told the Illinois congressman Isaac Arnold, "and the worship of truth is coming. My duty is to truth, man, and God. My mind is made up, and nothing but facts, experiences run and purified through reason, shall ever change my course."

In the weeks following Lincoln's death, Herndon found himself inundated by "enquires & interrogations by thousands of visitors as to Lincoln." True to his partner's memory, he attempted to answer them all and was soon compelled to "write dozens of letters weekly." He had been reduced to being "simply a talker—a babbler." As he patiently supplied the facts of Lincoln's life to all those who sought out his counsel, Herndon detected a common tendency to turn Lincoln into a divine figure.

No biographer was more guilty of this historical mischief than Josiah Holland, the deeply pious editor of the *Springfield Republican* in Massachusetts, who paid Herndon a visit in May 1865. Though Holland's *Life of Abraham Lincoln* was not published until the following year, Herndon may have detected strains of revisionism in his conversations with the author. Holland ultimately portrayed Lincoln as an "eminently Christian president"—the "basis of an ideal man." Relying on the stilted memories of Newton Bateman, a state official who occupied the office next door to Lincoln and Nicolay during the fall campaign in 1860, the author introduced Lincoln as a Bible-quoting evangelical whose hatred of slavery flowed from an eschatological belief that "the day of wrath was at hand." "I know that liberty is right, for Christ teaches it and Christ is God," he imaginatively quoted the future president. Here was the model of a righteous man. Repudiating the late president's reputation for unlearned, rustic charm, Holland deemed it a "great misfortune . . . that he was introduced to the nation as pre-eminently a rail-splitter." "It took years for the country to learn that Mr. Lincoln was not a boor." The book reinvented Lincoln from whole cloth, but the reading public eagerly bought up 100,000 copies, making it an overnight bestseller.

Joining Holland in the larger endeavor to apotheosize the late

president were a number of early biographers. The *New York Times* editor Henry Raymond (*The Life and Public Services of Abraham Lincoln*), the portrait artist Francis Carpenter (*Six Months at the White House*), the congressman Isaac Arnold (*The History of Abraham Lincoln, and the Overthrow of Slavery*)—all sought to enshrine Lincoln in the pantheon of the gods.

Herndon determined to strike a preemptive blow against the purveyors of fiction and religious fantasy. He complained that "the stories we hear floating around are more or less untrue in part or as a whole." Lincoln "was not God—was man," he insisted. "He was not perfect—had some defects & a few positive faults: [but] he was a good man—an honest man." In the late spring of 1865, just weeks after the assassination, Herndon traveled to Petersburg, Illinois, the county seat of Menard that housed many former residents of New Salem, the now-defunct river town where Abraham Lincoln first struck out on his own in the early 1830s. There, Herndon was amazed to encounter dozens of gray-haired old-timers who had known the future president when he was but an awkward, gangly young man dressed in pants that barely reached his ankles and crude, homespun shirt and shoes. Uncle Jimmie Short. Hardin Bale. N. W. Branson. Elizabeth Abell. Mentor Graham. All were still alive and eager to share their reminiscences of young Abraham Lincoln. "I have been with the people," Herndon reported excitedly, "ate with them—slept with them, & thought with them—cried with them too. From such an investigation—from records—from friends—old deeds & surveys &c. &c. I am satisfied, in Connection with my own knowled[ge] of Mr. L . . . that Mr. L's whole early life *remains to be written*."

Herndon was right. Most of the familiar personalities and episodes that make up the full body of early "Lincolniana" were still wholly unknown to most Americans. The pioneer boy who learned to write and cipher on the back of a shovel. The teenager who first encountered the barbarism of slavery while driving a barge full of goods down the Mississippi River. The New Salem postmaster who franked his neighbors' letters. The assistant Sangamon County surveyor who mapped out their farms. The storekeeper who walked miles to deliver money

to a customer whom he accidentally shortchanged. The wrestling match with the Clary's Grove boys. The Black Hawk War. The first run for political office. The more that Herndon learned, the hungrier he grew for new stories and new leads. Over the following two years, he all but gave up his law practice, devoting himself entirely to the Lincoln enterprise. He scoured county courthouses for records of cases that Lincoln tried both before and during their partnership. He tracked down Lincoln's cousins and interviewed them. He placed newspaper ads throughout Kentucky, Indiana, and Illinois and initiated correspondence with dozens of informants who responded to his requests for intelligence on the slain president's formative years. He even visited Lincoln's stepmother, Sarah Bush Lincoln, and recorded her teary-eyed reminiscences of Abe, "the best boy I ever saw." "I did not want Abe . . . elected," she mournfully told Herndon, "—felt in my heart that something would happen [to] him." At the end of their emotional talk, Sarah gripped Herndon's hands and, sobbing lightly, predicted that "I shall never see you again—and if you see Mrs. Abm Lincoln & family tell them I send them my best & tenderest love— Goodby my good son's friend—farewell." The entire enterprise demanded patience and diligence. Some informants, like George Spears, honestly conceded that "at that time I had no idea of his ever being President therefore I did not notice his course as close as I should have." Others remembered all too well—so much so that Herndon discounted their recollections as tall tales. The historical profession was still young in 1865, and Herndon had no formal training in the nascent practice of oral history. But he was a skilled attorney with years of experience in deposing and cross-examining witnesses. With time, he believed that he could separate the wheat from the chaff to uncover the real story of Abraham Lincoln.

The Lincoln family took a cautious view of Herndon's efforts but initially thought it safer to engage rather than ignore him. Robert, who had never been especially close to his father, thought little of Herndon and coolly but politely refused his requests for information, insisting that "even when I differ with anyone in his views of my

father's character, &c. unless it were something flagrantly wrong, I would not discuss the subject." Mary's relationship with her husband's former partner was toxic, and had been for many years. The two antagonists first met in 1837, when Mary was a young Southern belle, recently moved from Kentucky to live with her sister and brother-in-law in Springfield. At a fete thrown by Colonel Robert Allen, Herndon—then a young man just back from college—asked Mary to dance. As they locked arms, he offered the somewhat awkward compliment that she "seemed to glide through the waltz with the ease of a serpent." Thin-skinned in the extreme, Mary took umbrage at being likened to a snake, and so began a mutual enmity that lasted until her death. Never in the sixteen years that he worked alongside his partner did Herndon or his wife receive a dinner invitation to the Lincoln household. When Mary visited the law office, she and Herndon politely ignored each other. Predictably, during his one and only visit to the White House, the first lady snubbed him.

Though their relationship had long been a poisoned well, Mary understood that Herndon could not easily be ignored. Between the fall of 1865 and the winter of 1866, he had delivered several well-received lectures on Lincoln that garnered admiring reviews in the national press. Papers as far and wide as the *Chicago Tribune,* the *Missouri Democrat,* the *New York Times,* and the Washington *Chronicle* reprinted excerpts of his addresses and singled out Herndon as the nation's greatest authority on Lincoln. He alone seemed capable of locating the slain president's central humanity, without investing him with divine qualities. Some of what he revealed to his audience and readership must have rankled the family's nerves. Lincoln, he proposed, "was an exceedingly ambitious man—a man totally swallowed up in his ambitions." He had "general greed for office . . . then Mr. Lincoln preferred Abm Lincoln to any body else." He also revealed that "Mr. Lincoln read *less* . . . than any man in America." Yet Herndon also insisted that "Mr. Lincoln thought *more* than any man in America." He "led mankind by a profound policy," "used no tricks—no base arts—committed no frauds to accomplish his ends," though he "was not always—to all

persons & at all times *absolutely* Honest." His mother's hostility not-
withstanding, Robert privately acknowledged that he "saw noth-
ing . . . at which to take umbrage" after skimming the first lecture.

In August 1866, Mary, who was living in Chicago, agreed to sit for
an interview with Herndon the following month during a scheduled
visit to her relatives in Springfield. "The recollection of my beloved
husband's truly affectionate regard for *you* & the knowledge of your
great love & reverence for the best man that ever lived, would of *itself,*
cause you to be cherished with the sincerest regard by my sons & my-
self," she told him, somewhat disingenuously. Though she insisted that
Herndon keep her visit a secret, she asked him to call on her at the St.
Nicholas Hotel on September 4, at which time she would answer his
questions in "remembrance of years of *very very* great domestic happi-
ness with my darling husband & children." The two enemies seem-
ingly buried the hatchet and met for several hours at the appointed
time and place. It was a decision that Mary would live to regret.

Neither Mary nor her son knew that Herndon was preparing a lecture
that touched heavily on the Lincolns' marriage and that by the time of
their September meeting he had already formed his point of view.
While interviewing the former residents of New Salem the year be-
fore, Herndon heard several of them recount the story of Ann Rut-
ledge, the young, auburn-haired, blue-eyed daughter of the local
tavern keeper. One of his informants described Ann as "a woman of
exquisite beauty, but her intellect was quick—sharp—deep & philo-
sophic as well as brilliant." Lincoln probably first met Ann when he
boarded at the Rutledge Inn in 1831. She was eighteen years old, and he
was twenty-two. According to Herndon's informants, Lincoln fell hard
for Ann sometime around 1833 or 1834. Tragically, she reciprocated his
feelings but was already engaged to John McNeil, a local merchant
from New York with a suspect past. In 1832, while Lincoln was away
serving in the Black Hawk War, McNeil confided to Ann that his real
name was McNamar. He claimed that his family was deeply in debt
and that he had changed his surname to make a clean break of things.
Now that he had amassed a fortune of over $10,000, he planned to head

east, settle his family's accounts, and bring them back to New Salem. Upon his return, he and Ann would marry. As weeks turned into months, and months into years, McNamar's letters grew less frequent and less tender. According to Herndon's informants, Lincoln began courting the young woman around 1834, and by the following year they decided to marry—but only after she could break off her engagement to McNamar in person, and only after Lincoln completed his legal studies. Decades later, Ann's cousin James McGrady Rutledge told Herndon of a conversation he had in early 1835 while walking back from a Christian camp meeting nearby. Ann told him that "engagements made too far a hed sometimes failed, that one had failed, Ann gave me to understand, that as soon as certain studies were completed she and Lincoln would be married." Then a freshman legislator, Lincoln was attending session at the old state capitol at Vandalia when Ann suddenly contracted typhoid fever and died at the age of twenty-two. Some of Herndon's informants claimed that he returned to New Salem before her passing and had an opportunity to exchange last words at her deathbed; others remembered that he arrived home to find her already gone. "Mr. Lincolns friends after the sudden death of one whom his soul & heart dearly & [?] loved were compelled to keep watch and ward over Mr. Lincoln," one of the old-timers told Herndon, "he being from the sudden shock somewhat temporarily deranged. We watched during storms—fogs—damp gloomy weather Mr. Lincoln for fear of an accident. He said, 'I can never be reconcile[d] to have the snow—rains & storms to beat on her grave.'"

The tale astonished and fascinated Herndon, who had no inkling that the citizens of Petersburg had been trafficking in similar gossip for the better part of several decades. A year after his first visit, he returned to Menard County and tracked down none other than John McNamar, now an old man living quietly on the outskirts of what had once been New Salem. "Did you know Miss Rutledge," Herndon asked. "If so, where did she die?" The old man pointed his finger toward the western horizon and, choking back tears, replied, "There, by that—there, by *that* currant bush, she died." McNamar told Herndon that he had bought the desolate farm "in part, if not solely, because of

the sad memories that cluster over and around it." (That part was not entirely true. McNamar owned the land before Ann died and, as one skeptical historian later noted, "had since buried one wife and married another near that same currant bush.") No matter. Herndon was convinced that he had unlocked the mystery of Lincoln's deep melancholy. At McNamar's suggestion, he wandered to the desolate cemetery where Ann was buried, on a bluff overlooking the ruins of New Salem. There, "in the presence of Ann Rutledge, remembering the good spirit of Abraham," he described the intense rush of emotion that overcame him as he stood in the "presence of the ashes of . . . the beautiful and tender dead." The following morning, a "misty, cloudy, foggy and cold" autumn day, Herndon awoke early and walked through the remnants of the old town. A solemn, half-crumbled wood shack was all that remained. There, he sat down and once again took pen in hand to record the "ring of a lone cow-bell, rattling, tapping and sounding here and there," the "roll and roar of the Sangamon," as it cut a path in the valley below. "The frost had scorched the leaves of the forest, and they hung dry, curled and quivering in the winds as they sighed and moaned."

Herndon put to good use his forensic study of the physical surroundings of old New Salem when, on November 16, he delivered his much-anticipated lecture, mysteriously titled "A. Lincoln—Miss Ann Rutledge, New Salem—Pioneering, and the Poem Called Immortality—or, 'Oh! Why Should the Spirit of Mortal Be Proud.'" Dwelling intently on the physical splendor of "the eternal Sangamon, casting and rolling sand and clay, flint and lime-stone, animal and vegetable *debris,* on either shore as it half omnipotently wills, sometimes kissing the feet of one bluff and then washing the other," he laid out a geopolitical explanation of Lincoln's genius rooted in the distinct and rustic landscape of the Illinois prairie. An amateur but ardent student of history, Herndon was well acquainted with the work of Henry Thomas Buckle, the British historian whose recent book, *History of Civilization in England,* pioneered the use of geopolitical explanations of human progress. Buckle's thesis anticipated the work of later writers who have identified geography as a determining element of a civilization's economic and military competitiveness.

In 1865, these ideas were still very much in their nascent form, but Herndon was smitten with Buckle's thesis and applied it without precision or method to explaining Lincoln's "Western-ness." He regaled his audience with florid descriptions of the early-nineteenth-century frontier and its population of inventive and resourceful settlers who could "shave a horse's main [*sic*] and tail, paint and disfigure and offer him for sale to the owner in the very act of inquiring for his own horse . . . could hoop up in a hogshead a drunken man, they being themselves drunk, put in and nail down the head, and roll the man down New Salem hill a hundred feet or more. They could run down a lean, hungry wild pig, catch it, heat a ten-plate stove furnace hot, and putting in the pig, could cook it, they dancing the while a merry jig." If these early settlers were rough or crude, Herndon continued,

> What! are Grant and Jackson, Douglas and Benton, Clay and *Lincoln, inefficient men, coming west from the spirit of shiftless discontent! . . . the pioneers,* with their brave hearts and their defiant and enduring souls, are and were efficient men and women . . . [T]hey consumed and burnt the forest and cleared and cleaned it. They had and have energy and creative activity, with capacity, honesty and valor. They created states and hold them to the Union, to liberty and to justice. They and their children after them can and do point with the highest pride and confidence to the deep, broad-laid, tolerant, generous, magnanimous foundations of these mighty several western states, whereon our liberty and civilization so proudly and firmly stand.

Herndon's treatise on the geopolitical foundations of Lincoln's character would form the basis of almost all future biographies of the sixteenth president. Whether they agreed or argued with him, generations of scholars could not ignore his thesis, which was as original then as it is conventional now. Robert Todd Lincoln, for one, was unimpressed. Even as late as 1917, long after Herndon, Hay, and Nicolay had died, Robert strongly denied that his father was a simple, rough-hewn

relic of the frontier. That year, the city of Cincinnati unveiled a new statue of Lincoln by the sculptor George Grey Barnard. A minimal likeness, Barnard's statue showed the president as a clean-shaven western lawyer with plain clothes and a chiseled, rugged visage. The sculptor intended to portray "the mighty man who grew from our soil and the hardships of the earth." "He must have stood as the republic should stand, strong, simple, carrying its weight unconsciously without pride in rank and culture." Robert was livid. He thought the statue a "monstrous figure . . . grotesque as a likeness of President Lincoln . . . defamatory as an effigy." He had spent a half century attempting to burn a wholly different historical image of his father in the collective consciousness. His Abraham Lincoln was, figuratively, the distant father figure to a nation that he had been, literally, to his eldest son. These battles, in which John Nicolay and John Hay figured as central actors and which Robert would fight until his dying day, still lay far in the distance when Billy Herndon delivered his famous lecture.

For now, there was the matter of Herndon's more injurious storytelling. After framing the scene of Lincoln's youth in crude geopolitical terms, Herndon laid out for his Springfield audience and the national newspapers the tragic romantic story of young Abe Lincoln and Ann Rutledge, "the beautiful, amiable, and lovely girl of nineteen." "Abraham Lincoln loved Miss Ann Rutledge with all his soul, mind and strength," he continued. When she died, Abe "slept not . . . ate not . . . joyed not." For the rest of his years, the future president would bear the weight of an inconsolable sadness. He "*never* addressed another woman . . . 'yours affectionately'; and . . . abstained from the use of the word 'love' . . . He never ended his letters with 'yours affectionately,' but signed his name, 'your friend, A. Lincoln.'" The subtext of Herndon's argument, which he would later place in much sharper relief, time and again, was impossible to mistake: Lincoln had loved only one woman (Ann Rutledge), and his grief for her was so profound that he never loved another woman, including his wife.

The reaction to Herndon's lecture was swift and brutal. Though few of her old Springfield or Washington acquaintances harbored much love for Mary, Victorian-era convention held women in general,

and wives in particular, as immune from public scrutiny. It was one matter to criticize Mary when she was first lady, when her actions had some bearing on the public purse; it was another matter entirely to do violence to the memory of her marriage and family. Francis Carpenter, a painter who had lived in the Lincoln White House for several months while working on a presidential portrait, spoke for many respectable citizens when he scored Herndon's lecture as "an invasion of a sacred *chamber*—a tearing away of the veil which conceals the 'holy of ho-lies.'" Mary, of course, was enraged. "This is the return for all my husband's kindness to this miserable man!" she fumed. "Out of pity he took him into his office, when he was almost a hopeless inebriate and although he was only a drudge, in the place—he is very forgetful of his position and assumes a confidential capacity toward Mr. Lincoln." Robert was equally infuriated, but also concerned. "Mr. Wm. H. Hern-don is making an ass of himself," he told David Davis, and pleaded with his father's executor to intercede. Because Herndon "speaks with a certain amount of authority from having known my father for so long," his story, "even if it were . . . all true," would do great injury to his family's reputation.

In early December, Robert traveled to Springfield to try his hand with Herndon. The meeting did no good. With rumors flying of a new lecture in the works, he took a soft approach. "I have never had any doubt of your general good intentions," he wrote to Herndon, "but inasmuch as the construction put upon your language by everyone who has mentioned the subject to me was entirely different from your own, I felt justified to change your expression." Robert conceded that he had no "right" to censure Herndon's speeches and offered that "your opinion may not agree with mine but that is my affair . . . All I ask is that nothing may be published by you, which after *careful consid-eration* will seem apt to cause pain to my father's family, which I am sure you do not wish to do." On Christmas Eve, Robert sent another pleading letter, asking if it was true that he intended "to make some considerable mention of my mother in your work—I say I hope it is not so, because in the first place it would not be pleasant for her or for any woman to be made public property of in that way—With a man it is

very different, for he lives out in the world and is used to being talked of." Robert readily agreed that men like his father could be fairly "exposed to the public gaze," but he saw "no reason why his wife and children should be included—especially while they are alive . . . I hope you will consider this matter carefully, my dear Mr. Herndon, for once done there is no undoing."

It was all to no avail. In the coming years, Herndon devoted himself entirely to the project of remembering Abraham Lincoln to the nation. He let his law practice fall by the wayside, moved to a farm on the outskirts of Springfield, nearly went bankrupt, and neglected his family and career in the single-minded pursuit of "truth." The narrative that Herndon pushed was more damning than anything included in his original lectures. Over the next decade, Americans learned (incorrectly) that Abraham Lincoln's mother was a "bastard" and that she, like her own mother, had cuckolded her husband. The sixteenth president's father was not Thomas Lincoln but one Abraham Enlow. How else to explain the achievements of one born so low? Herndon also pressed the notion that his former partner was an atheist or deist and not a "technical Christian," quoting Mary out of context from the interview that she believed had been in the strictest of confidence. Her intention had been not to paint her husband as a nonbeliever but to suggest that his failure to join or regularly attend a formal church belied his more textured Christian spirituality. Herndon ignored the nuance and went for the direct punch. Worse still, from the Ann Rutledge story he drew the larger conclusion that the president never loved his wife and that she, in turn, knew it and made his domestic life a living hell. Lincoln's fidelity to Ann Rutledge was "sublime," he claimed, and all of the "struggles, difficulties, etc., between himself and his wife were partly, if not wholly, caused by Mrs. L's cognition that Lincoln did not love her, and *did love another*[.] Lincoln told his wife that he did not love her, did so before he was married to her; she was cognizant of the fact that Lincoln loved another." In Herndon's mind, *"Mrs. Lincoln's domestic quarrels . . . sprang from a woman's revenge which she was not strong enough to resist. Poor woman!"* As the years went by, Herndon's view of Mary hardened. "Jesus, what a home

Lincoln's was!" he told a friend some twenty years after the president's death. "What a wife!"

Fortunately for the Lincoln family, Billy Herndon lacked all of the necessary discipline to sit down and write a proper book. Unfortunately for them, by 1867 Herndon had recognized this shortcoming himself. "I need kicking, scolding, cussing, etc. in order to make me trot along briskly with head up and tail up," he acknowledged. In increasingly dire financial straits, he sold copies of his extensive collection of Lincoln materials—including interview transcripts, court records, testimonial letters, and newspaper clippings—to Ward Hill Lamon, the bluff, gregarious lawyer whom Lincoln had befriended on the circuit in the 1850s. Lamon came to Washington with Lincoln, served as U.S. marshal for Washington, D.C., during the war, and later established a prosperous law practice with Jeremiah Black, a prominent Democrat who had served in Buchanan's cabinet. After securing copies of the Herndon collection, Lamon, too, realized that he lacked the author's flair. So he joined forces with his partner's son, Chauncey Black, who undertook the protracted task of ghostwriting Lamon's history of Lincoln. No one had ever accused "Hill" of being a genius. The president kept him close because he enjoyed his company and because Lamon proved a familiar and comforting presence during the tumult and uncertainty of the war years. But his chronic lapses of judgment caused Lincoln frequent headaches, as when he continued arresting fugitive slaves long after it was the government's policy to encourage runaways to flee behind Union lines, or when he took it upon his (nonexistent) authority to divert an army unit from the military theater, to protect the capital. Now he displayed no better wisdom in entrusting the late president's memory to the Black family, which held the Republican Party and its martyr in low esteem. "He certainly does not compare well with the refined and highly cultivated gentlemen (fifteen in number) who preceded him in the executive chair," the elder Black scoffed. "He also lacked that lofty scorn of fraud and knavery which is inseparable from true greatness. He was not bad himself but he tolerated the evil committed by others when it did not suit him to resist it." For five years, Lamon engaged in a lively

correspondence with Herndon, who encouraged his old friend to "tell the truth and shame 'old Nick.'" On the eve of the book's publication in 1872, David Davis, who had learned of its contents, all but locked Lamon in a room for several hours and compelled him to excise an entire chapter—written, as were all of the chapters, by Chauncey Black—that portrayed the Buchanan administration's handling of the secession crisis of 1860–61 as deft and represented Lincoln as a bumbling, inept president-elect who inadvertently pushed the nation to war. Black was incensed by the eleventh-hour omission, but what remained in print proved sufficiently explosive. Folding all of Herndon's material into their dense volume, Black and Lamon were the first to publish in book form the full story of Lincoln's early life, including the New Salem stories, the alleged details of Lincoln's troubled marriage to Mary Todd, the depth of the future president's alleged atheism, and the charge—long thereafter disputed, and much later discredited—of Lincoln's illegitimate patrimony. On the eve of publication, Hay beseeched a mutual friend to intercede. "Can't you stop him?" he begged. "For the grave of the dead and the crime of the living prevent it if possible. Its effects will be most disastrous and men occupying intimate relations to Hill will be held more or less responsible." Robert, too, was furious. "It is absolutely horrible to think of such men as Herndon and Lamon being considered in the light that they claim," he told Hay.

Lamon's history of Lincoln attracted wide attention, much of it stingingly negative. James Russell Lowell dismissed the book as the work of "a vulgar man who vulgarized a noble subject." Writing for *Scribner's,* Josiah Holland called the book a disgrace. The Lincoln family was naturally disgusted by Lamon's apostasy. Before the book's publication, Jeremiah Black had the temerity to ask David Davis to grant his son access to the Lincoln presidential papers. Responding as delicately as possible, Davis explained that only Robert could grant the authors access and would certainly not do so, as "Mr. Herndon has troubled the family greatly, by his indiscreet letters & publications," and Lamon's use of these materials left Robert and Mary bitterly disposed toward the authors.

If Chauncey Black's motives were not difficult to ascertain, why did

Billy Herndon and Ward Hill Lamon disseminate such an unflattering account of a man for whom they professed nothing but loyalty? Lamon could be easily dismissed as a profoundly unsophisticated man boxing far above his weight. For Herndon, what began as devotion to "truth" morphed steadily into an obsession. The more resistance that he met with from respectable quarters, the more determined he was to introduce the world to a version of Lincoln that was complicated, flawed, and eminently human. "Would you have Mr. Lincoln a sham, a reality or what, a symbol of an unreality?" he asked a correspondent. "Would you cheat mankind into a belief of a falsehood by defrauding their judgments? Mr. Lincoln must stand on truth or not stand at all." By no means did Herndon believe that he was breaking a sacred trust with his former partner. On the contrary, as he told Lamon, "Mr. Lincoln was my good friend, well tried and true. I was and am his friend. While this is true, I was under an obligation to be true to the world of readers—living and to live during all coming time—as long as Lincoln's memory lived in this world." In his increasingly stilted historiographical view, Herndon was helping the world to appreciate the complex of hurdles that Lincoln overcame, including bastardy, poverty, and obscurity, to become "the noblest and loveliest man since Christ." Unsurprisingly, the Lincoln family took exception to his declarations of friendship. Robert also came gradually to understand that to tell the story his way, he would need help.

Hay and Nicolay had begun planning a biography of Lincoln as early as midway through their White House tenure. The president's death upended whatever initial scheme they had in mind, though from their posts in Europe the secretaries continued to keep the project in mind. "Read (+ send back) . . . my Herndon," Hay instructed Nicolay in late 1866, adding a disdainful aside that Herndon's Ann Rutledge lecture was, according to the publisher, " 'the only biography of Lincoln in whom the future will take any stock.' " While visiting the United States between diplomatic assignments in 1867, Hay heard from Schuyler Colfax that "Arnold is to publish the works of Lincoln . . . at the request of the family." The rumor proved untrue, as Hay would soon

learn from Robert Lincoln, but at the time he told Nicolay that it "dishes our chances at the papers." A few weeks later, after making inquiries in New York and Chicago, he reported with dismay that "nobody is keen for our book. We will have to write it and publish it on our own hook some day, when we can afford it." The joint venture would remain on the back shelf for an indefinite period of time, sidelined but not forgotten.

Over the next five years, the secretaries turned their attention to other endeavors. Nicolay took pleasure in his young family, while Hay kept busy as a newspaper editor and poet and devoted considerable time to his courtship of Clara. By 1872, however, Hay was "convinced that we ought to be at work on our 'Lincoln.' You might just as well be putting in your time collecting material as not. I don't think the time for publication has come, but the time for preparation is slipping away." The recent death of William Seward was a warning that an aging generation of public men would soon pass away, and if their memories and papers were not carefully preserved, the task of writing a definitive biography would prove all but impossible. Nicolay pressed the issue with Robert, who had vaguely committed use of his father's papers to the secretaries at some future date but had not yet relinquished them. "There are in this city every winter during sessions of Congress from one to two hundred individuals" who could still provide an invaluable record of the Lincoln administration. "Cameron, Blair, Sumner, Wade . . . and others, the list of whom is too long for this letter." The secretaries were prepared to begin interviewing dozens of public figures who could shed light on his father's life and presidency, but only if they were first granted access to his archives and could formulate a "definite inquiry to present. To ask them for general information, would be simply asking them to write a book." In the meantime, Nicolay went about the business of accumulating a vast library of manuscript collections, books, articles, and government documents, in anticipation of the heavy work that lay ahead.

Robert's resistance to unlocking his father's papers gave way to new urgencies. Having ceded the stage to Herndon, Lamon, and a

lesser band of Lincoln popularizers, the family had unwittingly al-
lowed the primary focus of historical inquiry to rest with topics that
fascinated the public but that invariably diminished the late president's
reputation and standing. Was he an atheist or a deist? Was Ann Rut-
ledge the only woman whom he ever loved? Did he engage in crude
wrestling matches with the Clary's Grove boys? Was his mother a
"bastard"? Was *he* a "bastard"? In the absence of state papers, no seri-
ous writer could hope to beat back the tide of amateur Lincolniana
with a scientific study of the president's public career.

It did not help matters that so many of Lincoln's friends in Spring-
field seemed ready to take potshots at his memory. Having stood by
his side and carried his banner throughout the political battles of the
1850s, many of these men felt betrayed when, as president, Lincoln
declined to furnish them with patronage and favor. Others harbored
lifelong resentments of Mary Todd Lincoln, who had never been deft
at mending fences. John Todd Stuart, Lincoln's first law partner and
political mentor, furnished Herndon with fodder when he described
his former protégé as "a kind of vegetable . . . the pores of his flesh
acted as an appropriate organ for . . . evacuations &c." N. W. Edwards,
Mary's brother-in-law and a prominent civic leader in the state capital,
offered that "Lincoln was not a warm hearted man—seemed to be
ungrateful." Jesse Dubois, a longtime confidant who once told Lincoln
that he was "for you against the world," later determined that the pres-
ident "has for 30 years past just used me as a plaything to accomplish
his own ends: but the moment he was elevated to his proud position
he seemed all at once to have entirely changed his whole nature and
become altogether a new being." Joining the chorus of critics was a
host of prominent Illinois politicians who once counted themselves as
Lincoln's allies and intimates—men like Lyman Trumbull, Orville
Browning, John Palmer, Leonard Swett, and even, to a certain degree,
David Davis—but who gradually came to assess the late president
with a more critical eye. Many of these figures had migrated to
the Democratic Party by the 1870s, driven by concerns over political
corruption and monetary policy. Lincoln's legacy was closely tied
to a political economy that they viewed with distrust. As the years

progressed, their opinions of the Great Emancipator became less approving.

If it were solely the Illinoisans who refused to canonize Lincoln, the matter could have been written off as a family squabble. But by the early 1870s, national voices had joined the conversation. In 1872, Charles Francis Adams—a scion of the famous Massachusetts family (and father of Henry Adams) who had served in the Lincoln administration as minister to Great Britain—delivered a memorial address on William Seward. Adams held up Seward as the glue that kept the government together in perilous times. "I must affirm, without hesitation," he avowed, "that in the history of our government, down to this hour, no experiment so rash has ever been made as that of elevating to the head of affairs a man with so little previous preparation for the task as Mr. Lincoln." Only by good grace and luck did Lincoln possess the wisdom to appoint as his first minister Seward, the "master mind" of the government and savior of the Union. The speech infuriated Lincoln's stalwart defenders, first among them Gideon Welles, who issued a stinging rebuke. But Adams was not alone in assessing Lincoln as an ill-prepared, weak wartime leader. In his popular account of the war years, *The American Conflict,* the ever-erratic Horace Greeley similarly portrayed Lincoln as a bungling leader who squandered multiple opportunities to end the war early, either on the battlefield or through negotiation. Lincoln acolytes might have rolled their eyes at the aging bomb thrower, but he sold books, so his opinion mattered.

Shortly after Seward's death, Nicolay wrote once more to Robert, denouncing the "contemptible assertions of Chas. Francis Adams" and urging him to allow for the "collection and arrangement of the materials which John and I will need in writing the history we propose. We must of necessity begin with your father's papers, because everything else must be grouped and accumulated around them." Still Robert dragged his feet. The dam finally broke in April 1874. From his perch in New York, where he was still writing editorial content for the *Tribune,* Hay shopped their project around the city and received tremendous interest from all corners. Richard Gilder, the editor of *Scribner's,* had sent Hay a brief note, asking if it were not "time about a 'Life of

Lincoln' & are you looking for publishers? Or they for you?" On the reverse side of Gilder's note, Hay scribbled a quick valedictory to Nicolay. "Bob promised to give us the papers as soon as we are ready to begin work on them." That summer, several dozen boxes finally made their way from Bloomington to Washington, D.C., where Nicolay deposited them in his office. There, in the vast marble confines of the Capitol building, they would be safe from fire, water damage, or theft. It would take years to cull through the voluminous correspondence and identify the documents on which their work would be based.

By 1875, the secretaries were fully immersed in research and slowly coming to appreciate the mammoth task for which they had volunteered. "The work is a heavy one," Hay informed the former vice president Schuyler Colfax, "continually growing on our hands. I have many misgivings about it, but we shall put in it all we can." Writing from Springfield, Milton Hay offered Nicolay some unsolicited but undoubtedly welcome advice. "The reading public in this country (those who mainly buy books)," he began, "were in full sympathy with Mr. Lincoln and his administration, and they believe and sympathize with the idea that he was the greatest figure in that revolutionary period which began with the repeal of the Missouri Compromise, and ended with the suppression of the rebellion and the emancipation of the slaves." Milton reminded Nicolay that the better sort of citizens were sincere in their religious convictions and would never consent to "bring into their family libraries, a book which shall either deprecate Lincoln, or clothe him with heterodox religious views." He was glad to know that the secretaries were committed to the Lincoln enterprise, because Americans "want a model for all the good little boys to follow, and Billy Herndon's model won't do."

Milton's counsel did not fall on deaf ears. Nicolay was disgusted, as was John Hay, by the ham-fisted way in which men like Lamon, Herndon, and even Charles Francis Adams had butchered Lincoln's reputation. They had known William Seward intimately and admired him greatly, but they could not concur that he was somehow the invisible hand guiding the Union war effort. They had worked beside Lincoln

for more than four years, day and night, and believed that they understood him better than nearly anyone else alive. Theirs would be a corrective enterprise, though they scarcely appreciated the immensity of the task to which they were committing themselves. The biography would consume their professional attention for the next fifteen years. During that time, both men held other jobs: Nicolay remained at the Supreme Court until 1887, while Hay worked for his father-in-law and served briefly as assistant secretary of state. Their labors were frequently interrupted by their own illnesses or those of their wives and children. Editors begged them for an advance peek at the work. Publishers courted them persistently. For the time being, they held their suitors at bay. "We [are] in no hurry to make arrangements," Hay told one hopeful. Heads down, they set themselves to the work of presenting the historical Lincoln to the world.

Our Ideal Hero

John Nicolay was forty-two years old when he started work on his life of Lincoln; by the time he completed the manuscript, he was fifty-seven. John Hay began drafting his portion of the collection at age thirty-six; he was fifty-one when the book went to print. In the years since the two secretaries first went to Washington with the president-elect, both had married and started families of their own. They held diplomatic positions in Paris, Vienna, and Madrid. One was appointed the chief executive officer of the Supreme Court. The other published acclaimed works of literature and served as assistant secretary of state. But more than the popular image of Abraham Lincoln had effectively frozen in time on April 15, 1865. Many people who remembered the secretaries as young men encountered difficulty in appreciating that they had grown up with the world around them. One newspaper critic, upon learning of their project, complained that "whoever attempts to limn for future ages the characteristics of Abraham Lincoln . . . must possess the ability to survey very much more than comes within scope of ordinary mortal vision." The secretaries, he concluded, fell short of the mark. "Time enough for them to try biography when they are forty." Hay was enraged. "That scoundrel . . . has persuaded these idiots that you and I are about nineteen years of age," he fumed in a letter to Nicolay.

Even Robert Todd Lincoln sometimes had trouble imagining them in their passage to middle age. Though he was several years younger

than Nicolay and Hay, Robert enjoyed meteoric career advancement
that owed much to the good fortune of his last name, a fact that led
many to believe—perhaps himself included—that he was wiser than
his years. A prominent Chicago attorney, he turned down an offer to
serve as assistant secretary of state in 1877 but entered the cabinet in
1881 as secretary of war just before his thirty-eighth birthday. Having
entrusted his father's archive to Nicolay, he kept close watch on the
secretaries' progress, sometimes to their consternation. "I beg of you
to no longer think of us as mere boys," Nicolay pleaded on one occa-
sion, "but as men who have learned something in the school of experi-
ence at least, and who believe ourselves capable of doing creditable
work." Nicolay reminded Robert that his father was "our ideal hero.
We wish to delineate the grandeur of the era in which he lived, the
far-reaching significance and influence of the events he led, and to set
him in history as the type, the Preserver and Liberator of the People."

Robert's sensitivity belied his personal fondness for Nicolay and
Hay. He had known them for a very long time and remained on close
terms with them over the years, exchanging personal well wishes on
the births of their children, sharing gossip about mutual friends, and
keeping them apprised of his family's milestones and hallmark mo-
ments. They were his closest partners in securing the Lincoln legacy.
When Bob's youngest brother, Tad, passed away in 1871 at the age of
eighteen, Hay acted in effect as the family's official spokesman, pen-
ning a widely read obituary for the *New-York Tribune,* still the paper of
record for Republican stalwarts. "Most of those who read the dispatch
announcing the death of Thomas Todd Lincoln will never think of the
well-grown gentleman who died on Saturday at Chicago," Hay began.
"The name of 'Tad'—a pet name given by himself with his first stam-
mering utterances and adopted by his fond parents and the world—
recalls the tricksy little sprite who gave to that sad and solemn White
House of the great war the only comic relief it knew." Hay remem-
bered fondly and vividly the "chartered libertine" who was "idolized
by both his father and mother, petted and indulged by his teachers,
and fawned upon and caressed by that noisome horde of office-seekers
which infested the ante-rooms of the White House. He had a very bad

opinion of books and no opinion of discipline, and thought very little of any tutor who would not assist him in yoking his kids to a chair or in driving his dogs tandem over the South Lawn." To the world, Tad had seemed a one-dimensional character, easy to know and easy to like, but Hay recalled that he could treat "flatterers and office-seekers with a curious coolness and contempt," even as he "often espoused the cause of some poor widow or tattered soldier, whom he found waiting in the ante-rooms, and it was most amusing to see the hearty little fellow dragging his shabby protégés into the Executive presence, ordering the ushers out of the way, and demanding immediate action from headquarters." "The Tad Lincoln of your history ceased to exist long ago," he observed. In his place had emerged a "well-grown gentleman," the "modest and cordial young fellow who passed through New-York a few weeks ago with his mother [but] who will never be known outside the circle of his mourning friends." In the annals of history, he would forever remain "the child whose gayety and affection cheered more than anything else the worn and weary heart of the great President through the toilsome years of the war." Robert was deeply moved by the effort. "John Hay's screed is like a picture," he told Noah Brooks. Pry and edit as he might, the president's sole surviving son trusted that the secretaries saw and understood his father, and the entire Lincoln family, with greater clarity and loyal purpose than anyone else.

For their part, the secretaries genuinely admired Robert and regarded him as a friend, but they never mistook him for his father's spirit incarnate. Robert kept a cool distance from the political ante-rooms where his father cultivated a studied appreciation of men and motives. The father made politics his avocation; the son held it at bay. Nicolay believed that Robert possessed that "latent power of observation and comparison which is evidently in the blood" but thought that he "still looks at politics through a reflecting medium—perhaps I should say an opaque one . . . making him incapable of assigning it a true estimate. Politics is a thing *à laisser ou à prendre,* but by no means to be despised, either in nobler or baser relations to the times we live in. Nobody had a clearer perception [on] that point than his father. A

little more age and experience will probably enable Bob to see it as well."

As their work progressed over the years, the authors routinely conferred with Robert on matters of style and emphasis. Hay, who was closer in age and with whom he had a more intimate bond, regularly assured Robert of their fidelity to his family. "I need not tell you that every line has been written in a spirit of reverence and regard," he insisted, when sending him an early draft of the opening chapters. "Still you may find here and there words or sentences which do not suit you. I write now to request that you will read with a pencil in your hand and strike out everything to which you object. I will adopt your view in all cases, whether I agree with it or not, but I cannot help hoping you will find nothing objectionable." These agreements were never made public, though astute observers like William Herndon suspected that the secretaries were "writing the life of Lincoln under the surveillance of Bob; he gives them materials and they in their turn play hush. That is my opinion and is worth no more than an honest opinion."

Though only fragmentary copies of the original drafts survive, letters between Nicolay, Hay, and Robert testify to the heir's "plenary blue pen powers"—in Hay's words—over every word that the secretaries wrote. From those few extant drafts that bear his line edits, Robert appears to have played his heaviest hand in dictating cuts to those chapters dealing with Lincoln's childhood and early career, most of which Hay composed on his own. He made liberal excisions to Hay's description of his grandfather Thomas Lincoln, whom he had never met. "It is beyond doubt that my departed grandfather was not an enterprising man," Robert conceded, "& it is likely that your graphic assaults upon him . . . are not undeserved but I could not help feeling better if you would 'let up' on him a little in a final revision. He did not have much chance to prepare & pose in the reflection of his son's fame & I feel sorry for him."

In his original draft, Hay judged Thomas "an idle, roving, inefficient, good natured man" and offered that he "appears never to have done [anything] especially deserving of mention." It was a gentle way of dealing with a sensitive topic. Robert ordered the offending lines

cut. Hay noted that "men like him may be seen every day in Western rural towns, fond of story-telling, of talking things over by the red-hot stove of tavern bar-rooms, or in the cool door ways of livery stables, according to the season. He was a Jackson Democrat, as those of his kind usually were. He was discursive in his religious affiliations, changing his church about as often as he changed his residence." This, too, Robert called out, though he did not object to Hay's observation that Thomas Lincoln was "generally called an unlucky man." Gone also was Hay's description of the family's early settlement in Indiana. "When we consider that a weeks work was all that was required to make a cabin habitable," read the offending passage, "and that Thomas Lincoln was a carpenter by trade, we can form some idea of the hopeless indolence which allowed him to live two years in a house without a door and without a floor." Instead, the final manuscript noted simply that Thomas Lincoln's "cabin was like that of other pioneers. A few three-legged stools; a bedstead made of poles stuck between the logs in the angle of the cabin . . . The boy Abraham climbed at night to his bed of leaves in the loft, by a ladder of wooden pins driven into the logs."

If Nicolay and Hay compromised the independence of their work in agreeing to grant Robert final editorial discretion, the standards of their day were unclear on the qualities that defined good history. They embarked on their project at a time when the American historical enterprise stood on the verge of a sea change in methodology and philosophical approach. Until the latter part of the nineteenth century, most U.S. universities and colleges were incubators of discipline and morality but bore little resemblance to the centers of formal inquiry and training that would characterize higher education in the next century. Inasmuch as students mastered classical literature and mathematics by rote memorization, they inherited knowledge and skill sets that prepared them for professional endeavors, but there was as yet no American counterpart to the scientific methods and formalized degree programs preferred by the great German universities. History, as practiced by George Bancroft and his generation of scholars, remained a linear story of providence and progress, and its view of America was of a land endowed by God with a certain destiny. There was less regard

for human agency in the development of political systems and govern-
ments and even less appreciation of impersonal economic or environ-
mental forces in the shaping of human choices.

The Civil War did much to shake the foundations of American his-
torical consciousness. As scholars began to chronicle its causes and
effects, it became impossible to escape the suspicion that the United
States might not be a perfect, divinely ordained society—or at least
that its progress might not yet be complete or strictly linear. New ex-
planations required new methodologies. Only with the inauguration
of new American institutions like Johns Hopkins and the University of
Chicago, and the wholesale overhaul of older establishments like Co-
lumbia and Harvard, did Americans import the rigorous approach of
the German academy. Underlying this transformation was a vogue for
"objective, verifiable and clearly communicable truths," as a contem-
porary scholar framed the challenge. Among historians, the earliest
practitioners of this approach were the students in Herbert Baxter Ad-
ams's pioneering history seminar at the Johns Hopkins University.
Adams, who earned his Ph.D. at Heidelberg, established the research
seminar in 1880 to help the university evolve "from a nursery of dogma
into a laboratory of scientific truth." That evolution would require an
abandonment of romantic and subjective uses of history for a reliance
on dispassionate and fact-driven analysis, grounded in evidence and
divorced from ideology or bias. It is unclear how successful Adams was
in inculcating his classroom with precisely this ethos. One of his stu-
dents, J. Franklin Jameson, whom Johns Hopkins would ultimately
award its first doctorate in history, complained that his professor was
undisciplined and his seminars "tiresome," given to "too much mutual
admiration and not enough savage criticism"; "the staple of the meet-
ings consists of outside 'attractions,' now a Confederate general to talk
on a campaign, now an elderly party exhumed to 'reminisce' to us."
But the enterprise was fast becoming a profession. The American His-
torical Association was founded in 1884, and by the turn of the century
increasing numbers of history professors claimed doctorate degrees
from institutions that trained them to research and think like "cool,

unbiased" social scientists. The era of romanticism had given way to a search for "objectivity" and "stern historical truth."

Nicolay and Hay were not among this new generation of professional historians. They claimed no formal training (Nicolay did not even have a college degree) and made little effort to mask their bias. But they did set out to write a history grounded in evidence and fact. In the early days of the project, Nicolay spent several months interviewing dozens of individuals who had known Lincoln in Illinois and Washington. The transcripts of these discussions informed their work, but with time they came to cast a skeptical eye on memories recorded years or decades after the fact. If a fact or an anecdote could not be confirmed by the written record, they usually discounted it entirely. Luckily, what they could not find in Lincoln's vast manuscript collection they often found in their personal archives. Writing to Nicolay in 1878, Hay reported that he had "devoted a day or two to looking over my notebooks" from the White House years. "I have a large amount of valuable notes—made on the spot, the extent and value of which I had quite forgotten. They are weak in 1861, not very good in '62 except in respect to 2nd Bull Run, but quite full and valuable for '63 and '64. They are not in good shape. I do not know but that I may try to have them copied by type-writer." On rare occasions they relied on their personal recollection of events to bring the pages of the biography to life. Nicolay's vivid description of the moment that Lincoln was nominated at Chicago was one such use of memory; their general descriptions of the Lincoln White House were another. In the final volume, Hay drew on his firsthand account of Lincoln's death. But in their general methodological approach, they could not have differed more sharply from Herndon, Lamon, and most other early Lincoln biographers, all of whom relied almost exclusively on interviews conducted long after the fact. When chapters of their work were serialized in the late 1880s, Charles Dana, who had served as assistant secretary of war under Edwin Stanton, publicly challenged their assertion that Hay had been with the president at the War Department telegraph office on the evening of the 1864 election—"in face of my diary which says I was,"

Hay wrote. "You see the sort of pig-headed contradiction we have got to go through on the part of conceited old men with bad memories, who have been lying for 20 years." Writing to the former vice president Schuyler Colfax, he wryly observed that people grew self-aggrandizing over time, as their memories betrayed them. "You know it is impossible for any old Illinoisan to talk for five minutes without letting you understand that he made Lincoln all he was," Hay said with a wink. Ultimately, the secretaries stopped conducting interviews altogether, Hay later explained to Charles Francis Adams Jr., "because it placed us in a dilemma of either being compelled to report a lot of worthless fiction, or of giving grave offense to our friends by declining to do so."

To supplement the Lincoln archives and their personal diaries and letters, Hay and Nicolay set about acquiring as much additional material as they could buy. Robert helped them gain access to Gideon Welles's diary and also granted them use of important genealogical documents. They scoured newspapers for speech transcripts. They collected vast quantities of government documents, both Union and Confederate, related to the war. They swapped materials with the War Department, which still retained copies of Lincoln's ingoing and outgoing telegrams. They asked the children of long-departed Civil War notables to look through their attics for important documents and purchased materials from manuscript and book dealers. "I am getting together quite a little lot of books," Nicolay reported as early as 1876. "I think I have the foundation for a Rebellion Library . . . There must be now between three and five hundred volumes, big and small, as you count, or omit to count, the trash in it." Over the next decade, the oversized first-floor study in Nicolay's Capitol Hill row house came to accommodate one of the largest private collections of Civil War documentation and secondary scholarship in the country. Both men paid out of pocket for the materials and conferred regularly to decide on the acquisition of particular items. To organize and store the vast stacks of paper and books that he consulted while writing, Hay ordered a custom-made desk, measuring seven feet by four feet. It was so bulky the workmen could not maneuver it up to the second-floor office in his Cleveland residence. "I shall get a carpenter to remove the

banisters of the back stairs to get it up!!" he relayed with childish delight. When Hay lived in Washington, between 1879 and 1881 as assistant secretary of state, and again from 1885 onward, he and Nicolay would walk between each other's homes to swap materials and chapter drafts. When Hay was in Cleveland, or traveling in Europe, and when Nicolay vacationed in New England or Colorado during the summers, they exchanged documents by post. Over the years, they both struggled with headaches, illnesses, and diminishing eyesight. By the mid-1880s, Hay found himself "breaking down with the nervous fatigue of writing & copying [and] therefore hired a stenographer—a dull young Englishman who has nothing in the world but handwriting." Yet given the impediments to progress and the many personal and professional distractions that might have derailed their work, the pair made astonishing progress. Nicolay began the drafting process by fashioning a schedule of chapters. Once Hay agreed to the contents and order, they divided up the topics and set to writing.

"The two would never divulge how the actual writing was divided between them," Helen Nicolay later explained. "They seemed to take a mischievous delight in keeping it a secret, saying they were co-authors, and that was all the public need know." In some cases they alternated chapters. In other cases, each might assume responsibility for an entire volume. Though strains of Hay's lyricism are evident in his chapters, particularly those dealing with Lincoln's childhood and early career in Springfield, he and Nicolay had been so long acquainted, both professionally and personally, that they were able to develop a common prose style with little effort. "I write with great labor," Hay admitted early in the process. "My imagination is all gone, a good riddance. I think my judgment is improved. I shall never write easily and fluently again." That was not quite true. Six years later, he dashed off *The Bread-Winners*. But Hay clearly compartmentalized the project from his literary efforts. The Lincoln biography was to be a work of politics and memory. It demanded a different kind of diligence. He was content to favor exposition and analysis over style.

Reporting from Cleveland in the summer of 1877, Hay, who was responsible for chronicling the majority of Lincoln's early life, promised

that "if nothing happens adversely, we can have Lincoln inaugurated by the 4th of March 1878."

By the time Nicolay and Hay began their writing in earnest, roughly fifteen years after the collapse of the Confederacy, prominent Southerners had already begun crafting a new narrative—one that would afford their people a modicum of self-respect in the wake of devastating defeat and inspire Northerners to embrace a revisionist history in which everyone was right and no one was wrong. In these efforts, the progenitors of America's reunion romance achieved considerable success. It was against this backdrop of apologia and reunion that the secretaries set out to fashion their interpretation of Lincoln's story.

In the immediate aftermath of the war, the business of recording and remembering the rebellion fell to a small group of hard-line, unreconstructed rebels. The first fomenters of Confederate revivalism included such figures as Jubal Early, B. T. Johnson, Fitz Lee, and W. P. Johnson, most of whom shared aristocratic credentials, nominally distinguished war records, and a venomous hatred of all things Northern. Although their calls for defiant commemoration met with widespread apathy throughout the 1860s and 1870s, these men ultimately formulated the ideological underpinnings of what would become, under new leadership in the 1880s, the standard Southern interpretation of the Civil War.

The prevailing themes of this Southern historical rendering were veneration of an antebellum South that was both aristocratic and, by implication, better mannered than the North, with its pervasive spirit of avarice and cruel economic competition; confirmation that secession had been a legal response to incursions against states' rights rather than a revolutionary action; and finally, insistence that slavery had been only a remote cause of the war. As one Hunter McGuire explained in a historical report for the Grand Camp of Confederate Veterans of Virginia, "however brave" rebel soldiers had been, to acknowledge that they fought to preserve slavery would only "hold us degraded rather than worthy of honor . . . [O]ur children, instead of revering their fathers, will be secretly, if not openly, ashamed." With

the nettlesome issue of slavery thus disposed of, new officials of the Confederate memory machine could stress more desirable subthemes of the Lost Cause saga, including Confederate respect for social discipline, Southern womanhood, and private property.

The 1880s and 1890s saw the rapid proliferation of Confederate commemoration as a new trio of associated organizations—the United Confederate Veterans (UCV), the United Daughters of the Confederacy (UDC), and the Sons of Confederate Veterans (SCV)—institutionalized the related themes of intersectional reconciliation and a vague form of Southern pride, rooted in heritage but devoid of overt ideology. These groups appealed to a far wider swath of the white Southern population than Early and Fitz Lee because they offered a compelling postwar epilogue in which almost everyone could believe. Rather than bewail what could have been, they worked to create a spirit of sectional reconciliation based on a unity of experience among combat veterans of the Blue and the Gray. The first large-scale manifestation of this new wave of Confederate commemoration occurred in May 1890, when between 100,000 and 150,000 onlookers gathered in Richmond for the unveiling of a statue of Robert E. Lee. Throughout the late 1880s and the 1890s, hundreds of towns across the South undertook the commission of similar monuments to their heroes and war dead. Unlike the initial wave of graveyard memorials that Southerners unveiled in the 1860s, these structures tended to be placed in town squares and by county courthouses, and in keeping with the new emphasis on comradeship in arms, more often than not they featured statues of Confederate veterans.

More sweeping still were the annual reunions of state UCV chapters and the perennial, section-wide UCV meeting, which drew crowds ranging as high as a hundred thousand. Confederate veterans were at the center of these celebrations, reinforcing the UCV's emphasis on military honor. Beyond their ability to draw impressive numbers at memorial events, the UCV, UDC, and SCV enjoyed considerable political influence in determining how future generations of Southerners would understand the events of the 1860s. During the war, for instance, Confederate soldiers had eagerly embraced the sobriquet "reb,"

but the new guardians of Southern memory insisted the term violated their revision of the war's status from revolution to constitutional conflict. "Was your father a Rebel and a Traitor?" asked a typical chapter leaflet. "Did he fight in the service of the Confederacy for the purpose of defeating the Union, or was he a Patriot, fighting for the liberties granted him under the Constitution, in defense of his native land, and for a cause he knew to be right?" Keeping to this revisionist tendency, rather than propagate undignified titles like "the late war" (too vague), the "Civil War" (too revolutionary), and "the War of Rebellion" (far too revolutionary), in the late 1880s the UCV and UDC approved resolutions encouraging the conflict's official designation as "the War Between the States." Successive generations of Southern schoolchildren would learn it as such.

At the same time that Southerners were reconceptualizing the war's meaning, many white Northerners acceded to a similar revisionist impulse influenced by a reverence for shared military experiences and progressively hardened racial sensibilities. Soured by the experience of Reconstruction and increasingly inclined to view biracial Southern democracy as a noble but failed experiment, many Northerners focused on what they shared with the Confederates, not on the bygone ideological differences that once caused them to raise arms against each other. A telling example of this transformation was Oliver Wendell Holmes Jr., a scion of Boston's Brahmin society who began the war as a firebrand abolitionist. After enduring four years of grim combat, Holmes found his faith in causes tempered. Decades later he reflected, "The faith is true and adorable which leads a soldier to throw away his life in obedience to a blindly accepted duty, in a cause which he little understands, in a plan of campaign of which he has little notion, under tactics of which he does not see the use." In effect, action, rather than belief, was the true test of faith and courage. In his intellectual journey from idealist to pragmatist, Holmes may have been similar to many other men of the Civil War generation.

Toward the close of the nineteenth century, veterans and the public at large came to view the martial achievements of both sections as equally praiseworthy. This spirit of reconciliation, and its emphasis on

combat over ideology, produced a new vogue in the late 1880s: Blue and Gray reunions. Over the next several decades, veterans and enthusiasts attended hundreds of battlefield and regimental reunions at which standard etiquette held that soldiers from both sides be honored guests. In 1887, Boston's Granddaughters of the American Revolution post hosted members of Richmond's Robert E. Lee Camp of Confederate Veterans, who were treated to a sightseeing tour of the city formerly regarded as the unofficial capital of abolitionism. That same year, the Seventh Connecticut held a reunion at which the honoree was the Confederate colonel Charles Olmstead, whom the regiment had captured during the war. Two years later, the Society of the Army of the Cumberland held a Blue-Gray reunion on a scale that would become increasingly common: twenty-five thousand people gathered at Crawfish Springs, near the Chickamauga Battlefield, for a picnic and public ceremony.

Further aiding the process of historical revisionism was a highly successful Southern literary assault on public memory. Beginning in the 1880s, a host of Southern writers—most notably Joel Chandler Harris, John Esten Cooke, Thomas Nelson Page, and Sara Pryor—flooded the nation's mass-circulation fiction market with local-color stories depicting the antebellum South's refinement and civilization. To court Northern readers (something they did exceedingly well), these writers scrupulously avoided topics that might rekindle old political flames and instead wove tales replete with beautiful plantation belles, dashing cavaliers, and dull-witted but cheerful black slaves. Between 1875 and 1900, Northern magazine fiction most commonly described black freedmen as "simple," "fervent," or "good-humored," qualities that harmonized with Page's stock story line: out-of-town traveler (often from the North) meets "old retainer" (a former slave remaining in his master's service) who, after a great deal of prodding, reminisces wistfully of a bygone age when "nuttin warn too good for the niggers." Above all, these writers celebrated the Southern heritage without dwelling on the nagging questions of slavery and treason. "For those who knew the old County as it was then," read one of Page's novels, "and can contrast it with what it has become since, no wonder

it seems that even the moonlight was richer and mellower 'before the war' than it is now." Such sentimentality and romance played well with Northern audiences, whose memory of slavery and capacity for race liberalism had evaporated considerably since Reconstruction. Over were the days when *Uncle Tom's Cabin* could enrage a nation of readers with its depiction of slavery's violent assault on the cherished institutions of family and Christianity.

Not everyone bought into the spirit of selective national amnesia. In 1894, shortly before his death, Frederick Douglass, the aging lion of the abolitionist movement, warned that "death has no power to change moral qualities . . . What was bad before the war, and during the war, has not been made good since the war . . . Whatever else I may forget, I shall never forget the difference between those who fought for liberty and those who fought for slavery." It was a theme he had been sounding for almost thirty years—that the spirit of intersectional reunion must not blot out the moral dimension of the Civil War, that "there was a right side and a wrong side in the late war which no sentiment ought to cause us to forget." Douglass was outraged by the willingness of the victorious North to forgive and forget the trespasses of the vanquished South. He was incredulous that Northerners seemed ready to permit Southerners to divest the bloody conflict of its ideological and moral components and to refashion the war as an epic family feud in which both Johnny Reb and Billy Yank fought courageously and honorably, buried the hatchet, and became brothers again. While Douglass vigorously rejected "that school of thinkers which teaches us to let bygones be bygones," by the late nineteenth century more Americans chose to treat the 1860s with wistful but selective retrospection. At battlefield reunions, in popular fiction, inscribed on war memorials, a single theme reverberated clearly: the war was over, its cause was moot, and all should be honored.

By 1885, Hay and Nicolay had reached a critical juncture. It had been a full decade since they embarked on the Lincoln project, and almost a quarter century since they left Springfield for Washington to take up their positions in the White House. They had already written some

500,000 words and were scarcely halfway through the Civil War. Hay grew increasingly concerned by the exhaustive scope and length of the undertaking. In late January he acknowledged receipt of a massive package of documents from Nicolay but confessed to "dread and terror" at its size. "I will try to tackle it next week," he promised, though he did not "know where or how to begin." With a light hand, he warned Nicolay that "if we give every incident a chapter, we will have a hundred volumes." In April, Hay pleaded once again for concision, remarking with apparent exasperation that Nicolay had plotted out five chapters for events that Hay had assigned one. "There is certainly matter enough to make 15 or 50 chapters of it," he wrote, "but I judge from my own weariness of the subject that no living man will read more than I am writing. We will be happy if they read as much." Nicolay disagreed. For the duration of their work on the life of Lincoln, he wrote long, while Hay tried to write short. But he had known his partner for almost four decades and understood how to manage him. He assured Hay that his organizational scheme was provisional and that he had no fixed opinion on the number or names of the remaining chapters. At the same time, he gently suggested that "you are giving yourself needless worry about the chapters not being read. I have not the remotest interest that any living man woman or child will read them all . . . They will be read if at all, either individually as chapters, or by short periods and campaigns, and to secure that, I think the rather careful working out of details, giving their separate dramatic unity, is desirable. But people *must* buy our book whether they read it or not. It will be, as the Debating Society said of Shakespeare, 'The best work on that subject,' and the subject they cannot remain ignorant of." Nicolay reminded his friend that they were writing for two "classes" of readers: those who experienced the war, knew a great deal about it, and expected new revelations, and those who were too young to have experienced the great events of the 1860s and who needed general instruction. Their mandate was to write large and thereby create a definitive record of events for all Americans and for all time.

What they needed was incentive to bring the project to a close. Roswell Smith and Richard Gilder provided just that motivation, and

they were not coy about their intent. "We want your life of Lincoln," Smith told Hay plainly. "We must have it. If you say so, I shall give you all the profit. We will take it, and work it for nothing . . . It is probably the most important literary venture of the time." As publisher of the *Century Magazine*, Smith knew whereof he spoke. The successor outlet to *Scribner's Monthly*, the *Century*, as it was formally rechristened in 1881, was America's fastest-growing and most popular periodical, overtaking both the *Atlantic* and *Harper's* in readership and literary influence. Edited by Gilder, who had apprenticed at the foot of Josiah Holland during the *Scribner's* days, the magazine became a leading arbiter of taste and values among the nation's growing postwar middle class.

Gilder was a native of Bordentown, New Jersey. Slim, debonair, and fashionably mustachioed, he was a poet of decent renown who had served briefly in the Union army. But his true genius was for reading the national mood, and by the early 1880s he realized that there was money to be made in the business of Civil War memory and national reunion. Under Gilder's tutelage, the *Century* became an avid promoter of Southern romance literature by such leading authors as George Washington Cable, Thomas Nelson Page, and Grace King. By far the most popular of the early New South authors, Cable soon became a cautionary tale for those trafficking in the risky enterprise of local color and regional memory. A veteran of the Confederate army, by the early 1880s he had evolved into a searing critic of the emerging Jim Crow system and a thoughtful observer of Southern class and race relations. The magazine's editors urged him to stick to stock story lines in which Union soldiers fell in love with, and married, Southern belles. "Hold up the best side of the South and North during the War of Secession," they advised. "Here is romance ready made." Cable resisted these calls to idealize the "invaded and desolated South," and Gilder gradually stopped publishing his work. More popular among the *Century's* readership were wistful (though manifestly ahistorical) descriptions of antebellum plantation life, in all its supposed harmony and beneficence. This type of literature attracted a growing Southern audience and encouraged the spirit of intersectional friendship that

emerged from the ashes of Reconstruction. "It is hard to explain in simple terms what Thomas Nelson Page meant to us in the South at that time," Grace King later observed. "He was the first Southern writer to appear in print as a Southerner, and his stories, short and simple, written in Negro dialect, and, I may say, Southern pronunciation, showed us with ineffable grace that although we were sore bereft, politically, we had now a chance in literature at least."

Recognizing the appeal of reunion and romance, in July 1883 two of Gilder's associate editors, Robert Underwood Johnson and Clarence Buel, hatched plans for a new series, Battles and Leaders of the Civil War, which would capitalize on the emerging vogue for battlefield reunions and personal memoirs. Running between 1884 and 1887, the series featured first-person accounts by high-ranking officers of both the Union and the Confederate armies. Gilder was willing to pay top dollar, and contributions by Ulysses S. Grant, William Tecumseh Sherman, George McClellan, P. G. T. Beauregard, Joseph E. Johnston, and James Longstreet, as well as many lesser-known veterans, helped expand the magazine's readership from 127,000 to 225,000, making it first among equals in the stable of American periodicals. Each installment featured upward of 160 pages of war material, effectively subsidizing the Century's serial efforts to acquaint its readership with the works of Mark Twain, Walt Whitman, Henry James, and William Dean Howells. By the time Roswell Smith and Richard Gilder began courting Lincoln's secretaries, their magazine had become America's foremost curator of Civil War memory.

The Century's editors believed that "no time could be fitter for a publication of this kind than the present, when the passions and prejudices of the Civil War have nearly faded out of politics, and its heroic events are passing into our common history where motives will be weighed without malice, and valor praised without distinction of uniform." The series would endeavor to show a generation that was too young to remember the war how men "who were once divided on a question of principle and State fealty" were now bound by a "respect for each other which is the strongest bond of a reunified people." As a magazine with a national readership, the Century, Gilder hoped, could

exert a "moral effect in helping to bring the once warring sections into a better understanding and a higher mutual regard." It was "time for the 'unveiling of all hearts,'" he confided to a potential Confederate contributor. "If the North can see the heart of the South, and the South's the North's they will love each other as never before! This is truth, and not sentimentalism." Opting to title the series "Battles and Leaders," rather than "Men and Events," Gilder told his staff that "'Battles' is the main thing. 'Events' might seem as if we were going into, say, the condition & action of the freedmen—the Emancipation Proclamation—& other events not connected with battles." Johnson agreed, promising to "soften controversy" through the "exclusion of all political questions." Thus sanitized of race, ideology, or partisanship, the result was pleasing to all concerned. Northern and Southern readers devoured the *Century*'s Battles and Leaders series, while the editors crowed that it "did more to bring together North and South than anything that had happened since they were torn apart in 1861."

Gilder began courting Hay and Nicolay as early as 1874, when he was an assistant editor at *Scribner's*. Over the years, he continued to send the secretaries hopeful letters, and in 1880, even before he launched Battles and Leaders, he approached them with an unusual offer to serialize their work. "Flattering as his suggestion is," Nicolay told Hay, "I do not after a week's reflection see that it is at all practicable. To begin with, we are not ready; second, the full work would occupy five magazines for five years—and finally, I think the historical *effect* of the work would be substantially lost if published serially in chapters." Hay was inclined to agree. It was not until five years later, after persistent entreaties from Gilder and Roswell Smith, that he entered into serious discussions with the magazine, though for rights to the entire book, not serial publication. Visiting New York, Hay met with the *Century*'s publishers, who proffered a 10 percent royalty on all sales. He was unimpressed by the proposed authors' cut and skeptical of their competency, as a magazine, to sell books along the subscription circuit. Like Nicolay, he felt that serialization was an acceptable format for other subjects, "but they are not on a level with Lincoln." He suggested that they entertain a competing offer from Harper.

The power of persuasion—and money—soon caused both men to think anew. Hay's palatial home in Washington, D.C., was near completion; it would require furnishings and trimmings. Nicolay, who lived in modest comfort, had his eye on land in Colorado and New Hampshire, where his family enjoyed spending summers. It was time to publish. "The unprecedented success of the *Century* articles," Hay told Nicolay, in reference to Battles and Leaders, "and the fair sale even of Stoddard's book"—a reference to the release of William Stoddard's White House memoirs—"show that the market is ready. I am getting anxious to print a volume or two." In late March, Hay instructed Nicolay to meet with representatives of the *Century* and "get from them as much information as possible & give them as little. I think it is best not to let publishers know anything about our methods of work—who writes what—&c. &c." Gilder's response was sufficient to earn him, at long last, an invitation to review the incomplete manuscript. Vacationing with his family in New England, Nicolay asked the editor to join him for several days of review. Gilder was "visibly interested," Nicolay reported. Poring over twelve chapters each day, he "said several times he was hoping to find a dull chapter which he could skip . . . We are only at about the middle of the reading as yet. G. has not said much, and I have put no questions to draw out the impressions which he may be gathering in his mind."

By fall, they had a contract. *Century* offered the secretaries terms unprecedented in the publishing industry. They would be paid $50,000 for the serial rights to their work, as well as royalties on sales of the full ten-volume set, which would be issued following the completion of the magazine run. All involved assumed that the serial run would last more than two years. If the first installment ran sometime in 1886, Hay and Nicolay would have almost three years to complete their life of Lincoln. "The work will have a great moral and political effect," Gilder crowed, "in that it will help unite the North and South as never before, around the story and experiences of the great President."

If Gilder hoped that the Lincoln serial would continue in the vein of Battles and Leaders by fostering greater understanding between North

and South, he was mistaken. He had read the first half of the secretaries' manuscript. He met multiple times with Hay and spent several days in seclusion with Nicolay at a New Hampshire farmhouse, poring over the completed chapters. He was perceptive enough to understand the mind-set of his new authors. Confiding to a friend, he explained that the Nicolay-Hay volumes were "the secret history of the secession conspiracy" and a "complete, authentic, and logical account of the great political struggle in connection with the subject of slavery," an assessment with which they would have heartily agreed. Yet he also believed—as Nicolay and Hay surely did not—that "Lincoln is now one of the most revered of our public men in the very South whose political unity he destroyed. They soon felt that in Lincoln's death they lost their best friend." (Had most Southerners believed it, the secretaries would not have cared.) Writing to Nicolay, Gilder struck the same optimistic note, wondering at the "universal tone of respect and even affection with which the memory of Lincoln seemed to be held in the South . . . It is hard to find the slavery or the secession sentiment in the South today." "As for the Negro," he added, liberal men like George Washington Cable and Thomas Dudley, the Episcopal bishop of Kentucky and outspoken supporter of black rights, were "fighting out the remaining problems in the pages of the *Century.*"

Thus began a delicate balancing act. Gilder was giddy at the prospect of following the highly successful Battles and Leaders series with a two- or three-year run of "the only authorized life of the greatest man this country has ever produced—at least since Washington—and not only the greatest, but by far the most interesting." But the aggressive Northernism of his authors was out of alignment with the *Century*'s ethos and diverse readership. At some point during their weeklong confab in New Hampshire, Nicolay casually offered the opinion that Robert E. Lee could or should have been shot for treason. This argument did not appear in the manuscript, but then, the manuscript was only half-complete. Gilder was "horrified" at the suggestion, Hay reported, and though he agreed that it was "a simple truth of law and equity," he reminded Nicolay that such extreme displays of Northern sectionalism would not do for a national publication. Seeking clarifica-

tion, Gilder sent a delicate note to Nicolay, who responded noncha-
lantly that he would "look up the exact language I used in reference to
Lee. I think the phrase you called my attention to was merely used in
conversation, and then only as a hypothesis on military law. I do not
mean to say even in conversation that as a matter of policy the penalty
he rendered himself legally liable to ought to have been inflicted. But
I do mean to say that his adherents and admirers ought to be grateful
to the people and the government of the U.S. for the Great Pardon
with which they have covered all these offenses against law and hu-
manity."

Nicolay and Hay spared Gilder's readership lengthy fulminations
on the crimes and applicable punishments of Robert E. Lee, but they
did suggest in fairly plain language that the widely esteemed Virginian
was a liar. Lee long maintained that when he was offered field com-
mand of the Union armies, he turned down the offer, for "though op-
posed to secession and deprecating war, I could take no part in an
invasion of the Southern States." "A flat contradiction exists as to the
character of Lee's answer," Nicolay and Hay wrote, citing the testi-
mony of Simon Cameron, Lincoln's first war secretary, and Montgom-
ery Blair, his first postmaster general, that Lee had in fact accepted his
promotion before subsequently reneging. "In the course of events,"
they continued, "we find him not alone defending his native State, to
which he owed nothing, but seeking to destroy the Union, which had
done everything for him; opposing war by promoting 'revolution,' and
redressing grievances by endeavoring to establish anarchy." True, the
authors did not call for Lee's head. But Gilder may have reeled in his
chair when he read their "contrast" between "the weakness and de-
fects of Lee" and "the honorable conduct and example of General
Scott." Nicolay ultimately thought that they did justice to the subject
and that their chapter on Lee could "hardly be objected to, except by
the utterly 'unreconstructed.' "

Though Southern partisans much preferred Lee, the general, to
Jefferson Davis, the politician, in the chapter describing Abraham Lin-
coln's death, Hay rankled Southern sensibilities by writing that Jeffer-
son Davis rejoiced at news of the Great Emancipator's murder. He later

defended this claim in the face of bitter criticism. In their assessment
of another Confederate icon, Thomas Jackson, the secretaries smiled
as they cut. Hay, who drafted most of the material on Stonewall,
thought that the late general was a "howling crank" but feared that it
would "be the greatest folly for me to say so." As it was, he told Nico-
lay, "I am afraid that I have come too near saying so in what I have
written about him." Offering that "Jackson was by far the most inter-
esting and picturesque figure in the Southern army" and "a man of
extraordinary qualities," he proceeded to dismiss the Confederate
"saint and hero" as a "slow, dull, unprepossessing youth" who, "had
the war not come to call him forth to glory and the grave . . . would
probably have lived and died in the mountain village known only to
his neighbors . . . 'as a sincere, odd, weak man.'" Jackson "believed
himself to be under the immediate and partisan protection of his Cre-
ator; he believed . . . that Heaven helped him plan his campaigns and
battles; his Creator was ever present to his mind, in his own image—as
a good Southerner, as earnest a hater of the Yankees, as stern a fighter
as himself." Stonewall was "a fanatical Sabbatarian; he would not read
a letter, which arrived Saturday night, until Monday; he would not
post one in such a way that it would travel on the Sabbath. Yet he
would not scruple to bring a bloody battle on Sunday." He was a hypo-
chondriac who believed that one of his legs was growing shorter than
the other, that he only perspired on one side of his body, and that he
needed to maintain his opposite limbs in perpetual motion to sustain
proper circulation. "If John Brown of Ossawatomie had been bred in a
slave State and had received a West Point training," he remarked,
evoking the South's greatest bête noire, "it is hard to see in what par-
ticular he would have differed from Stonewall Jackson."

The secretaries did not enjoy full leeway in hacking down the idols
of Confederate mythology. They were being paid handsomely for their
efforts and could not disregard the *Century*'s concerns. Though rarely
one for diplomacy, Nicolay assured Gilder that he agreed with "the
principles laid down in your letters." "I believe I have adopted all your
corrections," he added, "and I think the text the better for them . . . We

want to make the text as acceptable as we can without sacrificing essentials." In practice, the cuts and modifications irritated Nicolay. Defeated on several editorial points, and in a rare display of pique with Hay, who urged him to temper some of his language, Nicolay rued that he lacked the "grit to stand up against the demoralizing sugar coated historical principles you lay down. In fact, I think my wings had been sprouting just a little before that. Gilder's pencil went through a great many of my strong and most picturesque adjectives, and I agreed that on the whole it improved the text. When we come to revise I suppose that very few if any of them will go back." (Their friendship was too long-standing to suffer for a minor literary disagreement. In his next breath, Nicolay expressed concern at Hay's frequent illnesses and counseled him to take a month off from writing to restore himself to good health.)

The *Century* ran excerpts of the Nicolay-Hay enterprise between 1886 and 1890, ultimately exposing hundreds of thousands of readers to roughly one-third of the total work. Toward the end of the serial run, Gilder congratulated the authors on their success. "Lincoln's fame, for all time, has been more firmly established for your labors," he told them, and "the people now living, so many of whom were also living during his lifetime, have had an opportunity of knowing the man, such as would never have occurred if the history had only appeared in book form." As an aside, Gilder allowed that some critics had charged Hay and Nicolay with "partisanship," but

> even those most opposed to certain deductions and general remarks of the authors, would recognize that an honest attempt has been made to present the truth as you were convinced of it . . . It may be that future historians, and critics of history, will be less severe in the judgment of some you have thought it right to condemn;—and such historians or critics may be called upon to take into view the "personal equation";—but when all is said that can possibly be said in criticism, the fact will remain that you have followed your

convictions, and by your devotion and industry have pre-
sented a picture of the man, and of the times, which will
have an indistinguishable value.

Gilder wrote the letter in the spirit of friendship and as a valedic-
tory on the closing of an important chapter in the lives of his authors
and his magazine. Nicolay saw only criticism. In a blistering draft re-
ply, he asserted that neither he nor Hay was

> conscious of having written a word of censure of any per-
> son, party or principle which is not in accord with the stan-
> dard recognized by the civilized world. We fail to see how
> any secession conspirator can ask the tolerance of reason-
> able minds in claiming for South Carolina the right to se-
> cede from the United States . . . With what claim to pardon
> could Jefferson Davis incur the penalty of death or treason
> to the United States, and immediately thereafter take an
> oath to inflict the death penalty upon others for treason to
> the Confederate States? With what sense of military duty
> and honor could Robert E. Lee render himself liable to be
> shot for desertion from the U.S. Army and then take an
> oath to shoot a Southern soldier for desertion from the Con-
> federate Army?

After cooling his heels for a few days, Nicolay filed the letter away,
unsent, much as Lincoln often drafted dispatches that he later opted
not to transmit. Two weeks later, he mailed a gracious response to his
editor, agreeing heartily that the serial run had proven a great success.
In closing, he added, "As to the possible accusations of partisanship, we
stand in no awe of them. We deny that it is partisanship to use the
multiplication table, reverence the Decalogue, or obey the Constitu-
tion of the United States. When logic, morals and law all unite to con-
demn the secession of the rebellion of 1861, he will be a rash critic to
pronounce censure upon any who helped put down that secession and
rebellion, or who venture truthfully to record its incidents."

More so than Nicolay, Hay was sensitive to appearance. He worried that he and his co-author might appear to current and future readers as still being "in the gall and bitterness of twenty years ago." But on points of substance, there was little daylight between the two men. In its final form, *Abraham Lincoln: A History* presented in ten volumes, and 1.2 million words, the authorized biography of a slain leader and the unofficial Northern, Republican Party interpretation of the Civil War.

CHAPTER 16

We Are Lincoln Men All Through

The long-awaited serial publication of the Nicolay-Hay biography began in late 1886. Almost from the start, the work proved controversial. While many observers debated its treatment of specific persons or themes, others were baffled by its long digressions into general historical topics in which Lincoln emerged only as a minor player and sometimes not at all. One of Richard Gilder's correspondents privately lamented that because he had a "very great interest in Lincoln," he was "disappointed at finding so little concerning him" in the magazine's excerpts. Expecting to read a biography of the late president, this dissatisfied reader instead found "biographical remarks on the great men of Abraham Lincoln's time, with a few bits of irrelevancy about Lincoln himself thrown in. The historical narrative that Messrs. Hay and Nicolay are giving us is a great success as a picture of days gone by, and it is a great pity that it should be marred by those personal details of an obscure Illinois lawyer which we notice have crept into the story from time to time." One critical reviewer quipped that the book ought really to be titled "From Boone to Booth; or, The Surprising Adventures of Senator Tom, Governor Dick, and Congressman Harry, in the Early Days of the Roaring Republic." *Life* magazine even proposed a new game whereby players would spread copies of the *Century* out on a table and attempt to locate five references to Lincoln in a particular volume; a successful player could then jump to the next issue. "Chapters of the history which contain five allusions to the

subject must be provided for the game," the editors warned; "otherwise the evening is likely to go by without any winners, and drag correspondingly."

Odd, indeed, was a biography whose subject all but disappeared for an entire volume. Yet by virtue of their exhaustive treatment of Lincoln's political career, Nicolay and Hay seared into the national awareness episodes that were then largely unknown to the public, and themes and arguments that would influence Lincoln scholars and Civil War historians for generations to come. Among its many famous contributions to the nation's shared historical consciousness were revelations that William Seward drafted the closing lines of Lincoln's first inaugural address, which the president-elect then fashioned into a work of literary genius, and that early in his term Seward attempted to assert himself as "first minister" by provoking a war with Britain and France, in an ill-conceived attempt to unite North and South against a common enemy. Lincoln, they revealed, stopped the secretary in his tracks, rejecting his proposal outright and warning that even "if this must be done, I must do it." Nicolay and Hay were the first to report George McClellan's vainglorious assurance that he could "do it all" when Lincoln gave him command of the entire Union army. They were the first to write of Lincoln's great distress early in the war, when Washington, D.C., was cut off from the rest of the North and the president, keeping an anxious vigil for fresh troops, wondered, "Why don't they come!" They offered unprecedented insight into Lincoln's decision making around emancipation and the enlistment of black soldiers and an insider's view of his interaction with the Union's high military command. Few Americans knew that when Lincoln appointed Joe Hooker as commander of the Army of the Potomac, he also seized the opportunity to dress him down for having argued that "both the army and the Government needed a dictator. Of course, it was not for this, but in spite of it, that I have given you the command. Only those generals who gain success can set up dictators. What I now ask of you is military success, and I will risk the dictatorship."

The critics were not without reason. In some ways the term "biography" was a misnomer when applied to the Nicolay-Hay enterprise.

More accurately, it amounted to a "life and times" account that drew on vast and heretofore unreleased document collections to offer a comprehensive portrait of Lincoln's career and to situate the late president within the broader universe of actors and events that formed the backdrop of his tenure in office. In fifteen chapters (totaling more than three hundred pages) covering the period between October 5, 1860, and January 9, 1861, Nicolay admitted that he scarcely even addressed "the acts of Lincoln or the Republican Party."

Above all, Nicolay and Hay created a master narrative whose influence would ebb and flow over the years but that continues to command serious scrutiny and engagement more than a century after its initial introduction. Early in the writing process, Nicolay assured Robert Todd Lincoln, "We hold that your father was something more than a mere make-weight in the cabinet . . . We want to show that he formed a cabinet of strong and great men—rarely equaled in any historical era—and that he held, guided, controlled, curbed and dismissed not only them but other high officers civilian and military, at will, with perfect knowledge of men." This overarching theme pervades the ten volumes of their work. Populating his original cabinet with former opponents for the Republican presidential nomination, Lincoln demonstrated his discernment and magnanimity in choosing men whom he "did not know . . . He recognized them as governors, senators, and statesmen, while they yet looked upon him as a simple frontier lawyer at most, and a rival to whom chance had transferred the honor they felt to be due to themselves." Presaging by one hundred years the popular argument that Lincoln forged a "team of rivals," Nicolay and Hay insisted that the strong personalities and talents who constituted his inner circle did not always appreciate "the stronger will and . . . more delicate tact [that] inspired and guided them all." "The President was gifted by nature with a courtesy far excelling the conventionalities of an acquired politeness. With a delicacy which has rarely been equaled, he respected not merely their official authority but also their sentiments." With few exceptions, they, in turn, yielded to "the superior sagacity and authority of the President."

The Lincoln who filled the pages of the Nicolay-Hay volumes was

"almost a giant in physical stature and strength" and "combined in his intellectual nature a masculine courage and power of logic with an ideal sensitiveness of conscience and a sentimental tenderness as delicate as a woman's. The Presidential trust which he had assumed was to him not a mere regalia of rank and honor. Its terrible duties and responsibilities seemed rather a coat of steel armor." Though both authors died some twenty years before the completion of the Lincoln Memorial, their description of the slain president could not have anticipated its design more perfectly.

The *Century*'s Lincoln series started at the beginning, quite literally. To John Hay had fallen the task of writing most of Lincoln's early life, which made up the first volume of the joint enterprise. Despite his deep skepticism of oral history, Hay relied heavily on Lamon's work, which was in turn rooted in Herndon's extensive interviews. Supplementing these sources with genealogical materials, public records, and print sources, he devoted himself to the task of recasting an old story, rather than new digging for new research. The heart of the larger enterprise would concern Lincoln's presidential tenure, not the minutiae of his upbringing. "Of all these years of Abraham Lincoln's early childhood," Hay wrote, "we know almost nothing. He lived a solitary life in the woods, returning from his lonesome little games to his cheerless home. He never talked of these days to his most intimate friends." Hay's volume included lively accounts of familiar stories, from Lincoln's first arrival in New Salem, to his service in the Black Hawk War and the Illinois state legislature, to his courtship and marriage to Mary Todd and his one term in Congress. In no way did he contribute any new information, but in leaning on Herndon and Lamon for these details of Lincoln's early life, Hay fashioned a new interpretation rooted heavily in the antebellum western experience.

Unlike Herndon, who bought substantially into geopolitical explanations of Lincoln's personal development, Hay described a more complicated encounter between environment, blood, and circumstance in the formation of Lincoln's character. "The 'barbarous neighborhood' and the 'savage intercourse' " that early Kentucky settlers (like

Lincoln's grandfather and namesake) met with in the early 1780s "un-
doubtedly had their effect upon the manners and morals of the set-
tlers," he proffered, "but we should fall in error if we took for granted
that the pioneers were all of one piece. The ruling motive which led
most of them to the wilds was that Anglo-Saxon lust of land which
seems inseparable from the race . . . Accompanying this flood of emi-
grants of good faith was the usual froth and scum of shiftless idlers and
adventurers, who were either drifting with a current they were too
worthless to withstand, or in pursuit of dishonest gains in fresher and
simpler regions." Despite the savage influence of the land and its na-
tives, "near as they were to barbarism in all the circumstances of their
daily existence, they were far from it politically. They were the chil-
dren of a race which had been trained in government for centuries in
the best school the world has ever seen, and wherever they went they
formed the town, the county, the court, and the legislative power with
the ease and certainty of nature evolving its results."

In his youth, Hay had been deeply embarrassed by the "sharp points
and salient angles of Western life." As a White House aide, he came to
miss the rustic beauty and quiet charm of the place where he grew up.
Toward the close of the Civil War, on a visit home, he marveled at the
"beauty of our river society." "You can scarcely find a quieter place to
write your romance," he told Nicolay. "There is no society here. You
can pass a couple of months here entirely undisturbed by visitors . . . I
would give a great deal to pass a month here." Later, as poet and au-
thor, Hay became an accidental authority on western habits and mind-
sets. Always, his relationship to the region was complicated. He did
not romanticize the world of Lincoln's childhood. "In most respects
there had been little moral or material improvement since the early
settlement of the country," he wrote. "Their houses were usually of
one room, built of round logs with the bark on . . . Their dress was still
mostly of tanned deer-hide, a material to the last degree uncomfort-
able when the wearer was caught in a shower. Their shoes were of the
same, and a good Western authority calls a wet moccasin 'a decent
way of going barefoot.'" Kentucky and southern Indiana were "full of
strange superstitions," and a "vague and ignorant astronomy governed

their plantings and sowings." Pioneer residents were rough and unsophisticated. "Among these people, and in all essential respects one of them, Abraham Lincoln passed his childhood and youth. He was not remarkably precocious. His mind was slow in acquisition, and his powers of reasoning and rhetoric improved constantly to the end of his life, at a rate of progress marvelously regular and sustained. But there was that about him, even at the age of nineteen years, which might well justify his admiring friends in presaging for him an unusual career."

Hay's deep admiration and love for Lincoln shine through in his imagination of the future president's solitary childhood. Describing Lincoln's boyhood habit of reading and rereading *Aesop's Fables, Robinson Crusoe,* the Bible, and Parson Weems's *Washington,* he drew a moving portrait of a young boy sitting *"by the fire at night,"* covering his "wooden shovel with essays and arithmetical exercises, which he would shave off and begin again. It is touching to think of this great-spirited child, battling year after year against his evil star, wasting ingenuity upon devices and makeshifts, his high intelligence starving for want of the simple appliances of education that are now afforded gratis to the poorest and most indifferent." None of these morsels were new to the reading public, but Hay cast them in a new light. Whereas Herndon and Lamon sought to knock Lincoln off his godly pedestal, Hay presented the future president as a hero in the wilderness, doing solitary battle against the physical and emotional privations of his upbringing.

At times, he applied a simple western essentialism to explain Lincoln's personal attributes and characteristics. In describing Lincoln's "constitutional sadness," a trait that most of the late president's close associates readily acknowledged, Hay offered that "it may be said to have been endemic among the early settlers of the West. It had its origin partly in the circumstances of their lives, the severe and dismal loneliness in which the struggle for existence for the most part went on. Their summers were passed in the solitude of the woods; in the winter they were often snowed up for months in the more desolate isolation of their own poor cabins. Their subjects of conversation were limited, their range of thoughts and ideas narrow and barren." This

"generic tendency to melancholy," Hay surmised, could be traced to
the bleak world of the pioneer generation, to which Abraham Lincoln's
parents belonged and which the future president knew intimately in
his youth. "There was as little cheerfulness in their manners as there
was incentive to it in their lives." What could not be explained by ge-
ography could be ascribed to science. Malaria and other killer diseases
were rife in the woodlands and prairies of southern Indiana and Illi-
nois. "Abraham was exposed through all the earlier part of his life to
those malarial influences." In an effort to ward off sickness, pioneers
routinely consumed "various preparations of Peruvian bark . . . In
many instances this miasmatic poison did not destroy the strength or
materially shorten the lives of those who absorbed it in their youth;
but the effects remained in periodical attacks of gloom and depression
of spirits." William Herndon, who generally viewed such geographic
explanations favorably, dismissed as complete rubbish the suggestion
that "we of the great West of an early day were unsocial and never
smiled, only laughed . . . That Mr. Lincoln was a sad, gloomy, and mel-
ancholic man, I admit," but "his sadness, etc., were *principally* and
chiefly caused by his organism, his make-up and his constitution . . .
These, with the untimely death of Ann Rutledge, and his unfortunate
marriage to Miss Mary Todd, and the hell that came of it, caused Lin-
coln's sadness."

That Hay dispensed with the Ann Rutledge story in just two sen-
tences also struck Herndon as pure folly. On this topic, the authors
said only that during the New Salem days, Lincoln "made the acquain-
tance of the best people the settlement contained, and among them
had become much attached to a girl named Ann Rutledge, the daugh-
ter of one of the proprietors of the Rutledge place. She died in her girl-
hood, and though there does not seem to have been any engagement
between them, he was profoundly affected by her death." Of Mary
Todd, who had been dead for over a decade, Hay and Nicolay wrote
relatively little. They glossed over the often-told story of the Lincolns'
first, abortive intent to marry, in a fashion that reflected well on both
parties (arguing, in essence, that neither had been ready to take the
leap); they also withheld judgment as to Mary's character, or the

character of her marriage to Lincoln, and remarked simply that "on the 4th of November, a marriage license was issued to Lincoln, and on the same day he was married to Miss Mary Todd, the ceremony being performed by the Rev. Charles Dresser. Four sons were the issue of this marriage . . . Of these only the eldest lived to maturity." Given the unhappiness of her latter days, and his Victorian belief that the women behind public men should remain shielded from scrutiny or attention, Robert may well have preferred that they gloss over his mother's role with minimal fanfare or mention. An intensely private man, he may also have appreciated the infrequency of his own appearances throughout the Nicolay-Hay opus.

Neither Hay nor Nicolay believed that geographic or environmental influences could explain the entirety of Lincoln's character. Much of his course in life, they argued, owed to blood and providence. Remarking on the superficial similarities between Lincoln and Jefferson Davis—both roughly the same age and Kentucky-born, both claiming service in the Black Hawk War, each a successful politician in his own right—they offered that "if chance or fate had guided their parents to exchange their routes of emigration from Kentucky; if Lincoln had grown up on a Southern cotton plantation, and Davis had split rails to fence a Northern farm; if the tall Illinois pioneer had studied trigonometry at West Point, and the pale Mississippi student had steered a flat-boat to New Orleans, education might have modified but would not have essentially changed either. Lincoln would never have become a political dogmatist, an apostle of slavery, a leader of rebellion; Davis could never have become the champion of universal humanity . . . Their natures were antipodal."

Though Hay cautioned Nicolay that they must not seem like two ancient relics rehashing the great sectional crisis of their youth, his opening chapters were thoroughly unforgiving of Southern politics and character. Describing the end of the "pioneer period of Illinois," which coincided roughly with the Lincoln family's migration across the Indiana line, he noted matter-of-factly that "the earlier emigrants, principally of the poorer class of Southern farmers, shunned the

prairies with something of a superstitious dread. They preferred to pass the first years of their occupation in the wasteful and laborious work of clearing a patch of timber for corn, rather than enter upon those rich savannas which were ready to break into fertility at the slightest provocation of culture." These Southern pioneers, who dominated the settlement of Illinois until the late 1840s and the 1850s, "were mostly a simple, neighborly, unambitious people, contented with their condition, living upon plain fare, and knowing not much of anything better."

In dwelling on the cultural and political differences between Northerners and Southerners before the war, the authors presaged the larger sectional bias that ran through their work. Nicolay and Hay were writing against the popular grain of sectional reunion—a sentiment that their publisher, the *Century*, arguably did more to foster than any other institution. In 1881, even as he labored at their life of Lincoln, Nicolay found time to write the first volume of a popular series published by Charles Scribner's Sons, titled Campaigns of the Civil War. Nicolay's contribution, *The Outbreak of Rebellion*, flatly rejected the vogue for reconciliation and portrayed secession as a long-held, deeply laid plot to subvert the tenets of democratic government. Dismissing South Carolina as a "school of treason for thirty years," he assailed the "unthinking masses of the South" for their hysterical reaction to the 1860 presidential elections and for initiating a bloody and expensive war in the service of a "counterfeit philosophy." Identifying the "prominent office-holders, governors, senators, congressmen, [and] judges" as the "central clique of conspiracy," Nicolay laid wider blame on the "inexorable tyranny of Southern opinion." This was not an argument likely to win the hearts and minds of Southern readers, a fact that several reviewers pointed to in their sharp criticism of the volume.

"I confess I learned something from the criticisms of your book," Hay told Nicolay. "All the reviews acknowledged its merits of style, accuracy and readableness—but nearly every one objected to its tone of aggressive Northernism. This was a surprise to me. I read it in M.S. and thought it perfectly fair and candid—but I am of that age and

imbued with all its prejudices." His "prejudices" notwithstanding, Hay warned that they must not appear as "two old dotards fighting over again the politics of their youth." "The war has gone by," he counseled Nicolay. "It is twenty years ago. Our book is to be read by people who cannot remember anything about it . . . We must not write a stump speech in eight vols., 8vo. We will not fall in with the present tone of blubbering sentiment, of course. But we ought to write the history of those times like two everlasting angels who know everything, judge everything, tell the truth about everything, and don't care a twang of their harps about one side or the other. There will be one exception," he added. "We are Lincoln men all through."

Though "aggressive Northernism" pervades all ten volumes of the Nicolay-Hay history, it assumed full primacy in Nicolay's chapters on the sectional crisis of the 1850s and the secession winter of 1860–61. Largely a rehash of his book for Scribner's, Nicolay's account of this period featured only two kinds of Americans: traitors and patriots. The vast majority of Southerners fell into the former category, along with a despised fifth column of Northern doughfaces, while the Northern public embodied the spirit of the latter category, along with an unrepresentative number of brave Southern souls. Revealing their shared sectional bias, the authors did not merely denigrate Southern motives and mores, but also held up the antebellum and wartime North as an advanced and superior civilization. "The lion of the North was fully roused," Nicolay wrote of the immediate reaction to the fall of Fort Sumter. "Betrayed, insulted, outraged, the free States arose with a cry of pain and vengeance. War sermons from pulpits; war speeches in every assemblage; tenders of troops; offers of money; military proclamations and orders in every newspaper; every city radiant with bunting; every village-green a mustering ground; war appropriations in every legislature and in every city or town council; war preparations in every public or private workshop." Even Northern children "abandoned their old-time school-games, and played only at soldiering." Having anticipated a "'peaceable secession,'" the South was soon "fully awakened when regiment after regiment came pouring into Washington, when treason was choked in Maryland, when the

Western capitals became great camps, when the blockade began to close the seaports of the South. More alarming was that increasing activity of the Northern uprising, the earnestness of which could no longer be denied or mistaken."

In resisting the prevailing romance of sectional reunion, Nicolay and Hay gave a prominent place to the elephant in the room: slavery. Few white Americans were interested in discussing the question by 1885, but Nicolay and Hay resisted the popular consensus. They were not writing, however, as aging, unreconstructed abolitionists. In the years since they first engaged the issue as young men, both authors had evolved considerably in their thinking. They had always counted themselves as antislavery men, but they now remembered the war as having been rooted deeply in the moral offense of the peculiar institution, a position that they did not hold in 1861, or even as late as 1865. In his discussion of the sectional politics that formed the backdrop of Lincoln's political rise, Hay stated matter-of-factly that "it is now universally understood, if not conceded, that the Rebellion of 1861 was begun for the sole purpose of defending and preserving to the seceding States the institution of African slavery and making them the nucleus of a great slave empire." Rejecting out of hand the increasingly popular argument that the Civil War was about a great many things, but not slavery, Hay reduced the conflict to "that persistent struggle of the centuries between despotism and individual freedom; between arbitrary wrong, consecrated by tradition and law, and the unfolding recognition of private rights; between the thralldom of public opinion and liberty of conscience; between the greed of gain and the Golden Rule of Christ."

Addressing the causes of the war, Nicolay acknowledged that Jefferson Davis had written some fifteen years after the war that "the equality of the States," rather than slavery, had precipitated the conflict. "The generation which fought the war needs no proof of the incorrectness of this declaration," he scoffed, before devoting another twelve pages to dissecting Davis's public statements to the contrary. Nicolay decried the "spirit of bullying" and "resort to violence" that besmirched the halls of Congress in the mid-1850s, stipulating that "it

all came from the pro-slavery party." Revisiting the same theme that he had sounded as the young editor of the *Pike County Free Press,* he asserted that "proslavery sentiment rendered the constitutional right of 'freedom of speech or of the press,' and rights of domicile and of citizenship, practically a dead letter throughout the South." Of the antebellum South, he held that "the great plantation master dominated society and politics; there was no diffused and healthy popular action, as in the town-meetings of New England. Even the slaves of the wealthy proprietors spoke with habitual contempt of the 'poor white trash' who lived in mean cabins and hoed their own corn and cotton."

The authors were also strident in their consideration of slavery as a social and economic system. Paraphrasing Lincoln, Hay described the institution as "one of the many 'relics of barbarism'—like the divine right of kings, religious persecution, torture of the accused, imprisonment and enslavement for debt, witch-burning, and kindred 'institutions'—which were transmitted to that generation from former ages as so many burdens of humanity." Breaking his own rule against believing the memories of old men long after the fact, Hay gave credence to the claim of John Hanks, Lincoln's cousin, who told William Herndon about a trip that he and Lincoln had taken many years before. Hired to escort a barge full of goods down the Mississippi River in 1831, Hanks claimed that it was there that Lincoln first saw "negroes chained, maltreated, whipped, and scourged. Lincoln saw it; his heart bled; said nothing much, was silent, looked bad. I can say, knowing it, that it was on this trip that he first formed his opinion of slavery." The story may very well have been true, as many Northerners reacted with the same revulsion upon first laying eyes on Southern slave pens, but in all likelihood John Hanks had debarked from the journey before his party arrived in New Orleans.

In any event, Hay dismissed as "an idle waste of labor" any attempt to pinpoint with precision Lincoln's conversion to the antislavery cause, as these "sentiments came with the first awakening of his mind and conscience, and were roused into active life and energy by the sight of fellow-creatures in chains . . . on the wharf at New Orleans." Hay chronicled Lincoln's first public utterances against slavery, when

he and his fellow Whig legislator Dan Stone introduced a temperate resolution in the Illinois House, declaring that "the institution of slavery is founded on both injustice and bad policy; but that the promulgation of abolition doctrines tends rather to increase than to abate its evils." Having witnessed and experienced firsthand the evolution of Northern thought on slavery—as young men, after all, the authors had been more ambivalent about the morality of the institution—Hay knew that "there was a long distance to be traveled between the guarded utterances of this protest and the heroic audacity which launched the proclamation of emancipation. But the young man . . . had in him the making of a statesman and, if need be, a martyr. His whole career was to run in the lines marked out by these words, written in the hurry of a closing session, and he was to accomplish few acts, in that great history which God reserved for him, wiser and nobler than this."

On the subject of slavery, Hay and Nicolay sounded nothing like their younger selves. They did not summarize the Republican Party's platform as land "for white men *without* niggers," as Nicolay indelicately framed the matter in 1858; Hay no longer blamed the war on "traitors North and South" or maintained that "the life of the nation, and not the condition of the nigger, is at stake," as he did early in the war. They had long ago evolved on issues of race and equality. The sectional conflict, they insisted, was caused by America's sinful "traffic in human beings" and the need to blot out that crime. They roundly condemned the bygone Fugitive Slave Act, which elevated "the master's right to slave property" over "any black man's right to personal liberty," and recalled with disgust how "persons in the free States were pursued, seized, handcuffed, gagged, bludgeoned, or shot." In their discussion of the *Dred Scott* decision, the authors suffered a convenient bout of historical amnesia. Northerners, they now claimed, had viewed the court's abrogation of popular sovereignty as a grave moral transgression, but "much more offensive to the Northern mind than his conclusions of law were the language and historical assertions by which [Taney] strove to justify them." According to Nicolay, who wrote most of the chapters on the politics of the 1850s, Roger Taney's

infamous assertion that black men had no "rights which the white man was bound to respect" rankled the Northern conscience profoundly. "This cold and pitiless historical delineation of the bondage, ignorance, and degradation of the unfortunate kidnaped Africans and their descendants in a by-gone century, as an immutable basis of constitutional interpretation, was met by loud and indignant protest from the North," he claimed. Here, Nicolay's memory was highly selective. As a young antislavery editor, he, like most of his political compatriots, had deeply resented the *Dred Scott* decision, which, as he complained at the time, held that "white men, after running their race according to Democratic terms, and winning it under all these difficulties, are cheated out of the prize [western land] by three Democratic judges, who give it to the niggers." A quarter of a century later, he denounced Taney for denying African Americans "their birthright in the Declaration of Independence" and for "unmerciful logic [that] made the black before the law less than a slave; it reduced him to the status of a horse or dog, a bale of dry-goods or a block of stone. Against such a debasement of any living image of the Divine Maker the resentment of the North was quick and unsparing." The social revolution unleashed by the war had created a similar evolution in thought on the part of many Northerners, but within the space of twenty years the brief burst of racial liberalism that emerged from the ashes of the battlefield had given way to a hardening of sentiment. Writing at a time when the tide of popular racism was once again on the rise, Lincoln's secretaries were swimming against the currents.

In the Nicolay-Hay volumes, Lincoln walked a fine line between the radicals and the conservatives who made up the Republican Party's uneasy electoral coalition. Throughout late 1861 and 1862, he urged border-state congressmen to accept a compensated emancipation scheme. "The antislavery feeling at the North," they wrote, "excited by the ten-years' political contention, intensified by the outbreak of rebellion," weakened slavery with every passing day that the war visibly ate away at its very fabric and stability. "Conservative opinion could not defend a system that had wrought the convulsion and disaster through which the nation was struggling. Radical opinion lost no

opportunity to denounce it and attack its vulnerable points." According to the authors, Lincoln negotiated the tug-of-war between proslavery border-state unionists and antislavery Republicans, but "on the kindred policy of emancipation the President" pursued a course that was "in advance of the views of his entire cabinet." When he announced his intention to issue the preliminary Emancipation Proclamation, all of his ministers were stunned, save Seward and Welles, whom he had informed in advance. Introducing for the first time documents that later became familiar to generations of Civil War scholars, the authors cited Lincoln's own assertion that he was "naturally antislavery. If slavery is not wrong, nothing is wrong. I cannot remember when I did not so think and feel."

As young White House aides, Nicolay and Hay complained bitterly of the grief that radical Republicans visited upon the administration. Now, with the benefit of hindsight, they remembered the division between radical and conservative Republicans as "those who were anxious to destroy and those who were willing to preserve slavery." "Antislavery opinion in Congress not only had the advantage of overpowering numbers," they wrote, "but also of conspicuous ability . . . [A]mong those whose zeal gave them especial prominence in these debates, the names of Charles Sumner in the Senate and of Thaddeus Stevens and Owen Lovejoy in the House need only be mentioned to show what high qualities of zeal and talent pursued the peculiar institution with unrelenting warfare." The only difference between Lincoln and his radical critics, the authors argued, was one of time. Radicals could demand immediacy, because they did not live in the White House; Lincoln could not, because he did. "Could antislavery people not realize and rest content with the undreamed-of progress their cause had already made—slavery abolished in the District of Columbia, the Territories restored to freedom, almost wholesale emancipation provided through the Confiscation Act?" they wrote of the months preceding Lincoln's emancipation decree. "Had he not aided these measures, signed these laws, ordered their enforcement; and was he not, day and night, laboring to secure compensated emancipation in the border States? Had he not the very proclamation they sought

lying written in his desk, waiting only the favorable moment when he might announce it?"

In their treatment of black soldiers, Nicolay and Hay demonstrated the sweep of this ideological and moral evolution. Both men had encountered black regiments in and around Washington, but in his travels through the coastal South in 1863 and 1864, Hay enjoyed a special proximity to troops fresh from the front, as well as to the "contrabands" who pitched tents in Union army camps. He witnessed black regiments in battle, spoke with black enlisted men, and conferred with white officers who commanded black regiments. These experiences left an indelible mark on his thinking. "It had been a serious question with many thoughtful men whether the negro would fight," Hay and Nicolay noted. "Practical trial in skirmish and battle, however, proved the gallantry and reliability of the black soldier in the severest trials of devotion and heroism. Within half a year after Lincoln's order of enlistment the black regiments had furnished such examples of bravery on many fields that commanders gave them unstinted praise and white officers and soldiers heartily accepted them as worthy and trusted companions in arms." The authors were particularly unforgiving of Confederate war crimes against captured black soldiers. "Under the barbarous institution to perpetuate which they committed treason and were ready to die," white Southerners "had punished their human chattels with the unchecked lash, sold them on the auction block, hunted them with bloodhounds; and it is hardly to be wondered at that amid the license of war individuals among them now and then thought to restore their domination by the aid of military slaughter." Writing just before the dawn of the Jim Crow era, and in the wake of stark political violence that reversed the political gains of Reconstruction, Nicolay and Hay condemned the "revolting crimes" perpetrated against "captured colored soldiers" and unmanned those white Southern officers and enlisted men who "did not scruple to murder negro prisoners, and then lie about it to avoid retaliation . . . It is hard to enter into the minds of men to whom these things are possible, unless we reflect that an environment of slavery created peculiar ideas of humanity and morals."

The secretaries lamented that the term "contraband" "acquired much more than a mere slang value. One would be sadly puzzled to read the literature of the war in detail without knowing that 'an intelligent contraband,' or 'reliable contraband,' meant some man, woman, or child of the enslaved race." Lincoln's secretaries had long been shrewd observers of political and popular sentiment. They almost certainly understood that the humanity of African Americans, long a subject of debate among white Americans, was fast slipping back into disputed territory by the time they wrote these words. They were not alone in embracing a more advanced position on race in the aftermath of the Civil War, but their enduring consciousness, in the midst of a national retrenchment, likely owed in some fashion to their close association with Lincoln. As an antebellum politician, the late president—though not an abolitionist or a radical—had boldly affirmed that black Americans were fellow men and women. After four years of war, Lincoln's own thinking evolved even further. The secretaries followed his moral and intellectual lead. They also understood that his legacy would forever be linked with his emancipation agenda. In this regard, they were writing for posterity, not for the present day.

As young presidential aides, living and working in real time, Nicolay and Hay often missed the significance of the events that they witnessed and in which they participated. They were actors in "stirring times," Nicolay told Therena in the first weeks of the war, though "I hardly realize that they are so, even as I write them." In November 1863, the secretaries drank their way through a twenty-four-hour trip to Gettysburg, in part because it was their job to work the swing-state reporters and politicians who were on hand for the dedication of the cemetery, but also because they were young men who enjoyed a good time. In hindsight, they appreciated the gravitas of the moment.

It is unclear exactly when (let alone how) the Gettysburg Address became part of America's secular gospel, though the critical moment seems to have coincided roughly with the publication of the Nicolay-Hay serial. The term itself, "Gettysburg Address," appears less than

two dozen times in a search of major newspapers between 1864 and 1890; between 1891 and 1910 it appears well over five hundred times. By 1894, the speech had become sufficiently important in the popular mind that Nicolay felt compelled to write a stand-alone article in the *Century* debunking the common myth that Lincoln had written it on the train, while en route to Gettysburg. In 1900, he instinctively included the "immortal Gettysburg address" among a select list of milestone Lincoln moments that it was his "privilege to witness." After the secretaries died, Robert Todd Lincoln and Helen Nicolay spent the better part of a decade in vain pursuit of what they believed to have been the original manuscript; it had appeared as a facsimile in the Nicolay-Hay volumes but mysteriously disappeared after Helen transferred possession of the Lincoln papers to Hay in 1901. Alice Hay Wadsworth, John and Clara's younger daughter, found the document among her possessions in 1916 and donated it to the Library of Congress. It is possible, even likely, that her father removed the manuscript from the larger collection after Nicolay's death and retained it in his own files. Somehow, a speech that had not registered as seminal as late as the 1880s had become a national heirloom by the early twentieth century. Scholars and collectors—to say nothing of Robert Todd Lincoln, Helen Nicolay, and Clara Hay—devoted much energy to understanding the subtle differences between the several extant drafts, as well as the chain of custody of each copy.

In their history, Nicolay and Hay acknowledged the growing consensus around the magnitude of the Gettysburg Address when they devoted a stand-alone chapter, thirteen pages long, to the speech. They reproduced the entire address in their text, along with a photo facsimile of the original manuscript in Lincoln's hand. But after establishing the context of the occasion, the authors devoted eight pages to reviewing Edward Everett's peroration and only two pages to Lincoln's. Writing in the late 1880s, they understood that the speech was somehow an important one, "for then and there the President pronounced an address of dedication so pertinent, so brief yet so comprehensive, so terse yet so eloquent, linking the deeds of the present to the thoughts of the future, with simple words, in such living, original,

yet exquisitely molded, maxim-like phrases that the best critics have awarded it an unquestioned rank as one of the world's masterpieces in rhetorical art."

Nicolay and Hay did not single-handedly raise the profile of the Gettysburg Address, but they contributed to a growing consciousness of its importance. In 1863, Hay barely noted the contents of the speech in his diary, noting simply that "all the particulars are in the daily papers." Only long after the fact did he—along with millions of his fellow countrymen—understand the full import of what he had heard.

In securing Lincoln's historical legacy, Hay believed it was imperative that the biography diminish the reputation of George McClellan, the former Union general and Democratic presidential candidate. A thorn in Lincoln's side during the war, McClellan proved a lasting difficulty to the authors. In 1875, Prince Philippe d'Orléans, the comte de Paris, published the first volume of his highly influential military history of the Civil War. A French nobleman who had served on McClellan's general staff during the Peninsula Campaign, the count was a fierce partisan for his former commander, whose exploits and achievements he exaggerated beyond recognition. He also took frequent opportunity to denigrate Lincoln's skills as a political and military leader. Apart from these efforts, McClellan frequently put pen to paper, offering up his stilted version of events for magazines and, in 1887, his posthumously published memoirs. Perhaps because of his army service, or because he spent more time than Nicolay in the general's presence during the winter of 1861–62, Hay tackled most of the chapters dealing with Little Mac. "I think I have left the impression of his mutinous imbecility," he assured Nicolay, "and I have done it in a perfectly courteous manner . . . It is of the utmost moment that we should *seem* fair to him, while we are destroying him."

Hay portrayed McClellan at his worst—an inept general given to "delusions" and "hallucinations of overwhelming forces opposed to him," a man who "rarely estimated the force immediately opposed to him at less than double its actual strength." Hay disclosed for the first time McClellan's discourteous refusal to meet with Lincoln, when the

president called at his house in late 1861, and zeroed in mercilessly on the general's botched effort at the Battle of Antietam, where, thanks to a Union private's discovery of Lee's battle plans, he "knew not only of the division of his enemy's army in half, but he knew where his trains, his rear-guard, his cavalry, were to march and to halt, and where the detached commands were to join the main body." McClellan failed to act on this intelligence, Hay disclosed, and "every minute which he thus let slip away was paid for in the blood of Union soldiers the next day." McClellan's "deplorable shortcomings" were a constant source of agony, as was his "mutinous insolence" in routinely denigrating the president behind his back.

Taking care to seem "courteous," Hay assured his readers that Mc-Clellan was "as far from being the traitor and craven that many thought him as from being the martyr and hero that others would like to have him appear." He was a knowledgeable officer with a "pure and upright" character but a weak leader whose "native inability to use great means to great ends" led to repeated failure on the battlefield. In a coup de grâce, and to explain why Lincoln came to the conclusion that his commanding general had "no real desire to defeat the enemy," Hay reviewed at length McClellan's blunders and missteps, setting in stone an argument and chronology of events that have dominated Civil War historiography to this day:

> His lethargy of six months in front of Washington, to the wonder and scorn of the Southern generals; his standing at gaze at Yorktown, halted with his vast army by Magruder's men in buckram; his innocent astonishment at Williamsburg at finding the rebels would not give up Richmond without a fight; his station astride the Chickahominy, waiting for the enemy to grow strong enough to attack him, while his brave soldiers were fading to specters with the marsh fever; his failure to assume the offensive after the Confederate repulse at Seven Pines; his second refusal of the favors of the fortune of war when Lee took his army North of the Chickahominy . . . his starting for the James,

in this crisis of his fate, when he should have marched upon Richmond; his final retreat from Malvern Hill to Harrison's Landing, breaking the hearts of the soldiers who had won on that field a victory so complete and so glorious—all these mistakes proved how utterly incapable he was of leading a great army in a grand war . . . With such limitations as these it is not likely that posterity will rank him among the leading generals of the war.

If George McClellan stood out as Lincoln's chief tormentor, Salmon P. Chase ran a very close second. Here, the secretaries had to walk a fine line. McClellan had been a leading Democratic opponent of Lincoln's emancipation policy; Chase was a venerated public servant with unimpeachable antislavery credentials. Nicolay and Hay knew Chase intimately and remained on friendly terms with his family. He was going to be a "tough nut to crack," Hay admitted, especially given their solicitousness for the feelings of his surviving daughters. He informed readers that Chase brought "great natural abilities, unswerving integrity and fidelity, and unwearying industry" to his post as Treasury secretary and "grappled with the difficulties of the situation in a manner which won him the plaudits of the civilized world and will forever enshrine his name in the memory of his fellow-citizens." Comparing him with Seward, Hay acknowledged that the two cabinet secretaries developed a deep enmity for each other but judged that "Lincoln, Chase, and Seward were, by a long interval, the first three Republicans of their time, and each, by what would almost appear a special favor of Providence, was placed in a position where he could be of most unquestioned service to the country. Had either of the three, except Lincoln, been President, the nation must have lost the inestimable services of the other two." But for all of his "untiring zeal and perfect integrity," his "attitude towards the President . . . varied between the limits of active hostility and benevolent contempt. He apparently never changed his opinion that a great mistake had been committed at Chicago, and the predominant thought which was present to him through three years of his administration was that it was

his duty to counteract, as far as possible, the evil results of that mistake." Hay described in detail Chase's various machinations for the Republican nomination in 1864, revealing his chronic indiscretion and ineptitude at backroom political intrigue. In his description of the cabinet crisis of December 1862, in which radical members of Congress attempted to secure the dismissal of the president's secretary of state, Lincoln emerges, as always, the consummate strategist, cornering Seward and Chase into tendering their resignations, which he refused to accept but filed away for contingency purposes. "Now I can ride," Hay quoted Lincoln. "I have got a pumpkin in each end of my bag."

The Lincoln whom Hay and Nicolay introduced to the reading public was a deft operator. He exerted control "daily and hourly" over "the vast machinery of command and coordination in Cabinet, Congress, army, navy, and the hosts of national politics. To still the quarrels of factions, to allay the jealousies of statesmen, to compose the rivalries of generals, to soothe the vanity of officials, to prompt the laggard, to curb the ardent, to sustain the faltering, was a substratum of daily routine underlying the great events of campaigns, battles, and high questions of state." When the military high command failed to deliver victory, the president schooled himself in the art of battle, and "it is safe to say that no general in the army studied his maps and scanned his telegrams with half the industry—and, it may be added, with half the intelligence—which Mr. Lincoln gave to his." Unlike many of his generals, the president displayed a "larger comprehension of popular forces" and understood that "a free people . . . can stand reverses and disappointments; they are capable of making great exertions and great sacrifices. The one thing that they cannot endure is inaction on the part of their rulers." Yet Lincoln was no mere compass of public sentiment, nor a temporizing moderate. Unlike his conservative and radical critics, he "sagaciously" directed and "control[led] the average public sentiment of the country." He was, in the eyes of his secretaries, the most skilled executive ever to have lived in the White House.

Shortly before his death, John Hay, then secretary of state, urged Congress to construct a national monument to Lincoln on the still-undeveloped Potomac Flats site at the western edge of the Mall.

Perched on high land, in direct view of the Capitol, the memorial would occupy a space unto itself. "Lincoln of all Americans next to Washington deserves this space of honor," he argued. "He was of the Immortals. You must not approach too close to the Immortals. His monument should stand alone, remote from the common habitations of man, apart from the business and turmoil of the city; isolated, distinguished, and serene. Of all the sites, this one near the Potomac is most suited to the purpose." The Lincoln Memorial Lincoln whose creation owed so much to Nicolay and Hay would seem a plainly intuitive rendering to later generations. But at the time of his first introduction, he was an altogether new and novel invention. In his own time, Lincoln had been a tremendously popular, though also controversial, figure, loved by a comfortable majority of the electorate, scorned by a solid minority, and consistently underestimated by the political chattering class up to the day of his murder. After his death, friend and foe alike tried to humanize the man, in ways that often vulgarized his legacy. Others, like Charles Francis Adams and the comte de Paris, continued to see his political ascent as a mistake of fortune and his success as president the result of good counsel from a strong cabinet. Nicolay and Hay blasted the foundations of this narrative and in its place created a lasting image. The man on the $5 bill later became the abridgment of ten volumes and fifteen years of labor.

CHAPTER 17

Lincolniana

By and large, John Hay was pleased with the reception of the Lincoln biography. "They send me an occasional column of abuse from some friend of McClellan or Chase and I can only wonder at the merciful Providence which keeps my critics away from the weak joints in my armor," he told Henry Adams in 1889, toward the end of the serial run. "Laws-a-mercy! If I had the criticizing of that book, what a skinning I could give it!" To Robert Lincoln, Hay reported with relief that "we are nearly at the end of our life-long task and I hope you will think your father's fame has not suffered any wrong at our hands." "There will be ten volumes," he explained. "It will be dedicated to you. Now, in very fact, the fifteen-year-long task was drawing to a close." Hay was certain that in the end analysis, he and Nicolay had placed "the truth before the country . . . Year after year of study has shown me more clearly than ever how infinitely greater your father was than anybody about him, greater than ever we imagined while he lived. There is nothing to explain or apologize for from beginning to end. He is the one unapproachably great figure of a great epoch."

Reviews of the massive Nicolay-Hay work were mixed. Some reviewers were baffled by its length and scope, complaining that Lincoln ultimately played but a small part in his own biography. A critic for *Life* humorously assured readers that "the picture of the Pharaohs in the last *Century* must not be mistaken for illustrations in the 'Life of Lincoln.' The authors of that exhaustive biography passed the Pharaohs

several numbers back, and are understood to be well along in their retrospective summary of the Middle Ages." Others groused that the volumes were too "damn partisan," as the Irish American sculptor Augustus Saint-Gaudens complained to Richard Gilder over a meal at New York's Century Club. There was too much "pitching in, calling names, etc." for his taste. Even a friendly newspaper remarked that "no one will suspect the writers of being lukewarm Republicans." Such criticism might have stung Nicolay, but Hay showed little compunction in private about confessing to his political bias. The book, he conceded, was a "ponderous Republican history." Some critics disputed particular details or interpretations in the work. Alexander McClure, an aging Pennsylvania editor, claimed that Lincoln had told him of his intention to substitute Andrew Johnson for the incumbent vice president, Hannibal Hamlin, just prior to the 1864 convention. Relying on their diaries, memorandums, and letters, the secretaries insisted that, on the contrary, the president had maintained absolute neutrality in the matter, though he quietly made it known that he had no objections to another four-year term for Hamlin. "The whole thing is growing very ridiculous," Hay moaned. "Every old deadbeat politician in the country is coming forward to protest that he was the depository of Lincoln's inmost secrets and the engineer of his campaigns." (In 1903, toward the twilight of his life, Hay told Charles Francis Adams Jr.—Henry's older brother—that McClure "never had two hours' conversation in his life" with Lincoln.)

Some readers were also uncertain how to classify the Nicolay-Hay volumes. Charles Eliot, the president of Harvard, maintained that "these gentlemen did not write history. They were actors in many of the scenes they described, and therefore, could not be historians. They have prepared invaluable materials for the subsequent historian, and done an admirable piece of literary work: but I submit that they have not written history."

Others were generous in their praise. Writing from France, the American historian James Ford Rhodes sent a heartfelt "word of congratulation . . . I expect that your book will demolish the modern day theory that an author cannot write modern history impartially."

William Dean Howells, the dean of American literature who, as a young man, had written Lincoln's campaign biography in 1860, called it "not only . . . the most important work yet accomplished in American history" but also "one of the noblest achievements of literary art." By far, the critic whose opinion held the greatest sway with the authors was Bob Lincoln, and he was "much pleased . . . with the results of your long work," he told Hay. "It is what I hoped it would be." "Many people speak to me & confirm my own opinion of it as a work in every way excellent—not only sustaining but elevating my father's place in History," he assured his friend of three decades. "I shall never cease to be glad that the places you & Nicolay held near him & in his confidence were filled by you & not by others."

Hefty and expensive, *Abraham Lincoln: A History* sold only seven thousand copies, but for every person who bought the ten-volume collection, fifty others read extensive excerpts in its serial run. In 1902, the *Century* published a one-volume abridgment of the work; it quickly sold thirty-five thousand copies, a robust number in its day. But more important than sales was the book's intellectual reach. For at least half a century, the Nicolay-Hay volumes formed the basis of all major scholarship on Lincoln.

Roughly around the time that the Nicolay-Hay volumes appeared in book form, William Herndon and a co-author, Jesse Weik, tried to shop around their long-delayed edition of *Herndon's Lincoln,* the culmination of a quarter century of research and meditation. The response was not encouraging. Charles L. Webster & Co., Mark Twain's publishing house, turned them down, explaining that "Life of Lincoln, by General Hay and Mr. Nicolay, will give the public all that they wish to know of Lincoln, just at the present." Initially, Elder Publishing, a little-known entity, expressed interest, though its executives worried about the "risk we run in going into competition with the Century." In the end, they opted not to take the manuscript, as most of its important content had been revealed years before in Ward Hill Lamon's work.

Horace White, a journalist who covered the Lincoln-Douglas debates as a young man and who later developed a close relationship

with the president, remarked that the "most striking fact of our time, of a psychological kind, is the growth of Lincoln's fame since the earth closed over his remains." In the decades following the publication of *Abraham Lincoln: A History,* this fascination morphed into the growing field of Lincolniana. Collectors scoured the countryside for rails that Lincoln might or might not have split; furniture that once resided in his law office and Springfield residence; his family Bible; the rocking chair he sat in at Ford's Theatre on the night of his murder; his autograph book; his checkbook; his stovepipe hat. Under pressure to indulge the public interest, and increasingly disconnected from his birthplace, Robert donated the house at Eighth and Jackson to the state of Illinois, where Osborn Oldroyd, one of the premier collectors of Lincolniana, had established an exhaustive and not altogether tasteful display of the slain president's personal effects. At the Chicago World's Fair in 1893, tens, if not hundreds, of thousands of visitors gazed at a special installation of Lincolniana. No item was too small to mesmerize. Or too sacred. In 1890, enthusiasts raised money to have Ann Rutledge's body exhumed and reinterred in a nearby cemetery overlooking the Sangamon River. In place of a simple stone marker, they raised an imposing granite monument, later inscribed with the poet Edgar Lee Masters's verse in her honor.

One reason the field so quickly devolved into a collector's game was that there was little else scholars could hope to accomplish for the immediate time. Nicolay and Hay published Lincoln's *Complete Works* in 1894, comprising 1,736 of the president's speeches, state papers, and letters. But they had already analyzed and discussed the most important of these documents in their larger biographical work. The great body of Lincoln's manuscript collection, including tens of thousands of letters and communications sent *to* him—many containing valuable margin notes that the president scribbled in his own hand—remained off-limits, depriving Civil War historians of the same context and wide-angle view that Nicolay and Hay had enjoyed. In 1894, Nicolay opened his home at 212 B Street SE to a reporter for the New York *World,* who described the former secretary's "workroom, with its great desk and many bookcases," as "a place in which the present is not

known. There are gathered practically all the Lincoln manuscripts in existence. Some of them are owned by Mr. Nicolay, most of them are the property of the Lincoln family." Nicolay had moved the papers to the row house in 1887, shortly after relinquishing the marshal's post at the Supreme Court. There they remained until his death in 1901, when John Hay arranged for their temporary storage at the State Department. From there, they reverted to Robert's custody. Increasingly reclusive, the presidential son kept them near his person at all times, arranging for their movement between his mansion in Washington and his vacation home in Vermont whenever he relocated for a season. Many scholars appealed for access, but none succeeded in prying open the iron door.

Not everyone was willing to concede the last word to Nicolay and Hay. In 1895, Ida Tarbell, a young writer for *McClure's Magazine,* accepted an assignment to hunt down additional Lincoln materials and photographs and to edit them for a prospective documentary series. Noah Brooks assumed that "the stories were all told," as the number of men and women who knew the late president was fast diminishing with the passage of time. Tarbell set out to prove him wrong. At first, it was hard going. Nicolay rebuffed her request for assistance; according to Tarbell, he huffed, "You are invading my field. You write a popular Life of Lincoln, and you do so much to decrease the value of my property." (The language does not sound like him, but the tone does.) Robert was more polite but equally unhelpful. "Impossible," he told her, when she requested access to his father's papers. "I won't allow anybody to see them. There is nothing of my father's there, that is of value—Nicolay and Hay have published everything; but there are many letters *to* him which if published now would pain, possibly discredit able and useful men still living." As a peace offering, Robert gave her a previously unpublished daguerreotype taken sometime around his father's term in Congress. Its publication sparked enormous interest in the larger series. Though the aging experts scoffed at her labors—Henry Whitney, a Lincoln confidant, claimed that she "*sponged* more or less Lincoln afflatus," while Richard Gilder said with a laugh that S. S. McClure had "got a girl to write a Life of Lincoln"—Tarbell

proved a deft investigator. She hired a team of researchers, placed ad-
vertisements soliciting new documents in newspapers throughout the
country, and rummaged through courthouses, attics, and family col-
lections. The result was a steady stream of speeches, legal documents,
telegrams, and letters—roughly 275 in number—that Nicolay and Hay
never knew existed. Initially a skeptic, Robert Todd Lincoln readily
acknowledged that Tarbell's series, ultimately aggregated in a two-
volume book, *The Life of Abraham Lincoln,* was "an indispensable ad-
junct to the work of Nicolay and Hay."

"Adjunct" was the operative word. While Tarbell contributed new
material on Lincoln's childhood and early adult years, disproving or
qualifying many of William Herndon's most controversial claims, she
offered little original insight into his public career in the 1850s and
1860s. Without access to Lincoln's manuscript collection, neither she
nor those who followed in her footsteps could hope to break much
new ground. Still, for several decades, others tried. Carl Sandburg, the
famed poet, earned wide acclaim and financial success for his two-
pronged work: *Abraham Lincoln: The Prairie Years* (1926) and *Abraham
Lincoln: The War Years* (1939). The first volume drew liberally on earlier
writers, including Herndon, Lamon, and Tarbell, and offered a pre-
dictably earthy rendering of the sixteenth president. Claiming no for-
mal historical training, Sandburg used his sources uncritically, giving
credence to many anecdotes and remembrances that scholars then and
since dismissed as non-credible. This shortcoming was particularly
evident in his first volume. But his lyricism gripped the imagination of
readers. "Out of the pages of this book emerges no heroic figure, no
epic character, no titan towering above puny men," wrote the critic
Harry Hansen. "This is the book of the railsplitter, of the country
storekeeper, the young lawyer, the frontier advocate, the practical
backwoods politician." In *The War Years,* a four-volume affair that Ste-
phen Vincent Benét called "a mountain range of a book," Sandburg
was more attentive to scholarly accuracy, even submitting portions of
the manuscript to academic historians so he could vet his work for
inaccuracies. But the much-acclaimed war volumes suffered the same
credulous approach to sourcing. James G. Randall, who reviewed *The*

War Years for the *American Historical Review,* admitted privately to a friend, "I really deal too leniently with [Sandburg]. There seems to be a tendency, almost a conspiracy, among reviewers to do this."

By the time Sandburg completed his study, the body of known Lincoln documents had grown by roughly one-third since the *Complete Works* appeared in 1894. But most of the new discoveries only refocused popular attention on the president's formative years. By World War II, Nicolay and Hay, who had focused almost singularly on fashioning an image of Lincoln's public career from the 1850s onward, continued to dominate the field.

If Nicolay and Hay prevailed in their effort to define the meaning of Abraham Lincoln's public career, and particularly his presidency, their contribution to the historiography of the Civil War fared less consistently. Initially, *Abraham Lincoln: A History* met with approval from most scholars of American life. Their tone of "aggressive Northernism" ran against the popular current of sectional reunion, but professional historians and political scientists largely concurred with Nicolay and Hay's argument that slavery was the driving cause of the war. James Ford Rhodes, the unofficial dean of the American historical profession, was a Bourbon Democrat who held African Americans and radical Republicans in low regard; he nevertheless asserted that "the question may be isolated by the incontrovertible statement that if the negro had never been brought to America, our Civil War could not have occurred." The clash between "opposing moral and social forces" created an "inevitable" war between slave states and free states. Edward Channing, a Harvard professor who held one of the first doctorates in American history, similarly determined that while the "war was not begun to secure the destruction of slavery," fundamentally, "slavery was at the bottom of the social and material distinctions which separated the country into two irreconcilable sections." The very notion that slavery rendered the North and the South "irreconcilable" traced its roots to William Seward's famous remark in 1858 that there was an "irrepressible conflict between opposing and enduring forces," to wit, the slave South and the free-labor North. This

assumption informed almost all serious writing on the Civil War through the early twentieth century, including the Nicolay-Hay volumes.

In the early twentieth century, a new generation of scholars began to question the idea that the war had been an inevitable clash between two irreconcilable civilizations. Instead, slavery became an aggravating factor but not a central cause of intersectional conflict. This shift in interpretation owed partly to the success of Southern writers in enshrining the romance of reunion in the popular consciousness, partly to the hardening of racial sensibilities in the decades following the Civil War, and partly to the advent of new scientific approaches to historical inquiry. As historians learned to sift through new types of evidence and plucked emerging theoretical frameworks from other fields in the social sciences, they began to search out interpretive patterns that may have eluded their predecessors. Charles Beard, the intellectual father of the "progressive" school of American history, viewed the war as a result of "inherent antagonisms" between an urban and industrializing North and an agrarian South. Inasmuch as the Southern economy was deeply reliant on slavery, the institution was a cause of the great conflict, but more central to the war were competing legal and economic interests that led to a "transfer of the issues from the forum to the field." The Civil War and Reconstruction were the "Second American Revolution," Beard claimed, not because they obliterated slavery, but because they saw the forces of industrial capitalism vanquish and effectively colonize the agrarian South. In his thinking, Beard was deeply influenced by social scientists who applied a Marxist lens to the examination of past events, though by no means did Beard or his fellow progressives regard themselves as Marxists. Rather, they searched for discontinuities associated with economic development and change, whereas previous scholars, including Nicolay and Hay, tended to emphasize the slow and evolutionary nature of history. Products of their own social context, progressive historians viewed the past through the lens of conflict between urban and rural—industrial and agrarian—interests.

Progressive historiography dominated university life in the

opening decades of the new century and subjected almost every major phenomenon in American history—from colonial-era politics and the framing of the Constitution to Jacksonian-era politics and the Civil War itself—to an analysis that favored economic motivation as a driver of cause and action. Although they relegated slavery to a supporting role in provoking the Civil War, progressive historians did not completely overturn prevailing interpretations of the conflict. Slavery was still at the heart of the problem, but the problem was now economic rather than moral in nature.

In the 1920s, many of the nation's best and brightest scholars began to embrace an alternative theory of Civil War causality. Rather than view the war as an inevitable conflict between two incompatible civilizations, they came to believe that it had been an entirely avoidable, repressible conflict. Slavery, according to Frank L. Owsley, a Southern-born scholar who spent most of his career at Vanderbilt, was a "red herring" that Northerners had long used to deflect attention from the aggressive expansionism of their region's industrial capital complex. Owsley was more avowedly in sympathy with the Confederacy than most revisionists, but as a pathbreaking practitioner of emerging research methodologies, he cast wide influence in the field. Equally prominent was the Iowa-born Avery Craven, the most powerful proponent of this new tendency in Civil War–era historiography. Arguing that the dissimilarities between North and South were "not much greater than those existing between the East and West," he concluded that "a generation of well-meaning Americans . . . permitted their short-sighted politicians, their over-zealous editors, and their pious reformers to emotionalize real and potential differences and to conjure up distorted impressions of those who dwelt in other parts of the nation." In reality, he argued, there existed no "inherent difference great enough to make war 'inevitable' or 'irrepressible' . . . That was to be an artificial creation of inflamed minds." Instead, the "conflict was the work of politicians and pious cranks!" In the 1850s, popular democracy had been almost as young as the country itself, and by Craven's rendering, a generation of ambitious office seekers and newspaper editors stoked the fires of public opinion for private gain. In effect, they elected

for war, when no war had been necessary. Craven was a committed Quaker who privately bemoaned that humans should ever "settle differences by shooting at each other." The Civil War was no different. But he also embodied the racial insensitivities that pervaded the American academy—and most of American life—in the 1930s and 1940s, when he was most active as a historian. While Craven conceded that "the idea of holding men in bondage and buying and selling them as property" violated the tenets of "the democratic and Christian ideal of the modern world," he argued that the system was more harmful in theory than in practice. Slaves, he believed, "went on with [their] tasks generally unconscious of the merits or lack of them in the system under which [they] toiled." "Perhaps the idea [of slavery] was always worse than the fact itself." It was inconceivable to him that men should kill each other over a benign, perhaps even dying, institution.

Like Craven, James G. Randall, a professor at the University of Illinois and the leading Lincoln scholar of the mid-twentieth century, took a skeptical view of abolitionism. Slaves, he wrote, "adapted . . . to bondage with a minimum of resistance, doing cheerfully the manual work of the South." If slaves were occasionally mistreated, "there was truth in the common declaration that Southern abuse of the slave was often a matter of mistreatment through leniency." By Randall's estimation, a "blundering generation" of politicians unwittingly provoked a "great American tragedy [that] could have been avoided, supposing of course that something more of statesmanship, moderation, and understanding, and something less of professional patrioteering, slogan making, face-saving, political clamoring, and propaganda had existed on both sides." Ultimately, it was "fanaticism (on both sides), misunderstanding, misinterpretation, or perhaps politics" that caused the war, not, as Nicolay and Hay maintained, a fundamental clash between slavery and freedom.

Randall exempted Lincoln from his broad censure of antebellum politicians, singling him out as "moderate, temperate, and far-seeing." This notion was not new. Since the early twentieth century, popular Southern writers and their allies in the academy—particularly Columbia University's William Dunning and his many intellectual

followers—had drastically revised the history of Reconstruction, por-
traying the abolitionists and radical Republicans of the 1860s as singu-
larly vicious individuals whose overriding agenda was revenge against
the vanquished South. In the popular novels of Thomas Dixon, and in
respectable academic histories of Reconstruction, flawed, profane men
like Thaddeus Stevens were the sworn enemies of Abraham Lincoln,
the "great heart" (in Dixon's words) who, had he lived, would have
welcomed the South back with open arms and charity. African Amer-
icans, in turn, were congenitally and culturally ill-prepared for free-
dom and plunged the postbellum South into a deep political and
economic crisis. This interpretation held up through the early years of
the modern civil rights era, when the racial egalitarianism of radicals
and abolitionists, and the fervent self-assertion of the freedmen, began
to look better in the light of day, especially when compared with the
crude violence and political usurpation that Southern whites employed
to overthrow the gains of the Civil War. In Randall's time, it was still
popular to think of Lincoln as a misfit in his own house, doing battle
with radical Republicans even as he prosecuted the war with the Con-
federacy. In his influential Fleming Lectures at Louisiana State Univer-
sity in 1945, Randall emphasized Lincoln's Kentucky heritage and
posited that he was at his core more sympathetic to the South than
most of his Republican brethren.

Like his contemporaries, Randall wrote in an era when racial senti-
ments had hardened and few Americans any longer appreciated the
moral strains of the war and its aftermath. As an academic historian,
he also labored to create a counterintuitive model. So much had been
said about Lincoln, he observed, that "the historian must turn revi-
sionist." Thus, Randall's Lincoln was "essentially a Douglas Demo-
crat" who "did not fundamentally differ" from his Democratic
archrival on matters pertaining to race and slavery. As president, Lin-
coln repeatedly (and to his country's detriment) caved to radical pres-
sure and interfered in military matters that he scarcely understood.
His dismissal of George McClellan, Randall wrote, was "the act of a
buffeted President." As for the "stock image" of Lincoln as the Great
Emancipator, Randall held that the president's true "blueprint for

freedom" never envisioned the sweeping program of political and eco-
nomic equality forced on the South by the radical Republicans who
survived him.

These revisionist strains in Civil War historiography cannot be under-
stood outside the context of Jim Crow culture and politics. The brief
window in time when many Americans reappraised their thinking on
race relations had closed by the late 1880s. In its place arose a new and
elaborate system of enforced racial hierarchy that pervaded nearly ev-
ery facet of American life until the mid-twentieth century.

 Jim Crow, in all of its unprecedented intricacy, sprang from multi-
ple sources. In part, it was a political phenomenon and reflected popu-
lar disillusionment with Reconstruction, but it was also an intellectual
movement that drew strength from the academy. As American univer-
sities matured into modern centers of social and scientific inquiry,
scholars grew interested in using emerging methodologies to catego-
rize difference. This trend gained force from the arrival of millions of
new immigrants, many of whom originated from southern and east-
ern Europe. They seemed darker skinned than earlier arrivals and
practiced religions that had gained little foothold in America before
this time. They were different, and their ambiguous racial designation
fed the country's renewed obsession with blood and origins—not only
on the part of older Americans, but also on the part of new Americans
who struggled to assert their whiteness, and thus their fitness for citi-
zenship. As well, for many Americans, Jim Crow provided a way to
reorder life amid bewildering change. In the antebellum South, it had
been largely unnecessary to separate white and black Americans. In-
equality had been sufficiently interwoven with slavery. But the same
wave of economic growth that the Civil War helped catalyze now in-
troduced confusion in the ranks. In a new world of railway and street
cars, public amusements and thoroughfares, department stores and
shared urban spaces, it was less clear who was on top and who was on
the bottom. White Americans, both North and South, devised a com-
plicated and brutal system to reassert dominion. They advertised it
on rice boxes (Uncle Ben) and syrup bottles (Aunt Jemima). They

enshrined it in laws governing the physical separation of black and white citizens. They built it into the electoral system by disenfranchising millions of black voters. They enforced it through thousands of gruesome spectacle lynchings.

There was never a single, solitary white America. Different people claimed different levels of complicity in the system and enjoyed widely divergent levels of wealth and power. But very few nonblack Americans operated entirely outside the cultural and intellectual assumptions of Jim Crow. Writing in the context of their own time, historians in the first decades of the twentieth century looked for alternative theories to explain the Civil War, because it no longer seemed intuitive to assume that slavery was its central and inexorable cause. From *The Birth of a Nation* (1915) to *Gone with the Wind* (1939), American culture reinforced many of the core tenets of the Southern revisionism that Nicolay and Hay had written against. In a climate so inhospitable to African Americans, it was little wonder that scholars moved far afield from the true roots of the conflict.

After World War II, the dawn of the modern civil rights movement prompted historians to rediscover the moral struggle that lay at the heart of the Civil War and Reconstruction. New and successive generations of scholars now placed black slaves and freedmen at the heart of a more complicated narrative that emphasized the agency of ordinary African Americans in forcing the Union to embrace emancipation as a tool, and later an aim, of war. Whereas mid-century scholars largely viewed the sectional conflict as "repressible," historians working in the shadow of Birmingham and Selma rediscovered the inescapable clash between two civilizations built on oppositional theories of political economy. Unlike Nicolay and Hay, modern scholars of the Civil War era readily acknowledged the economic symbiosis between the slaveholding South and the free-labor North. They also documented the deeply seated racism that pervaded Northern culture and politics and explored the halting and unsteady progression of the conflict as it evolved from a war for union into a war against slavery. Contemporary Civil War scholarship in many ways bears only dim resemblance to the "Northern" or "Republican" interpretation that

Nicolay and Hay helped pioneer, but the seeds of their argument—a now-commonsense assertion that secession and states' rights always operated in the service of slavery and that slavery was "somehow" (in Lincoln's word) the primary cause of the war—have for several decades underpinned most historical analyses of the Civil War. In some fashion, Nicolay and Hay enjoyed the final word.

In their description of the sixteenth president, the secretaries left an even more lasting impression. Over the past half century scholars have expanded the study of Lincoln into its own field. The modern civil rights movement inspired historians to reconsider the Great Emancipator's lasting image as the man who freed the slaves. A new focus on the agency of the slaves themselves cast doubt on the centrality of white politicians in effecting the abolition of slavery. Likewise, some historians have found Lincoln to be too moderate, too temporizing, and too much an ordinary politician. Before the civil rights era, the question "What would Lincoln do?" assumed that the sixteenth president, and he alone, was the repository of all political and moral wisdom. In recent decades, scholars have tended more often to turn the question on its head. What would Lincoln have done in the face of massive resistance—George Wallace's stand at the schoolhouse door or the massacre of black children in a Birmingham church? It is hard to escape the conclusion that Lincoln felt a kinship, but was not at one, with the radical Republicans of his own time—those who drove what Charles Sumner once called the "antislavery enterprise." Would he have been on the side of the angels in *our* time?

From these debates has emerged a nuanced, and now predominant, historical portrait of a master politician who evolved personally over the years in his capacity to envision a biracial democracy and who used his mastery of politics to build and then use popular opinion against an institution that he had always despised on a gut level. He was not a passenger on the train, but neither was he the conductor. From the vantage point of today, it is as impossible to imagine the destruction of slavery without Lincoln as it is to imagine it without the tireless agitation of slaves and freedmen, or abolitionists and radicals.

In the final chapter of their ten-volume biography, Hay remarked on the coincidental timing of Lincoln's murder. "If he had died in the days of doubt and gloom which preceded his reelection," he wrote, "he would have been sincerely mourned and praised by friends of the Union, but its enemies would have curtly dismissed him as one of the necessary and misguided victims of sectional hate . . . But as he had fallen in the moment of a stupendous victory, the halo of a radiant success enveloped his memory and dazzled the eyes of even his most hostile critics." At home and abroad, those who had "persistently vilified" Lincoln now raised a "universal chorus of elegiac praise."

In the darkest hours of the Civil War, Hay had been struck by Lincoln's deep connection to the ordinary farmers and soldiers of the North. "I know the people want him," he told Nicolay in 1863. "There is no mistaking that fact. But politicians are strong yet & he is not their 'kind of cat.'" Almost a quarter century later, he continued to believe that it was "among the common people of the entire civilized world that the most genuine and spontaneous manifestations of sorrow and appreciation were produced, and to this fact we attribute the sudden and solid foundation of Lincoln's fame."

"There are two classes of men whose names are more enduring than any monument," Hay claimed, "—the great writers; and the men of great achievement, the founders of states, the conquerors." Lincoln was both. "Nothing would have more amazed him while he lived than to hear himself called a man of letters; but this age has produced few greater writers." His prose ran "from the wit, the gay humor, the florid eloquence of his stump speeches to the marvelous sententiousness and brevity of the letter to Greeley and the address at Gettysburg, and the sustained and lofty grandeur of the Second Inaugural." Yet it was "principally as a man of action that the world at large will regard him." Master politician, he was "bitterly denounced and maligned" throughout his term but "bore himself with such extraordinary discretion and skill, that he obtained for the Government all the legislation it required." He outgeneraled his generals and outmaneuvered his foes.

"After times will wonder, not at the few and unimportant mistakes he may have committed, but at the intuitive knowledge of his business that he displayed."

Nicolay and Hay had devoted ten volumes, and over a million words, to establishing Lincoln's everlasting greatness. But they would insist to the end on his humanity. In Lincoln's "case, as in that of all heroic personages who occupy a great place in history, a certain element of legend mingles with his righteous fame," Hay observed. But Lincoln was "a man, in fact," not a God. Recalling his trip to the South Carolina coast in 1863, he described for readers "a religious meeting among the negroes of the Sea Islands," where he heard a young man "wish that he might see Lincoln. A gray-haired negro rebuked the rash aspiration: 'No man see Linkum. Linkum walk as Jesus walk—no man see Linkum.'" As a young man, he had been held rapt by the spiritual fervor that freedmen had for their president. Older now, he understood that these "fables" were but a "natural enough expression of popular awe and love." He agreed with Emerson, in whose final estimation Lincoln was a "plain man of the people," the "true history of the American people in his time."

In the decades after their deaths, Nicolay and Hay left behind a thesis that remains embedded in historical consciousness to this day. Their rendering of Lincoln—the Lincoln Memorial Lincoln—was endowed with uncommon sagacity and humanity, but he was flesh and blood. Nicolay and Hay could fairly claim to have known Lincoln better than any other men of his day. It is therefore little wonder that their rendering has withstood the test of time.

PART V

The Fellows Who Came of Age
in the Lincoln Years

Though in his final years John Hay waxed eloquent about his upbringing along the Mississippi River, fondly recalling the forts and snow huts that he and his friends built along its wooded banks, he never shared George Nicolay's boundless enthusiasm for outdoor life. In the lonely days of his childhood, Nicolay developed a love of nature during long walks through the woods. As a young presidential secretary, he delighted in visiting the far reaches of Minnesota and Colorado, where he hiked, rode along dirt trails, and slept under the stars or in crude canvas tents for weeks at a time. Later in life, he brought Helen and Therena to Colorado nearly every summer, where the family "hid away from the hot weather" and enjoyed weeks of rugged living. He managed to drag Hay with him several times, assuring his chronically laid-up friend that the cool mountain air would do wonders for the mysterious ailments that always seemed to sap him of his strength, and after several years of debating the issue, the two men went in together on a parcel of land near present-day Colorado Springs. They intended to build summer houses there but never did. Helen and Therena evidently enjoyed the setting as much as George, for in 1885 Nicolay reported that "the family council" had decided on "tent life pure and simple" during its upcoming trip to Crystal Park. Not the Hays. The whole family went west in 1888, where they stayed at a nearby hotel. (As Helen Nicolay delicately explained some years later, "Mrs. Hay could scarcely have been comfortable in that wild

country.") The children enjoyed themselves thoroughly, riding horses at "Buffalo Bill speed" and pretending to rough it, but Hay felt "under par" from the "air, or water, or age" and apologetically told Nicolay that he would "never again have the courage" to come back. Instead, John and Clara bought a large plot of land in New Hampshire, where they constructed a stately summer mansion, the Fells.

Tragedy struck the Nicolay family in November 1885 when Therena took ill and died suddenly, after a painful struggle of just two weeks. George was grief stricken. "You can appreciate my loss," he wrote to Hay, "when I tell you that since the day you assisted me at my wedding she has kept me young and allowed one to smile complacently at my grey hairs. Now I am sundered from the past by a chasm, which can never be bridged. How I will walk in the twin shadows of conscious age and loneliness is more than my oppressed heart can now divine." George and Therena had known each other for well over thirty years and had been married for twenty. "Maggie," as he affectionately called her, had waited patiently through his years of service to Lincoln, proving his constant and steady confidante through the darkest days of the war. In the years since they left Pittsfield behind, George and Therena traveled Europe, hiked and camped in the Rocky Mountains, raised a daughter, and built a vibrant life for themselves in Washington. Therena shared in George's passions, working by his side for the better part of a decade as he wrote his portion of the Lincoln biography. She copied, researched, and edited with tireless energy, Nicolay reminded Hay, and when the work was done, it would stand as a "monument to her zeal and labor, as well as our own." December found him struggling to move past his loss. "For the present," he told Hay, "Helen and I are filling up the hours with the habitual daily routine . . . I suppose too the sooner I get back to business of whatever nature, the nearer I will get to mental and bodily quiet."

Helen was nineteen years old when Therena passed away. A younger brother had died in infancy. She would never marry, and until his death in 1901 she remained her father's closest companion, travel partner, and research assistant. In later years, she picked up George's work and wrote extensively on Lincoln, as well as other American

historical topics. Hay had always been fond of Helen, whom he affectionately dubbed "Butterfly" during their days in Paris. Now he and Clara took care to include her in their lives. There were invitations to lunch and tea, and when vacationing at the Fells, Hay made sure to identify motifs that Helen, a budding artist, might want to paint. Before Helen set sail for Europe in 1900, Hay, who was by then secretary of state, told her, "As I shall probably never have any more fun on my own account, I want to have a little vicarious enjoyment." He enclosed a check and instructed her to " 'blow it' in any way that may seem to you amusing."

In his twilight years, George traveled often, spending most summers either in Colorado or in New Hampshire, where he and Helen eventually built a small cottage that could have doubled as servants' quarters at the Fells but that "suited our needs perfectly," Helen later remarked. There were frequent trips to Europe, and in 1900 George fulfilled a long-deferred dream when he and his daughter visited Egypt in the company of S. S. McClure, the publisher of *McClure's Magazine* (and Ida Tarbell's editor). For two months, their small party traveled the Nile on a well-appointed dahabeah. Though growing frail, George was able to climb the Cheops, from which he could "look down on the wounded Sphinx." Father and daughter "dropped completely out of the present, while centuries long ago became real and vital."

It did not require a trip to Egypt to make George Nicolay drop out of the present and live in the past. While Hay spent his last decade deeply engaged in statesmanship and politics, Nicolay continued to labor in Lincoln's shadow. He contributed articles on various matters of Lincoln lore and legend. He condensed the ten volumes of his joint effort with Hay, creating an abridged history that achieved robust sales. At Hay's suggestion, Lord Acton, the Regius Professor of Modern History at Cambridge University, invited him to contribute chapters on the American Civil War for *The Cambridge Modern History*. Nicolay eagerly took to the task. Following on the heels of the Princeton University professor Woodrow Wilson, a Virginia-born scholar whose chapters on the sectional crisis of the 1850s offered a charitable portrayal of the antebellum South's political position but maintained a

ponderous, academic distance from the passions of the bygone era, Nicolay provided a roughly 150-page account of the war, largely drawn from the Nicolay-Hay work. (Hay had no qualms about this approach, advising his friend to "take most of it out of our book . . . as any body else would do the same.") In his conclusion, Nicolay returned to the meaning of Abraham Lincoln's life, explaining to English readers that the sixteenth president "was beloved by his countrymen because he was the full embodiment of American life, American genius, American aspiration." A self-made man whose experience proved that the son of the humblest farmer could one day rise to the White House, he wielded frightening power but used it judiciously and without arrogance. Foreigners might not readily understand Lincoln's "typical American characteristics," Nicolay conceded, but they grasped his "greatness and achievements for more universal reasons." Though it was no longer fashionable to say so, Nicolay would go to the grave believing that it was Lincoln's "great act of Emancipation that raised his administration to the plane of a grand historical landmark, and crowned his title of President with that of Liberator."

That his life had become an extension of Lincoln's did not seem to trouble Nicolay in the least. He had not grown as rich as Hay (though he surely understood that Hay married, rather than earned, his money). He was by no means as famous. He never held high office or seemed even to aspire to it. In the last decade of his life, Nicolay observed with pride his friend John Hay's late but spectacular political ascension, first as minister to Great Britain and then as secretary of state. "Of course I am proud of Hay's success," George wrote to William Stoddard, "especially as it is fully merited both by his ability and experience." He and Helen lived a comfortable and fulfilling life, he assured his old White House colleague, "and I do not let any unsatisfied ambitions worry me."

As George Nicolay settled contentedly into retirement, John Hay, now approaching sixty, finally achieved the political heights that many of his friends had expected of him decades earlier. Though he and Clara spent very little time in Cleveland, preferring to split the majority of

their time between Washington, New Hampshire, and Europe, they remained deeply connected to Euclid Avenue. By happy coincidence, Ohio had been a powerhouse in national Republican politics since the Civil War era. Two Ohioans served as president (Rutherford B. Hayes and James Garfield; three, if one includes Benjamin Harrison, who was born in Ohio but built his political career in Indiana), and by the early 1890s it was clear to most careful observers that Governor William McKinley, a Civil War combat veteran and former congressman, would likely make a run for the White House. First, however, there was the matter of avoiding bankruptcy, for McKinley had carelessly co-signed a series of banknotes for an old friend whose business interests had collapsed because of bad luck and poor management, leaving the governor on the hook for $100,000 that he could not afford to repay. Quietly, a group of wealthy businessmen, organized by the Cleveland industrialist Mark Hanna, McKinley's chief political strategist and backer, arranged a bailout fund. Hay's initial contribution of $3,000 was one of the largest, but more important it was one of the first. Hanna never forgot the gesture, and neither did McKinley, who gratefully told Hay that he could find "no words with which to adequately thank you." Two years later, Hanna called on Hay to line up delegates in advance of the 1896 Republican convention, particularly in delegate-rich Pennsylvania, where Hay enjoyed a longtime relationship with Senator Don Cameron, his neighbor on Lafayette Square (and the son of Lincoln's first war secretary, Simon Cameron). "I think you are as good at the game as either of the Penna Senators," Hanna told Hay, "and I am perfectly willing to leave them in your hands."

Hay also contributed liberally to the McKinley campaign, as he had to most earlier Republican canvasses. Henry Adams, a Democrat in a family of Republicans, later rued the way in which prior administrations had abused his good friend. "The Republican leaders treated Hay as one of themselves," he observed with a scowl. "They asked his services and took his money with a freedom that staggered even a hardened observer; but they never needed him in equivalent office." He was the "only competent man in the party for diplomatic work," Adams continued angrily, but a long succession of Republican presidents

"were always using him; always invited his services, and always took his money." That trend stopped with William McKinley, who valued Hay's long record of service and deeply appreciated his past fidelity. In the weeks following the 1896 presidential election, Hay's name was widely circulated as a contender for secretary of state or ambassador to Great Britain. Mark Hanna was eyeing one of Ohio's seats in the U.S. Senate. Because neither was up for grabs that year, McKinley moved the aging senator John Sherman over to the State Department in order to clear the path for his campaign manager. After some jockeying, Hay was offered England, a post for which he had aggressively lobbied.

John and Clara would in many regards consider the next year and a half one of the best periods in their life together. Having spent many extended visits in the country, they were familiar with the ways of England's wealthiest subjects and determined to make a good showing for themselves, as well as for the U.S. government. The ambassador's salary of $17,000 per annum did not even begin to cover the cost of their extravagant lifestyle. After renting a stately home that over-looked St. James's Park, they shipped over silver, carriages, and horses from the United States; once arrived in England, they secured the ser-vices of three footmen, a butler, several housemaids, and a chef. "The scale of expenditure on which he has established his household and the gorgeousness of his entourage causes even the English people to gape," one newspaper reported with wonder. Hay was an instant success at his job. He charmed English audiences with a grueling schedule of speaking engagements, dispatched his official duties with the ease and skill of a veteran diplomat, and surprised even himself when he proved a favorite with Queen Victoria. Clara was shocked—and pleasantly so—when the aging monarch shook her hand upon first meeting, and when the ambassador and his wife were later invited to dine and spend the evening at Windsor Castle, the queen herself rearranged the seat-ing chart to ensure that Hay would be situated next to her. "She was extremely gracious and talked freely with me for an hour," Hay re-ported to the president. Victoria, who had known every American envoy since Martin Van Buren's administration, privately called Hay "the most interesting of all the Ambassadors I have known."

Ironically, Hay, who is best remembered by many students of American history for declaring the Spanish-American conflict of 1898 a "splendid little war," played almost no part in its precipitating events. Instead, he was out of pocket for most of the buildup, vacationing with Clara, their daughters, Helen and Alice, and Henry Adams in Egypt. Their party was sailing down the Nile when the USS *Maine* exploded in Havana Harbor, and even when word reached him, Hay decided there was little he could do by returning to London and instead chose to spend several days in Cairo and Athens. In the coming weeks, Hay observed from afar the events that led to America's acquisition of an overseas empire, including Admiral George Dewey's defeat of Spain's Pacific naval forces and the brief, three-month engagement that led to Spain's ejection from Cuba. In his famous letter to Theodore Roosevelt dated July 27, Hay did in fact hail the successful conclusion of a "splendid little war," but not in the spirit of conquest and empire that many readers then and since ascribed to him. Instead, he was relieved that the conflict had ended quickly and with minimal loss of American life, and he believed that it had been "begun with the highest motives, carried on with magnificent intelligence and spirit, favored by that Fortune which loves the brave. It is now to be concluded, I hope, with that fine good nature, which is, after all, the distinguishing trait of the American character."

That fall, McKinley forced the increasingly senile John Sherman out of the State Department and tapped John Hay to replace him. Over the next six and a half years, until the day of his death, Hay played an instrumental role in expanding America's economic and strategic position over two oceans and two hemispheres. He orchestrated treaties that extended American control over the Philippines, Puerto Rico, and Guam; he authored the famous Open Door note, which asserted America's trade rights in China; he negotiated first with Britain, then with Colombia, and then with the breakaway state of Panama, to facilitate the construction of a canal across the Panamanian isthmus. Raised to consciousness by the war against slavery, the onetime champion of democratic reform in Europe became an architect of American imperialism. How to square his transformation?

In the 1890s, Americans straddled opposite instincts. The country was in many ways brimming with confidence, the product of unparalleled size, economic output, wealth, and innovation. "We are sixty-five million of people," declared one member of Congress, "the most advanced and powerful on earth." John Hay shared this feeling of buoyancy, proudly averring that the "greatest destiny the world ever knew was ours." The World's Columbian Exposition of 1893, known popularly as the Chicago World's Fair, stood as a literal monument to America's glory and triumph. But alongside this spirit of optimistic chauvinism ran a parallel sense of dread. Too much had gone wrong in recent years, from the panic of 1893, which bankrupted untold American businesses and households, to major class disturbances—the Pullman strike, the Homestead massacre, the unprecedented march on Washington by Jacob Coxey's army of unemployed workers. Large corporations like Standard Oil and Carnegie Steel seemed to have bought or co-opted public institutions that should have been looking out for the public interest. Equally alarming, in 1890 the U.S. census declared the western frontier officially "closed." At the Chicago fair—seemingly the apex of national greatness—the historian Frederick Jackson Turner delivered a disturbing lecture that seemed to augur poorly for the coming century. The frontier, he claimed, was the source of American democracy and ambition. In taming wild and unsettled lands, earlier generations had developed the spirit and institutions that underpinned American greatness. Now, with no more territory to conquer and civilize, the country's raw ambitions and talent would surely dissipate. The speech struck a resonant chord, for already many people saw signs of weakness in the culture. As more men worked as clerks and professionals, they let atrophy the muscle, brawn, and sheer courage that it took to break the land. Even manual laborers were now more likely to be employees of other men, rather than self-sufficient yeoman farmers or shop owners, whom earlier generations of Americans regarded as the foundation of the republic. With women enjoying more prominent roles in churches and reform organizations, and even entering the workforce in sizable numbers, the old barrier between the public and the private spheres no longer seemed

impenetrable. Worse still, millions of new immigrants from southern and eastern Europe threatened to dilute the heritage that many "old-stock" Americans viewed as central to the nation's past success. The United States was losing its edge, or so people worried.

Popular culture in the 1890s and early twentieth century reflected a backlash against trends that seemed to have reduced the country to a state of weak-kneed neurasthenia. This was an age of what one historian called "noisy nationalism and spread-eagle patriotism." John Philip Sousa found success with his soldierly marching music. Harry Houdini held audiences rapt with his displays of strength and courage. Theodore Roosevelt captured the imaginations of urban readers with his sweeping accounts of ranching and hunting in the unsettled West. College football, a relatively new, always rough-and-tumble game, grew more popular and more dangerous, as young men who had not had the opportunity to prove themselves at Gettysburg or Antietam sought to test their mettle on the gridiron. Not everyone bought into the new cult of masculinity. Visiting his son Del at Yale in 1894, John Hay dropped in on football practice but instantly recoiled in "anguish" at the sight of his "first-born son [being] rolled and tumbled and pulverized until he became a sorry spectacle of dirt and misery." It was not just the violence that repulsed Hay. He saw in his children and their friends a marked immaturity when compared with the young men he had known during the Civil War. "I am sure that you and I were never so young as the boys of to-day," he told Whitelaw Reid. "The riddle of the painful world suggested itself to us earlier and more imperatively. The fellows who came of age in the Lincoln years were forced to look at life in wider aspects than the Sophomores of to-day."

Neither did Hay share much enthusiasm for the real-life corollary to college football and marching bands—that is, actual war. Alfred Thayer Mahan, the celebrated naval strategist whose work influenced a rising generation of policy makers, reflected the prevailing spirit of jingoism when he warned that "no greater danger could befall civilization than the disappearance of the warlike spirit (I dare say *war*) among civilized men." Members of Congress from both sides of the aisle agreed with an Illinois Republican that "war is healthy to a nation" and

with a Kentucky Democrat that "a little blood-letting would be an admirably good thing about this time for the people of the United States." Chief among the saber rattlers were Assistant Secretary of the Navy Theodore Roosevelt, whom Hay had known for years (and whose father he had befriended during the Civil War), and Henry Cabot Lodge, a young Republican lawmaker who was part of Hay's social set in Washington but who would prove a stubborn antagonist in the Senate. Like many ultra-expansionists, Lodge believed that military adventurism offered an antidote to domestic malaise. It would "knock on the head . . . the matters which have embarrassed us at home." Like his close friend and collaborator Theodore Roosevelt, and like many in the imperialist camp, Lodge had been too young to fight in the Civil War. "I was a boy of ten years old when the troops marched away to defend Washington," he recalled with both fondness and reverence. His "broken but vivid memories" of seeing Robert Gould Shaw lead the all-black Massachusetts Fifty-fourth through the streets of Boston left an indelible mark on Lodge's consciousness. Soldiers were "heroes and patriots." "War is a bad thing," he conceded, "but there are far worse things both for nations and for men."

Roosevelt and Lodge would never quite understand the more cautious approach of their elders. Hay and McKinley shared their faith in America's greatness. As long as traditional European powers like Britain, France, and Spain reaped the benefits of empire, and with new aspirants like Germany and Japan thirsting for a broader sphere of influence, they had no objection to taking measures to ensure America's access to resources and markets. They also shared a condescending belief in America's responsibility to civilize and elevate the residents of Puerto Rico and the Philippines. Theirs was an aggressive, economic expansionism. But they did not invite or romanticize war. In his first two years in office, McKinley resisted the entreaties of war-hungry Republicans who wanted to intercede militarily on behalf of Cuban rebels who were fighting a bloody war with Spanish troops. He wanted the Spanish out of Cuba, if for no other reason than to safeguard American business interests on the island, but he preferred negotiation to saber rattling. "I shall never get into a war until I am sure that God

and man approve," he promised. "I have been through one war; I have seen the dead piled up; and I do not want to see another." Even after the explosion of the *Maine,* the president resisted cries for immediate retaliation and awaited the report of an investigative commission. Only when pressure became insurmountable did he call up a volunteer army to invade Cuba. For his part, Hay had little love of war. He surely remembered the youthful enthusiasm of his good friend Elmer Ellsworth, a young law student who had clerked with Lincoln before raising a troop of "Zouave" soldiers in New York. Just a year older than Hay, Ellsworth rode with Nicolay and Hay as part of Lincoln's official entourage in February 1861 and dazzled Washington with his swashbuckling demeanor and contagious passion. In May 1861, Ellsworth and his Zouaves led a Union invasion of Alexandria, Virginia, where his outfit tore down a rebel flag that had been flying atop the Marshall House hotel in full sight of government buildings. Descending the stairway, Ellsworth encountered the inn's proprietor, who shot him dead. The first casualty of the Civil War, he became an instant hero throughout the North. His body lay in state at the White House, where Hay and Nicolay looked grievously upon their old friend, and his death became a rallying cry for the Union. He was celebrated in verse and song and memorialized in hundreds of newspapers. Hay still remembered Ellsworth, and he remembered the wounded and dying soldiers he had encountered in South Carolina and Florida in 1863. He remembered nursing his brother Charlie—like so many other soldiers, a victim of battlefield disease—back from death. "I detest war and had hoped I might never see another," Hay wrote in the early days of the Spanish-American conflict, "but this was as necessary as it was righteous."

In the first days of the Spanish-American War, Roosevelt implored Lodge to "prevent any talk of peace until we get Porto Rico [*sic*] and the Philippines as well as secure the independence of Cuba." McKinley, on the other hand, moved slowly, deliberating cautiously over the decision to take over the former Spanish islands. When in the end he embraced annexation, he did so with the patronizing intent to "educate the Filipinos, and uplift them and civilize them." Of course, many

Filipinos *were* Christians, and they most likely regarded themselves as
already sufficiently civilized, but McKinley's motives were both self-
serving and sincere. The United States reaped enormous economic
benefits from its colonial project, but it also constructed millions of
dollars of schools, roads, hospitals, and public buildings that served the
islands well.

As McKinley's secretary of state, from September 1898 until the
president's death three years later, Hay was an active participant in
annexation and empire building, but he ran repeatedly into a brick
wall with ultra-imperialists in his own party. Like McKinley's, his zeal
for empire was more temperate than that of certain younger Republi-
can officeholders. When he brokered a treaty with Britain that would
allow the United States to build a canal across the Panamanian isth-
mus, Lodge killed the agreement in the Senate, objecting to a provi-
sion that would keep the canal zone demilitarized and open to ships
from all countries. "The American people can never be made to un-
derstand that if they build a canal at their own expense and at vast
cost," fumed Lodge, "which they are afterwards to . . . keep open and
secure for the commerce of the world at equal rates, they can never be
made to understand, I repeat, that the control of such a canal should
not be absolutely within their own power." When Roosevelt, now
serving as governor of New York, joined the chorus of disparagement,
Hay protested. *"Et tu!"* he complained with scorn. "Cannot you leave
a few things to the President and the Senate, who are charged with
them by the Constitution?" So bitter was the feud between Hay and
Lodge that the Massachusetts senator soon began interfering with
consular appointments, going so far as to eliminate appropriations for
certain offices when he objected to Hay's selections. In early 1900, Hay
offered his resignation to McKinley, finding that "the action of the Sen-
ate indicates views so widely divergent from mine in matters affecting,
as I think, the national welfare and honor, that I fear my power to
serve you in business requiring the concurrence of that body is at an
end." The president refused Hay's offer, seeing him as indispensable.
They were, after all, fellows who came of age in the Lincoln years.

The White House had changed markedly since the Civil War. Upon reporting to the president for duty, Hay was surprised to find the bedroom that he formerly shared with George Nicolay now converted into a massive office, brimming with a dozen bright-eyed clerks. Nicolay's old office had been converted into a telegraph room. Telephone lines crisscrossed the walls and ceilings. The president's office, where Lincoln first presented his draft of the preliminary Emancipation Proclamation to the cabinet, still looked much the same, but an electric chandelier had replaced the old gas fixtures.

Hay admired the president even before he took his place in the cabinet. Now he came to respect him. Regarded for many decades after his death as a stodgy conservative of limited abilities, McKinley has undergone a modest historical revision in recent years, as scholars have come to see in him the same strong, able executive and master politician that Hay detected during his tenure at State. The first president since Lincoln to expand the authority of his office, McKinley wielded power quietly but ably. "The President rules [his cabinet] with a hand of iron in a mitten of knitted wool," Hay wrote to a friend. "It is delightful to see the air of gentle deference with which he asks us all our opinions, and then decides as seemeth unto him good. He is awfully like Lincoln in many respects." In public, Hay declared that it "may well be doubted if in any century of the glorious future before us, there will ever appear two such sincere, high-minded, self-respecting lovers of the people as the last fifty years have shown us in Abraham Lincoln and William McKinley." He was not just saying it for effect; he meant it. For his part, McKinley saw something invaluable in Hay's pedigree. When the administration's opponents attacked Hay, the president testily asked his staff why they did not reply, "Yes, he was trained under Abraham Lincoln."

McKinley's murder in 1901 deeply affected Hay. By a "strange and tragic fate," three presidents in his day had been cut down by an assassin's bullet. He had worked for two of them and turned down an invitation to work for the third. He knew them all intimately and counted

them as friends. Chosen to deliver McKinley's official memorial ad-
dress before a joint session of Congress, Hay dwelled extensively on
the straight line that ran between the martyred presidents. "The men
who are living to-day and who were young in 1860 will never forget
the glory and glamour that filled the earth and the sky when the long
twilight of doubt and uncertainty was ending and the time of action
had come," he intoned. "A speech by Abraham Lincoln was an event
not only of high moral significance, but of far-reaching importance;
the drilling of a militia company by Ellsworth attracted national atten-
tion." Invoking McKinley's military service, Hay placed the late presi-
dent in the generation of men whose hearts and minds were shaped by
the experience of the Civil War. "He was a Republican," he said of
McKinley. "He could not be anything else. A Union soldier grafted
upon a Clay Whig." "There is not one of us but feels prouder of his
native land because the august figure of Washington presided over its
beginnings; no one but vows it a tenderer love because Lincoln poured
out his blood for it; no one but must feel his devotion for his country
renewed and kindled when he remembers how McKinley loved, re-
vered, and served it."

By all outward appearances, Hay established a warm and cordial
relationship with the new president. "If the Presidency had come to
you in any other way," he told Roosevelt in September 1901, "no one
would have congratulated you with better heart than I. My sincere
affection for your father—would he could have lived to see you where
you are!—would have been deeply gratified . . . With your youth, your
ability, your health and strength, the courage God has given you to do
right, there are no bounds to the good you can accomplish for your
country and the name you will leave in its annals."

In their personal correspondence, Hay alternated between address-
ing Roosevelt as "Theodore" and "Mr. President." In his diary, quite
probably meant for the prying eyes of historians, Hay spoke of him
only as "the President." The two men took care to keep in each other's
best graces. "I wonder if you realize how thankful I am to you for hav-
ing stayed with me," Roosevelt wrote to his secretary of state. "I owe
you a great debt, old man." In a fawning reply, Hay assured TR that it

was "a comfort to work for a President who, besides being a lot of other things, happened to be born a gentleman." "As Secretary of State, you stand alone," Roosevelt said in all flattery. "It is hard for me to answer your kind letter," Hay responded. "I know better than any one how far I am from deserving all that you say; but I am nonetheless proud and glad of your confidence." Roosevelt's accidental ascendance to the presidency made John Hay an essential anachronism. As one of the most economically conservative members of the cabinet, Hay gave cover to the president's increasingly progressive domestic agenda. The wise elder statesman and senior member of the cabinet, he was indispensable to TR, who even today remains the youngest president ever to have occupied the White House. Hay played the part expertly, saluting the "young, gallant, able, brilliant president" before the Ohio Society of New York. The president responded, "Edith and I were saying last night that if I died we could wish that others would put on my tomb the words you spoke . . . [T]hey describe what I wish I were, not what I am; no one else has ever so spoken of me."

Abraham Lincoln loomed large over the relationship between the president and his secretary of state. On summer vacation at his family's estate at Oyster Bay, Long Island, Roosevelt breezed through all ten volumes of the Nicolay-Hay biography. He professed to have learned much and to have been humbled by the example of his predecessor. In 1904, as the president stood before the voters to earn his own term in office, Hay showed him the original copy of the now-famous "blind memo," in which Lincoln pledged to cooperate with George McClellan in the event that the general should defeat him at the polls. "He was much impressed," Hay noted, "and went on as he often does to compare Lincoln's great trials with what he calls his little ones." When Roosevelt was inaugurated in 1905 in his own right, Hay presented him with a ring. Inside the setting was a strand of hair "from the head of Abraham Lincoln. Dr. Taft cut it off the night of the assassination, and I got it from his son—a brief pedigree. Please wear it to-morrow; you are one of the men who most thoroughly understand and appreciate Lincoln. I have had your monogram and Lincoln's engraved on the ring." Roosevelt was "deeply moved" by the gesture. He

likely had no idea that Hay had presented McKinley with his own Lincoln ring in 1896 and that in 1877 he had bestowed upon Rutherford B. Hayes a ring consisting of a lock of hair clipped from George Washington's head. It was John Hay's winning way with presidents-elect.

Roosevelt and Hay needed each other, but they were different men of entirely different generations. Theirs was in some measure a marriage of convenience. Privately, Hay groused that when "McKinley sent for me, he gave me all his time till we got through, but I always find T.R. engaged with a dozen other people, and it is an hour's wait and a minute's talk—and a certainty that there was no necessity of my coming at all." Just three weeks after Hay's death, Roosevelt told his friend Henry Cabot Lodge that Hay had not been a "great Secretary of State . . . He had a very ease-loving nature and a moral timidity which made him shrink from all that was rough in life and therefore from practical affairs. He was at his best at a dinner table or in a drawing room; and in neither place have I ever seen anyone's best that was better than his." But as "Secretary of State under me he accomplished little . . . In the Department of State his usefulness to me was almost exclusively the usefulness of a fine figurehead." In later years, Roosevelt complained to Lodge that Hay had been too ill to serve effectively as America's chief diplomat. "His name, his reputation, his staunch loyalty, all made him a real asset of the administration. But in actual work I had to do all the big things by myself, and the other things I always feared would be done badly or not done at all."

It is true that Hay grew increasingly frail as his term in office wore on, but Roosevelt's memory, which became more self-aggrandizing with time, did him a disservice. Certainly he felt that he needed Hay in 1904, when he beseeched his aging secretary of state to take to the hustings for one last canvass. In a highly reported speech delivered on the fiftieth anniversary of the Republican Party's founding, Hay returned to the theme that he knew best and felt most intimately.

"The Republican party had a noble origin," he said to much applause. "It sprang directly from an aroused and indignant national conscience. Questions of finance, of political economy, of orderly administration, passed out of sight for the moment, to be taken up and

dealt with later on. But in 1854 the question that brought the thinking men together was whether there should be a limit to the aggression of slavery; and in 1861 solemn inquiry turned to one still more portentous, 'Should the nation live or die?'" The party that was born five decades earlier forced a "discussion of the right and wrong of slavery . . . the light was let in, fatal to darkness. A system which degraded men, dishonored women, deprived little children of the sacred solace of home, was doomed from the hour it passed into the arena of free debate. And even if we shut our eyes to the moral aspects of that heartless system, and confined ourselves to its economic merits, it was found to be wasteful and inefficient."

They were the party that freed the slaves, built the transcontinental railroad, passed the Homestead Act, redeemed the nation's paper currency, presided over its historic postwar economic and geographic expansion. "The Republican party," he proclaimed, "in the mass and in detail, has shown its capacity to govern."

But if there was "one thing more than another in which we Republicans are entitled to a legitimate pride," he continued, "it is that Lincoln was our first President; that we believed in him, loyally supported him while he lived, and that we have never lost the right to call ourselves his followers. There is not a principle avowed by the Republican party to-day which is out of harmony with his teaching or inconsistent with his character."

John Hay was not the last living link between Lincoln and Roosevelt—1854 and 1904—or even the Civil War and the Progressive Era. But he was one of his generation's most powerful memoirists, if only for the history he had seen and made. After his death, the distance between the two ages would grow longer.

Days after William McKinley's death, John Hay rode by carriage from his home on Lafayette Square to Capitol Hill, where his oldest friend, George Nicolay, lay dying. He wore black crape on his arm, a sign of mourning for the president. Helen greeted him in the hall and explained that her father did not have long to live. She asked that Hay not tell him of the president's assassination, for fear that the news would

only agitate him. "I must take this off before I go up to him," Hay said
as he removed his armband. "I had to tell him that my father would
not see it—that he was already more in the other world than in this,"
Helen later wrote. "He mounted the stairs slowly. I stayed below. He
came down more slowly still, his face stricken with grief. He never
saw his old friend again, for before my father died, Colonel Hay had
left town, and it was impossible for him to return in time for the fu-
neral." After settling her father's estate, Helen turned over the Lincoln
papers to John Hay, who deposited them in the State Department
vault. They remained there until Hay's death in 1905, whereupon Clara
remanded them to Robert Lincoln's care.

Shortly following Theodore Roosevelt's inauguration in 1905, Hay
took a protracted leave of absence from the State Department and trav-
eled to Europe with Clara, where he hoped that doctors might help
cure him of mounting heart trouble. The sojourn seemed to have had
a restorative effect, though the family proved unsuccessful in holding
various monarchs and ministers at bay. Yet by the time John and Clara
boarded the RMS *Baltic* for the journey home, the old troubles seemed
to afflict him once again. On June 14, a day after he dreamed one last
time of Abraham Lincoln, Hay took stock of his life. "I say to myself
that I should not rebel at the thought of my life ending at this time,"
he wrote in his diary.

> I have lived to be old, something I never expected in my
> youth. I have had many blessings, domestic happiness being
> the greatest of all. I have lived my life. I have had success
> beyond all the dreams of my boyhood. My name is printed
> in the journals of the world without descriptive qualifica-
> tion, which may, I suppose, be called fame. By mere length
> of service I shall occupy a modest place in the history of my
> time. If I were to live several years more I should probably
> add nothing to my existing reputation; while I could not
> reasonably expect any further enjoyment of life, such as
> falls to the lot of old men in sound health.

I know death is the common lot, and what is universal ought not to be deemed a misfortune; and yet—instead of confronting it with dignity and philosophy, I cling instinctively to life and the things of life, as eagerly as if I had not had my chance at happiness and gained nearly all the great prizes.

After conferring with the president in Washington, Hay left for the Fells with Clara. He died there in the early hours of July 1.

Epilogue

July 25, 1947

On July 25, 1947, some thirty scholars and scions of the Civil War era gathered in the Whittall Pavilion of the Library of Congress for a gala dinner. Carl Sandburg was there—so were James G. Randall and Paul Angle, the leading expert on Lincoln's Springfield years. Ulysses S. Grant III was pleased to attend; Helen Nicolay, now eighty-one years old, was compelled by poor health to send her regrets. "Not since that morning in the Petersen House have so many men who loved Lincoln been gathered together in one room," remarked one of the attendees. Shortly before midnight, the party took leave of the banquet and walked across the street to the annex. There, on the third floor, they waited for the clock to strike twelve, signaling the twenty-first anniversary of Robert Todd Lincoln's death. Among the crowd of two hundred onlookers, newspaper cameramen lit the room with their flashbulbs, while CBS Radio News interviewed several of the dignitaries. At the appointed hour, the library staff unlocked the vaulted doors that had for many years guarded the Lincoln collection, and the scholars rushed the card catalog. Overpowered by the grandeur of the moment, Randall recited a line from Keats—"Then felt I like some watcher of the skies / When a new planet swims into his ken." Upon first inspection, Randall was delighted to discover that Nicolay and Hay had used and cited only a fraction of the collection. "Little of what was basically

known has had to be discarded," he explained, "but in vividness and glowing detail we have much more of Lincoln and his period than before." Elated, he felt as though he were "living with Lincoln, handling the very papers he handled, sharing his deep concern over events and issues, noting his patience when complaints poured in, hearing a Lincolnian laugh." What Randall *sensed,* only two men before him had truly experienced. Many of the Lincoln papers were written in their hand and signed by the late president. Most had passed through their fingers at least twice—during the war, when they were young men, and decades later, when they were old. Randall could close his eyes and imagine Lincoln's laugh. In their lifetimes, they had heard it.

Soon after the release of the Lincoln manuscript collection, Roy P. Basler, the forty-one-year-old secretary of the Abraham Lincoln Association, entered into an agreement with the Library of Congress to edit *The Collected Works of Abraham Lincoln*. Armed with a doctorate in literature (his dissertation was a study of Lincoln literature) and an exhaustive knowledge of his subject, he devoted the next six years to his task. The result, a nine-volume edition comprising 6,870 documents—triple the number that Nicolay and Hay produced in their *Complete Works*—sold forty thousand copies and netted a small fortune for its academic publisher, Rutgers University Press. Basler, who died in 1989, never authored a Lincoln biography of his own, but he was among a handful of individuals, then and since, who could claim to have read almost every extant scrap that Lincoln ever wrote—from the mundane to the truly profound—with the exception of the late president's legal papers. In 1974, speaking as "one of the few people yet alive who once read Nicolay and Hay complete," he judged their work "indispensable" and predicted that it "will not be superseded." Theirs was "not merely a biography of a public man but a history of the nation in his time." It "stands up today in my opinion better than any other work so comprehensive, written by any historian contemporary of Nicolay and Hay." Sandburg and Randall "fill in many niches, of course," but they did "not . . . ma[k]e revisions of the essential story told by N. & H." The secretaries, he concluded, made "use of the stuff of history" in a way that few of their successors could claim.

Acknowledgments

Books like this are not written in a vacuum. They are the product of years of collaboration with friends and colleagues. Along the way, I've benefited greatly from the advice, counsel, training, and critical feedback of countless historians. The best parts of this book come from their influence; the errors are all mine.

At Brown University, where I conducted my graduate studies, I was fortunate to work with James T. Patterson, Gordon S. Wood, Howard Chudacoff, and John L. Thomas. Their professionalism and intellectual rigor set a high standard to which all of their students continue to aspire. Sean Wilentz, whom I've had the privilege of knowing through my political work, has influenced my thinking about the role of history (and historians) in public life. During my tenure at Cambridge, Tony Badger and John Thompson were great mentors, both as teachers and as writers.

During my time as a contributing editor at *American Heritage,* I was fortunate to work with Richard Snow and Fred Allen, both stellar writers, editors, and historians. Many of my early chapters on the antislavery movement grew out of conversations with them. Ken Burns, the great filmmaker and chronicler of American life, has been a constant source of encouragement.

I owe thanks to editors at the *Atlantic Monthly,* for whom I reviewed

the 2012 film *Lincoln*. They afforded me the opportunity to set down some early observations about Nicolay's and Hay's roles in forging a lasting historical image of the sixteenth president. Thanks are also due to the editors of *Dissent,* who kindly allowed me to adapt and include portions of my article on Civil War memory in the 1880s and 1890s.

To my good friend Troy Rondinone I owe enormous gratitude. A fine scholar of nineteenth-century America, Troy gave my manuscript a close read and offered insightful feedback that saved me from errors of fact and interpretation.

At Princeton University, where I taught between 2010 and 2012, Christina Paxson (then the dean of the Woodrow Wilson School of Public and International Affairs, and now the president of Brown) offered both great encouragement and resources that aided me in my research.

Special appreciation goes to several archivists and librarians who gave freely of their time and expertise. Holly Snyder of the John Hay Library was an early and frequent source of wisdom about the Hay Papers. The professional staff at the Library of Congress was indispensable as I sifted through both the Nicolay and Hay collections. Jane Gastineau, the Lincoln librarian at the Lincoln Financial Foundation Collection in Fort Wayne, Indiana, was more than generous in identifying and providing me with access to rare manuscripts and photographs associated with Nicolay.

I began this book under the thoughtful and steady guidance of Scott Moyers and later had the great fortune of working with Andrew Wylie, who has proven a great champion of the project. Wendy Wolf, my estimable editor at Viking, was a source of both tough criticism and calm encouragement. Her positive influence is everywhere in these pages. Wendy's deputy, Maggie Riggs, has been a great colleague throughout, as has production editor Bruce Giffords, who ushered the project from rough manuscript to finished product. Ingrid Sterner is probably the finest copy editor whom I've had the opportunity to work with. She saved me from many a poorly turned phrase and more errors than I'd like to admit.

My wife, Angela, offered me love and encouragement throughout.

Her support, in turn, gave me the confidence to keep at it. On many a Saturday and Sunday, our daughter Lily crawled (then toddled, and later sprinted) into my office to inform me that it was time to stop writing and start playing. She occasionally hopped into my chair and, when no one was looking, typed her own observations into the manuscript. This book is dedicated to Angela and Lily, and to Naomi, who joined our world just as the final touches went to press.

Notes

Abbreviations

AL-CW Roy P. Basler, ed., *The Collected Works of Abraham Lincoln* (New Brunswick, N.J.: Rutgers University Press, 1953).

ALS Michael Burlingame, ed., *At Lincoln's Side: John Hay's Civil War Correspondence and Selected Writings* (Carbondale: Southern Illinois University Press, 2000).

CF *A College Friendship: A Series of Letters from John Hay to Hannah Angell* (Boston: privately published, 1938).

Hay Diary Michael Burlingame and John R. Turner Ettlinger, eds., *Inside Lincoln's White House: The Complete Civil War Diary of John Hay* (Carbondale: Southern Illinois University Press, 1997).

HN-ACPL Helen Nicolay MSS, Allen County Public Library, Fort Wayne, Ind.

JGN John George Nicolay.

JGN-LC John G. Nicolay MSS, Library of Congress, Washington, D.C.

JH John Hay.

JH-BU John M. Hay MSS, John Hay Library, Brown University, Providence, R.I.

JH-LC John M. Hay MSS, Library of Congress, Washington, D.C.

JH-LL William Roscoe Thayer, *The Life and Letters of John Hay,* 2 vols. (Boston: Houghton Mifflin, 1915).

LJOUR Michael Burlingame, ed., *Lincoln's Journalist: John Hay's Anonymous Writings for the Press, 1860–1864* (Carbondale: Southern Illinois University Press, 1998).

N&H-AL John G. Nicolay and John M. Hay, *Abraham Lincoln: A History,* 10 vols. (New York: Century, 1890).

PCFP *Pike County Free Press.*

RTL Robert Todd Lincoln.

TB Therena Bates.

TR *The Letters of Theodore Roosevelt,* 8 vols., selected and edited by Elting E. Morison (Cambridge, Mass.: Harvard University Press, 1951–54).

WH Emanuel Hertz, *The Hidden Lincoln: From the Letters and Papers of William H. Herndon* (New York: Blue Ribbon Books, 1940).

Prologue: June 13, 1905

1 three weeks before his death: JH-*LL*, 2:404.
2 "I dreamed last night": JH Diary, June 13, 1905, box 1, JH-LC.
2 in the words of Noah Brooks: Burlingame, *Lincoln Observed*, 83–84; *Hay Diary*, Aug. 25, 1864.
3 "decidedly German in his manner": Stoddard, *Inside the White House in War Times*, xi, 57.
3 Hay cultivated a softer image: Donald, *We Are Lincoln Men*, 183.
3 worked hard at being inscrutable: Current, *Lincoln Nobody Knows*, 6, 12–13.
4 "came from Illinois to Washington": N&H-*AL* (repr., New York: Century, 1918), 1:xii.
5 Leading into the 1864 election cycle: Donald, *Lincoln*, 524, 531.
6 "died in the days of doubt": N&H-*AL*, 10:341.
7 "help unite the North and South": Peterson, *Lincoln in American Memory*, 119.
7 "an uprising of the national conscience": N&H-*AL*, 10:352.

Chapter 1: Exile in the West

11 "As I am now": JH to "Friends," Sept. 30, 1855, reel 5, frames 1219–21, JH-BU.
11 Springfield, Illinois: Angle, *"Here I Have Lived,"* 91, 165.
12 John Hay was born: *Christian Advocate*, July 20, 1905, 1130.
12 "The days of my boyhood": JH, "The Press and Modern Progress," in *Addresses of John Hay*, 244–45.
12 It was clear from the start: JH-*LL*, 1:6–7.
13 Writing to his sister: JH to "My Dear Sister," March 5, 1854, reel 5, frames 1213–15, JH-BU.
14 With backing from his uncle Milton: JH to "Dear Friends," Nov. 28, 1855, reel 5, frames 1222–24, JH-BU.
14 "red-cheeked, black-eyed, sunshiny boy": Sears, *John Hay, Author and Statesman*, 8.
14 recollections of other contemporaries: *LJOUR*, xxv; William Leete Stone, "John Hay, 1858," in Brown et al., *Memories of Brown*, 153–54.
15 "In those days, all text": JH-*LL*, 1:41.
15 Hay's senior-year roommate: Stone, "John Hay, 1858," 154.
15 College library records: Dennett, *John Hay*, 22.
15 outsized personality and charm: JH-*LL*, 1:35, 47.
15 "love for and appreciation": Ibid., 41–42.
16 Anna Ridgely: Anna Ridgely Hay, "Springfield, Illinois, in 1860," Dec. 1913, reel 7, frame 662, JH-BU.
16 "which you could look into": JH-*LL*, 1:29.
16 "I have no news to write you": JH to Hannah Angell, June 26, 1858, in *CF*, 10.
16 As they walked together by the Ponaganset River: JH to Hannah Angell, July 6, 1858, in *CF*, vi, 12.
17 After three successful years: Dennett, *John Hay*, 20.
17 "In heathen wilds": JH to Hannah Angell, n.d., ca. May/June 1858, in *CF*, 6.
18 "in a remarkably good humor": JH to Hannah Angell, June 2, 1858, in *CF*, 3.
18 "Oft let the poet": Dennett, *John Hay*, 22.
19 "When I look around me": JH to Hannah Angell, Aug. 13, 1858, in *CF*, 26.
19 "go to my room": JH to Perry, Aug. 30, 1858, reel 5, frames 1250–53, JH-BU.

19 "turn my eyes Eastward": JH to Perry, Jan. 2, 1859, reel 5, frames 1266–74, JH-BU.

20 "a dreary waste of heartless materialism": JH to Perry, Oct. 12, 1858, reel 5, frames 1254–59, JH-BU.

20 "give up my dreams": JH to Whitman, Dec. 15, 1858, reel 5, frame 1260, JH-BU.

20 "somewhat undecided": Charles Hay to Milton Hay, Sept. 6, 1858, reel 5, frames 990–92, JH-BU.

21 "I am not making the most rapid progress": JH to Milton Hay, Jan. 28, 1859, reel 5, frames 1275–78, JH-BU.

21 "They would spoil a first-class": JH-LL, 1:68.

21 "I am hardly in a situation": JH to Hannah Angell, May 2, 1859, in CF, 45.

21 "insanity has not yet changed": JH to Hannah Angell, May 5, 1860, in CF, 55.

22 "I am very easily contented": JH to Milton Hay, Jan. 28, 1859, reel 5, frames 1275–78, JH-BU.

Chapter 2: The Homes of Free White People

23 "the grand theme is politics": Nevins, *Ordeal of the Union*, vol. 1, *Fruits of Manifest Destiny* (New York: Charles Scribner's Sons, 1947), 57.

23 John noted in passing: JH to Milton Hay, March 30, 1856, reel 5, frames 1225–27, JH-BU.

23 Whigs and Democrats: Holt, *Political Crisis of the 1850s*. See also Gienapp, *Origins of the Republican Party*, 3–12; Potter, *Impending Crisis*. The above argument is drawn principally from Holt's work.

24 Wilmot Proviso: Cong. Globe, 29th Cong., 1st Sess., 1217.

24 "As if by magic": McPherson, *Battle Cry of Freedom*, 54.

25 "the United States will conquer Mexico": Edward Waldo Emerson and Waldo Emerson Forbes, eds., *The Journals of Ralph Waldo Emerson*, vol. II (Boston: Houghton Mifflin, 1912), 206.

26 new Fugitive Slave Act: Nevins, *Ordeal of the Union*, 1:381–82.

26 resistance to the Fugitive Slave Act: Ibid., 388.

26 federal marshals in Boston: Nevins, *Ordeal of the Union*, vol. 2, *A House Dividing, 1852–1857* (New York: Charles Scribner's Sons, 1947), 151–52; Clarke, *Anti-Slavery Days*, 172

27 "We went to bed one night": McPherson, *Battle Cry of Freedom*, 199–20.

27 "morbid sympathy for the slave": Ibid., 55.

28 "The whole nation is interested": Goldfield, *America Aflame*, 102.

28 local, rather than national: Oakes, *Freedom National*, 21.

29 "exhausted soil": Foner, *Free Labor, Free Soil, Free Men*, 41.

29 "Enslave a man": Ibid., 46.

29 "Slavery always degrades labor": *Speech of the Hon. Thaddeus Stevens of Pennsylvania on the Subject of the Admission of Slavery in the Territories*, Feb. 20, 1850, Stevens ms., Library of Congress, Washington, D.C.

29 "Go ask Virginia": Foner, *Free Labor, Free Soil, Free Men*, 44.

29 "To the New England mind": Adams, *Education of Henry Adams*, 47.

29 Southerners responded: McPherson, *Battle Cry of Freedom*, 196–97.

31 "manifest destiny": Hine and Faragher, *Frontiers*, 80.

31 "raise a hell of a storm": Potter, *Impending Crisis*, 160.

31 "a terrible outrage": McPherson, *Battle Cry of Freedom*, 124.

32 "the North had got its back up": Nevins, *Ordeal of the Union*, 2:111, 126.

Chapter 3: It Was My Privilege to Witness

33 **"a hamlet too small":** Helen Nicolay, *Lincoln's Secretary*, 4–5; JGN, Autobiographical sketch dictated to Helen Nicolay, Oct. 24, 1897, box 1, Scrapbook, JGN-LC.

34 **"found little companionship":** JGN speech cited in Helen Nicolay, *Lincoln's Secretary*, 6–7.

34 **"I fancy my father was not sorry":** Helen Nicolay, *Lincoln's Secretary*, 9–10; "Hon. John G. Nicolay," *Pike County Democrat*, June 19, 1910.

35 **"Franklin the Printer":** JGN, "Franklin the Printer," JGN-LC.

35 **"next to typesetting":** JGN, autobiographical fragment, JGN-LC.

35 **politics and journalism:** Howe, *What Hath God Wrought*, 225–29, 696; McGerr, *Decline of Popular Politics*, 14–18; Morr, *American Journalism*; Sellers, *Market Revolution*, 370.

37 **"the mere money value":** Helen Nicolay, *Lincoln's Secretary*, 10–11; Wayne Temple, "Abraham Lincoln and Pittsfield, Illinois," *Illinois Heritage*, May/June 2010, 35–41.

37 **sharp takedowns:** *PCFP*, Oct. 25, 1854.

38 **"Let it then be remembered":** *PCFP*, Sept. 21, 1854.

38 **"great evil":** *PCFP*, Sept. 14, 1854.

38 **"free and have committed no crime":** *PCFP*, April 21, 1853; JGN, 1858 notebook, box 1, JGN-LC.

38 **"Without showing legal authority":** *PCFP*, March 16, 1854.

39 **"life or progress":** *PCFP*, May 16, 1852.

39 **"the rich inheritance of Freedom":** *PCFP*, June 19, 1856.

39 **state of extreme confusion:** Donald, *Lincoln*, 178–79.

40 **"This is a disputed point":** Lincoln to Joshua Speed, Aug. 24, 1855, in AL-CW.

40 **"A less good humored man":** Donald, *Lincoln*, 183–84.

40 **"We have the pleasure of informing":** *PCFP*, Feb. 16, 1855.

41 **"the game must be played boldly":** White, *"It's Your Misfortune and None of My Own,"* 160.

41 **"take up those fertile prairies":** Nevins, *Ordeal of the Union*, 2:306.

41 **assaulting Free-Soil men:** Goldfield, *America Aflame*, 113.

42 **Charles Sumner rose on the Senate floor:** Nevins, *Ordeal of the Union*, 2:437–44.

43 **"No meaner exhibition of Southern cowardice":** Goldfield, *America Aflame*, 116.

43 **"cowardly and atrocious":** *PCFP*, May 29, 1856.

43 **"In the coming campaign":** *PCFP*, June 19, 1856.

44 **Hoisting banners:** Gienapp, *Origins of the Republican Party*, 413.

44 **"full of fire":** Donald, *Lincoln*, 191–92.

45 **"good fortune":** JGN to Ezra M. Price, May 11, 1900, box 1, Scrapbook, JGN-LC.

Chapter 4: The Prairies Are on Fire

47 **"assiduous student of election tables":** JGN, Autobiographical sketch dictated to Helen Nicolay, n.d., box 1, Scrapbook, JGN-LC.

47 **"funeral sermon":** McPherson, *Battle Cry of Freedom*, 176.

48 **"moral weight [as] the judgment":** Nevins, *Ordeal of the Union*, vol. 3, *The Emergence of Lincoln* (New York: Charles Scribner's Sons, 1950), 96.

48 **Hay and Nicolay explained:** N&H-AL (repr., New York: Century, 1918), 2:74.

48 **"broken-down political hacks":** Nevins, *Ordeal of the Union*, 3:230.

49 **"treachery and juggling":** Ibid., 250–53.

49 "Talk of 'sectionalism' ": Fehrenbacher, *Prelude to Greatness*, 5–6.

49 **North and South agreed:** Ibid., 98; Donald, *Lincoln*, 214.

50 "The prairies are on fire": Fehrenbacher, *Prelude to Greatness*, 101.

50 "his favorite misrepresentations": *Chicago Press and Tribune*, Aug. 13, 1858.

51 " 'the nigger equality' dodge": Ibid., July 20, 1858.

51 "the negro was made his equal": Fehrenbacher, *Prelude to Greatness*, 106.

51 "no reason in the world": *Political Debates Between Abraham Lincoln and Stephen A. Douglas*, 42–43.

51 "black Republicans": Ibid., 84–85.

51 "White, white!": Donald, *Lincoln*, 219–20.

52 **facility for research:** Helen Nicolay, *Lincoln's Secretary*, 28.

52 **campaign rallies:** JGN to Schuyler Colfax, Oct. 23, 1858, HN-ACPL.

52 "In 1854": JGN, 1858 Journal, box 1, JGN-LC.

53 "Pro-Slavery Black Democracy": PCFP, June 19, June 26, Aug. 14, 1856.

53 "an outlet for *free white people everywhere*": *Political Debates Between Abraham Lincoln and Stephen A. Douglas*, ix, 352.

54 "territories [were] for free white men": JGN, 1858 Journal, box 1, JGN-LC.

54 **enormous crowds assembled:** Fehrenbacher, *Prelude to Greatness*, 102; Nevins, *Ordeal of the Union*, 3:376.

54 "over long, weary miles": Nevins, *Ordeal of the Union*, 3:385.

54 **In Galesburg:** Ibid., 387.

55 **Carl Schurz:** Schurz, Bancroft, and Dunning, *Reminiscences of Carl Schurz*, 89–91.

56 "After a hundred consecutive days": N&H-*AL*, 2:166–67.

56 "wished, but . . . did not much expect": Lincoln to Dr. Henry, Nov. 19, 1858, in AL-*CW*.

56 "that the negro is no longer a man": Donald, *Lincoln*, 233.

56 "He came into the law office": *ALS*, 115.

57 "Let us stand by our duty": Donald, *Lincoln*, 238–39; Holzer, *Lincoln at Cooper Union*.

57 "The taste *is* in my mouth": Donald, *Lincoln*, 214.

Chapter 5: Wide Awake

58 "life of listless apathy": JH to Stone, May 20, 1859, reel 5, frames 1296–99, JH-BU; JH to Hannah Angell, Sept. 1, 1858, in *CF*, 31.

58 **settled in quickly enough:** JH-*LL*, 1:83; Caroline Owsley Brown, "Springfield Society Before the Civil War," 497–98.

59 "a very pleasant young fellow": *LJOUR*, xxv.

59 "I scarcely know what I shall do": JGN to TB, Nov. 25, 1860, box 7, JGN-LC.

60 "It's been raining all day": JGN to TB, Dec. 9, 1860, box 7, JGN-LC.

60 "I have rarely ever": JGN to TB, Jan. 20, 1861, box 7, JGN-LC.

60 **the view from inside the "wigwam":** N&H-*AL*, 2:266.

61 "Our policy": Donald, *Lincoln*, 244.

61 "united voice of a great crowd": N&H-*AL*, 2:271.

61 **the chairman began to call the roll:** Ibid., 273–77.

62 "Well Gentlemen": Donald, *Lincoln*, 250–51.

62 "the central city of the north": *Providence Journal*, May 21, 1860, in *LJOUR*, 1–3.

63 "filled with an ambitious desire": Helen Nicolay, *Lincoln's Secretary*, 34; JGN to TB, June 7, 1860, box 7, JGN-LC.

64 "*never, never, never*": *New York Times*, Apr. 27, 1860.

64 **bound by tradition:** McGerr, *Decline of Popular Politics*, 35–36; Wilentz, *Rise of Popular Democracy*, 60, 301; Wood, *Radicalism of the American Revolution*, 297; Wood, *Empire of Liberty*, 62, 210.

65 **"bored—*bored badly*":** Donald, *Lincoln*, 254.

65 **Wide-Awake Clubs:** Howland, "Organize! Organize! Organize!"; Rinhart and Rinhart, "Prairies A-Blaze"; Grinspan, "'Young Men for War.'"

65 **"Party lines were as strictly drawn":** McGerr, *Decline of Popular Politics*, 13.

66 **"Everybody was intensely excited":** Ibid., 5, 29–30.

66 **"the greatest political demonstration":** *Providence Journal*, Aug. 9, 1860, in *LJOUR*, 3–6.

67 **"effect of the glorious news":** *Chicago Tribune*, Oct. 13, 1860.

68 **heady times:** Helen Nicolay, *Lincoln's Secretary*, 41; JGN to TB, July 16, 1860, box 7, JGN-LC.

68 **"if ever there was a man":** Taliaferro, *All the Great Prizes*, 32.

68 **Douglas rally:** *Chicago Tribune*, Oct. 20, 1860.

69 **"watchfires of liberty":** *Providence Journal*, Aug. 23, 1860, in *LJOUR*, 7.

69 **"the dense crowd":** *LJOUR*, 69.

69 **"Here in this little room":** N&H-*AL* (repr., New York: Century, 1918), 3:345.

69 **"the crowd had speeches and songs":** *Providence Journal*, Nov. 7, 1860.

70 **"shouting, yelling, singing":** JGN to TB, Nov. 8, Nov. 11, 1860, box 7, JGN-LC.

70 **John Hay began showing up:** JGN to TB, Nov. 25, 1860, box 7, JGN-LC.

70 **"gratified to tell you":** JGN to TB, Dec. 9, 1860, box 7, JGN-LC.

71 **"We can't take all Illinois":** Donald, *We Are Lincoln Men*, 180.

71 **"a decided disposition":** JGN to TB, Dec. 2, 1860, box 7, JGN-LC.

72 **"bluntly replied":** N&H-*AL*, 3:280.

73 **"The tug has to come":** Holzer, *Lincoln, President-Elect*, 158.

73 **"We have just carried an election":** Ibid., 222–23.

73 **"Give them that":** Ibid., 240.

73 **"If that is true":** JGN to TB, Dec. 22, 1860, box 7, JGN-LC.

74 **"Just think of it!":** JGN to TB, Dec. 30, 1860, box 7, JGN-LC.

74 **"weak, pottering old man":** *Providence Journal*, March 2, 1861, in *LJOUR*, 50–51.

74 **"Muddy boots and hickory shirts":** Holzer, *Lincoln, President-Elect*, 84.

75 **"He reads letters constantly":** *Providence Journal*, Jan. 9, 1861, in *LJOUR*, 18.

75 **"The President's whiskers":** *Providence Journal*, Jan. 7, 1861, in *LJOUR*, 17.

75 **"good room":** JGN to TB, Dec. 30, 1860, box 7, JGN-LC.

76 **"there he wrote his first inaugural":** Holzer, *Lincoln, President-Elect*, 265.

76 **specially outfitted railcar:** "For the Reception of the President Elect," box 1, Scrapbook, JGN-LC.

76 **"The scene at the depot":** *Providence Journal*, Feb. 11, 1861, in *LJOUR*, 23.

76 **"Lincoln appeared on the platform":** N&H-*AL*, 3:291.

77 **"To this place":** Holzer, *Lincoln, President-Elect*, 300–301.

77 **"something of the gloom":** *Providence Journal*, Feb. 11, 1861, in *LJOUR*, 23.

78 **"don't I feel at home?":** JGN to TB, Feb. 11, 1861, JGN-LC, box 7.

78 **polar dispositions:** JGN to TB, Feb. 11, 1861, box 7, JGN-LC; *Providence Journal*, Feb. 11, 1861, in *LJOUR*, 23.

78 **Over the next ten days:** Holzer, *Lincoln, President-Elect*, 389–90.

79 **"Such crowds":** *Providence Journal*, Feb. 18, 1861, in *LJOUR*, 28.

79 **"utterly inadequate":** JGN to TB, Feb. 17, 1861, box 7, JGN-LC; *Providence Journal*, Feb. 18, 1861, in *LJOUR*, 28.

79 **"I'm a millionaire myself":** Holzer, *Lincoln, President-Elect*, 362.

79 At Trenton: *Providence Journal,* Feb. 21, 1861, in *LJOUR,* 40.

80 "This trip of ours": JH to Annie E. Johnston, Feb. 22, 1861, reel 5, JH-BU.

80 "[T]here is something *up*": Holzer, *Lincoln, President-Elect,* 388.

81 Nathaniel Hawthorne said: Furgurson, *Freedom Rising,* 45–47.

81 "all of the party except": JGN to TB, Feb. 24, 1861, box 7, JGN-LC.

81 Walking from the hotel: *Providence Journal,* Feb. 25, 1861, in *LJOUR,* 46–47.

82 Monday, March 4: Holzer, *Lincoln, President-Elect,* 447–52.

82 Back inside the Capitol: JH, "The Heroic Age in Washington," unpublished manuscript, JH-BU.

Chapter 6: A Young Man of His Age

85 "As you see from the heading": JGN to TB, March 5, March 7, 1861, box 7, JGN-LC.

85 Washington was the largest city: Baker, *Mary Todd Lincoln,* 167–77; Furgurson, *Freedom Rising,* 13–14.

86 "the town is a congeries of hovels": *Providence Journal,* March 1, 1861, in *LJOUR,* 48.

86 "beautiful on a moonlight night": Dicey, *Six Months in the Federal States,* 98.

87 "very meagerly furnished": Burlingame, *Lincoln Observed,* 83–84.

87 "very pleasant offices": Burlingame, *Abraham Lincoln,* 2:249–50; JGN to TB, March 7, 1861, box 7, JGN-LC.

88 "extremely unmethodical": JH to Herndon, Sept. 5, 1866, in *ALS,* 109–11; Burlingame, *Abraham Lincoln,* 2:255–56.

88 "took quite a stroll": JGN to TB, March 31, 1861, box 7, JGN-LC.

89 "being continually haunted": JGN to TB, March 24, 1861, box 7, JGN-LC.

89 "grounds, halls, stairways, closets": Bancroft, *Life of William H. Seward,* vol. II (New York: Harper & Brothers, 1900), 94; JH to William Leete Stone, March 15, 1861, in *ALS,* 5.

89 inordinate attention to patronage: Holzer, *Lincoln, President-Elect,* 234–37; Burlingame, *Abraham Lincoln,* 2:69; Donald, *Lincoln,* 285. For an opposing argument, see Fehrenbacher, *Lincoln in Text and Context,* chap. 3.

89 "Mr. Lincoln owes a higher duty": Burlingame, *Abraham Lincoln,* 2:72.

90 "It is morally impossible": Ibid., 69.

90 "snobby and unpopular": *ALS,* xii–xiv.

90 the position of secretary: Pendleton Herring, *Presidential Leadership,* 101–10; Price, "Secretaries to the Presidents."

91 "the bull-dog in the anteroom": Burlingame, *Abraham Lincoln,* 2:73.

92 "the thin, frail body": Ibid.; *Pittsburgh Dispatch,* Aug. 23, 1891; Helen Nicolay, *Lincoln's Secretary,* 84.

92 "sour and crusty": Stoddard, *Inside the White House in War Times,* 57, 151.

92 "brilliant and chivalrous": *ALS,* xxii; Burlingame, *Abraham Lincoln,* 2:74.

93 "a young, good-looking fellow": *ALS,* xii–xiv.

93 struggled to conceal their self-satisfaction: JGN to TB, Dec. 9, 1860, Sept. 24, 1861, box 7, JGN-LC; JGN to the Tribune Company, June 19, 1863, box 7, JGN-LC.

93 "showed part of your last letter": JH to Hannah Angell, Jan. 6, March 29, Aug. 12, 1861, in *CF,* 56–62.

94 Nathaniel Hawthorne scorned: Nevins, *Ordeal of the Union,* vol. 5, *The Improvised War* (New York: Charles Scribner's Sons, 1959), 188.

94 "Keeper of the President's Conscience": Burlingame, *Abraham Lincoln,* 2:74.

94 "it still seems queer": JGN to TB, March 31, 1861, box 7, JGN-LC.

94 **"Lincoln loved him as a son":** DuBois and Matthews, *Galusha A. Grow,* 266–67.

95 **"a little after midnight":** *Hay Diary,* April 30, 1864.

95 **"the Mona Lisa of my stage":** Ibid., April 18, 1861.

96 **"was little gaiety in the Executive house":** "Life in the White House in the Time of Lincoln," in *ALS,* 134.

96 **"the whole floor [was] as silent":** Stoddard, *Inside the White House in War Times,* 94.

96 **frequent dinner guests:** JGN to TB, Sept. 2, 1861, June 27, 1862, Jan. 15, Feb. 1, 1863, Jan. 13, 1865, box 7, JGN-LC.

97 **"as gay, as jolly":** *Missouri Republican,* Nov. 24, 1861, in *LJOUR,* 146–47; JGN to TB, June 30, 1861, box 7, JGN-LC.

97 **"obtained a position":** JH-LL, 2:152–53.

97 **"stirring times":** JGN to TB, April 14, 1861, box 7, JGN-LC.

97 **"all the excitement":** JGN to TB, April 7, April 11, 1861, box 7, JGN-LC.

98 **attack on Fort Sumter:** McPherson, *Battle Cry of Freedom,* 284–85.

98 **"the first bloodshed":** JGN, Memorandum of Events, April 19, 1861; JGN to TB, April 19, 1861, box 7, JGN-LC.

98 **"Why don't they come!":** *Hay Diary,* April 24, 1861.

99 **"The contrast":** Ibid., April 20, 1861.

99 **"with the city perfectly demoralized":** JGN to TB, April 26, 1861, box 7, JGN-LC.

99 **"*efficiency*—to perfection in drill":** JGN to Hatch, April 26, 1861, in Burlingame, *With Lincoln in the White House,* 38–39.

99 **the population of Washington swelled:** Nevins, *Ordeal of the Union,* 5:223–24, 227–29, 291.

100 **elaborate reviews:** Ibid., 293.

100 **"Went out to-day":** JGN, Memorandum, Nov. 20, 1861, box 7, JGN-LC.

100 **"I had tired myself out":** JGN to TB, Nov. 21, 1861, box 7, JGN-LC.

100 **"We could hear the explosion":** JGN to TB, May 10, June 2, 1861, box 7, JGN-LC.

101 **"The battle is lost":** JGN to TB, July 21, 1861, box 7, JGN-LC.

101 **"with the ushering in of daylight":** *New York World,* July 22, 1861, in *LJOUR,* 75–79.

101 **In Missouri:** Foner, *Fiery Trial,* 176–79; Nevins, *Ordeal of the Union,* 5:331–33.

102 **Lincoln's action:** Foner, *Fiery Trial,* 178; Nevins, *Ordeal of the Union,* 5:338.

102 **"quiet earnest":** *Hay Diary,* Aug. 28, 1861.

102 **"one of the most troublesome affairs":** JGN, Memorandum, Sept. 17, 1861, box 7, JGN-LC.

103 **"neither [General John] Pope":** JGN to Lincoln, Oct. 17, 1861, Burlingame, *With Lincoln in the White House,* 60.

103 **"taken some pains to learn":** JGN to Lincoln, Oct. 21, 1861, ibid.

103 **"I intend to be careful":** *Hay Diary,* Oct. 10, 1861.

103 **"you must not fight":** Ibid., Oct. 26, 1861.

103 **extreme derision:** McPherson, *Battle Cry of Freedom,* 359; Donald, *Lincoln,* 319.

104 **"portent of evil to come":** *Hay Diary,* Nov. 13, 1861.

105 **back on his heels:** JGN, Memorandum, Oct. 2, 1861, box 7, JGN-LC.

106 **"The people are impatient":** Donald, *Lincoln,* 30.

106 **"John and I are moping":** JGN to TB, Dec. 25, 1861, box 7, JGN-LC.

Chapter 7: Despotic Act in the Cause of Union

107 **"the best preparation in the world":** JGN to TB, Jan. 2, Jan. 3, 1862, box 7, JGN-LC.

108 **$70,000 of his official salary:** Baker, *Mary Todd Lincoln*, 186–92; Donald, *Lincoln*, 309, 312.

108 **"hideously dull":** JH to Fanny Campbell Eames, Aug. 21, 1861, in *ALS*, 11–12.

109 **"the Hellcat":** JH to JGN, March 31, 1862, reel 5, frame 1336, JH-BU.

109 **"I told her to kiss mine":** JH to JGN, April 4, 1862, reel 5, frames 1339–40, JH-BU.

109 **"The devil is abroad":** JH to JGN, April 5, 1862, reel 5, frame 1342, JH-BU.

109 **"The Hellcat is getting":** JH to JGN, April 9, 1862, reel 5, frame 1344, JH-BU.

110 **" 'Well, Nicolay,' said he":** JGN, Journal Entry, Feb. 20, 1862, JGN-LC.

110 **In the months that followed:** Baker, *Mary Todd Lincoln*, 208–17; Donald, *Lincoln*, 336.

111 **The western campaign:** McPherson, *Battle Cry of Freedom*, 392–427; Guelzo, *Fateful Lightning*, 200–213; JGN to TB, April 4, 1862, JGN-LC.

112 **"upon the highest principles":** McClellan to Lincoln, July 7, 1862, ALP.

113 **"You cannot if you would":** Foner, *Fiery Trial*, 200.

114 **"half the army":** Ibid., 211.

114 **"paramount object":** Ibid., 228; Lincoln to Greeley, Aug. 22, 1862, AL-*CW*.

114 **"by mere friction and abrasion":** Foner, *Fiery Trial*, 212–13.

114 **"military necessity absolutely essential":** Welles, *Diary of Gideon Welles*, 1:70.

115 **"Broken eggs":** Foner, *Fiery Trial*, 218–20; Lincoln to Belmont, July 31, 1861, ALP.

115 **"flaying the Abolitionists":** JH to "Friends," Sept. 30, 1855, reel 5, frames 1219–21, JH-BU; JH-*LL*, 1:82.

115 **Like Nicolay:** JGN to JH, Aug. 17, 1863, box 7, JGN-LC.

115 **"a jolly-hearted old Shaker":** *Hay Diary*, April 25, 1861.

115 **frequent, anonymous dispatches:** *Missouri Republican*, June 14, July 22, 1862, Oct. 19, 1861, in *LJOUR*, 111, 192–95, 283–85.

115 **visit to Yorktown:** *Missouri Republican*, June 14, June 27, 1862, in *LJOUR*, 192–95, 271–75.

116 **"fanatics and fire-eaters":** *Missouri Republican*, July 22, 1862, in *LJOUR*, 284.

116 **"this bloody revolution":** *Missouri Republican*, March 27, 1862, in *LJOUR*, 235.

117 **"slavery offers itself":** *Hay Diary*, May 10, 1861.

117 **"the General says":** JH to JGN, April 4, 1863, reel 5, frame 1379, JH-BU.

117 **presidents communicated at large:** Carwardine, "Abraham Lincoln and the Fourth Estate."

117 **"one thing we have certainly gained":** *Missouri Republican*, April 27, 1862, in *LJOUR*, 253–57.

118 **"How gloriously":** JH to Jay, July 20, 1862, in *ALS*, 22–23.

119 **"far more nearly sympathize[d]":** *Missouri Republican*, Jan. 28, 1862, in *LJOUR*, 239, 202.

119 **"They are nearer to me":** *Hay Diary*, Oct. 28, 1863.

119 **"I walked up this morning":** JGN to TB, Jan. 25, 1863, box 7, JGN-LC.

119 **"a party at Mrs. Hoopers":** JGN to TB, March 3, 1863, box 7, JGN-LC.

120 **"In the garden":** JGN to TB, May 31, 1861, box 7, JGN-LC.

120 **"Some of our northerners":** *Hay Diary*, May 7, 1861; JGN, Memorandum, May 7, 1861, box 7, JGN-LC.

121 **"The dogmas of the quiet past":** Abraham Lincoln, Annual Message to Congress, Dec. 1, 1862, AL-*CW*.

121 **The preliminary Emancipation Proclamation:** Foner, *Fiery Trial*, 231, 242; Welles, *Diary of Gideon Welles*, 1:141–43; *Hay Diary*, Sept. 24, 1862.

122 **"extremists from the North":** *Missouri Republican*, Sept. 26, 1862, in *LJOUR*, 311.

122 **"I told you so":** Donald, *Lincoln*, 380, 382.

123 **"things look badly":** JH to JGN, Oct. 28, 1862, reel 5, frames 1360–65, JH-BU.

124 **"This temple of our idolatry":** *Washington Daily Morning Chronicle,* Jan. 2, 1863.

124 **"We shall never agree":** JH to Charles G. Halpine, Aug. 14, 1863, in *ALS,* 50–51.

Chapter 8: God Placed Him Where He Is

125 **worried constantly about their health:** JGN to TB, July 18, July 20, 1861, box 7, JGN-LC.

126 **"flat of my back":** JH to JGN, Aug. 24, 1861, reel 5, frame 1320, JH-BU.

126 **"all bugdom outside":** JGN to TB, July 20, 1862, box 7, JGN-LC.

126 **"The ghosts of twenty thousand":** JH to JGN, June 20, 1864, in *ALS,* 85.

126 **"almost too numb to write":** JGN to TB, Feb. 17, 1864, box 7, JGN-LC.

126 **"So Washington weather goes":** JGN to TB, April 24, 1864, box 7, JGN-LC.

127 **"a very quaint and old place":** JGN to TB, Aug. 11, Aug. 18, 1861, box 7, JGN-LC.

127 **In August 1862:** See Wilson and Moe, "Secretary Nicolay's Souvenir Album."

127 **"The trip is truly delightful":** JGN to JH, Aug. 9, 1862, box 7, JGN-LC.

128 **"Our point of destination":** JGN to TB, n.d. [ca. Aug. 9, 1862], Aug. 19, 1862, box 7, JGN-LC.

128 **"the mess with Hole-in-the-Day":** JGN to TB, Sept. 1, 1862, box 7, JGN-LC.

128 **"Since I wrote you last":** JGN to TB, Sept. 8, 1862, box 7, JGN-LC.

128 **"there is positively nothing":** JH to JGN, Aug. 1, 1862, JH-BU.

128 **"horribly hot":** JH to JGN, Aug. 11, 1862, JH-BU.

129 **"Where is your scalp?":** JH to JGN, Aug. 27, 1862, in *ALS,* 25.

129 **"I could not afford to hang":** Donald, *Lincoln,* 394–95.

129 **"scalp was yet safe":** JGN to JH, Sept. 12, 1862, box 7, JGN-LC.

130 **On April 2:** JH to Mrs. Charles Hay, March 19, 1863, JH-BU; JGN to TB, April 5, 1863, box 7, JGN-LC.

130 **"The President and Mrs. L.":** JGN to JH, April 16, 1863, JGN-LC.

130 **"solitary agony":** *Hay Diary,* April 4, 1863.

130 **Hay interviewed Du Pont:** JH to JGN, April 8, April 10, April 16, April 23, 1863, JH-BU; JH to Lincoln, April 10, May 2, 1863, JH-BU.

130 **"I am a Colonel":** JH to JGN, May 1, 1863, JH-BU.

130 **"Write to me":** JH to JGN, April 16, 1863, JH-BU.

130 **"getting browned by equitation":** JH to Mrs. Charles Hay, April 23, 1863, JH-BU.

131 **"the land of the rebels":** JH to John Hay, May 2, 1863, JH-BU.

131 **"I wish you could be down here":** JH to JGN, April 8, 1863, JH-BU.

131 **"As we sat in the shade":** JH to JGN, May 1, 1863, JH-BU.

131 **"The sunset scene":** *Hay Diary,* May 14, 1863.

132 **"pomegranate at Major Dormans":** *Hay Diary,* April 29, 1863.

132 **"Secesh women":** Ibid., April 12, 1863.

132 **thirteen hundred contrabands:** Ibid., April 24, 1863.

132 **Robert Smalls:** Ibid., April 12, 1863.

132 **"Eugene, an intelligent contraband":** Ibid., May 10, 1863.

132 **"Talk about Linkum!":** Ibid., April 19, 1863.

133 **"Williams says they work better":** Ibid., May 21, 1863. The term "rehearsals for Reconstruction" is taken from Foner, *Reconstruction.*

133 **"Song by a Florida slavegirl":** *Hay Diary,* April 19, 1863.

133 **"Went to the colored Schools":** Ibid., April 27, 1863.

134 *"Genl. Hunter sitting":* Ibid., May 23, 1863.

135 **"Why is not authority given":** JH to JGN, May 24, 1863, JH-BU.
135 **"Pennsylvania and Maryland":** JGN to TB, June 21, June 30, 1863, box 7, JGN-LC.
135 **"The Prest was deeply grieved":** *Hay Diary*, July 14, 1863.
136 **draft riots:** Bernstein, *New York City Draft Riots*.
136 **Colorado Territory:** JGN to William P. Dole, July 22, 1863, box 7, JGN-LC.
136 **"in a coach":** JGN to TB, Aug. 17, 1863, box 7, JGN-LC.
136 **"Off to the west":** JGN to JH, Aug. 17, 1863, box 7, JGN-LC.
136 **"frailly built of knotty pinelumber":** JGN to JH, Aug. 21, 1863, box 7, JGN-LC.
136 **"I have not experienced":** JGN to TB, Aug. 23, 1863, box 7, JGN-LC; JGN to JH, Aug. 25, 1863, box 7, JGN-LC.
137 **"Today we spent 6 hours":** JH to JGN, July 28, 1863, JH-BU; *Hay Diary*, July 18, 1863.
137 **"The house is gradually going to the bad":** JH to JGN, July 18, Sept. 11, 1863, JH-BU.
137 **"The newspapers say":** JH to JGN, Aug. 7, Sept. 11, 1863, reel 5, frames 1420–22, 1434, JH-BU.
137 **"You are a fortunate man":** *Hay Diary*, Nov. 18, 1863.
137 **"The Tycoon is in fine whack":** JH to JGN, Aug. 7, 1863, reel 5, frames 1434–37, JH-BU.
138 **"The old man sits here":** JH to JGN, Sept. 11, 1863, reel 5, frame 1448, JH-BU.

Chapter 9: New Birth of Freedom

139 **modicum of order:** Boritt, *Gettysburg Gospel*, 5–9.
140 **without regard for rank:** Ibid., 39.
140 **"we had a great many pictures":** *Hay Diary*, Nov. 8, 1863.
141 **"Spent the evening at the theatre":** Ibid., Nov. 9, Nov. 11, 1863.
141 **"It was a time when [the president]":** JGN, "Lincoln's Gettysburg Address."
142 **"Except during its days of battle":** Ibid., 598–601.
142 **"a straggled, hungry set":** Young, *Men and Memories*, 59–61. For a firsthand description of Gettysburg on the eve and day of the speech, see Klement, "Milwaukeean Witnesses Lincoln's Gettysburg Address."
142 **"ugly and dangerous":** *Hay Diary*, Nov. 18, 1863.
143 **"when that cause is removed":** JGN, "Lincoln's Gettysburg Address," 601.
143 **"taking more decided anti-slavery grounds":** *Detroit Free Press*, Nov. 21, 1863.
143 **Days later the *Chicago Tribune*:** Boritt, *Gettysburg Gospel*, 78.
144 **"large and clamorous":** *Hay Diary*, Nov. 18, 1863.
144 **had not yet seen a draft:** Young, *Men and Memories*; Boritt, *Gettysburg Gospel*, 77.
144 **"In the morning I got a beast":** *Hay Diary*, Nov. 19, 1863.
145 **Initial reviews were mixed:** Burlingame, *Abraham Lincoln*, 2:575–77.
145 **still mere prophecy:** Reid, "Newspaper Response to the Gettysburg Address"; George, "World Will Little Note?"
146 **"He says they will carry Ohio":** JH to Lincoln, Oct. 4, 1863, reel 5, frame 1451, JH-BU.
147 **Behind the scenes:** Burlingame, *Abraham Lincoln*, 2:488, 558, 560–61, 564–65.
147 **"a good man":** *Hay Diary*, n.d. [ca. July–Aug. 1863].
147 **Ten Percent Plan:** See Donald, *Lincoln Reconsidered*, 57–81.
148 **"a lonesome sort of Christmas":** *Hay Diary*, Dec. 25, 1863.
148 **"about the matter of reconstruction":** Ibid., Dec. 28, 1863.
148 **"that fellow five feet tall":** Burlingame, *Abraham Lincoln*, 2:601.

149 **"Great good luck"**: *Hay Diary*, Jan. 13, 1864.

149 **"Variety of complexions"**: Ibid., Jan. 15, 1864.

149 **"held the President's letter"**: JH to JGN, Jan. 21, 1864, reel 5, frames 1466–68, JH-BU.

150 **"The people are ignorant and apathetic"**: JH to Lincoln, Feb. 8, 1864, in *ALS*, 76.

150 **"I came down the St. John's River"**: JH to JGN, Feb. 8, 1864, reel 5, frames 1469–70, JH-BU.

150 **"a few men straggled in"**: *Hay Diary*, Feb. 6, 1864.

151 **"dirty swarm of grey coats"**: Ibid., Feb. 11, 1864.

151 **"Some wrote [in] good hands"**: Ibid.

151 **"The fact that more than 50 per cent"**: Ibid., Feb. 12, 1864.

151 **"I find nearly everybody"**: JH to Nathaniel P. Banks, March 7, 1864, in *ALS*, 78.

151 **"a gigantic humbug"**: Burlingame, *Abraham Lincoln*, 2:602.

152 **"simply . . . for the purpose"**: Ibid.

152 **"The original lie"**: JH to Charles G. Halpine, April 13, 1864, in *ALS*, 80.

152 **"I have seen some rather rough incidents"**: JH to JGN, Feb. 8, Feb. 23, 1864, in *ALS*, 78.

153 **"glad the President has sloughed off"**: *Hay Diary*, July 1, 1864.

153 **"There was a pic-nic yesterday"**: Ibid., July 5, 1864.

154 **"made a mistake"**: Ibid., June 30, 1864.

154 **He sent Nicolay to Baltimore**: JGN to JH, June 6, 1864, box 7, JGN-LC.

154 **"weak-kneed d——d fools"**: JGN to JH, Aug. 25, 1864, box 7, JGN-LC.

154 **"unless *something* was done"**: JGN to TB, Aug. 28, 1864, box 7, JGN-LC.

154 **"*badly beaten*"**: Burlingame, *Abraham Lincoln*, 2:658.

154 **Lincoln bandwagon**: JGN to Lincoln, Aug. 29, Aug. 30, Aug. 31, 1864, in Burlingame, *With Lincoln in the White House*, 154–56; JGN to TB, Sept. 4, 1864, box 7, JGN-LC.

156 **"Lose ten times as much"**: *Hay Diary*, Oct. 11, 1864; Taliaferro, *All the Great Prizes*, 86–88.

156 **collect and disburse party funds**: JH to Henry J. Raymond, Oct. 17, 1864, in *ALS*, 98; JH to JGN, Oct. 8, 1864, reel 5, frames 1521–24, JH-BU.

156 **"an encouraging view"**: JGN to TB, Sept. 11, 1864, box 7, JGN-LC.

157 **"The Republicans here are talking better"**: JH to JGN, Sept. 7, 1864, reel 5, frames 1508–10, JH-BU.

157 **"this nation may have sinned grievously"**: JH to George Wilkes, Sept. 2, 1864, reel 5, frames 1508–14, JH-BU.

157 **"It is a little singular"**: *Hay Diary*, Nov. 8, 1864.

159 **"haunting strain of poetry"**: *ALS*, 169, 184.

159 **"wrote very few letters"**: JH to Herndon, Sept. 5, 1866, in *WH*, 307–8.

159 **A subsequent analysis**: *ALS*, 169–84.

Chapter 10: His Heart Was Too Sad

161 **"because I have written nothing of it"**: JGN to TB, Feb. 10, 1865, box 7, JGN-LC.

162 **"When it came time to direct"**: JGN to JH, Jan. 18, 1864, box 7, JGN-LC.

162 **"the afternoon of the dinner"**: JGN to JH, Jan. 29, 1864, box 7, JGN-LC.

162 **Noah Brooks**: Burlingame, *Lincoln Observed*.

163 **"As the case now stands"**: JGN to TB, Feb. 10, 1865, box 7, JGN-LC.

163 **George could wait**: JGN to TB, Sept. 20, 1863, Feb. 12, Feb. 17, 1864, Jan. 26, 1865, box 7, JGN-LC. On January 26, 1865, Nicolay made reference to an occasion "after

my return from Colorado, and while you were here." It is unclear whether "here" was the White House or Washington, D.C., more generally.

163 **"What did you mean"**: JGN to TB, May 22, 1864, box 7, JGN-LC.

164 **"You have probably seen"**: JGN to TB, March 12, 1865, box 7, JGN-LC.

164 **The evidence establishes otherwise:** Brooks to Isaac P. Langworthy, May 10, 1865, in Hugh McClellan, *Character and Religion of President Lincoln*, 9–10. In a letter dated several weeks after Lincoln's assassination, Brooks told a friend that "the death of our beloved Lincoln changes all my plans. At first, when it appeared doubtful if Nicolay could be induced to go abroad, I accepted from Mr. Lincoln the promise of a lucrative place in San Francisco, and had well-nigh concluded to go there when Nicolay concluded to go abroad. The President was then anxious for me to take the place near him."

164 **"sail as soon as the President can spare me"**: JH to Manning Leonard, April 13, 1865, reel 6, frames 5–7, JH-BU; JH to Charles Hay, March 31, 1865, quoted in Dennett, *John Hay*, 57.

165 **"a day of deep and tranquil"**: *The Century*, vol. 39, no. 17, 428.

166 **"breathed with slow and regular"**: Ibid., 436.

167 **"took a pilot on board"**: JGN to TB, April 17, 1865, box 7, JGN-LC.

167 **"describe the air of gloom"**: JGN to TB, April 18, 1865, box 7, JGN-LC.

167 **"After the funeral"**: JGN to TB, April 24, 1865, box 7, JGN-LC.

168 **Thaddeus Stevens and James Buchanan:** Power, *Abraham Lincoln*, 131.

168 **"He looked very much fatigued"**: Corneau, "Girl in the Sixties," 445.

169 **the grand review:** JGN to TB, May 24, 1865, box 7, JGN-LC.

169 **"sorry to say"**: JGN to TB, May 5, 1865, box 7, JGN-LC.

169 **"We will have the ceremony"**: JGN to TB, May 30, 1865, box 7, JGN-LC.

169 **"to Pike so as to be there"**: JGN to JH, June 1, 1865, reel 9, frames 638–39, JH-BU.

170 **"The storm passed"**: Helen Nicolay, *Lincoln's Secretary*, 241.

170 **"The White House was full"**: Taliaferro, *All the Great Prizes*, 5.

Chapter 11: Europe

173 **"I learned yesterday"**: Bigelow to JGN, March 31, 1865, in Bigelow, *Retrospections of an Active Life*, 2:440–42.

174 **"an intelligent, honorable man"**: Weed to Bigelow, April 26, 1865, in Bigelow, *Retrospections of an Active Life*, 2:520–21.

174 **"Paris of the Second Empire"**: Helen Nicolay, *Lincoln's Secretary*, 241–45; Taliaferro, *All the Great Prizes*, 109.

175 **"the literary lady"**: JGN to TB, Aug. 21, 1866, box 4, JGN-LC.

175 **"a great city"**: JGN to Charles Walker, Dec. 14, 1865, box 3, JGN-LC.

175 **"I wish you could take a look"**: TB to Emma Westlake, Dec. 1, 1868; TB to Dorus Bates, Aug. 14, 1867, Nov. 13, 1868, boxes 3, 4, JGN-LC.

176 **"George has been gone"**: TB to Dorus Bates, Sept. 26, 1867, box 3, JGN-LC.

177 **"Business is dull"**: JGN to John Bigelow, April 21, 1868, box 4, JGN-LC.

177 **"I won't flatter you"**: JGN to TB, Aug. 13, 1866, box 4, JGN-LC.

177 **"Kiss Helen for me"**: JGN to TB, Aug. 18, 1866, box 4, JGN-LC.

177 **"appears like [Dickens's] Major Bagstock"**: JGN to TB, Aug. 23, 1866, box 4, JGN-LC.

177 **"I received your letter"**: JGN to TB, Aug. 16, 1866, box 4, JGN-LC.

178 **"There is a little tot"**: JGN to JH, July 17, 1868, box 4, JGN-LC.

178 **"One torment":** JH-*LL*, 1:229–30.
178 **Christmas reception at the palace:** Ibid., 1:237–38.
180 **"I must begin to occupy myself":** JH to Seward, n.d. [ca. Sept. 1866], reel 6, frames 21–23, JH-BU; Taliaferro, *All the Great Prizes*, 67.
180 **"got as much out":** JH to Milton Hay, Sept. 30, 1866, reel 6, frames 28–31, JH-BU.
181 **"Well, John Hay":** JH-*LL*, 1:247–59.
183 **"would ruin the best cause":** JH to Milton Hay, Sept. 30, 1866, reel 6, frames 28–31, JH-BU.
184 **"more richly and carefully furnished":** JH-*LL*, 1:257, 263.
184 **"digging some, planting":** Ibid., 276.
184 **"a little at sea":** JH to JGN, Feb. 14, 1867, reel 6, frames 33–36, JH-BU.
184 **"stay where you are":** JH to JGN, March 18, 1867, reel 6, frames 44–47, JH-BU.
185 **"You ought to come see this town":** JH to JGN, Sept. 2, 1867, reel 6, frame 63, JH-BU.
185 **"poked around Poland":** JH to JGN, Oct. 19, 1867, reel 6, frames 64–67, JH-BU.
185 **"I hate the water":** JH to JGN, Nov. 24, 1867, reel 6, frames 69–74, JH-BU.
185 **"It is curious":** JH to Bigelow, April 27, 1868, in Bigelow, *Retrospections of an Active Life*, 4:178–79.
186 **In the coming months:** JH to Bigelow, Feb. 27, 1868, reel 6, frames 82–85, JH-BU.
186 **"of prime talents and ambition":** JH to JGN, June 30, 1868, reel 6, frames 104–6, JH-BU.
186 **"I have been hoping":** JGN to JH, Aug. 9, 1868, box 4, JGN-LC.
186 **By late summer:** JH to Charles B. Norton, Sept. 17, 1868, reel 6, frame 115, JH-BU; JH to JGN, Oct. 14, 1868, reel 6, frames 117–19, JH-BU.
186 **"as close-mouthed as ever":** JH to JGN, Dec. 8, 1868, reel 6, frame 120, JH-BU.
187 **selling poems:** JH to JGN, May 14, 1869, reel 6, frames 125–27, JH-BU.
187 **"I have determined":** Dennett, *John Hay*, 66.
187 **"blind reverence":** JH, *Castilian Days*, 56, 60.
187 **"new and beneficent spirit":** Ibid., 369–70.
187 **"Necessity of the Republic":** Ibid., 406.
188 **"every month that my father":** Helen Nicolay, *Lincoln's Secretary*, 252.
188 **"central idea pervading":** *Hay Diary*, May 7, 1861.
188 **"The heap will smoulder":** Helen Nicolay, *Lincoln's Secretary*, 252–53.
188 **"I am glad I committed":** JH to JGN, Oct. 7, May 1869, reel 6, frames 140–45, JH-BU.
189 **"I was never so thoroughly":** JH to Bigelow, Feb. 20, 1870, reel 6, frames 150–53, JH-BU.

Chapter 12: Pike County Balladeer

190 **"Should the worse come":** Helen Nicolay, *Lincoln's Secretary*, 225–26.
191 **"Small water lilies":** Ibid., 263–64.
191 **William Dean Howells:** Howells to JGN, Sept. 24, 1871, box 4, JGN-LC.
192 **"Daniel Boones and the Davy Crocketts":** *New York Times*, March 2, 1871, 6; Feb. 13, 1871, 2; Jan. 27, 1871, 2.
192 **Bogotá:** JGN to Harlan, June 29, 1872; Colfax to JGN, July 2, 1872; Boutwell to JGN, July 5, 1872; Chandler to JGN, July 19, 1872, box 4, JGN-LC.
192 **marshal of the U.S. Supreme Court:** *Philadelphia Public Ledger and Daily Transcript*, Dec. 16, 1872.
192 **"few more desirable":** Milton Hay to JGN, Dec. 24, 1872, box 4, JGN-LC.

193 **"M. Hay told me":** JH to JGN, Nov. 22, 1872, reel 6, frames 348–50, JH-BU.

193 **"I have a sure income":** JH to Bigelow, July 9, 1870, in Bigelow, *Retrospections of an Active Life*, 4:369.

193 **"Nicolay and I agreed":** JH to Howells, Oct. 2, 1870, reel 6, frames 176–77, JH-BU.

193 **"I will try to shin around":** JH to JGN, Oct. 13, 1870, reel 6, frames 178–80, JH-BU.

194 **"I cannot regard it":** JH to JGN, Dec. 12, 1870, reel 6, frames 185–88, JH-BU.

194 **"Greeley does the thinking":** O'Toole, *Five of Hearts*, 43; JH-*LL*, 1:331–34.

194 **"six miles, more or less":** *New-York Tribune*, Oct. 17, 1871, 1.

195 **"done as well as I could":** JH to Reid, Oct. 15, 1871, JH-*LL*, vol. 1, 338–39.

195 **"waste[d] two-thirds of my time":** JH to Bigelow, March 12, 1871, reel 6, frames 199–201, JH-BU.

195 **as many as four columns each day:** JH to Clara Stone, Oct. 23, 1873, reel 6, frames 332–35, JH-BU.

195 **second-in-command:** JH to Bigelow, March 12, 1871, reel 6, frames 199–201, JH-BU.

195 **"It was a liberal education":** Dennett, *John Hay*, 91–93.

196 **"ridiculous rhyme":** JH to JGN, Dec. 12, 1870; JH to JGN, n.d. [ca. 1871], reel 6, frames 185–88, 196–98, JH-BU; Dennett, *John Hay*, 71.

198 **"a number of dialects":** Stevenson and Stevenson, "John Milton Hay's Literary Influence," 21–25.

199 **"Plain Language from Truthful James":** Taliaferro, *All the Great Prizes*, 134–35.

199 **"sense of the backwoods":** Howells, "John Hay in Literature," 345–47.

201 **"The Foster-Brothers":** JH, "Foster-Brothers."

204 **"an immense favorite of the ladies":** Taliaferro, *All the Great Prizes*, 120.

204 **"I have been brought down":** Ibid., 150.

204 **"I have sometimes gazed":** JH to Clara Stone, March 4, 1873, reel 6, frame 250, JH-BU.

204 **"There will be an internecine war":** JH to JGN, Aug. 27, 1873, reel 6, frame 369, JH-BU.

205 **"obliged to leave":** RTL to JGN, June 16, 1873, box 4, JGN-LC.

205 **"My work in journalism":** JH to Alvey A. Adee, Nov. 28, 1874, reel 6, frames 397–400, JH-BU.

205 **"merely the care of investments":** JH to Alvey A. Adee, Dec. 14, 1875, reel 6, frames 41–46, JH-BU.

205 **"Known best as a verse-maker":** O'Toole, *Five of Hearts*, 128; Dennett, *John Hay*, 106.

205 **"My wife keeps well and lovely":** JH to Alvey A. Adee, Dec. 14, 1875, reel 6, frames 413–16, JH-BU.

206 **"He was so tender-hearted":** Taliaferro, *All the Great Prizes*, 273.

206 **"prize it [and] wear it":** Hayes to JH, Feb. 27, 1877, reel 7, frame 696, JH-BU.

207 **"All Euclid Avenue":** Taliaferro, *All the Great Prizes*, 183–84.

207 **ushered into his secretary's office:** JH to Clara Stone Hay, Nov. 21, 1879, reel 6, frames 493–96, JH-BU.

207 **"Think of that":** JH to Clara Stone Hay, Nov. 24, 1879, reel 6, frame 502, JH-BU.

207 **"Today was an important one":** JH to Clara Stone Hay, Nov. 25, 1879, reel 6, frames 505–8, JH-BU.

208 **"Friends are born":** Adams, *Education of Henry Adams*, 106.

208 **"chats for two":** O'Toole, *Five of Hearts*, 68–70.

209 **"I cannot really say I regret":** JH to Clara Stone Hay, Feb. 7, 1880, reel 6, frames 623–26, JH-BU.

209 **"clamorous greedy host"**: JH to Clara Stone Hay, March 2, 1880, reel 6, frame 665, JH-BU.

209 **"a little tiresome"**: JH to Clara Stone Hay, March 3, 1880, reel 6, frame 671, JH-BU.

209 **cabinet meetings grew routine:** JH to Clara Stone Hay, June 20, 1880, reel 6, frame 712, JH-BU.

209 **"glad all my life"**: JH to Clara Stone Hay, Feb. 15, 1880, reel 6, frame 644, JH-BU.

209 **"Mrs. Hay, gravely clad"**: Twain, *Autobiography of Mark Twain*, 233–34.

210 **"I should have been nominated"**: JH to Clara Stone Hay, Dec. 18, 1879, July 25, 1880, reel 6, frames 559, 733, JH-BU.

210 **"The more I see the life"**: JH to Clara Stone Hay, Dec. 8, 1879, reel 6, frames 538–41, JH-BU.

210 **equal in rank and pay:** Garfield to JH, Dec. 10, 1880, reel 4, frame 1397, JH-BU.

210 **"To do a thing well"**: JH to Garfield, Dec. 25, 1880, in JH-LL, 1:443–444.

Chapter 13: Breadwinners

212 **two mansions but no home:** Taliaferro, *All the Great Prizes*, 157, 167, 243–49; O'Toole, *Five of Hearts*, 153–57.

213 **more wealth:** Taliaferro, *All the Great Prizes*, 223.

213 **"literary society"**: JH to Clara Stone Hay, Dec. 8, Dec. 22, 1879, Feb. 8, June 20, 1880, reel 6, frames 542, 567, 629, 712–14, JH-BU.

214 **"Had they been Tyrian traders"**: Adams, *Education of Henry Adams*, 237.

214 **"In April 1861"**: Foner, *Reconstruction*, 19.

214 **"great gulf"**: Keller, *Affairs of State*, 2.

215 **dramatically accelerated economic transformations:** Ibid., 19–21, 462; McPherson, *Battle Cry of Freedom*, 428–53; Curry, *Blueprint for Modern America*; Richardson, *Greatest Nation of the Earth*; Lawson, *Patriot Fires*, 40–64.

217 **"rendered very valuable service"**: Richardson, *West from Appomattox*, 129.

218 **"Every greenback"**: Keller, *Affairs of State*, 191.

218 **The boom proved lucrative:** Hays, *Response to Industrialism*, 150–51; Painter, *Standing at Armageddon*, chaps. 1–2.

219 **"The Democratic party is our Evil"**: JH to Reid, Oct. 15, 1879, in JH-LL, 1:434.

219 **"liked Tilden very much"**: JH to Howells, Feb. 20, 1877, in Monteiro and Murphy, *John Hay–Howells Letters*, 22–23.

219 **dismissed most congressmen:** JH to Alvey A. Adee, Feb. 20, 1877, reel 6, frames 433–36, JH-BU.

220 **"I am utterly opposed"**: Foner, *Reconstruction*, 481.

220 **Godkin:** Ibid., 489.

220 **Parkman:** Ibid., 489.

221 **a region that would struggle:** Foner, *Reconstruction*, 125; McPherson, *Abraham Lincoln and the Second American Revolution*, 17.

221 **"the masses will never be"**: Foner, *Reconstruction*, 478.

221 **"communistic war"**: Ibid., 518.

222 **"the most extensive and deplorable"**: Ibid., 583.

222 **"The strikers have been put down"**: Ibid., 585.

222 **In their zeal:** Rondinone, *The Great Industrial War*, 38–57.

222 **"During my two terms of office"**: Grant to Daniel Ammen, Aug. 26, 1877, in Simon, *Papers of Ulysses S. Grant*, 28:251–53.

223 **"We at the North":** Keller, *Affairs of State,* 4.

223 **"A few shots fired":** JH to Amasa Stone, July 24, 1877, in JH-*LL,* 2:1–3.

224 **"the law-and-order men":** JH to Amasa Stone, July 27, 1877, in JH-*LL,* 2:3–4.

224 **"The very devil":** JH to Amasa Stone, Aug. 23, 1877, in JH-*LL,* 2:5.

225 **"Thackeray and Dickens":** Dennett, *John Hay,* 112.

225 **"free-hand sketch":** Vandersee, "Great Literary Mystery of the Gilded Age," 244.

225 **"been accustomed to earning":** Dennett, *John Hay,* 112–13.

226 **"We think we have done":** Dennett, *John Hay,* 127.

Chapter 14: A Model for All the Good Little Boys to Follow

231 **"Please come to Washington":** Mearns, *Lincoln Papers,* 15–17, 45, 139.

232 **"not any letters":** Ibid., 11.

233 **"I believe Lincoln":** JH to Herndon, Sept. 5, 1866, in *WH,* 307–8.

234 **"The age of blind hero worship":** Herndon to Arnold, Nov. 20, 1866, in *WH,* 39.

234 **"enquires & interrogations":** Donald, *Lincoln's Herndon,* 168.

234 **"eminently Christian":** Peterson, *Lincoln in American Memory,* 67–69; Donald, *Lincoln's Herndon,* 170–71, 212–13.

235 **all sought to enshrine:** Thomas, *Portrait for Posterity,* 7.

235 **"was not God":** Donald, *Lincoln's Herndon,* 170.

235 **"I have been with the people":** Ibid., 184–85.

236 **"the best boy":** Ibid., 168, 182–83.

236 **"even when I differ":** Mearns, *Lincoln Papers,* 49.

237 **"seemed to glide through":** Clinton, *Mrs. Lincoln,* 344.

237 **Herndon could not easily be ignored:** Thomas, *Portrait for Posterity,* 17.

237 **"general greed for office":** Donald, *Lincoln's Herndon,* 202–6.

238 **"The recollection of my beloved":** Ibid., 190.

238 **Ann Rutledge:** Ibid., 185–86; Wilson and Davis, *Herndon's Informants,* 21.

239 **"There, by that—there":** Donald, *Lincoln's Herndon,* 218.

240 **"in the presence of Ann Rutledge":** Ibid., 219.

240 **ardent student of history:** Turner, *Frontier in American History;* Potter, *People of Plenty;* Jared Diamond, *Guns, Germs, and Steel: The Fates of Human Societies* (New York: W. W. Norton, 2005).

241 **"shave a horse's main":** Donald, *Lincoln's Herndon,* 226–27.

242 **"monstrous figure":** Peterson, *Lincoln in American Memory,* 209–10.

242 **"Abraham Lincoln loved":** Herndon, *Abraham Lincoln.*

242 **swift and brutal:** Donald, *Lincoln's Herndon,* 230, 237.

243 **"I have never had any doubt":** Mearns, *Lincoln Papers,* 50–51.

243 **"to make some considerable mention":** Ibid.

244 **Abraham Enlow:** Herndon to Ward Hill Lamon, March 6, 1870, in *WH,* 73.

244 **"struggles, difficulties":** Herndon to Isaac Arnold, Nov. 20, 1866, in *WH,* 37.

244 **"*Mrs. Lincoln's domestic quarrels*":** Herndon to Charles Hart, Nov. 26, 1866, in *WH,* 40.

245 **"What a wife!":** Herndon to Jesse Weik, Nov. 19, 1885, in *WH,* 105.

245 **"I need kicking":** Thomas, *Portrait for Posterity,* 26.

245 **"He certainly does not compare well":** Jeremiah Black to David Davis, July 9, 1870, in Mearns, *Lincoln Papers,* 59.

246 **"tell the truth":** Donald, *Lincoln's Herndon,* 256–57.

246 **"Can't you stop him?":** Thomas, *Portrait for Posterity*, 44.

246 **"It is absolutely horrible":** RTL to JH, April 7, 1872, reel 8, JH-BU.

246 **"a vulgar man":** Peterson, *Lincoln in American Memory*, 80.

246 **"Mr. Herndon has troubled the family":** Jeremiah Black to Davis, July 9, 1870; Davis to Jeremiah Black, Aug. 19, 1870, in Mearns, *Lincoln Papers*, 59–61.

247 **"Would you have Mr. Lincoln":** Herndon to Isaac Arnold, Nov. 20, 1866, in *WH*, 38.

247 **"Mr. Lincoln was my good friend":** Herndon to Lamon, March 6, 1870, in *WH*, 71.

247 **"the noblest and loveliest man":** Herndon to Francis Carpenter, Dec. 11, 1866, in *WH*, 48; JH to JGN, March 5, 1867, reel 6, frames 37–39, JH-BU.

247 **"Read (+ send back)":** JH to JGN, Dec. 1866, reel 6, frame 32, JH-BU.

248 **"dishes our chances":** JH to JGN, March 5, 1867, reel 6, frames 37–39, JH-BU.

248 **"nobody is keen":** JH to JGN, March 18, 1867, reel 6, frames 44–47, JH-BU.

248 **"convinced that we ought":** JH to JGN, Nov. 22, 1872, reel 6, frames 348–49, JH-BU.

248 **"There are in this city":** JGN to RTL, March 3, 1872, box 4, JGN-LC.

249 **so many of Lincoln's friends:** Donald, *Lincoln's Herndon*, 172–73; Guelzo, "Come-Outers and Community Men."

249 **prominent Illinois politicians:** Donald, *Lincoln's Herndon*, 263. See also Josephine Louise Harper, "Post-Lincoln Party Attitudes of Lincoln's Friends" (master's thesis, University of Illinois, 1943).

250 **"I must affirm":** Welles, *Lincoln and Seward*, 24–25.

250 **Horace Greeley:** Peterson, *Lincoln in American Memory*, 86.

250 **"contemptible assertions":** JGN to RTL, n.d. (ca. 1872), box 4, JGN-LC.

250 **"time about a 'Life of Lincoln' ":** Gilder to JH, April 25, 1874; JH to JGN, April 26, 1874, reel 6, frames 381–82, JH-BU.

251 **"The work is a heavy one":** JH to Colfax, July 20, 1875, reel 6, frame 404, JH-BU.

251 **"The reading public in this country":** Milton Hay to JGN, Dec. 24, 1872, box 4, JGN-LC.

252 **"We [are] in no hurry to make arrangements":** JH to JGN, April 26, 1874, reel 6, frame 381, JH-BU.

Chapter 15: Our Ideal Hero

253 **"whoever attempts to limn":** Helen Nicolay, *Lincoln's Secretary*, 280–81.

254 **"I beg of you":** JGN to RTL, July 17, 1874, box 4, JGN-LC.

254 **obituary for the *New-York Tribune*:** ALS, xv, 111–13.

255 **"latent power of observation":** JGN to JH, April 24, 1868, box 4, JGN-LC.

256 **"I need not tell you":** JH to RTL, Jan. 27, 1884, in JH-*LL*, 2: tktk

256 **"writing the life of Lincoln":** Herndon to Jesse Weik, Jan. 22, 1887, in *WH*, 156–59.

256 **"plenary blue pen powers":** Thomas, *Portrait for Posterity*, 111.

256 **"It is beyond doubt":** RTL to JH, April 17, 1885, reel 8, JH-BU.

256 **In his original draft:** Thomas, *Portrait for Posterity*, 114–15; N&H-*AL*, 1:23.

257 **"cabin was like that":** Thomas, *Portrait for Posterity*, 117; N&H-*AL*, 1:30.

258 **shake the foundations of American historical consciousness:** Novick, *That Noble Dream*, 21–22, 25, 33, 48–49; Ross, "Historical Consciousness in Nineteenth-Century America."

259 **interviewing dozens of individuals:** Reel 9, frames 625–745, JH-BU.

259 **"I have a large amount":** JH to JGN, Feb. 28, 1878, reel 6, frame 452, JH-BU.

259 **On rare occasions:** N&H-*AL*, 1:266–78.

260 **"You see the sort of pig-headed":** JH to JGN, Oct. 14, 1889, reel 6, frame 1141, JH-BU.

260 **"You know it is impossible":** JH to JGN, Nov. 23, 1876, reel 6, frame 432, JH-BU.

260 **"because it placed us":** Dennett, *John Hay*, 137.

260 **To supplement:** JGN to JH, Jan. 18, 1876, box 4, JGN-LC.

260 **"I think I have the foundation":** JGN to JH, Nov. 11, 1876, box 4, JGN-LC; JGN to JH, Sept. 3, 1875, reel 9, frames 746–48, JH-BU.

260 **"I shall get a carpenter":** JH to JGN, Feb. 28, 1878, reel 6, frame 452, JH-BU.

261 **"breaking down with the nervous fatigue":** JH to JGN, Aug. 10, 1885, reel 6, frame 941, JH-BU.

261 **"The two would never divulge":** Helen Nicolay, *Lincoln's Secretary*, 283.

261 **"I write with great labor":** JH to JGN, Aug. 9, 1877, reel 6, frame 443, JH-BU.

262 **"if nothing happens adversely":** Ibid.

262 **"however brave":** Foster, *Ghosts of the Confederacy*, 119.

264 **"The faith is true and adorable":** Holmes, "Soldier's Faith."

265 **"For those who knew":** Page, *Red Rock*, viii.

266 **"death has no power":** Faust, *This Republic of Suffering*, 269.

267 **"I will try to tackle it":** JH to JGN, Jan. 17, 1885, reel 6, frame 908, JH-BU.

267 **Hay pleaded once again for concision:** JH to JGN, April 22, 1885, reel 6, frames 925–27, JH-BU.

267 **"you are giving yourself needless worry":** JGN to JH, April 26, 1885, reel 9, frames 828–30, JH-BU.

268 **"We want your life of Lincoln":** Smith to JH, March 3, 1885, box 4, JGN-LC.

268 **George Washington Cable:** Caron, "'How Changeable Are the Events of War,'" 153, 157–58, 164–65.

269 **Battles and Leaders of the Civil War:** Ibid., 152, 156–57.

269 **The *Century*'s editors:** Foster, *Ghosts of the Confederacy*, 69; Caron, "'How Changeable Are the Events of War,'" 154–57; Blight, *Race and Reunion*, 173–81.

270 **Gilder began courting:** JH to JGN, April 26, 1874, reel 6, frame 381, JH-BU.

270 **"Flattering as his suggestion is":** JGN to JH, Aug. 21, 1880, reel 9, frames 780–81, JH-BU.

270 **"but they are not on a level":** JH to JGN, March 20, March 21, 1885, reel 6, frames 913, 915–16, JH-BU.

271 **"The unprecedented success":** JH to JGN, March 2, 1885, reel 6, frames 912–13, JH-BU.

271 **"get from them as much information":** JH to JGN, March 29, 1885, reel 6, frame 918, JH-BU.

271 **"visibly interested":** JGN to JH, July 19, 1885, box 4, JGN-LC.

271 **"The work will have a great":** Peterson, *Lincoln in American Memory*, 117–19.

272 **"the secret history":** Gilder to Edmund Gosse, Nov. 2, 1885, in Gilder, *Letters of Richard Watson Gilder*, 174–76.

272 **"universal tone of respect":** Gilder to JGN, June 11, 1885, box 4, JGN-LC.

272 **"the only authorized life":** Gilder to Edmund Gosse, Nov. 2, 1885, in Gilder, *Letters of Richard Watson Gilder*, 175.

272 **"a simple truth of law":** JH to JGN, Aug. 10, 1885, reel 6, frame 944, JH-BU.

273 **"look up the exact language":** JGN to Gilder, Aug. 5, 1885, box 4, JGN-LC.

273 **"the weakness and defects":** N&H-*AL*, 5:97–102.

273 **"hardly be objected to":** JGN to Gilder, Aug. 13, 1885, box 4, JGN-LC.

273 **Hay rankled Southern sensibilities:** JH to "Dear Sir," April 22, 189?, reel 6, frame 1159, JH-BU.

274 **"I am afraid that I have come":** JH to JGN, Aug. 10, 1885, reel 6, frames 941–46, JH-BU.

274 **"If John Brown":** N&H-*AL*, 5:393–99.

274 **"I believe I have adopted":** JGN to Gilder, Jan. ?, 1887, box 4, JGN-LC.

275 **"grit to stand up against":** JGN to JH, Aug. 16, 1885, reel 9, frames 847–48, JH-BU.

275 **"Lincoln's fame":** Gilder to JGN, Jan. 2, 1890, box 4, JGN-LC.

276 **"conscious of having written":** JGN to Gilder, Jan. 8, 1890 (unsent), box 4, JGN-LC.

276 **"As to the possible accusations":** JGN to Gilder, Jan. 24, 1890, box 4, JGN-LC.

277 **In its final form:** JH to JGN, Aug. 10, 1885, reel 6, frames 941–46, JH-BU.

Chapter 16: We Are Lincoln Men All Through

278 **baffled by its long digressions:** Burlingame, "Nicolay and Hay," 1.

279 **Among its many famous contributions:** N&H-*AL*, 7:87–88, 4:152–53, 466, 3:448.

280 **In fifteen chapters:** JH to JGN, Jan. 20, 1879, March 8, 1882, reel 6, frames 485, 811–13, JH-BU; JGN to JH, n.d. [ca. Nov. 1876], box 4, JGN-LC.

280 **"We hold that your father":** JGN to RTL, July 17, 1874, box 4, JGN-LC.

280 **"did not know":** N&H-*AL*, 3:443.

280 **"the superior sagacity":** Ibid., 4:129, 139.

281 **"almost a giant":** Ibid., 151.

281 **"Of all these years":** Ibid., 1:26–27.

281 **"The 'barbarous neighborhood' ":** Ibid., 16–19.

282 **"sharp points and salient angles":** JH to Hannah Angell, Oct. 20, 1858, in *CF*, 33.

282 **"beauty of our river society":** JH to JGN, Sept. 7, 1864, reel 5, frames 1508–10, JH-BU.

282 **"In most respects there had been":** N&H-*AL*, 1:39–42.

283 *"by the fire at night":* Ibid., 35–36.

283 **"constitutional sadness":** Ibid., 189–90.

284 **"we of the great West":** Herndon to Jesse Weik, Jan. 30, 1887, in *WH*, 163–65.

284 **"made the acquaintance":** N&H-*AL*, 1:191–92.

285 **"on the 4th of November":** Ibid., 186–202.

285 **"if chance or fate":** Ibid., 3:208.

286 **"were mostly a simple, neighborly":** Ibid., 1:51–52.

286 **Campaigns of the Civil War:** Charles Scribner's Sons to JGN, July 17, 1880, box 4, JGN-LC.

286 **"inexorable tyranny":** JGN, *Outbreak of Rebellion*, 3, 6, 9.

286 **"I confess I learned":** JH to JGN, Aug. 10, 1885, reel 6, frames 941–46, JH-BU.

287 **"The lion of the North":** N&H-*AL*, 4:85, 261.

288 **"that persistent struggle":** Ibid., 1:315.

288 **"The generation which fought":** Ibid., 3:199–200.

288 **"spirit of bullying":** Ibid., 2:52, 3:32, 176.

289 **"one of the many 'relics of barbarism' ":** Ibid., 3:314–15.

289 **"an idle waste of labor":** Ibid., 1:72–73; Foner, *Fiery Trial*, 10–11.

290 **"there was a long distance":** N&H-*AL*, 1:152–53.

290 "traffic in human beings": Ibid., 285.
290 "the master's right to slave property": Ibid., 3:29.
291 "white men, after running": JGN, 1858 Journal, box 1, JGN-LC.
291 "their birthright": N&H-*AL*, 2:76–77.
291 "Conservative opinion": Ibid., 6:96–97.
292 "on the kindred policy": Ibid., 125.
292 "naturally antislavery": Ibid., 430–31.
292 "those who were anxious to destroy": Ibid., 148.
292 "Antislavery opinion in Congress": Ibid., 106–7.
292 "Could antislavery people": Ibid., 157.
293 "Practical trial": Ibid., 469.
293 "Under the barbarous institution": Ibid., 477.
293 "revolting crimes": Ibid., 7:453–55.
294 "acquired much more": Ibid., 4:389.
294 "stirring times": JGN to TB, April 14, 1861, box 7, JGN-LC.
294 **critical moment seems to have coincided:** A ProQuest Historical Newspapers search of eleven newspapers, including the *New York Times, New-York Tribune,* and *Chicago Tribune,* produces 20 mentions of the Gettysburg Address between January 1864 and January 1891, and 575 mentions between January 1891 and January 1911.
295 **stand-alone article:** JGN, "Lincoln's Gettysburg Address."
295 "privilege to witness": JGN to Ezra M. Price, May 11, 1900, box 1, Scrapbook, JGN-LC.
295 **in vain pursuit:** Johnson, "Who Stole the Gettysburg Address?"
295 "for then and there": N&H-*AL*, 8:199–202.
296 "all the particulars are in the daily papers": *Hay Diary,* Nov. 19, 1863.
296 **comte de Paris:** Comte de Paris, *History of the Civil War in America.*
296 **stilted version of events:** George B. McClellan, *McClellan's Own Story.*
296 "I think I have left the impression": JH to JGN, Aug. 10, 1885, reel 6, frame 941, JH-BU. For background on Hay's enmity for McClellan, see Monteiro, "John Hay and the Union Generals."
296 "hallucinations of overwhelming forces": N&H-*AL*, 4:449, 5:154–56, 364.
297 "mutinous insolence": Ibid., 6:135–38, 147, 5:443.
297 "as far from being the traitor": Ibid., 6:188–93.
298 "tough nut to crack": JH to JGN, Aug. 10, Aug. 29, 1885, reel 6, frames 941–46, 958, JH-BU.
298 "Lincoln, Chase, and Seward": N&H-*AL*, 6:224–25.
299 "Now I can ride": Ibid., 254, 262, 265–71.
299 "daily and hourly": Ibid., 4:367–68.
299 "it is safe to say": Ibid., 6:114.
299 "larger comprehension": Ibid., 5:151–52.
299 "control[led] the average public sentiment": Ibid., 6:107.
300 "He was of the Immortals": Mechlin, "Proposed Lincoln Memorial."

Chapter 17: Lincolniana

301 "Laws-a-mercy!": JH to Henry Adams, Aug. 4, 1889, in JH-*LL*, 2:43.
301 "There will be ten volumes": JH to RTL, April 22, Dec. 22, 1889, in JH-*LL*, 2:44–46.

301 **"the truth before the country":** JH to RTL, Jan. 6, 1886, in Mearns, *Lincoln Papers,* 75.

301 **A critic for *Life:*** Burlingame, "Nicolay and Hay," 1–2.

302 **"damn partisan":** Helen Nicolay, *Lincoln's Secretary,* 298.

302 **"no one will suspect":** Gilder to JGN, March 30, 1887, box 4, JGN-LC.

302 **"ponderous Republican history":** Burlingame, "Nicolay and Hay," 2.

302 **"The whole thing is growing":** JH to JGN, July 25, 1891, reel 6, frame 1233, JH-BU.

302 **"never had two hours' conversation":** Dennett, *John Hay,* 136.

302 **"these gentlemen did not write history":** O'Toole, *Five of Hearts,* 226.

303 **"one of the noblest achievements":** *Harper's Magazine,* Feb. 1891, 479.

303 **"much pleased":** Mearns, *Lincoln Papers,* 80.

303 **"Many people speak to me":** Burlingame, "Nicolay and Hay," 12.

303 **seven thousand copies:** Peterson, *Lincoln in American Memory,* 126.

303 **"risk we run":** Donald, *Lincoln's Herndon,* 312–13.

304 **"most striking fact":** Peterson, *Lincoln in American Memory,* 67–69; Donald, *Lincoln's Herndon,* 141.

304 **"a place in which the present":** Mearns, *Lincoln Papers,* 86.

305 **Ida Tarbell:** Peterson, *Lincoln in American Memory,* 149–55; Thomas, *Portrait for Posterity,* 178–202.

306 **"Out of the pages":** Peterson, *Lincoln in American Memory,* 275.

307 **"I really deal too leniently":** Ibid., 307–8.

307 **James Ford Rhodes:** Stampp, "The Irrepressible Conflict," in *Imperiled Union,* 191.

307 **Edward Channing:** Channing, *United States of America, 1765–1865,* ix–x.

308 **Charles Beard:** Stampp, "Irrepressible Conflict," 193–94.

308 **discontinuities associated with economic development:** Novick, *That Noble Dream,* 92–100.

310 **"worse than the fact itself":** Craven, *Coming of the Civil War,* 93; Stampp, "Irrepressible Conflict," 199, 204–5; Novick, *That Noble Dream,* 237.

310 **"blundering generation":** Randall, *Civil War and Reconstruction,* vii; Randall, "A Blundering Generation," in *Lincoln the Liberal Statesman,* 49–52.

311 **revised the history of Reconstruction:** Peterson, *Lincoln in American Memory,* 302; Foner, "New View of Reconstruction"; Weisberger, "Dark and Bloody Ground of Reconstruction Historiography."

311 **"essentially a Douglas Democrat":** Peterson, *Lincoln in American Memory,* 308–10.

312 **disillusionment with Reconstruction:** Richardson, *Death of Reconstruction;* Foner, *Reconstruction,* chaps. 11–12.

312 **strength from the academy:** Fredrickson, *Black Image in the White Mind,* chaps. 8, 10; Sitkoff, *New Deal for Blacks,* 29–30.

312 **millions of new immigrants:** Jacobson, *Whiteness of a Different Color.*

312 **confusion in the ranks:** Hale, *Making Whiteness,* introd., chaps. 4, 5; Litwack, *Trouble in Mind,* chaps. 1, 6.

313 **oppositional theories of political economy:** Foner, *Free Labor, Free Soil, Free Men;* McPherson, *Battle Cry of Freedom.*

315 **"If he had died":** N&H-*AL,* 10:341.

315 **"I know the people want him":** JH to JGN, Sept. 11, 1863, reel 5, frame 1448, JH-BU.

315 **"among the common people":** N&H-*AL,* 10:344.

315 **"Nothing would have more amazed him":** Ibid., 351–52.

315 "**principally as a man of action**": Ibid., 352–53.
316 "**a man, in fact**": Ibid., 346–47.
316 "**fables**": Ibid., 347–48.

Chapter 18: The Fellows Who Came of Age in the Lincoln Years

319 **upbringing along the Mississippi River:** JH, "The Press and Modern Progress," in *Addresses of John Hay*, 244–45.
319 "**hid away from the hot weather**": JGN to Schuyler Colfax, Aug. 16, 1878, reel 9, frame 767, JH-BU.
319 "**the family council**": JGN to JH, April 11, 1885, reel 9, frame 821, JH-BU.
319 "**Mrs. Hay could scarcely have been comfortable**": Helen Nicolay, *Lincoln's Secretary*, 339–40.
320 "**Buffalo Bill speed**": Taliaferro, *All the Great Prizes*, 249, 257.
320 "**You can appreciate my loss**": JGN to JH, Nov. 25, 1885, box 4, JGN-LC.
320 "**For the present**": JGN to JH, Dec. 9, 1885, box 4, JGN-LC.
321 **include her in their lives:** JH to JGN, March 12, 1888, Nov. 10, 1892, reel 6, frames 1057–58, 1281–84; JH to JGN, Nov. 4, 1898, reel 7, frame 55, JH-BU.
321 "**As I shall probably never**": JH to Helen Nicolay, Oct. 5, 1900, reel 7, frame 202, JH-BU.
321 "**suited our needs perfectly**": Helen Nicolay, *Lincoln's Secretary*, 340.
321 "**dropped completely out of the present**": Ibid., 341.
322 "**take most of it**": JH to JGN, Dec. 27, 1897, reel 6, frames 1537–40, JH-BU.
322 "**was beloved by his countrymen**": A. A. Ward, G. W. Prothero, and Stanley Leathes, eds., *The Cambridge Modern History* (New York: Macmillan, 1903), 7:548.
322 "**Of course I am proud**": JGN to Stoddard, Nov. 13, 1898, reel 9, frames 950–51, JH-BU.
323 "**no words with which**": McKinley to JH, Feb. 26, 1893, reel 8, frame 1170, JH-BU.
323 **1896 Republican convention:** JH to Hanna, Dec. 20, 1895, reel 6, frames 1371–1374, JH-BU.
323 "**I think you are as good**": Hanna to JH, Dec. 21, 1895, reel 5, frame 315, JH-BU.
323 "**The Republican leaders treated Hay**": Adams, *Education of Henry Adams*, 323–24.
324 "**The scale of expenditure**": Taliaferro, *All the Great Prizes*, 315–16.
324 "**She was extremely gracious**": Ibid., 323–24.
324 "**the most interesting**": JH-LL, 2:181.
325 "**splendid little war**": JH to Roosevelt, July 27, 1898, in JH-LL, 2:337.
326 "**We are sixty-five million**": George C. Herring, *From Colony to Superpower*, 299.
326 "**greatest destiny the world**": LaFeber, *New Cambridge History of American Foreign Relations*, 2:126.
326 **parallel sense of dread:** Bederman, *Manliness and Civilization*, 1–44; Kasson, *Houdini, Tarzan, and the Perfect Man*, 3–20.
327 "**noisy nationalism**": George C. Herring, *From Colony to Superpower*, 302.
327 "**first-born son**": JH to Whitelaw Reid, Oct. 26, 1894, in Hay and Adams, *Letters of John Hay and Extracts from His Diary*, 2:337.
327 "**I am sure that you and I**": JH to Reid, in JH-LL, 2:123.
327 **prevailing spirit of jingoism:** Hoganson, *Fighting for American Manhood*, 36.
328 "**knock on the head**": George C. Herring, *From Colony to Superpower*, 302.

328 **"I was a boy":** Lodge, "The Blue and the Gray," in *Speeches and Addresses, 1884–1909*, 25–30.

328 **"War is a bad thing":** George C. Herring, *From Colony to Superpower*, 302.

328 **"I shall never get into a war":** Richardson, *West from Appomattox*, 336.

329 **Elmer Ellsworth:** Goodheart, *1861*, 280–91.

329 **"I detest war":** JH to Theodore Stanton, May 8, 1898, in JH-LL, 2:168.

329 **"prevent any talk of peace":** George C. Herring, *From Colony to Superpower*, 318.

329 **"educate the Filipinos":** Ibid., 332.

330 **"The American people can never be made":** Lodge to JH, March 28, 1901, in JH-LL, 2:259–60.

330 **"Et tu!":** JH to Roosevelt, Feb. 12, 1900, in JH-LL, 2:225.

330 **"the action of the Senate":** JH to McKinley, March 13, 1900, reel 7, frame 155, JH-BU.

331 **"The President rules":** Taliaferro, *All the Great Prizes*, 337.

331 **"may well be doubted":** JH, "American Diplomacy," in *Addresses of John Hay*, 111–27.

331 **"Yes, he was trained":** O'Toole, *Five of Hearts*, 312.

331 **"strange and tragic fate":** JH to Lady Jeune, Sept. 14, 1901, in JH-LL, 2:266.

332 **"The men who are living":** JH, "William McKinley," in *Addresses of John Hay*, 135–90.

332 **"If the Presidency had come":** JH to Roosevelt, Sept. 15, 1901, in JH-LL, 2:344.

332 **The two men took care:** Taliaferro, *All the Great Prizes*, 455–56.

333 **economically conservative:** Rauchway, *Murdering McKinley*, 37.

333 **"young, gallant, able":** Taliaferro, *All the Great Prizes*, 455–56.

333 **"He was much impressed":** JH Diary, Oct. 23, 1904, JH-LC.

333 **"from the head of Abraham Lincoln":** JH to Roosevelt, March 3, 1905, in JH-LL, 2:363.

333 **"deeply moved":** JH Diary, March 4, 1905, JH-LC.

334 **"McKinley sent for me":** Dennett, *John Hay*, 347.

334 **"great Secretary of State":** Roosevelt to Lodge, July 21, 1905, TR.

334 **"His name, his reputation":** Roosevelt to Lodge, Jan. 28, 1909, TR.

334 **"The Republican party":** JH, "Fifty Years of the Republican Party," in *Addresses of John Hay*, tktktk.

335 **Days after William McKinley's death:** Helen Nicolay, *Lincoln's Secretary*, 342.

336 **"I say to myself":** JH Diary, June 14, 1905, JH-LC.

Epilogue: July 25, 1947

338 **"Little of what was basically known":** Peterson, *Lincoln in American Memory*, 327–30; Mearns, *Lincoln Papers*, 135–36.

339 **"one of the few people":** Burlingame, "Nicolay and Hay," 12.

Selected Bibliography

Adams, Henry. *The Education of Henry Adams: An Autobiography.* Boston: Houghton Mifflin, 1918.

Angle, Paul M. *"Here I Have Lived": A History of Lincoln's Springfield.* Rev. ed. Chicago: Abraham Lincoln Bookshop, 1971.

Baker, Jean H. *Mary Todd Lincoln.* 1987. New York: W. W. Norton, 2008.

Bancroft, Frederic. *The Life of William H. Seward.* New York: Harper & Brothers, 1900.

Basler, Roy P., ed. *The Collected Works of Abraham Lincoln.* New Brunswick, N.J.: Rutgers University Press, 1953.

Bederman, Gail. *Manliness and Civilization: A Cultural History of Gender and Race in the United States, 1880-1917.* Chicago: University of Chicago Press, 1995.

Bernstein, Ivar. *The New York City Draft Riots: Their Significance for American Society and Politics in the Age of the Civil War.* New York: Oxford University Press, 1990.

Bigelow, John. *Retrospections of an Active Life.* Vol. 2. New York: Baker & Taylor, 1909.

————. *Retrospections of an Active Life.* Vol. 4. Garden City, N.Y.: Doubleday, Page, 1913.

Blight, David W. *Race and Reunion: The Civil War in American Memory.* Cambridge, Mass.: Belknap Press, 2001.

Boritt, Gabor. *The Gettysburg Gospel: The Lincoln Speech That Nobody Knows.* New York: Simon & Schuster, 2006.

Brown, Caroline Owsley. "Springfield Society Before the Civil War." *Journal of the Illinois State Historical Society* 15, nos. 1–2 (1922): 477–500.

Brown, Robert Perkins, et al., eds. *Memories of Brown: Traditions and Recollections Gathered from Many Sources.* Providence: Brown Alumni Magazine, 1909.

Burlingame, Michael. *Abraham Lincoln: A Life.* 2 vols. Baltimore: Johns Hopkins University Press, 2008.

————, ed. *At Lincoln's Side: John Hay's Civil War Correspondence and Selected Writings.* Carbondale: Southern Illinois University Press, 2000.

————, ed. *Lincoln Observed: Civil War Dispatches of Noah Brooks.* Baltimore: Johns Hopkins University Press, 1998.

————, ed. *Lincoln's Journalist: John Hay's Anonymous Writings for the Press, 1860–1864.* Carbondale: Southern Illinois University Press, 1998.

————. "Nicolay and Hay: Court Historians." *Journal of the Abraham Lincoln Association* 19, no. 1 (Winter 1998): 1–20.

————, ed. *With Lincoln in the White House: Letters, Memoranda, and Other Writings of John G. Nicolay, 1860–1865.* Carbondale: Southern Illinois University Press, 2000.

Burlingame, Michael, and John R. Turner Ettlinger, eds. *Inside Lincoln's White House: The Complete Civil War Diary of John Hay.* Carbondale: Southern Illinois University Press, 1997.

Caron, Timothy P. "'How Changeable Are the Events of War': National Reconciliation in the *Century Magazine's* 'Battles and Leaders of the Civil War.'" *American Periodicals* 16, no. 2 (2006): 151–71.

Carwardine, Richard. "Abraham Lincoln and the Fourth Estate: The White House and the Press During the American Civil War." *American Nineteenth Century History* 7, no. 1 (March 2006): 1–27.

Channing, Edward. *The United States of America, 1765–1865.* London: Macmillan, 1896.

Clarke, James Freeman. *Anti-Slavery Days.* New York: John W. Lovell Company, 1883.

Clinton, Catherine. *Mrs. Lincoln: A Life.* New York: Harper Perennial, 2009.

A College Friendship: A Series of Letters from John Hay to Hannah Angell. Boston: privately published, 1938.

Corneau, Octavia Roberts, ed. "A Girl in the Sixties: Excerpts from the Journal of Ridgely (Mrs. James L. Hudson)." *Journal of the Illinois State Historical Society* 22, no. 3 (Oct. 1929): 401–46.

Craven, Avery. *The Coming of the Civil War.* New York: Charles Scribner's Sons, 1942.

Current, Richard N. *The Lincoln Nobody Knows.* New York: Hill & Wang, 1958.

Curry, Leonard. *Blueprint for Modern America: Nonmilitary Legislation of the First Civil War Congress.* Nashville: Vanderbilt University Press, 1968.

Dennett, Tyler. *John Hay: From Poetry to Politics.* New York: Dodd, Mead, 1933.

Dicey, Edward. *Six Months in the Federal States.* London: Macmillan, 1863.

Donald, David Herbert. *Lincoln.* New York: Touchstone, 1996.

————. *Lincoln Reconsidered.* New York: Vintage Books, 1956.

————. *Lincoln's Herndon.* New York: Alfred A. Knopf, 1948.

————. *We Are Lincoln Men: Abraham Lincoln and His Friends.* New York: Simon & Schuster, 2004.

DuBois, James T., and Gertrude S. Matthews. *Galusha A. Grow: Father of the Homestead Law.* Boston: Houghton Mifflin, 1917.

Faust, Drew Gilpin. *This Republic of Suffering: Death and the American Civil War.* New York: Vintage Books, 2008.

Fehrenbacher, Don E. *Lincoln in Text and Context: Collected Essays.* Stanford, Calif.: Stanford University Press, 1987.

————. *Prelude to Greatness: Lincoln in the 1850s.* Stanford, Calif.: Stanford University Press, 1962.

Foner, Eric. *The Fiery Trial: Abraham Lincoln and American Slavery.* New York: W. W. Norton, 2010.

————. *Free Labor, Free Soil, Free Men: The Ideology of the Republican Party Before the Civil War.* New York: Oxford University Press, 1970.

————. "The New View of Reconstruction." *American Heritage,* Oct./Nov. 1983, 10–15.

———. *Reconstruction: America's Unfinished Revolution, 1863–1877.* New York: Harper & Row, 1988.

Foster, Gaines. *Ghosts of the Confederacy: Defeat, the Lost Cause, and the Emergence of the New South, 1865 to 1913.* New York: Oxford University Press, 1987.

Fredrickson, George M. *The Black Image in the White Mind: The Debate of Afro-American Character and Destiny, 1817–1914.* New York: Harper & Row, 1971.

Furgurson, Ernest B. *Freedom Rising: Washington in the Civil War.* New York: Vintage Books, 2004.

George, Joseph, Jr. "The World Will Little Note? The Philadelphia Press and the Gettysburg Address." *Pennsylvania Magazine of History and Biography,* July 1990, 385–98.

Gienapp, William E. *The Origins of the Republican Party, 1852–1856.* New York: Oxford University Press, 1987.

Gilder, Rosamond, ed. *The Letters of Richard Watson Gilder.* New York: Houghton Mifflin, 1916.

Goldfield, David. *America Aflame: How the Civil War Created a Nation.* New York: Bloomsbury Press, 2011.

Goodheart, Adam. *1861: The Civil War Awakening.* New York: Alfred A. Knopf, 2011.

Grinspan, Jon. "'Young Men for War': The Wide Awakes & Lincoln's 1860 Presidential Campaign." *Journal of American History* 96 (Sept. 2009): 357–78.

Guelzo, Allen C. "Come-Outers and Community Men: Abraham Lincoln and the Idea of Community in Nineteenth-Century America." *Journal of the Abraham Lincoln Association* 21, no. 1 (Winter 2000).

———. *Fateful Lightning: A New History of the Civil War and Reconstruction.* New York: Oxford University Press, 2012.

Hale, Grace Elizabeth. *Making Whiteness: The Culture of Segregation in the South, 1890–1940.* New York: Vintage Books, 1999.

Hay, Clara, and Henry Adams, eds. *Letters of John Hay and Extracts from His Diary.* Vol. 2. Washington, D.C.: privately published, 1908.

Hay, John. *The Addresses of John Hay.* New York: Century, 1906.

———. *Castilian Days.* Boston: James R. Osgood, 1871.

———. "The Foster-Brothers." *Harper's New Monthly Magazine,* Sept. 1869, 535–44.

Hays, Samuel P. *The Response to Industrialism, 1885–1914.* Chicago: University of Chicago Press, 1957.

Herndon, William. *Abraham Lincoln: Miss Ann Rutledge, New Salem, Pioneering, and the Poem, a Lecture Delivered in the Old Sangamon County Court House, November 1866.* 1866. Reprint, Springfield, Ill., 1910.

Herring, George C. *From Colony to Superpower: U.S. Foreign Relations Since 1776.* New York: Oxford University Press, 2008.

Herring, Pendleton. *Presidential Leadership: The Political Relations of Congress and the Chief Executive.* New York: Rinehart, 1940.

Hertz, Emanuel, *The Hidden Lincoln: From the Letters and Papers of William H. Herndon.* New York: Blue Ribbon Books, 1940.

Hine, Robert V., and John Mack Faragher. *Frontiers: A Short History of the American West.* New Haven, Conn.: Yale University Press, 2007.

Hoganson, Kristin L. *Fighting for American Manhood: How Gender Politics Provoked the Spanish-American and Philippine-American Wars.* New Haven, Conn.: Yale University Press, 1998.

Holmes, Oliver Wendell. "The Soldier's Faith." *Harvard Graduates' Magazine* 4 (1895–96): 179–86.

Holt, Michael. *The Political Crisis of the 1850s.* New York: Wiley, 1978.

Holzer, Harold. *Lincoln at Cooper Union: The Speech That Made Abraham Lincoln President.* New York: Simon & Schuster, 2006.

———. *Lincoln, President-Elect: Abraham Lincoln and the Great Secession Winter, 1860–1861.* New York: Simon & Schuster, 2008.

Howe, Daniel Walker. *What Hath God Wrought: The Transformation of America, 1815–1848.* New York: Oxford University Press, 2007.

Howells, W. D. "John Hay in Literature." *North American Review* 181, no. 586 (Sept. 1905): 343–51.

Howland, Glenn C. "Organize! Organize! Organize! The Lincoln Wide-Awakes in Vermont." *Vermont History* 48, no. 1 (Jan. 1980): 28–32.

Jacobson, Matthew Frye. *Whiteness of a Different Color: European Immigrants and the Alchemy of Race.* Cambridge, Mass.: Harvard University Press, 1999.

Johnson, Martin P. "Who Stole the Gettysburg Address?" *Journal of the Abraham Lincoln Association* 24, no. 2 (2003): 1–19.

Kasson, John F. *Houdini, Tarzan, and the Perfect Man: The White Male Body and the Challenge of Modernity in America.* New York: Hill & Wang, 2001.

Keller, Morton. *Affairs of State: Public Life in Late Nineteenth Century America.* Cambridge, Mass.: Belknap Press, 1977.

Klement, Frank L. "A Milwaukeean Witnesses Lincoln's Gettysburg Address." *Milwaukee History* 9, no. 2 (June 1986): 34–49.

LaFeber, Walter. *The New Cambridge History of American Foreign Relations.* Vol. 2. New York: Cambridge University Press, 2013.

Lawson, Melinda. *Patriot Fires: Forging a New American Nationalism in the Civil War North.* Lawrence: University of Kansas Press, 2002.

Litwack, Leon F. *Trouble in Mind: Black Southerners in the Age of Jim Crow.* New York: Alfred A. Knopf, 1998.

Lodge, Henry Cabot. *Speeches and Addresses, 1884–1909.* Boston: Houghton Mifflin, 1909.

McClellan, George B. *McClellan's Own Story.* New York: Charles L. Webster, 1887.

McClellan, Hugh, ed. *The Character and Religion of President Lincoln: A Letter of Noah Brooks.* Champlain, N.Y.: privately printed, 1909.

McGerr, Michael E. *The Decline of Popular Politics: The American North, 1865–1928.* New York: Oxford University Press, 1986.

McPherson, James M. *Abraham Lincoln and the Second American Revolution.* New York: Oxford University Press, 1991.

———. *Battle Cry of Freedom: The Civil War Era.* New York: Oxford University Press, 1988.

Mearns, David C. *The Lincoln Papers: The Story of the Collection with Selections to July 4, 1861.* New York: Doubleday, 1948.

Mechlin, Leila. "The Proposed Lincoln Memorial." *Century Magazine,* Jan. 1912, 367–69.

Monteiro, George. "John Hay and the Union Generals." *Journal of the Illinois State Historical Society* 69, no. 1 (Feb. 1976): 46–66.

Monteiro, George, and Brenda Murphy, eds. *John Hay–Howells Letters: The Correspondence of John Milton Hay and William Dean Howells, 1861–1905.* Boston: Twayne, 1980.

Morison, Elting E., ed. *The Letters of Theodore Roosevelt.* 8 vols. Cambridge, Mass.: Harvard University Press, 1951–54.

Morr, Frank Luther. *American Journalism, 1690–1960.* 3rd ed. New York: Macmillan, 1962.

Nevins, Allan. *Ordeal of the Union.* 8 vols. New York: Charles Scribner's Sons, 1947–71.

Nicolay, Helen. *Lincoln's Secretary: A Biography of John G. Nicolay.* New York: Longmans, Green, 1949.

Nicolay, John G. "Lincoln's Gettysburg Address." *Century Magazine,* Feb. 1894, 596–609.

———. *The Outbreak of Rebellion.* New York: Charles Scribner's Sons, 1881.

Nicolay, John G., and John M. Hay. *Abraham Lincoln: A History.* 10 vols. New York: Century, 1890.

Novick, Peter. *That Noble Dream: The "Objectivity Question" and the American Historical Profession.* New York: Cambridge University Press, 1988.

Oakes, James. *Freedom National: The Destruction of Slavery in the United States, 1861–1865.* New York: W. W. Norton, 2012.

O'Toole, Patricia. *The Five of Hearts: An Intimate Portrait of Henry Adams and His Friends, 1880–1918.* New York: Simon & Schuster, 2006.

Page, Thomas Nelson. *Red Rock: A Chronicle of Reconstruction.* New York: Charles Scribner's Sons, 1904.

Painter, Nell Irvin. *Standing at Armageddon: The United States, 1877–1919.* New York: W. W. Norton, 1987.

Paris, Comte de. *History of the Civil War in America.* Philadelphia: J. H. Coates, 1875–88.

Peterson, Merrill D. *Lincoln in American Memory.* New York: Oxford University Press, 1994.

The Political Debates Between Abraham Lincoln and Stephen A. Douglas. New York: G. P. Putnam's Sons, 1913.

Potter, David M. *The Impending Crisis: America Before the Civil War, 1848–1861.* New York: Harper & Row, 1976.

———. *People of Plenty: Economic Abundance and the American Character.* Chicago: University of Chicago Press, 1954.

Power, John Carroll. *Abraham Lincoln.* Chicago and Springfield: H. W. Rokker, 1889.

Price, W. W. "Secretaries to the Presidents." *Cosmopolitan,* March 1901, 487–92.

Randall, James G. *The Civil War and Reconstruction.* Boston: D. C. Heath, 1937.

———. *Lincoln the Liberal Statesman.* New York: Dodd, Mead, 1947.

Rauchway, Eric. *Murdering McKinley: The Making of Theodore Roosevelt's America.* New York: Hill & Wang, 2003.

Reid, Ronald F. "Newspaper Response to the Gettysburg Address." *Quarterly Journal of Speech* 53 (1967): 50–60.

Richardson, Heather Cox. *The Death of Reconstruction: Race, Labor, and Politics in the Post–Civil War North, 1865–1901.* Cambridge, Mass.: Harvard University Press, 2001.

———. *The Greatest Nation of the Earth: Republican Economic Policies During the Civil War.* Cambridge, Mass.: Harvard University Press, 1997.

———. *West from Appomattox: The Reconstruction of America After the Civil War.* New Haven, Conn.: Yale University Press, 2007.

Rinhart, Floyd, and Marion Rinhart. "The Prairies A-Blaze: The Iowa Wide-Awakes Carry Torches for Lincoln." *Iowa Heritage Illustrated* 77, no. 1 (March 1996): 42–48.

Rondinone, Troy. *The Great Industrial War: Framing Class Conflict in the Media, 1865–1950.* New Brunswick, N.J.: Rutgers University Press, 2011.

Ross, Dorothy. "Historical Consciousness in Nineteenth-Century America." *American Historical Review* 89, no. 4 (Oct. 1984): 909–28.

Schurz, Carl, Frederic Bancroft, and William Archibald Dunning. *The Reminiscences of Carl Schurz, 1852–1863.* New York: McClure, 1907.

Sears, Lorenzo. *John Hay, Author and Statesman.* New York: Dodd, Mead, 1914.

Sellers, Charles. *Market Revolution: Jacksonian America, 1815–1846.* New York: Oxford University Press, 1991.

Simon, John Y., ed. *The Papers of Ulysses S. Grant.* 31 vols. Carbondale: Southern Illinois University Press, 2005.

Sitkoff, Cornell. *A New Deal for Blacks: The Emergence of Civil Rights as a National Issue.* New York: Oxford University Press, 1978.

Stampp, Kenneth. *The Imperiled Union: Essays on the Background of the Civil War.* New York: Oxford University Press, 1980.

Stevenson, James D., Jr., and Randehl K. Stevenson. "John Milton Hay's Literary Influence." *Journal of the Illinois State Historical Society* 99, no. 1 (Spring–Summer 2006): 19–27.

Stoddard, William O. *Inside the White House in War Times: Memoirs and Reports of Lincoln's Secretary.* Edited by Michael Burlingame. Lincoln: University of Nebraska Press, 2000.

Taliaferro, John. *All the Great Prizes: The Life of John Hay, from Lincoln to Roosevelt.* New York: Simon & Schuster, 2013.

Thayer, William Roscoe. *The Life and Letters of John Hay.* 2 vols. Boston: Houghton Mifflin, 1915.

Thomas, Benjamin P. *Portrait for Posterity: Lincoln and His Biographers.* New Brunswick, N.J.: Rutgers University Press, 1947.

Turner, Frederick Jackson. *The Frontier in American History.* Rev. ed. Ithaca, N.Y.: Cornell University Press, 1956.

Twain, Mark. *The Autobiography of Mark Twain.* New York: Harper & Row, 1917.

Vandersee, Charles. "The Great Literary Mystery of the Gilded Age." *American Literary Realism* 7, no. 3 (Summer 1974): 245–72.

Weisberger, Bernard A. "The Dark and Bloody Ground of Reconstruction Historiography." *Journal of Southern History* 25, no. 4 (1959): 427–47.

Welles, Gideon. *The Diary of Gideon Welles.* Vol. 1. Boston: Houghton Mifflin, 1911.

———. *Lincoln and Seward: Remarks upon the Memorial Address of Chas. Francis Adams on the Late Wm. H. Seward.* New York: Sheldon, 1874.

White, Richard. *"It's Your Misfortune and None of My Own": A New History of the American West.* Norman: University of Oklahoma Press, 1993.

Wilentz, Sean. *The Rise of Popular Democracy: Jefferson to Lincoln.* New York: W. W. Norton, 2005.

Wilson, Bonnie, and Richard Moe. "Secretary Nicolay's Souvenir Album." *Minnesota History* 58, no. 7 (Fall 2003): 368–72.

Wilson, Douglas L., and Rodney O. Davis, eds. *Herndon's Informants: Letters, Interviews, and Statements About Abraham Lincoln.* Urbana: University of Illinois Press, 1998.

Wood, Gordon S. *Empire of Liberty: A History of the Early Republic, 1789–1815.* New York: Oxford University Press, 2009.

———. *The Radicalism of the American Revolution.* New York: Vintage Books, 1993.

Young, John Russell. *Men and Memories: Personal Reminiscences.* Vol. 1. New York: F. Tennyson Neely, 1901.

Index